Liam Swords was a priest of the diocese of Achonry. He spent some years in the Irish College, Paris, as archivist, *proviseur* and finally as the Irish Chaplain in Paris. He researched and wrote the scripts for the Radharc/RTÉ historical series on the Irish *diaspora* in Europe. He is the author of *Soldiers, Scholars, Priests* (1985), *The Green Cockade* (1989), *A Hidden Church* (1997), *In Their Own Words* (1999) and *A Dominant Church* (2004). He was editor of *The Irish-French Connection* (1977), and *Protestant, Catholic and Dissenter* (1997).

A PEOPLE'S CHURCH

Liam Swords

A People's Church

The Diocese of Achonry: From the
Sixth to the Seventeenth Century

the columba press

First published in 2013 by
the columba press
55A Spruce Avenue,
Stillorgan Industrial Park,
Blackrock, Co. Dublin

Layout and cover design by Bill Bolger and Columba
Printed and bound by CPI Group (UK) Ltd, Croydon, cr0 4yy

ISBN 978 1 85607 727 9

CONTENTS

List of Abbreviations

Abp	Archbishop
Abps of Dublin	Archbishops of Dublin
Anal. Hib.	*Analecta Hibernica*
Arch. Hib.	*Archivium Hibernicum*
ASV	*Archivio Segreto Vaticano*, Vatican City, Rome
Bp	Bishop
Cal. Docs Ire	Calendar of Documents of Ireland
Cal. Pat. Rolls	Calendar of Patent Rolls
Cath. Encyclopedia	Catholic Encyclopedia
Coll. Hib.	*Collectanea Hibernica*
Comp. Bke of Conought	Complete Book of Connaught
Conc. Trid.	*Concilii Tridentini Actorum*
CP	*Congregazioni Particolari, APF*
CPL	Calendar of Papal Letters
CPR: Petitions	Calendar of Papal Registrations: Petitions
CSP (Ire)	Calendar of State Papers
Dict. Mid. Ages	Dictionary of the Middle Ages
DNB	Dictionary of the National Library
Hib. Dom.	*Hibernia Dominicana*
IAS Miscell	Miscellany of the Irish Archaeological Society
IER	*Institut d'Etudes Religieuses?*
JRSAI	The Journal of the Royal Society of Antiquaries of Ireland
Martyr Don.	The Martyrology of Donegal
Martyr Tall.	The Martyrology of Tallaght
Onomast.	*Onomasticon*
Ord. Surv.	Ordnance Survey
Pont. Hib.	*Pontificia Hibernica*
PRO	Public Records Office, London
RIA	Royal Irish Academy
RIA Proc(s)	Proceedings of the Royal Irish Academy
SC Irlanda	*Scitture riferite nei Congressi, APF*
SOCG	*Scitture originali riferite nelli Congregazioni Generali, APF*
SP	State Papers
TCD	Trinity College, Dublin
Vat Lib	Vatican Library

Preface

Fr Liam Swords passed away in Dublin on 19 February, 2011. The volume here published, alas posthumously, is the third and final volume of his history of the Diocese of Achonry. Just before Christmas 2010, I received a note from him advising me that he had finished writing and asking if I would consider providing a foreword to this volume, which at that time he was beginning to prepare for publication.

The next we heard in January 2011 was that Liam was back in hospital. The illness he had been battling over many years had returned, and this time eventually got the better of him. The very last thing he was doing on the day he passed away was correcting proofs of this book.

There is sadness in the fact that Fr Liam himself did not live to see in print this final volume of what truly is a magnum opus. The diocese itself however, – and all who appreciate the availability of this history – are deeply grateful for the fact that he had, for all intents and purposes, completed the work.

Fr Liam began working on his history of the diocese of Achonry in 1993. He spent the year 1993–4 in Rome doing research on the project. The Bishop at that time, Most Reverend Thomas Flynn, had asked him to take on the task. It was an inspired request by Bishop Flynn, for Fr Liam embraced the project with enthusiasm and unrelenting commitment. It was a task for which Fr Liam was entirely suited and well-equipped. The result of his research bore fruit initially with the publication of *A Hidden Church – The Diocese of Achonry 1689–1818* in 1997. Two years later, in 1999, he published *In Their Own Words – The Famine in North Connacht 1845–1849*. Then in 2004, the second volume of the history of the diocese appeared: *A Dominant Church – The Diocese of Achonry 1818–1960*.

From then on, Fr Liam continued to work on the story of the first thousand years of the diocese. In spite of the fact that bouts of serious illness took a heavy toll on his energies, he managed to complete the work and so we now have '*A People's Church – The Dioces of Achonry from the Sixth to the Seventeenth Century*.

The moment of publication has finally come around, and we naturally feel a certain emptiness because Liam is no longer amongst us. But there is also a deep sense of gratitude for the fact that the Lord left him with us till the substantial work of research and writing was complete. Like St Paul in the second letter to Timothy (4:7), Fr Liam 'fought the good fight, finished the course, kept the faith'. Our prayer is that the 'crown of righteousness' which St Paul goes on to talk about, will be the Lord's gift to him now in that place where all our histories, *le cúnamh Dé*, will find their full meaning and completion.

This volume completes the historical picture, as it were, of the diocese of Achonry, from the sixth century right up to 1960. We live in times when the subject of history is, in the education system for example, under pressure to say the least. It is also a time of some crisis for the church in Ireland. I think it can be argued that we were never more in need, as human beings and as Christians, of the historical perspective. Modern culture has little patience with the long view. But where is life without roots and origins? Pressure, threat and crisis are not new phenomena at all. Familiarity with the struggles our ancestors engaged in, their successes and their sins, nurtures resilience and brings hope in the midst of current dilemma. So it is a very real blessing for us in the diocese to have the invaluable resource that Fr Swords has provided precisely at this juncture in our history. It will instruct and nourish, too, way beyond the borders of this small diocese. After all, the local is the universal in many ways, and Fr Swords' History can be read with profit way beyond Achonry boundaries.

Ins an litir dheireannach sin chugam ag iarraidh réamhrá uaim, d'iarr Liam orm cuid éigin den réamhrá sin a scríobh as Gaeilge, mar gurb shin é teanga mhuintir an deoise seo le linn an tréimhse ar fad atá faoi chaibidil sa leabhar seo. Tá an ceart aige, ar ndóigh, agus léiríonn an t-iarratas sin uaidh an t-ómós agus an báidh a bhí ag an stairí seo leis na daoine ar a raibh sé ag déanamh taighde. Tugann sin le fios dúinn go mba fíor-stairí é Liam Swords. Bhí an t-ádh ar Dheoise Achadh Conaire a leithéide a bheith againn i mbun na h-oibre seo. Bhí an dúchas ann don ábhar a bhí dhá láimhseáil aige. San áit a mbíonn ómós, is feidir muinín a chuir.

Ar bharr leathanach 71 sa leabhar, insítear dúinn 'Achonry was valued by Rome at 33 1/3 florins, one of the poorest dioceses in Ireland' san 15ú aois. Má ba bhocht é Achadh Chonaire mar dheoise san aois sin ó thaobh airgid de agus más beag fós é mar dheoise, is saibhir é mar dheoise san 21ú aois ó thobh na staire scríofa dhe, níos saibhre ná deoise ar bith éile in Éirinn. A bhuíochas sin don oidhreacht atá fagtha againn ag an Athair Liam Swords. Faoi shuan le Dia go raibh sé i measc naoimh agus ollúna na hÉireann.

✠ *An tEaspag Breandán Ó Ceallaigh,*
Bishop of Achonry

Introduction

A People's Church is the third and final volume of Fr Liam Swords' history of the diocese of Achonry. In publishing this work we now complete the first entire history of any diocese in Ireland from the first arrival of Christianity, right up to the modern era.

Sadly, this book is published posthumously, but it does complete the great mission which Fr Swords embarked on when he undertook this task at the behest and inspiration of Bishop Thomas Flynn. The collection now includes this volume, *A People's Church*, covering the sixth to the seventeenth century, *A Hidden Church*, which covered the period from 1689–1818, *A Dominant Church 1818–1960*, and *In Their Own Words, The Famine in North Connaught*, which covered the Great Famine period in the 1840s.

As this final volume was edited and completed in the absence of the author, the reader will notice a small number of changes from previous works, most particularly the fact that this volume remains unillustrated. We have however, maintained the marginalia, which are designed to help those who will dip in and out of the book, rather than read it in its entirety from cover to cover. We have also maintained the stylistic conventions as outlined in earlier volumes, i.e. language used in quotations is generally modernised, e.g. 'ye' is changed to 'the', and one form of each surname is adopted throughout the book. For place names, the modern postal spelling is adopted.

Similar to the previously published volumes, this book is a social and political history of the diocese as much as an ecclesiastical history. The intertwining of the social, political, and ecclesiastical lives of the people over this long period is very clear from the archives available. The records of the time covered in this volume vary from the very rare in the 7th to 11th centuries, to the more readily available in the 1600s as the bureaucracies of both Churches and States developed their record keeping on an increasingly systematic basis. Fr Liam Swords' intimate knowledge of the sources for the history of the church, held in Ireland, Britain, France, Spain, Italy, and the Vatican is striking throughout the book, and only a lifetime of dedication to this task could possibly have gleaned so much information on the history of his homeplace.

Like the other volumes in this series, this history is not strictly chronological and is divided into a number of identifiable sections.

The book starts with *What Patrick Found,* giving an outline of the political and social makeup of Ireland at the time of the arrival of Christianity, and the implications that this would have for the spread of the new religion. *Achonry Saints* deals with the earliest known local saints including Attracta, Finnian and Fechin, amongst others whose names are given to townlands and settlements across the diocese to this day. How the church became organised along the lines of parishes, rectories, and diocese, and the development of the monasteries is examined in chapters Three and Four. The arrival of the *Monks* to Ballysadare and the *Friars* to Straide are then examined in chapters Five and Six, while the spread of *Roman Tentacles* in the thirteenth century, *Matters Sexual* in medieval Ireland and *Crusading Knights* conclude the first thematic section of the book.

The second section of the book takes a chronological run through the bishops of the thirteenth to fifteenth centuries looking at both local developments and the impact of world events on Achonry. Fr Swords' extensive research through the Vatican archives shines here in showing the level of influence which Rome had locally in Achonry, and the level of reporting back to Rome which took place at a time when communication was by handwritten letter.

Bishop Eoghan Ó hAirt, whose life spanned the entire 16th century is the key character in the third section of the book, chapters Seventeen to Twenty-Two. Swords' knowledge of, and work on, the documents of the Council of Trent, which Ó hAirt attended, shows clearly the contribution which this bishop from the west of Ireland made at this crucial time in the history of the church. This section also covers the impact of King Henry VIII and Queen Elizabeth I's conquest of Ireland, the Reformation, and the confiscation and suppression of the monasteries.

The final section of the book brings us into the 1600s, starting with the Nine Years' War and its impact on Achonry. Swords particularly examines the role of Irish seminaries in Europe and the return of these Counter-Reformation priests in the survival of Catholicism in Ireland at a time when the rest of Europe was following the dictum *cuius regio, eius religio* ('whose realm, his religion'). Fascinating is the decision of Rome not to appoint a bishop to Achonry during the entire 17th century, for fear of provoking the anger of the English crown. The Rebellion of 1641 locally is addressed here, as is the violence that continued right through that decade, and the impact of the Cromwellian settlement.

This volume ends with a summary of where things stood for the people of Achonry at the end of the Restoration period. The events of 1685 onwards, with the accession of the Catholic James II to the throne are dealt with in *A Hidden Church*.

In previous volumes, Liam Swords acknowledged the help and support of all those who had assisted him in any way with his work. Sadly he had not prepared a list for this work, however reading the acknowledgements in *A Hidden Church* and *A Dominant Church* it is clear that many, if not most of those named there are also to be credited with assistance in this production. To this list may I add the names of John McCafferty, School of History and Archives, UCD, who read the Latin appendices, Sean O Boyle, who has overseen this entire series as Publisher at Columba Press, Patrick O'Donoghue, Leeann Gallagher and Shauna Nimmo who produced the book, and the late Bill Bolger who designed each cover in this series and who coined the title *A People's Church*, the last of Liam Swords' contributions to the store of human knowledge on the history of our church and people.

Final thanks go to the people of the diocese of Achonry, their clergy, Bishop Emeritus Thomas Flynn, and Bishop Brendan Kelly, who have supported the publication of this history, and in so doing have created their own piece of history by becoming the first diocese in Ireland to have a full history from earliest times to the modern day.

Fearghal O Boyle
Managing Director
The Columba Press

CHAPTER ONE

What Patrick Found

Ireland at the time was divided into about a hundred little kingdoms, called *túatha.* The present diocese of Achonry is almost exactly coterminus with the former kingdom of Luighne, which was inhabited by a people called the *Corcothri* (alias *Corcu-Firthri*). *The Book of Ballymote* has a reference to the King of Corcothri in the year AD 60 (see also Ogygia, iii, 69; AU, i, 500.) Later in the Middle Ages it was ruled by the O'Hara family who lived in a ringfort erected on a prominent hill, commanding an impressive view of the surrounding countryside. The name 'Luighne' is still preserved in the village and barony of Leyny. Within each kingdom the population was divided into social classes ranging from agricultural labourers at the bottom to the royal family at the summit of the hierarchical system. In between, there were professional orders who derived their support and protection from the rulers. Druids occupied a pre-eminent position among the professional classes. They were priests, an intellectual elite who may have exercised certain judicial powers.

There were no cities, towns or even villages of any size. The inhabitants lived in isolated ringforts scattered throughout the *túatha* or kingdoms. They were the typical medieval homesteads dating from about AD 400–1100, while the majority of them were constructed from the seventh to the end of the ninth century. A ringfort was an enclosure, usually circular, within which stood one or more buildings; it was protected by a high bank of earth called a *rath* or a *caiseal.* They were made of stone as a protection from wild animals or cattle raiders. The earthen bank of the *rath* was made up of material thrown up from a ditch in the interior of the enclosure. Forts ringed by two or three earthen banks are thought to have been the homes of kings and their families. Such a ringfort with enormous ramparts was called a *dún.* A three-ringed fort is sited in Carramore in Killasser, while there is a two-ringed *rath* in a field nearby.

Houses of a circular design were made of timber or turf sods and thatched with reeds or rushes. The hearth was usually near the centre of the house and away from the walls. Souterrains are often found associated with raths. The souterrain consisted of a stone passage and small chamber or chambers under the house probably used for storing meat and milk. Of the 243 souterrains or

Ringforts

possible souterrains identified in south Sligo, seventy-six per cent are associated with ringforts. Household vessels like bowls, mugs and plates were generally made of wood and skin. Buckets were made with staves.

Some large ringforts accommodated a community of cattle-ranchers with a population of forty or fifty, while others were small single-family enclosures. As the population varied considerably from one to another, they provide very little help in determining the population of a region. Ringforts were primarily farmsteads and produced their own food supplies, supplemented by hunting and fishing as is clear from the bones of fish and birds, and antlers found during excavations. They were usually built on good agricultural land. Cows provided the basic staples – milk in the summer and meat in the winter – as well as being the usual units of exchange in trade or barter, which was carried on in kind. Another unit of exchange was the *cumal* or slave-girl who was valued at four cows. The better-off farmer, known as the *bóaire* (cow-lord), lived in these *raths*. There were also pigs and boars, who foraged for themselves in the all-pervasive forests, and some hens. Sheep were important, but it seems it was mainly for their wool, as indicated by the relatively few sheep bones found. Wheat, barley, rye and oats were grown, harvested with knives, sickles and shears, and then stored and ground to make food. Each farmer made his own iron tools which is revealed by the traces of iron-smelting found in many small ringforts. Spindles have also been found, showing that thread was spun from sheeps' wool and woven into cloth to provide clothes for the family. Occasionally, in the ringforts which housed the aristocratic class, some luxury goods such as glass beads, bone-combs, bracelets, bronze and iron pins were found.[1]

Raths   Some of these early ringforts can be identified today by townland names with the prefixes *Cashel, Rath, Dún, Lios* and *Cathair*: the Irish words for ringforts. There are about seventy-four such townlands in the diocese. A detailed archaeological inventory has been carried out, covering south Sligo including about half the diocese; it was published in 2005. *Archaeol. Invent. of County Sligo, vol. I, South Sligo* acknowledges the contributions of the Sligo Field Club, the Ballymote Heritage Group, and local individuals including Mary and Martin Timoney, James Flanagan of the *Corran Herald*, Madame Felicity MacDermot, James P. McGarry, Gerry Carr, Cathal Coleman, Betty and John Conlon, Joyce Enright, Catherin Flynn, Jack Flynn, Dan Healy, Dr Patrick Heraughty, John J. Higgins, Gerry Keaney, James Kearns, Eamon

1.   Much of the above has been gleaned from Kathleen Hughes, *Early Christian Ireland: Introduction to the Sources*, 17–33.

Keeney, Sheila Kitchin, Aidan Mannion, Margaret McBrien, Roger McCarrick, Jim McGill, Michael Joe McGovern, Jimmy Mullaney, Patrick E. O'Brien, Seamas and Colm O'Donnell, Paddy O'Hara, Pat-Ann and Nicholas Prins, Michael Rochford, Eileen Tighe, Frank Tivnan, Pat Ward and Martin Wilson. Much of the present material is drawn from that work. It records over 1,200 *raths* of which 580 were in the diocese, plus another 110 sites which have been identified as possible *raths*, as well as 110 *cashels* bringing the total number of ringforts to over 800. The pre-Reformation parish of Achonry had the largest number of *raths* with 168 and a further twenty possible – giving a total of 188. The lowest number were identified in Keash with forty-four and two others possible. The number in the other parishes varied from fifty-three to sixty-nine. The diameters of most of them varies from twenty to sixty metres and they were sited generally on hilltops or hillside slopes.

There were 215 *cashels* recorded in south Sligo, of which 110 were in the diocese. The surrounding walls, constructed mainly from stones collected in the area, were sometimes six metres wide and three metres high and often served as walkways. The greatest number, with twenty-eight, was in the parish of Ballysadare, closely followed by Achonry with twenty-seven, while the least, with three each, were identified in Collooney and Ballymote. *Cashels*

Some families lived in lake-dwellings called *crannógs*. 115 *crannógs* have been identified in south Sligo, with no less than seventy-six in Lough Gara. Most of them are man-made islands with an average diameter of twenty-five metres, sited in low-lying lakes like Lough Gara. *Crannógs* were dated from the early to the late medieval period. While some of the *crannógs* were royal residences, many of them were occupied by less wealthy people. Some of the *crannógs* had causeways just beneath the surface of the water leading to the shore. *Crannógs*

No comparable archaeological inventory of the Mayo section of the diocese has yet been published. Some local histories provide information on the ringforts and *crannógs*, particularly, in Killasser and Kiltimagh.[2] Forty-two ringforts were identified in Kiltimagh while the 1838 Survey identified 113 forts in Killasser, a figure which has been questioned as underestimating the real number.

The ecclesiastical settlements established by St Patrick in Ireland could not follow the models existing elsewhere in Christendom where bishops established their seats in a *civitas* or city, as there were none in Ireland. The Irish were a completely rural community with people living in ringforts or *crannógs*, mostly *Ecclesiastical Settlements*

---

2   Bernard O'Hara, ed., *Killasser, a History*; Peter Sobolewski and Betty Solon, eds, *Kiltimagh, Our Life and Times*.

isolated but sometimes in small clusters. Royal residences were in larger ringforts but only accommodated the members of the royal family and their servants and retainers. Patrick had to establish his fledgling church in enclosures like the rest of the population. These were about 140 metres in diameter, surrounded by a high earthen mound within which were three buildings: a house for the bishop and his helpers, a church or oratory and a kitchen-*cum*-refectory. Diminutive though these ecclesiastic settlements were, they were still called *civitates*. The districts ruled by the bishops appointed by St Patrick were not very extensive and thus the number of bishops was quite high, possibly somewhere between forty and sixty.

Churches   Early church buildings were small. The 'great church of Saint Patrick' in Meath measured only sixty feet in length, the same as the medieval ruins of the Kilmorgan church (*c*.60ft l & 24ft w) in Ballymote. Kilturra church in Bunninadden had similar dimensions (*c*.20m E–W; 5m N–S) while those of Kilshalvey in the same parish were much smaller (int. 13.9m E–W; 5m N–S). The dimensions of the monastery church founded by St Fechin in the parish of Drumratt in Knockbrack were *c*.9.5m E–W; 5.5m N–S. The stone church in Killedan, which probably replaced the original wooden structure later in the Middle Ages, was calculated to be 15ft x 13ft x 9ft. These churches could accommodate relatively few in addition to the priest. The material usually used was wood, but where it was not available the walls were constructed of clay or mud and the roofs were thatched. St Nathy's church in the townland of Achonry followed the ringfort pattern consisting of a circular enclosure around a group of three buildings: a dwelling house for priests, a church or oratory where Mass was said and a kitchen which also served as a refectory, all built of wood and thatched with reeds or rushes.

Very little is known about the rite of the Mass used in the early Middle Ages. The best manuscript text survives in the *Stowe Missal* in the Royal Irish Academy. It is described as 'highly Romanised' and is probably not unlike the Gallican in form, containing numerous apology-type prayers. The Irish were fond of litanies which were repeated in the course of the Mass.

Creating   When Patrick arrived, Ireland was a pre-literate Iron Age civilisation where
Literacy   the only script in use was *ogham* which consisted of a series of strokes. As Christianity was based on scriptures and the written gospel, to christianise the people, it was necessary to teach them reading and writing. The Irish people spoke a Celtic language while Latin was spoken throughout the Roman world and was the language of the Church. Ireland was the first non-Latin speaking country in the western world to be thus converted. Conversion to Christianity involved a huge cultural change, introducing the alphabet and the Latin

language and thus bringing Ireland out of its isolation and into contact with the rest of the Latin-speaking world. Simple instruction based on the Bible was given by Patrick and his helpers to converts and those destined for the priesthood. To enable them to read, they were given an elementary grounding in Latin. It has been argued that Britons were their chief Latin teachers from the particularly British way in which Latin was pronounced in Ireland and which reflects itself in the orthography of the native language.

Patrick was assisted by a large number of bishops, all Britons like himself. *Bishops* Tirechán enumerated forty-two in his *Catalogue*, but added that there were many others. Some names like Auxilius, Isserninus, Secundinus, Cethiacus, Sachell and Assicus have survived. Bishops could scarcely be chosen among the first generation of Irish converts. Celibacy was also a problem and Patrick had to accept something less. He asked his friend to point out 'a man of one wife [u]nto whom one child hath been born,' and Dubthach replied that only one man possessing such a quality was known to him. As a result Patrick entrusted many of the churches he founded to priests. He and his assistant bishops travelled from ringfort to ringfort and their success was seemingly phenomenal, amounting to thousands of all classes baptised. Women were prominent among converts and Patrick had a special regard for slave-girls. Many of them became consecrated virgins though forbidden by their owners to do so.

In the century following the death of Patrick, the Irish Church underwent *Monasteries* a remarkable change. Monasteries sprang up everywhere, attracting huge numbers. The tradition of hermits originated in Egypt in the fourth and fifth centuries when Christians, wishing to escape the evil influences of cities like Alexandria, took refuge in the desert. As their number grew they came together to form monasteries. The Irish became greatly attracted to this more demanding form of Christianity. Apart from Finnian of Clonard, other great monastic founders were Enda of Aran, Columbanus of Bangor, Columba of Derry, Kevin of Glendalough, Ciaran of Clonmacnois, Mobi of Glasnevin and Fechin of Fore. The latter two were natives of Luighne. The great monastic founders had complete ecclesiastical control not only over their monasteries but probably also over districts that regarded the monastery as their chief church. The hierarchy set up by St Patrick became a monastic hierarchy in the sixth century and non-monastic bishops were of almost negligible importance.

The monastery, like early churches, was set within a large ringfort. Within the enclosure the chief building was the church or oratory, a rectangular building made of oak planks and thatched with reeds. The huts or cells of the monks, usually of wickerwork, were scattered around the enclosure. Other buildings included a guesthouse, refectory and, at least in the more important ones, a school and *scriptorium*, where monks copied manuscripts. Because the buildings were made of perishable materials, no traces of them remain except on treeless islands where they were constructed of stone. Some of them, like Clonmacnois, grew into very large settlements, making them Ireland's first cities.

Scriptorium   Boys who aspired to become monks were expected to have mastered the alphabet before entering a monastery. 'To the Irish mind an illiterate monk was a contradiction in terms.' In monasteries their studies included Latin, ecclesiastical rules and the Bible. Once able to read, each was given a copy of the psalms which they memorised. Later, they studied the gospels and the Acts of the Apostles. Copying the gospels was a common occupation for monks and most monasteries had a *scriptorium* where copies were made with pen and ink on to vellum. Irish monasteries were highly regarded as centres of learning. The Venerable Bede describes the crowds of English students who flocked to Ireland in the seventh century to study in the monasteries.

Monks' Habits   Irish monks wore tunics or inner garments over which they wore coarse woollen coverings, with hoods and outside cloaks in bad weather or on journeys. When travelling they always carried a staff or stick with a crook at the top, called a *bachall* in Irish, used to ward off wild dogs and other savage beasts. The standard of personal cleanliness was high and both clothes and persons were frequently washed.

Fasting   Food was very limited in Irish monasteries and consisted mainly of vegetables and a little bread. This was washed down with water or thin beer at the only meal of the day, usually at three o'clock, and the midday pangs of hunger were so severe that monks referred to them as the 'noon-day devil'. The fare was better on Sundays and feastdays or when guests arrived. There were two fastdays every week, Wednesday (*Céadaoin*) and Friday (*Aoine*) though there was a dispensation if there were guests. Fasting was also observed during Lent. In fact, there were three Lents, the first, forty days before Christmas, 'the Lent of Elias', the second as now before Easter, 'the Lent of Jesus', and the last, forty days after Whitsunday, 'the Lent of Moses'. Silence was regarded as very important for a monk, who spoke only when it was necessary or useful. Sleep was also strictly curtailed and monks rose during the night to sing the office. Other austerities included praying for lengthy period with arms outstreched, in imitation of Christ on the cross and repeated genuflections and immersion in cold water.

CHAPTER TWO

Achonry Saints

There is some slight evidence that St Patrick visited the *túath* of Luighne. The *St Attracta* seventh-century *Tripartite Life of Saint Patrick* states that he did. 'Pátric came from the west over the Moy into Gregraigi, where he was overtaken at Ráith Rígbaird.'[1] Various locations have been suggested for Ráith Rígbáird but the most likely is the townland called Rath-Ríghbaird situated east of Easky in County Sligo. It was recounted that while in Connacht, Patrick was resolved to visit Moylurg and for this reason he passed through Bearnas Hua nOililla or the gaps of Collooney and moved on to the River Boyle which rises in Lough Gara. A young woman, Adrochta, the daughter of Talan Cathbadi, was said to have received the veil from him and he set up a nunnery for her in Killaraght (*Cill Athrachta*), then the territory of the Gregraige on Lake Techet, now Lough Gara. St Attracta, through her father, was descended 'from the noble and ancient stock of Irius'. Talan was the father of St Coeman, as well as St Attracta. *The Life of Saint Attracta* is supposed to have been written by a Cistercian monk in Boyle at the beginning of the twelfth century, considered worthless by experts.[2] Crecraige, alias Gregraige, east of the River Moy was supposed to have been co-extensive with the barony of Coolavin but anciently more extensive and comprised the baronies of Leyny and Corran as well. '*Perrexit ad Tramitem Gregrege et fundavit aecclesiam in Drummae … patina et calix sunt in Cella Adrochtae.*'[3]

Attracta may well have been similar, if not the same, as the woman he described in his *Confession*:

> Among others, a blessed Irishwoman of noble birth, beautiful, full-grown, whom I baptised, came to us after some days for a particular reason: she told us that she had received a message from a messenger of God, and he admonished her to be a virgin of Christ and draw near to God. Thanks be to God, on the sixth day

---

1.   Hogan, *Onomast.*, 576–7.
2.   Colgan, *Acta Sanctorum Hiberniae* under the date 9 February; O'Hanlon, *Life of the Irish Saints*, iv, 31, viii, 150–62, *Onomast.*, 450, 'Tuatha crecraige, in Luighni, about Loch Teched', *Book of Ballymote*, 140, MacFirbis' *Book of Genealogies* written in 1650–66, 52.
3.   *Book of Armagh*, 13.

after this she most laudably and eagerly chose what all virgins of Christ do. Not that their fathers agree with them; no – they often even suffer undeserved reproaches from their parents; and yet their number is ever-increasing.

St Attracta established a hospital there and the convent survived until after the general suppression of the monasteries at the end of the sixteenth century. Attracta herself seems to have survived long after St Patrick as she was still active in Killaraght early in the sixth century. In the Middle Ages the Ó Mocháin family were erenaghs and keepers of St Attracta's Cross. Ó Mocháin was a man-servant of Attracta.[4] It was said that when Patrick was about to celebrate Mass the paten was missing. A paten with the impress of a cross miraculously rested on Attracta's shoulder.

St Finnian   Bishops were placed over the more important centres while churches of lesser significance were placed under the control of a priest or deacon. 'The ordinary hierarchy established by Saint Patrick became transformed in the sixth century into a monastic hierarchy. Non-monastic bishops and bishoprics were small and of almost negligible importance.' This was probably the case of Achonry where the church was established towards the middle of the sixth century. Founded by St Finnian, himself a bishop while most of his disciples remained priests, the founder of Clonard monastery which became one of the most important centres of monasticism, soon after his return from Britain.

The Life of Saint Finnian recounts the circumstances of the foundation of the church in Achonry. The *Lives of the Saints* is heavily laced with *thaumaturga* or miraculous happenings which have no basis in reality, and the majority are regarded by leading authorities as entirely fictitious. Finnian travelled through Connacht as far as the boundaries of Tirerrill where he was given hospitality by two brothers, Moysi and Ainmiri. Their sister had died that day and – as his biographer claims – Finnian resuscitated her. From there he went to the place 'where the man of God by the name of Nathy, a priest stayed. Here the Angel of the Lord appeared and said to him: "Wheresoever the man of God speaks of his family; it is a pleasant place to dwell, there will I found a church".' The king of Luighne, appropriately called Wolfhead, tried to expel him but Finnian worked a miracle which so impressed the king that 'the wolf became a lamb' and granted him the land called *Achad-chonaire*, formerly called Achadcaoin. Finnian's foundation at Achonry may well have been a monastery and the author of the *Life of Fechin* calls the place 'the monastery of Achad-

---

4.   *Onomast.*, *Muintir Mochain Chille hAthracht, Maoir na Croise Athracht;* O'Donovan, *Tribes and Customs of Hy-Fiachrach.*

Conair'. Colgan, 134: *Cum autem vir sanctus caepisset Monasterii fundamenta jacere, S. Nathineus eius institutor in monasterio de Achad-Conair existes …*

'Here the man of God left as head the priest by the name of Nathy.' Little is known about Nathy (in Irish *Nath Í*, 'nephew of yew') and no biography has survived. He is described as a priest in the *Life of Saint Finnian* and the *Life of Saint Corbmac;* the *Life of Saint Attracta* called him 'Saint Nathy Cruimthir', that is 'the Priest' making it most unlikely that he was a bishop. In fact, priests surpassed bishops, both in number and importance, in the Irish Church in the sixth century and Nathy was one of them. Nathy's feast is observed on 9 August. His name occurs in a stanza in *Leabhar Breac*:

St Nathy

> *Feith lat pais Antoni*
> *Firmi Fortren muinter*
> *In Achud cain clantar*
> *Nahii credal cruimther.*

'Remember thou the passion of Antoninus (and) of Firmus a mighty family. In Achad Cáin is buried Nathi a pious priest.'[5]

Fechin, whose feastday occurs on 29 January, was a native of Luighne, born of noble parents Coelcharno and Lassara in Bella in the present parish of Collooney and received his early education from St Nathy.[6] Sometime before the Norman invasion it became St Mary's Abbey of Augustinian Canons which lasted down to the general suppression of the monasteries during the Reformation. After Ballysadare Fechin founded a church in his home place, Billa (*Bile-fechin*) and a monastery nearby in Kilnemanagh, *Cill na manach*, 'the church of the monks', the next townland north of Billa which later became a small cell of the Ballysadare Augustinian Canons which appears to have ceased to exist before the suppression. The sites of both the church in Billa and in Kilnamanagh have been recently identified.[7] Fechin founded another monastery at Drumrat in the parish of Keash and this site has been identified in Knockbrack where the outline of a rectangular church with the interior

St Fechin

5.   Colgan, *Vita S. Finniani*, cap. xxvi, 396, *Vita S, Corbmaci*, cap. xv, 753, no. 31, 756; O'Hanlon, 123–30; *Martyr. Tall.*, '*Nathi sac, Achadh Conaire*.'; *Book of Leinster*. 'Nathi Presbyter in Achud Chonaire'; Irish Calendar, *RIA*, '*Crumthar Nati ó Achadh Conare i Luighnibh dnas.'*
6.   Colgan, i, 130–43; *Vita S, Corbmaci*, 753, no. 33, 756; O'Hanlon, i, 356–82; for a detailed and fairly lengthy account of the life of Fechin see O'Rorke, *Ballysadare*, 435–69. He became a noted founder of monasteries, one of the earliest in Ballysadare situated on 'a noble and beautiful tract of land which was called Tearmann Fechin,' Colgan, 141.
7.   *Arch. Invent.*, 2618 and 2650.

measurements of *c*.9.5m E–W; 5.5m N–S. Four cross-inscribed slabs were located in the church.[8] St Maelruain of Druim-Raithe appears in the *Martyrology of Tallaght* under 6 March and some experts believe this to be Drumrat in the parish of Keash which is translated as 'the church of the fort'.[9] Before the suppression at the end of the sixteenth century the Abbot of Ballysadare held the vicarages of Drumrat and Kilgarvan.[10] Outside the diocese of Achonry, Fechin's name is closely associated with Cong (*Cunga-Feichin*), where he is said to have been abbot, though it had been founded by Domnall, a nephew of the King of Ireland, in AD 624. His most prestigious foundation was in Fore, Co. Westmeath, from where he has forever been named 'Saint Fechin of Fore'. His last foundation was in Termonfeckin, County Louth, which later became a monastery of Augustinian Canons as did so many of the early Irish monasteries. He died on 20 January 664 as a result of a 'great plague' known as *Buidhe Connail* and described in the *Annals of Ulster* as *magna mortalitate*.[11]

St Aidan   Despite popular belief, Monasterredan has no connection with Aidan. Sites associated with him have been located in Ballynaglogh and Monasterredan. The latter, an ecclesiastical enclosure known as 'Cashelnamonastragh' is 77m E-W and *c*.71m. N-S and contained a graveslab with simple incised Greek cross and a bullaun stone which are usually associated with such sites. In Ballynaglogh the ruin of a rectangular church, 21.5m E-W; 7.65m N-S has been located which was the medieval parish church of Cloonoghill probably on the site of a sixth century monastery.[12]

St Columba   Columba founded a monastery in Emlefad over which he placed his disciple, Enna, and Columba's name survived there down to the sixteenth century when the rectory of Emlefad continued to be called after him. Columba had returned from Iona to attend a great Council held at Drumceat in Derry. Afterwards he sailed from Lough Foyle to Sligo Bay and proceeded from there to the region of Carbury where he founded a church at Drumcliff (*Druim-chliabh*). From there he went to Ballysadare where he was greeted by a large group of saints, men and women, including St Muredach, Bishop of Killala, Manius, Bishop of Tirerrill, and St Farannan of Easky. As Enna of Emlefad is not named among this group, Columba probably founded the monastery there after his visit to

8.   Ibid., 2687, 2936.
9.   O'Donovan, Ord. Surv.; O'Hanlon, i, 356–82, iii, 200.
10.   *Onomast.*; Swords, *Register, Coll. Hib.*, nos 39 and 40, 20.
11.   O'Hanlon, i, 20 Jan.
12.   *Martyr. Don.*, 271; Colgan, 753, notes 35, 756; O'Donovan, 36–7, note 38–9, notes i–l, 40–1, notes m-q, 486; O'Hanlon, x, 121–3; Gwynn and Hadcock, 377, 398; O'Rorke, *Sligo*, ii, 192, 380–1; *Arch. Invent.*, 2614, 2662, 2688.

Ballysadare. He made several foundation in the west at this time. After leaving Ballysadare he visited the territory of Hy-Fiachrach where he established monasteries on lands granted him by the prince there.[13]

Kilmorgan, *Cill Murchon* or *Murchaidh*, 'the church of Murchon or Murchadh' a townland in Ballymote parish, was itself a medieval parish and the ruins of a medieval rectangular church (*c.*60ft L & 24ft W) have been located in a corner of Kilmorgan graveyard. Murchon's name is entered in the *Martyrology of Tallaght* under the date 12 June when his festival was celebrated, and is probably the founder of the church of Kilmorgan. He is also mentioned in the *Martyrology of Donegal* as follows: 'There is a Murchu of the race of Conall Cremthainne, son of Niall of the Nine Hostages and there is a Cill Murchon in Corann, near Céis Corann in Connacht; and consider whether this is his festival.'[14] *St Murchon*

Killasser, *Cill Lasrach*, takes its name from a sixth century virgin, Lasair or Lassera, a native of Aghavea, Fermanagh, daughter of Ronán Mac Ninneadha, a descendant of Niall of the Nine Hostages and Dubhlaca, daughter of Donn Mac Murchadha, king of Leinster. She was probably part of a small group of virgins living under the care of a neighbouring bishop or abbot, a common feature of the sixth century Irish church. She later settled with her father Rónan in a *crannóg* in Loch Melagh in Kilronan parish near Boyle. She and her father were asked to assist in the rescue of a priest who had been seized and for whom a ransom was demanded. 'Then Lasair and Rónán, the release of the priest having been refused them, came to Duibhthir Mór in the Gailenga (Gallen) and stayed there the night ... then came the priest to the house ... and Lasair gave her blessing to a church there in the Gailenga from that day to this: so from her is Cill Lasrach, commonly called ever since in Gailenga.' There was an old church in ruins in Killasser in 1838.[15] O'Hara surmises that she was eighth century but John Ryan opts for the sixth century as she is brought into connection with St Molaise of Devenish who died in 564 or 561. *St Lasair*

Graffy in Killasser has the ruins of what was probably the medieval church, Kilsheshnan, *Cill Seiscnén*. It was recorded in the annals under the date 1263 that 'Meachair Ó Ruadháin was killed by treachery, in the door of the church *St Seiscnén*

13.   Colgan, *Vita S. Faranni*, 336–40; O'Hanlon, ii, 557–61.
14.   169; *Martyr. Tall.*, xxvii, xxxix, 454–5; Martyr. Don., 169; O'Hanlon, vi, 642–3; Swords, *Register, Coll. Hib.*, nos 39 and 40, 16; Gwynn and Hadcock, 383; O'Rorke, *Sligo*, ii, 184, 188.
15.   *Beatha Lasrach*, ed. L. Gwynn, *Ériu*, v, 73–109, according to Ó Muraíle, 60, her Life 'must be treated with a fair degree of caution, if not outright scepticism'; O'Donovan, 485; see also *Onomast.*; O'Hara, Killasser, 8.

of Cill Seisnén, *Tempall cille Sescnen.*' This gives credence to the tradition in 1838 that this church was founded by Cisneán Ó Ruadháin who belonged to a family that may have given two thirteenth-century bishops to the diocese, Giolla na Naomh and Tomás. Apparently, there were two parish churches and two vicars, that of Seiscnén and that of Killasser in the what is now the modern parish of Killasser. Leo X agreed to unite both of them in December 1515 and grant them to Aodh Ó hÉineacháin. On his death or resignation, the parishes were to revert to their original position.[16] No St Seiscnén is recorded in either of the martyrologies though a man of that name is mentioned. He was father of St Benignus or Benen, a disciple of St Patrick, and was described as 'of the race of Cian, son of Oilioll Olum'.[17]

St Luathrenna   Killoran, *Cill Luathrenn*, is called after St Luathrenna or Luaithrenn, the daughter of Colmán, descended from Lugha who gave his name to the *túath* called Luighne. He in turn was descended from Corbmac Gaileng who gave his name to the present barony of Gallen.[18] Luathrenna's name is entered in the Martyrologies of Tallaght and Donegal under the date of 8 June and according to the latter 'Luaithrenn, Virgin of Cill Luaithrenn, in Coraun (Corran) of Connacht' was venerated on that day. She is mentioned in the *Life of Saint Corbmac*, who was reputed to have predicted her future sanctity when he visited Luighne and the adjacent regions of Galenga in the sixth century. The ruins of the medieval church of Killoran have been located in Killoran North townland.[19]

St Mobí   Kilmovee, *Cill Mobhí* ('Mobí's church'), was called 'Kelmoby' in the 1307 Taxation. Mobí, founder of a monastery in Glasnevin, was one of twelve disciples of St Finnian, founder of the church in Achonry, who included among others, Ciarán of Clonmacnois, Columba of Iona, Brendan of Clonfert and Colmán of Terryglass. If, as has been stated, Mobí Cláireineach ('the flat-face') was son of Beoaed of Corcothri, the inhabitants of Luighne and born in Kilmactigue, his claim to have founded Kilmovee is greatly strengthened. Mobi, also known as Berchan, was of the race of Eochaidh Finn Fuathairt 'of whom Brighit is descended'. His mother was Uanfinn, daughter of Finnbarr.

His monastery at Glasnevin had a school with fifty pupils which included the saints Canice, Comgall and Kieran. With St Finnian's permission St

16. *CPL*, xx, 399, Roman scribe wrote Cilsersgnaien.
17. *Martyr. Don.*, 301; ALC, AC; O'Donovan, 486; *Onomast.*; *Arch. Invent.* 2640; Ord. Surv. Letters, 146–7; O'Hara, Killasser, 146 (visual); JSRAI (1898), 405f.
18   *Onomast.*, 434
19. *Martyr. Tall.*, xxvi; *Martyr. Don.*, 148–9; Colgan, *Vita S, Corbmaci* (25 March), cap. xv, 753, n 32, 756; *Félire of Gorman*, 112; O'Hanlon, vi, 244–5; *Onomast.*; O'Rorke, *Sligo*, ii, 60–1; Farry, Killoran and Coolaney; *Arch. Invent.*, 2646; Ord. Surv. Letters, 155, 157.

Columba joined Mobí's school and while there, a great pestilence broke out, probably the *Buidhe Chonaill* which occurred in AD 548, and Mobí had to disperse his pupils. The *Life of Columba* states that Mobí asked him not to accept any grant of land without his permission. Subsequently, when the king of Erin offered him Derry he refused to accept it without Mobí's permission. Mobí died of the bubonic plague in AD 544 or AD 545 in his monastery in Glasnevin. The *Annals of Inishfallen* record his death thusly: 'The first mortality, which is called "blefed" in which Mo Bí Chlárainech fell asleep' (*mortalitas prima quae dicitur blefed Mo-Bi Chlarannech*). As Columba was leaving Derry he was met by two of Mobí's disciples who offered him Mobí's girdle as well as his permission to accept land. Accepting the girdle, Columba said: 'Good was the man who had this girdle, for it was never opened for gluttony, nor closed on falsehood.'

Mobí is also mentioned together with Nathy, Fechin and Luathrenna and Aidan in the *Life of Saint Corbmac* where he is described as the nephew of Finnbarr 'from the line of Huanflinna'. His feastday was celebrated on 12 October. The ruins of the old church in Kilmovee were noted in 1838 which appeared to the observer 'comparatively modern'.[20]

Achonry has one townland called Kilcummin (*Cill Cumain*) 'church of   *St Cumain*
Cumain'. There is another Kilcummen near Killala and there is a tomb in the churchyard there which is said to be that of St Commyn; his feast is celebrated on 22 August. This may be the founder of Kilcummin in Achonry. A site of an abbey has been located in Kilcummin graveyard and in 1836 it was recorded as 'an old abbey in ruins'. Later, in the middle of the fifteenth century, a cell of the Third Franciscan Order at Court was established nearby. There was a holy well known as *Tobar Cuimín*.[21]

Attymas has two townlands with the prefix Kil-, Kilgellia, *Cill Creig Oilí*,   *St Diarmaid*
'church of ?', where there is an old burial ground and Kildermot, *Cill Diarmata*,

20.   Colgan, 753, no. 34, 756; O'Hanlon, vi, 294–5; *Martyr. Don.*; *Leabhar Breac*, 19; *Book of Ballymote*, 122b; *Book of Lecan*, 109; *Onomast.* on Corcothri, Corcortri, Corca-Firthri, the people of the modern baronies of Gallen, Leyny and Corran; the *Book of Ballymote* mentions the king of Corcorthri under the year AD 60, 128b.; see also *Ogygia*, iii, 69, AU, i, 500, *Book of Lecan*, 349, *Book of Leinster*, TCD, *Martyr. Tall.*, 36, O'Flaherty's *Ogygia*, 334, *AFM*, 11, 656, ed. Hennessy, *Chronicon Scotorum*, 207, *Leabhar Gabhála*, 148, ed. O'Donovan, *Topical Poems of O'Dugan and O'Heerin*, Keating, 32, *RIA Procs.*; Ryan, 123–4; Ord. Surv. Letters, 153; *Annals of Innisfallen*, 70, a, 544 Ó Muraíle, 'Mayo Placenames' in O'Hara, *Mayo*, 67, 68, 69, 70, 72. Ó Muraíle states that Mobí is a pet name of Brénainn; *JRSAI* (1902), 188f.
21.   O'Hanlon, viii, 330–1; O'Rorke, *Sligo*, ii, 130–1; Gwynn and Hadcock, suggest the founder may have been St Caemen or St Coemgen, 390; *Arch. Invent.*, 2640, 2641, 2744.

'church of Dermot', a small twelfth century church. The Ordnance Survey Letters of 1838 describe a small church in ruins on the north side of Ballymore lake which was said to have been a chapel attached to an abbey. St Diarmaid was a brother of St Evinus, the reputed author of the *Tripartite Life of Saint Patrick*. More probably, he may have been St Dermitius, the eldest brother of St Corbmac who had emigrated from Munster to Connacht before Corbmac visited the region in the sixth century. The church of St Dermitius was said to have been in Kilmackeon near Sligo.[22]

St Gall of Lough Gara, St Subach of Corran and St Colmán of Drumrat

Another early Irish saint associated with the diocese and in particular with Lough Gara in Coolavin, originally known as Loch Techet, was Gall or Gallus. His name appears in the *Martyrology of Tallaght* and that of Donegal under the date of 4 or 5 April. There are two entries for St Subach of Corran, 1 August and 21 November, and the latter provided the description, 'virgin'. The Irish word *subach* means 'merry' and not surprisingly, her name was rendered in Latin as 'Hilarius'. St Colman of Druim-rath is also mentioned in the *Martyrology of Donegal* as well as the *Martyrology of Tallaght* where he is described as Colman mac Baeith in Druim Raith. This is probably Drumrat in the present parish of Keash. His feastday was celebrated on 9 August.[23]

St Lughaidh, Sts Niadh and Berchan, St Colman of Drumlias, St Mainchinn of Corran, Bishop Rodan of Kildalough, St Sealbach'

There were other early Irish saints who were natives of, or had some association with, the diocese. St Lughaidh, whose feastday occurred on 6 October, was bishop of several places including 'Tuaim-Fobhair in Luighne'. This could either be Toomore (Foxford) or more likely Toomour (Keash). O'Donovan, Hy-Fiachrach, gives *Tuaim dá bhodhar* for Toomore and *Tuaim dá bhodar* for Toomour; Ó Muraíle, 83, doubts O'Donovan's equation preferring rather *Tuaim Mhór*, 'big mound'. A papal letter in 1440 names the parish in Keash as Tuaimfaubar.[24] He was son of Lucht and his mother was Medhbh, daughter of Garbhan of *Ciarraighe Luachra* which is the modern County Kerry.[25] Sts Niadh and Berchan, whose feasts were celebrated on 5

22.   Colgan, 751, n 9, 756: *S. Dermitius qui inter hos fratres erat primo genitus, ad Borealles & maritimos Connaciae fines profectus, Ecclesia de Rosredheadh excitavit in regione Carbriae. Haec Ecclesia postea ab ipso aliisq(ue) fratribus ea(dem) cum ipso aliquandiu incolentibus, Kill-mac-neoguin, id est, cella filiorum Eugenii (Corbmac's father), appelata est; eaq(ue) amplis praediis dotavit & ditavit unus Dynasta ex familia Hi-Fiacgriachorum oriundus, alias versis terminis, Dubh-Fhlán, qui ex Muredacio filio fuit Lugadii Aengusio nati nepos. Consecravit namq(ue) illi Ecclesiae dotandae totum tractatum, qui inter Droiched Martra & Brugh-chinnslebhe versus occidentem & a Murbhuch de Ros-Birn, usque ad Ail-choidbin interjacet.*

23.   *Martyr. Don*, 9, 94–5, 215, 315; *Martyr. Tall.* (copy in *Book of Leinster*) 147, 214–15, 472–3; O'Hanlon, iv, 31, viii, 19, 138–9, 140, 209, 214–15, 315, *Saint Lughaidh, Saints Niadh and Berchan, Saint Colman of Drumlias, Saint Mainchinn of Corran, Bishop Rodan of Kildalough, Cruimthir Riagan.*

24.   *CPL*, ix, 89.

25.   O'Donovan, 39, note k *Martyr. Don*, 267.

June, were 'of Cluain Aedha Aithmet in Luighne'. It may be the present townland of Clooneagh in County Sligo.[26] St Colman of Drumlias [in Luighne (March)] had his feast celebrated on 19 June.[27] St Mainchinn was described as 'son of Collan in Corran'. His mother Deidi was the daughter of Tren and great-granddaughter of Dubhach Ua Lughair, chief poet to Laoghaire, son of Niall, 'king of Erinn at the coming of Patrick'. Mainchinn's festival was 13 January.[28] It has been argued that the ancient church of Kildalough in the townland of Streamstown in the parish of Ballysadare was in fact Kileaspuig-Rodain. Bishop Rodan, whose feast occurs on 24 August was said to have been St Patrick's *armentarius* or herd.[29]

Kilshalvy (*Cill Sealbhaigh*) was the 'church of Saint Sealbach'. Muintir Shealbhaigh were tenants in 160 acres of church land in that parish up to the sixteenth century. The ruins of a rectangular church (int. 13.9m E–W; 5m N–S) were located there.[30]

Meelick marks the site of an early monastery dedicated to St Broccaidh whose feastday was celebrated on 9 July. He is described in the *Martyrology of Donegal* as 'Broccaidh of Imleach-Broccadha in Maigheo' which has been identified as Emlech or Emlagh in the barony of Costello. The *Life of Patrick* by Tíreachán states 'Broccaidh of Imleach Each in Ciarraighe of Connacht' was brother of Lomán of Ath-Truim and son of Gollit, sister of Patrick who was mother of Lomán as well as Muiris, Broccaidh, and Brogan or Brocan. Broccaidh was Bishop of Emlagh and was with Patrick at 'Magh Sealgas in Connacht'.[31] Ciarraighe was a large region just south and east of Kilkelly and Urlaur with Maigheo, a village in the south-west of the region. Meelick was situated in Gailenga, north-west of Ciarraighe; Magh Sealga, Uí Briúin in Connacht, descendants from Brian, king of Connacht, the O'Conors, MacDermots, O'Flahertys, of Uí Briúin Seala, O'Rourkes, O'Reillys. The whole Uí Briúin territory extended from Cenannus to Drumcliff.[32]

Almost all round towers in Ireland are associated with ecclesiastical sites and one in Meelick marks the site of an early monastery dedicated to St Broccaidh.

St Broccaidh of Meelick

26. *Onamast.*, 254; *Félire O'Gorman; Martyr. Don.*; 146; O'Donovan, 147.
27. Ibid., 173, a note added that what was in brackets was in a more recent hand and professed to be from the *Martyrology of Marianus O'Gorman*.
28. *Martyr. Don.*, 15; O'Hanlon, i, 194–5.
29. O'Rorke, *Sligo*, ii, 336–8, *Martyr. Don.*, 227. One strange entry in the *Martyr. Tall.* under 10 August reads 'Cruimthir Riagan [patron of Achadh Conaire, with Indulgence]'. An explanatory note states the 'words in brackets are by a more recent hand'.
30. Selbhach the Elder, the only one mentioned in the *Martyrology of Donegal*, wrote an elegy on Corbmac Mac Cuilenain, king of Munster killed in 908.
31. *Martyr. Don.*, 191, n 5; *Life of Patrick*, lib 2, ch. 2.
32. O'Donovan, Map of Hy-Fiachrach.

An early gravestone there with crudely interlaced cross and border, is inscribed OR[oit] DO GRIENI ('A prayer for Griene'). While some round towers date from the tenth century, the majority were built in the twelfth. The interior was divided by wooden floors into several storeys with four substantial windows on the top floor. Their primary function was as belfries calling monks to prayer for different hours of the office. The raised doorway suggests that it might have been used to protect valuable monastic goods from raiders. Ruins of an old church in Meelick and in the townland of Ballintemple (*Baile an Teampaill*), were noted in the Ordnance Survey.

St Liadhain

Described as 'daughter of Eochaidh of the race of Laeghaire, son of Niall' and of St Muredach, Bishop of Killala, also of the race of Laeghaire, son of Niall, she apparently had Mayo associations.[33] Ó Liodáin, anglicised Lydon or Leydon, is a Connacht surname. A small, stone church (15ft x 13ft x 9ft) replacing the original wooden church is located today in Killedan townland. Another place name in Killedan parish is *Cill cinn iubhar*, 'the church of the hill of yews', the ruins of which are in the graveyard in Oxford townland. 'Only the vestiges of the church of Killkevne, *Cill Cuimhne*' were traceable in 1838.

Unassociated Cill churches in Parishes and Townlands

Other churches cannot easily be associated with early Irish saints. Such is the case with Kilbeagh, *Cill Beitheach*, 'birchen church', and Kilconduff (*Cill Chon Duibh*) 'Cú Dubh's church'. The location of some of the early churches might be pinpointed from place names today with the prefix of Kill- or Kil-, from the Irish *Cill*, meaning 'church'. However, many Kil- names derive from *Coill*, 'wood'. There are fifteen such parishes and approximately thirty-seven townlands with the prefix Kil or Kill (Cell). Bunninadden has the greatest number, with eight, followed by five in Kilmovee and four in Ballaghaderreen. Where they are named after a saint, it does not necessarily prove that these churches were founded by these saints. Their cult may have been promoted there at some later stage.

Kilturra (*Cill Toraidhi*), 'church of Toraidhi', is the name of a townland and parish in the present parish of Bunninadden. Fragments of the foundations of a church (*c*.20m E–W; 5m N–S) have been found in the Kilturra townland. In the same townland there is a cross-slab close to a holy well. Killavil (*Cill a bhaill*) is a townland in Kilshalvy, as well as five others with the prefix Kil- (*Cill*) and another in Cloonoghill in the modern parish of Bunninadden; Kilfree (*Cill fraoich* or *na friuich*), 'the church of the heather', which together with Killaraght, forms the modern parish of Gurteen, possessed a quarter of land in the Middle Ages. There is a cross-slab there near a holy well. In the

---

33.   Ó Muraíle, 60–3.

1307 Taxation, the parish is called Kelnafruch. Kilmactigue (*Cill mhic Thaidhg*), 'the church of Teige's son' is the ancient name of the present parish of Tourlestrane while Killure is a townland in the same parish. A cross-slab has been located in Kilmactigue graveyard.[34]

Other early church sites can be identified by the word temple or *teampall*. Templemore, the traditional name of Straide parish, was named after a medieval church *Teampall Mór*, 'the big church'. Part of the south wall could still be seen in 1838 and the tradition then was that it pre-dated Straide Abbey by 250 years or the beginning of the eleventh century. Also in 1838, ruins of an old church called *Teampall Rómhuc* in Carrowgalda were recorded. At the same time, church ruins were noted in Bohola townland and the same in Kilmovee appeared 'comparatively modern', similarly in Kilkelly. In Templevanny graveyard in Toomour 'ruins of an old church or monastery called *Teampall a Mhánaigh* were noted in 1836 and Templehouse ('*teach teampla*') was the location of a prebendary of the Knights Templar. Temple (*Teampall*) in Charlestown may have been the location of an ancient church. In the Survey of 1633, church land in Kilfree in Gurteen was called "Carrowentemple" where the old church of Killfroy standeth'.[35]

Teampall

34. O'Donovan, 484–5, 846; *Onomast.*; Swords, 12; *Arch. Invent.*, 2469, 2653, 2654, 2683, 2684.
35. Qtd in O'Rorke, *Sligo*, ii, 364, Ord. Surv. Letters, 148, 150, 151, 153, 158.

CHAPTER THREE

Troubled Times

Viking Invasions The diocese probably largely escaped the Viking attacks on Irish monasteries in the ninth and tenth centuries as the raiders came from the sea and Achonry has only one narrow sea-opening at Ballysadare. They came from Scandinavia where the population had grown too large for the amount of farmland available. Those who arrived on our shores came from the fjords of western Norway and had already colonised the islands of Shetland and Orkney from where they made their first raids along the Atlantic coast of Scotland. Iona was first attacked in AD 795, again in 801 and once more in 806 when they murdered no less than sixty-eight of the monks. Afterwards, the abbot and other survivors retreated to Ireland where they re-assembled their monastery in Kells. They brought with them their brilliantly illuminated manuscript which had been largely produced in Iona and which as a result became known as the *Book of Kells*.

From Scotland, they extended their raids down the east coast of Ireland and the first Viking fleets appeared in the Irish Sea in 837 with sixty longboats at the mouth of the Boyne and another sixty on the Liffey. These longboats were able to navigate the larger rivers and thus were able to attack and plunder larger monasteries like Clonmacnois. The worst period of the Viking raids lasted only about fifty years but they made a marked impact on Irish society. Warfare was endemic in early Irish society but Viking warfare was of a totally different calibre. They rounded up inhabitants, whom they killed indiscriminately. They had no intention of establishing settlements, apart from trading-posts which were confined to a few large ports and coastal strips. In Ireland their main endeavour was to plunder and monasteries were attacked because they were reputed to be depots of valuable gold and silver ornaments.

Laicisation of the Monasteries, Coarbs and Erenaghs In the ninth, tenth and eleventh centuries, many of the Irish monasteries were gradually laicised. Lay successors of abbots were known as coarbs or *coarba*, 'co-heirs of the abbot' or erenaghs (*airchinneach*), 'ecclesiastical stewards'. The distinction between coarb and erenagh seems to be one of degree rather than kind. Coarbs were the successors of abbots of the more important monasteries while erenaghs were of abbots of lesser institutions. Though laymen, they were held in reverence by the people as the successors of saintly founders. They acquired substantial lands of former monasteries from which they acquired tithes and paid a tax to the bishop from the twelfth century on. Coarbships were hereditary and coarbs were 'usually married, and if he were not married he had children, and after his death if any of his sons were qualified with learning he was chosen … to be coarb, and if none of his sons were capable, another of that sept and surname was chosen'. The Ó Beolláin family were coarbs of Drumcliff for almost 500 years.

With the twelfth century reform, an attempt was made to absorb coarbs and erenaghs into the new diocesan system. Some became abbots of new religious orders, like the Augustinian Canons, which replaced old Irish monasteries. The First Synod of Cashel in 1101 decreed that 'no layman should be an erenagh in Ireland and that no erenagh of the church of Ireland should have a wife'.[1] From then on they became clerics in minor orders though not priests and many of them became rectors without care of souls. Rectors or parsons were somewhat persons of leisure, often very young and handsomely rewarded with a portion of tithes which were 'divided into four parts. Whereof the parson, being commonly no priest, hath two parts, the vicar who is ever a priest and serveth the cure hath one fourth part and the bishop hath another fourth part, which God knoweth in these poor waste counties, doth arise to very small portions.'[2]

Absorption of Coarbs and Eerenaghs into the New System

One of his principal duties was to provide hospitality as the original monasteries did and his main burden was to provide the bishop with entertainment which could be very costly. 'And indeed, by these refections did the bishops chiefly maintain themselves, and their followers, spending the most part of the year in this wandering kind of life, among their tenants, receiving from them meat and drink for 100 and sometimes 200 people that followed the bishop …'[3] Another duty of erenaghs-*cum*-rectors was to collect rents owed to the church and they were also expected to contribute to the upkeep and repair of the parish churches on their lands.

Duties

The deaths of Flaithgel, abbot of Drumrat (Druim-ratha), and the erenagh of Drumrat (Druimrathe) in 793 and 1017 respectively and that of Ceallach Ua Maelmidhe, erenagh of Druim-raithe, in 1016 indicates that the monastery was still in existence at the end of the eighth century and that it was certainly

Obituaries

1. On coarbs and erenaghs see Barry, John, *IER*, 88, 17–25; 89, 24–35, 424–32; 91, 27–39; 93, 361–5; 94, 90–5, 147–53, 211–18; Sir John Davies, 'Letter to Salisbury', in Morley, *Ireland under Elizabeth and James I* (London 1890), 365.
2. Gwynn, 'The First Synod of Cashel', *IER* (Aug. 1945), 82ff.
3. Montgomery, 'Account of the bishops …', in Shirley, ed., *Papers relating to the Church of Ireland*, 26.

laicised by early eleventh century and probably much earlier. The death of Maelfinnian, described as the 'coarb of Fechin and bishop of Tuath-Luighne,' in 993 was also recorded by the *Annals of Ulster*. The obituary of another coarb of Fechin who was abbot of the Augustinian Canons is mentioned by the same annals in 1230 while that of an erenagh is recorded by the *Annals of the Four Masters* in 1158.

Ó Mocháin family

Erenagh families were often transformed into great ecclesiastical dynasties, providing numerous clerics in the diocese. Such was the case with the Ó Mocháin family who were erenaghs of Killaraght. *Muintir Mochain Chille hAthracht* were described as *maoir na Croise Athracht*, 'keepers of the Cross of Saint Attracta'. They were described as descended 'from Cuboirne, fifth son of Eochaidh' who was brother of Sts Aidan and Colman.[4] The relics of St Attracta were variously described as paten inscribed with a cross; the 'Cross and Paten' of Attracta were much revered relics of the saint in Killaraght. Early in the fifteenth century the parish priest complained to Rome that they were taken from the church by clerics and laity to use for their own profit. Some time later they disappeared. Benedict Ó Mocháin who died in 1361 was described as 'archdeacon of Killaraght'.[5] He probably acted as steward of the lands of the hospital and nunnery. The family provided the diocese with one bishop, Conn, a Cistercian, who ruled the diocese from 1448–63. In that century some twenty-five of the name are recorded in papal documents, three of them, Cathal, Éinrí and Ruaidhrí, vicars of Killaraght and three others, Fearghal and two Ruaidhrís, separated from each other by fifty years, rectors of Coolavin where Killaraght is situated. Coincidentally, a well-known family of travellers in the diocese, called Maughans, may be Ó Mocháin descendants.

4.   Donovan, 41, 'Others say that the Cuboirne from whom Ó Mocháins were descended was son of Eoghan Aidhne, son of Eochaidh Breac.' Elsewhere Eochaidh Breac is called 'Eochaidh of the Moy', 46–7, Pedigree of Ó Mochain to Gregory, Abp of Tuam, d.1392, 42–3 notes q-r The Cross and Cup.
5.   ALC, AU.

CHAPTER FOUR

A Diocesan Church

The twelfth century was a time of enormous change in Ireland, both politically and ecclesiastically. At the beginning of the century, Irish church governance was brought into line with practice elsewhere, i.e. dioceses over which bishops ruled. Up to now, the practice was to chose a monk to be ordained bishop largely for the purpose of ordaining priests, while power and authority were vested in the abbot. This changed at a synod held in Rathbreasail in Tipperary in 1111 held during the pontificate of Pascal II (1099–1118). The *Annals of Ulster* give the fullest account of what happened: 'A synod was assembled at Fiad-mic-Oengusa (Rathbreasail in the great central plain of Tipperary) by the nobles of Ireland around Cellach, coarb of Patrick and Mael Muire Ua Dúnáin, noble senior bishop of Ireland, with fifty bishops or a little more, together with 300 priests, and 3,000 ecclesiastics around Muirchertach Ua Briain together with the nobles of the half of Moga, to enjoin rule and good conduct upon everyone, both layman and clerk.' Muirchertach Ua Briain was king of Munster and recognised as high-king by the kings of Leinster, Ossory, Meath and Connacht which probably explains the choice of Rathbreasail as the venue for the synod.

Synod of Rathbreasail 1111

Here the country was divided into two halves, following its traditional division of *Leath Cuinn* and *Leath Mogha*, one ruled by the Archbishop of Armagh and the other by the Archbishop of Cashel, each with twelve suffragans, with twenty-six dioceses in all. The northern ecclesiastical province included three secular provinces of Ulster, Meath and Connacht while the southern half consisted of Leinster, Munster and a small section of Connacht. The kingdom of Connacht was divided into five dioceses, Tuam, Clonfert, Cong, Killala and Ardcarne. Achonry was not included but a decree of Rathbreasail added a proviso that the Connacht clergy were free to change this division, provided that there were not more than five dioceses in the province. Connacht was, perhaps, less strongly represented than any of the other four provinces. However, twenty-six dioceses was a large number by European standards seeing that England with a much larger population had less than half that number. From the beginning most Irish dioceses were too small to be economically viable. The reason for that large number was that the country was divided into

Dioceses

a hundred or so petty kingdoms and each of them were eager to have its own bishop. The synod did well to reduce the figure to twenty-six, almost half of the fifty bishops present at the synod.

Connacht Hegemony

The death of Muirchertach Ua Briain in 1119 marked the end of the dominance of Munster in Ireland. Toirdelbach Ua Conchobhair (1088–1156) had succeeded his brother as king of Connacht in 1106 and almost immediately began to flex his muscles wider afield. Three years in a row, 1114, 1115 and 1116, he raided Munster with such severity that a contemporary annalist reported that he 'caused Munster to cry aloud' and carried away hostages, finally succeeding in dividing Munster into two parts: Thomond and Desmond. The rise of Connacht in the twelfth century as a major political power was due in large part to the singular ability of Toirdelbhach as a strategist and tactician.

Synod of Kells 1152

Another synod was held in 1148 off Skerries with fifteen bishops and a few hundred lesser clergy, presided over by Maeleachlainn (Malachy) of Armagh. A synod was held at Kells in 1152 during the pontificate of Eugene III (1145–53) in the presence of the papal legate, Cardinal John Paparo. The synod established four ecclesiastical provinces, Armagh, Cashel, Dublin and Tuam and thirty-two other dioceses bringing the total to thirty-six; this arrangement has endured with a few changes to the present. Armagh had nine suffragans, Dublin had four, Cashel had fourteen and Tuam had six which were Mayo, Killala, Roscommon, Clonfert, Achonry and Kilmacduagh.[1] Maol Ruadain O'Ruadan, who was present at Kells was appointed Bishop of Achonry.

Cistercians

Over the centuries many abuses had crept into the Irish church. As monasteries grew in wealth they attracted the interest of lay predators and many of them fell into the hands of laymen. Other abuses included simony or selling church positions. Maeleachlainn Ó Morgair (St Malachy) had gone to Rome in 1139 seeking approval for the new diocesan arrangement. On his way, he stayed with St Bernard at his Cistercian monastery of Clairvaux. As a result, the Cistercians were introduced into Ireland. Maeleachlainn had left a few companions in Clairvaux to be trained as Cistercians. They returned to Ireland in 1142 with some French confrères and set up their first abbey at Mellifont. Numbers flocked to join the new abbey as monks or lay brothers. Between 1147 and 1153 seven new communities were established in different parts of the country.

1.   The bishop of Achonry was recorded as two, which in fact should be joined into one, Achad Conaire (field of Conaire). Ms 92 of School of Medicine, Montpellier, qtd in H. D. Lawlor, 'A fresh authority for the Synod of Kells', in *RIA Procs.*, xxxvi, no. 3 (1922), 18.

Their nearest abbey to Achonry was established at Boyle in 1161 after several changes of sites beginning in 1148. It was to have close connections with the diocese. Some of its monks became bishops of Achonry while the abbey itself set up a dependant cell with a few monks in Templevanny in Keash. One Bishop of Achonry, Aengus Ó Clúmháin, resigned in 1248 and became a monk in Boyle where he died in 1263. *Boyle Abbey*

Maeleachlainn had also visited an abbey of Augustinian Canons at Arras in northern France and he also introduced these into Ireland. Most of the old Irish monasteries like Ballysadare adopted this Augustinian rule. Ruins of a church called Kildalough can be seen on the Corhownagh–Streamstown road and was said to have been a sister church of Killaspugbrone in Strandhill. A raised path near Springfield is locally called the Friar's Walk and a lake in the area was described in ordnance survey maps as *Loch na Bráthar,* 'the Friars' Lake'. St Mary's Abbey was built some time before the Norman invasion, a short distance from the site of an earlier monastery founded by St Fechin. St Mary's continued in existence until the general suppression of the monasteries in 1585. *Abbey of Augustinian Canons, Ballysadare*

The Premonstratensian Canons were founded in France early in the twelfth century and established a monastery at Lough Key early in the next century. One of the Canons, Clarus MacMailin O'Mulconry, founded a cell, Kildermot Abbey, overlooking Ballymore Lake in Attymas. *Abbey of Premonstratensian Canons, Lough Key*

In the twelfth century a momentous political change took place, the Norman invasion of Ireland, which marked the beginning of the long involvement of England in the affairs of Ireland. A group of Normans invaded Ireland in 1169, 1170 and 1171. The Normans, descendants of Norsemen, had settled in northern France, now called Normandy, in the tenth century. The duke of Normandy, William the Conqueror, invaded England where he won the Battle of Hastings in 1066 and assumed the throne of England. By 1100 most of Wales was conquered and it was from there that Strongbow with other Norman barons invaded Ireland. Their aim was to carve out an independent Norman kingdom for themselves and, fortuitously, they were invited by Dermot MacMurrough who, banished from his kingdom of Leinster, took refuge in Bristol in 1166. *The Norman Invasion*

Henry II, who ruled England, Scotland and Wales and half of France, was a Frenchman who spent most of his time in France and spoke only French. He had no intention of allowing the establishment of an independent Norman kingdom in Ireland. Like William the Conqueror, Henry sought and was given papal approval for his conquest of Ireland. The pope then was Nicholas Breakspeare, who took the name Adrian IV (1154–9), the only Englishman *Henry II* ever to occupy Peter's throne. He issued the bull *Laudabiliter* praising Henry's intent to conquer Ireland 'to extend the bounds of the church, to proclaim to a rude and untaught people the truth of the Christian faith and to root out the nurseries of vice from the field of the Lord'. The Pope's claim to the sovereignty of Ireland was based on a forgery, the 'Donation of Constantine', which purported to grant the Pope possession of 'all the islands'.

Henry had another pressing reason for his Irish adventure. Archbishop Thomas à Beckett had been murdered on the steps of his cathedral in Canterbury and Henry, deeply implicated, was threatened with a papal interdict. To evade the consequences he crossed to Ireland in 1171 and landed about eight miles from Waterford with a large army on 17 October. The kings of various regions, except the king of Connacht, came to Waterford and swore allegiance to him. Henry II could not wage war on the king of Connacht in winter time 'on account of the floods of water, the steepness of the mountains and the remoteness of the lands between them'. He promised to return the following summer with an army and force the king of Connacht into submission. All the archbishops and bishops of Ireland also came there and swore fealty to Henry.

Council of Cashel 1172

He received from each of them sealed letters confirming the lordship of Ireland to himself and sent ambassadors to the Pope, Alexander III (1159–81), with the bishops' letters accepting his lordship and the Pope duly confirmed it. The bishops included Giolla Íosa, Archbishop of Armagh and his eight suffragans; Domhnall, Archbishop of Cashel, with eleven suffragans; Lorcán Ó Tuathail, Archbishop of Dublin, with five suffragans; and Catholicus, Archbishop of Tuam, also with five suffragans, the last of which mentioned was the Bishop of Achonry (*Achahthonrensis episcopus*).[2] Henry summoned the bishops to a council of the Irish church at Cashel early in 1172. It decreed that 'children should be baptised in a church in the name of the Father and of the Son and of the Holy Spirit by a priest'. Up to this in certain places in Ireland immediately a child was born, 'his father or someone else immersed him three times in water, and if a son, three times in milk, and afterwards it was customary to throw that water and milk into his drains or other unclean places'. It also decreed that laymen who wished to have wives should be joined together according to ecclesiastical law. 'The majority of them have as many wives as they wish and even are accustomed to have wives who are related to them.' The council also ordered the payment of tithes, i.e. one-tenth of the annual value of their crops and animals, for the support of the church. This was to provide the necessary foundation of another Norman innovation, the

2.   *Council of Cashel 1172*, Stubbs (ed.), *Gesta Regis Henrici Secundi*, 26–7.

introduction of the parish system into Ireland. The system existing today was gradually established in the late twelfth and thirteenth centuries.

The Norman penetration was not evenly distributed throughout the country. At least one-third of the country in 1300 remained unoccupied by Normans and in Connacht they represented little more than the imposition of isolated military outposts in the form of stone castles. In Achonry one castle was built by the de Angulo family at Castlemore in the barony of Costello and another by Jordan de Exeter at Ballylahon. Ballymote Castle was built about 1300 by the Anglo-Norman Richard de Burgo and was one of the strongest in Connacht, with walls about ten feet thick. It was held later at different times by the families of O' Connor Sligo, the MacDermots and the MacDonaghs.

The division of the church into parishes in Western Europe occurred between the ninth and eleventh century but was introduced much later into Ireland and certainly after the Norman invasion. They began in the east and south at the end of the twelfth and early thirteenth century and later still in the west and the north. Parishes had rectors and vicars. The care of souls was provided by vicars, the equivalent of modern parish priests. Tithes, the principal income of the clergy all over Christendom, was the way laity supported the church by contributing one-tenth of their produce. This in turn was divided into three or four parts with the bishop getting one-third or one-fourth while the rest was divided between the rector and vicar, two-fourths to the rector and one-fourth to the vicar. In addition the vicar got all the offerings for baptisms, marriages and funerals.[3]

Parishes

Rectories usually consisted of a number of parishes and often rectors were sinecures, i.e. they had no responsibility for the care of souls, for celebrating Mass and administering the sacraments. Many were clerics in minor orders and never ordained priests. In the barony of Leyny the rectory of Hy-Fiachrach and Banada covered the parishes of Kilmactigue, Killoran and a portion of Achonry as well as Attymas and Kilgarvan (Bonniconlon) which then formed part of the kingdom of Hy-Fiachrach. This was coterminous with the lordship of Ó hEadhra and when that family split into two branches in the middle of the fifteenth century, Ó hEadhra Buidhe and Ó hEadhra Riabhach, so did the rectory into Killoran (Coolaney) in the territories of Ó hEadhra Buidhe and Kilmactigue (Tourlestrane) in those of Ó hEadhra Riabhach. The rectory of Dachorand (*Dá Chorann*, the two Corrans) and *Mota*

Rectories

3.   I am heavily indebted to K. W. Nicholls, 'Rectory, Vicarage and Parish in the Western Irish Dioceses' in *The Journal of the Royal Society of Antiquaries of Ireland, JRSAI*, ci (1971), 53–76; 'Medieval Irish Cathedral Chapters' in *IER*, xxxi, 103–11; see also Swords, 'A sixteenth century Register of Achonry' in *Coll. Hib.*, nos 39 and 40 (1997–8), 7–22.

(Ballymote) covered the barony of Corran and ran through the parishes of Emlefad and Kilmorgan (Ballymote), Cloonoghill, Kilshalvey, Kilturra (Bunninadden), Drumrat and Toomour (Keash). The rectory of Coolavin and Ranna consisted of Kilfree and Killaraght while the rectory of Sliabh Lugha comprised the parishes of Castlemore and Kilcolman (Ballaghaderreen), Kilbeagh (Charlestown) and Kilmovee. The rectory of Athleathain (Ballylahon) included all parishes in Gallen barony. By the sixteenth century this rectory was divided into the rectory of St Delphinus of Bohola, which ran through the parishes of Bohola, Killedan (Kiltimagh), Kilconduff (Swinford), Meelick and a portion of Killasser and the rectory of St Nicholas of Templemore, which included the parishes of Straide, Attymas, Toomore (Foxford), Kilgarvan (Bonniconlon) and twelve quarters of the parish of Killasser.

Chapters   Cathedral chapters, i.e. a group of Canons with a few other dignitaries attached to the cathedral, established in Ireland in the late twelfth and early thirteenth centuries, were an important feature of the medieval church. Canons were largely drawn from old ecclesiastical families with the families of Ó Clúmháin, Ó hEadhra, Mac Donnchadha and above all Ó Mocháin providing the largest number in the fifteenth and early sixteenth centuries. The number at any given time was indeterminate, usually hovering between twelve and fourteen.

Prebend   Canons were usually assigned prebends, parcels of lands throughout the diocese from which they drew their income. There were fourteen such prebends by the sixteenth century. Prebends were lands occupied by rent-paying tenants, five in the barony of Leyny, five in Corran barony, two in the half-barony of Coolavin and one each in Costello and Gallen, and in the fifteenth century were valued generally at two marks, though Killoran was three to four marks.[4] The amounts of land varied from a third of a quarter to one, two, three, or four quarters. The chief function of canons, including dean, chantor, chancellor and treasurer, was to assist daily in choir in the cathedral and sing the divine office. Canons were clerics, not always or even often priests, and their incomes from prebends supported them during their studies while in their late teens or early twenties.[5]

Some non-resident canons employed choral vicars to fulfill their functions in the cathedral choir. They also had a vote in the chapter which gave them the decisive voice in the election of bishops. By the end of the papacy of

4.   Kilmactigue, Killoran, Kilvarnet, Moymlough, Dougharne, Kilmorgan, Emlefad, Cloonoghill, Kilturra. Kilshalvey, Killaraght, Kilfree, Kilmovee, Kinaffe and Killedan.
5.   Swords, 'A sixteenth century Register of Achonry', in *Coll. Hib.*, nos 39 and 40 (1997–8), 17–18.

Innocent III (1198–1216) the rules for the election of bishops throughout the whole church were completed. The Fourth Lateran Council (1215) had laid down the church's law governing the election of bishops and they favoured the election by the chapter as the norm. The vast majority of bishops in Ireland in the thirteenth century were elected by the canons. If rules were not followed the election was declared invalid and the pope nominated the bishop.

An agreement was reached in 1215 between Innocent III and King John of England on the roles of the pope and the king in the election of bishops. Canons were obliged to seek a licence from the king to hold the election and the candidate they chose was to be presented to the king for his approval before his election was confirmed by the pope. The temporalities, i.e. the revenues of the diocese, were to be held by the king during the vacancy and restored once the new bishop had been duly installed and swore an oath of fealty to the king. This arrangement recognised the dual role played by a bishop who was not only pastor of his diocese by virtue of ecclesiastical appointment but he also was a secular landlord and thus a tenant of the crown because of his temporalities – the rents he received from diocesan lands. This remained the standard practice until the Reformation in the sixteenth century.

Election of Bishops

The dean and chapter notified King Edward I (1239–1307) in April 1286 that Achonry was vacant following the death of Denis (*correcté* Tomás) Ó Miadhacháin and asked for a licence to elect his successor which he granted accordingly. He instructed them 'to elect a bishop who shall be devout, fit for the rule of that church and useful and faithful to the King and Ireland'. Further, he empowered Stephen, Bishop of Waterford, justiciary of Ireland, to give the royal assent on behalf of the king after the election and to signify to the Archbishop of Tuam 'to do what depends on him in this matter'. The newly-elected bishop was then to take an oath of loyalty to the king and the temporalities were restored to him when the king received from him 'letters patent under his and the chapter's seal that this election shall not tend to the King's prejudice, nor be drawn into a precedent'. The chosen candidate was then automatically appointed by the pope who sent letters confirming his appointment to the chapter, *Hodie ecclesie vestre,* the clergy and people of the city and diocese, and the vassals (tenants) of Achonry church lands, *Hodie ecclesie Achadensi,* the Archbishop of Tuam, *Ad cumulum,* and the King of England. It is noteworthy that in December 1461 when Donnachadha Ó Conchobhar was appointed Bishop of Killala there was no letter to the King of England, indicating the waning of English power in Gaelic areas.[6]

6.   A. F. O'Brien, 'Episcopal elections in Ireland, *c.*1254–72' in *RIA Procs.*, lxxiii, section C, no. 5 (1973), 129–56.

Local interests predominated in the election of bishops in Ireland, whereas in England both the papacy and the crown controlled most episcopal appointments. In Gaelic Ireland native Irish rulers exercised a power that was a force to be reckoned with and English influence was virtually non-existant. All five dioceses of the Dublin province as well as Meath, where the king's power was paramount, had English or Anglo-Irish bishops from the early thirteenth century. Thus the Irish episcopacy was divided on racial grounds. Though Achonry diocese was politically divided with Leyny, Corran and Coolavin baronies in County Sligo under the control of the Ó hEadhra, Mac Donnachada and Ó Gadhra clans, and the two baronies in East Mayo, Costello and Gallen controlled by the Norman families of de Angulo and de Exeter, all its bishops were native Irish. A relatively small number of clergy were of Norman extraction, mostly from the de Exeter family, lords of Ballylahan.

The pope only intervened in cases where elections were not held according to the laws, in which cases he made good the canonical defects in the electoral process. By the end of the thirteenth century the king insisted that bishops-elect renounce those clauses in their papal appointments that suggested that the temporalities were in the bestowal of the pope and not of the king. In subsequent centuries the pope's role in choosing bishops became increasingly paramount and eventually he directly made all appointments.[7]

Dean   Three other dignitaries made up the chapter: dean, archdeacon and provost. The dean was vicar or parish priest of Achonry where he had two parcels of land in the east of the parish as well as a fourth of the tithes of the parish with the usual other parish offerings for christenings, marriages and funerals. The deanery described as a 'major elective dignity with cure', was estimated to be worth ten silver marks. In the sixteenth century he had a house there called *Teampaill Muire*, without a garden but he had two portions of land known as *Gort Sagart*, 'situated in the eastern part of Achonry on both sides of the king's highway'. He also got a quarter of the tithes and the other usual parish fees.

Archdeacon   The archdeacon was vicar of Kilturra (part of the modern parish of Bunnin-adden) where he had a quarter of land let out to tenants and in addition to their annual rent of 13s 4d, he was paid annually fourpence by the dean, provost and all rectors. The estimated value of the archdeaconry an 'elective non-major dignity with cure', was only three marks.

Provost   The provost (precenter or chantor), a 'non-major elective dignity with cure', was a canon with a prebend and a priest as the position involved the care of souls. His income was estimated at eight marks and he had two quarters of

7.   *Cal. Docs. Ire.* (1285–92), 92, 107, 228; *CPL*, xx, 369.

land, 'commonly called *Cill Easbaig*', probably surrounding the cathedral and a portion of the parish tithes.

The official, whose duties were concerned with the bishop's judicial court, was not a member of the diocesan chapter but a judge in the bishop's court. He received a mandate from Rome in February 1396 to appoint Con Mac Oireachtaidh (Gerraghty), cleric, to the rectory of Coolavin, 'if found fit after the usual examination in Latin'.[8] Henry Hart, who helped to compile the Register of Achonry at the end of the sixteenth century, was described as *jurisperitus et olim dicti episcopatus officialis*, 'a legal expert and one-time official of the said diocese'.

Official

There was also a treasurer (*oeconimus*), a 'non-major dignity with cure', whose job was to collect the monies owed to the bishop by the dean, archdeacon and the rectors, from each of which he received fourpence. He also received from a penny to sixpence from tenants in the bishop's lands.

Treasurer

Parish priests or perpetual vicars, were responsible for the care of souls. They were perpetual because they were vicars for life and not removable except for some canonical offence. Every parish had a 'glebe', a small portion of land, not more than a few acres, where the vicar kept a cow and grew food for his household. Vicars' remuneration was precisely defined at least in the sixteenth century but probably the norms were largely the same in previous centuries. They were given the first fruits from the land which consisted of *beart arrabh*, a sheaf of oats, which they got in the form of oat-flour at harvest time and *cuid Carghas*, Lenten dues, which were the first-born of livestock due in spring. They were also given *meascán príomh*, the first pat of butter after churning. The laity paid twopence at Christmas and Easter and a penny for the priest's houseboy who made his bed and looked after his horse. Offerings were made for baptisms and marriages and also for the funerals of the better-off which were shared between priests and friars. From all this each priest was obliged to pay the bishop ten testilia and also provide the usual *cuid-oíche*, overnight accommodation for the bishop and entourage.[9]

Perpetual Vicars

How parish boundaries were determined is lost in obscurity. It has been suggested that some were based on pre-existing monastic termons of which coarbs were rectors. Killaraght may have been such a case, where the Ó Mocháin clan continued to be erenaghs. Others may have been based on lesser secular divisions of the *túatha* while some might have been based on grants of lands made to monasteries by Irish or Norman lords after the Synod of Kells.[10]

Parish Boundaries

8.   *CPL*, iv, 530.
9.   Swords, *Coll. Hib.*, nos 39 and 40 (1997–8), 17–18; *Pat. Rolls, 16 Jas. I.*, qtd in Tracts relating to Ireland, 49n.
10. Gleason, *Killaloe*, 308–9.

Vicarages   There are references in the papal letters in the fifteenth century to some twenty-one vicarages, all easily identifiable with the present parishes. But these represent only those parishes to which Rome made appointments.[11] A few parishes are not recorded, notably three in the Norman barony of Costello, Castlemore, Kilcolman (Ballaghaderreen) and Kilmovee and two, Toomore (Foxford) and Kilgarvan (Bonniconlon) in the other Norman barony of Gallen. Vicarages were valued from one mark for Attymass to eight marks for Emlefad, while most vary from four to six marks.

11.   Achonry (mensal parish), Attymass, Ballysadare, Bohola, Cloonoghill (Bunninadden), Drumrat (Keash), Emlefad (Ballymote), Kilbeagh (Charlestown), Kilconduff (Swinford), Kilfree (Gurteen), Killaraght (Gurteen), Killasser, Killedan (Kiltimagh), Killoran (Coolaney), Kilmactigue (Tourlestrane), Kilmorgan (Ballymote), Kilshalvey (Bunninadden), Kilturra (Bunninadden), Kilvarnet (Collooney), Athleathan (Straide), Teampullmuire (Straide), Toomour (Keash).

CHAPTER FIVE

Monks

Augustinian Canons came into existence in the eleventh century under the influence of the Gregorian reform and adopted the Rule of St Augustine in the following century. By the end of the Middle Ages there were more than 4,500 foundations throughout Christendom and they were the largest religious order in England. The abbey of Augustinian Canons was built in Ballysadare a short distance from a church of an earlier Irish monastery. The date is uncertain but it probably pre-dated the Norman invasion in the twelfth century as the terms 'coarb' and 'erenagh' continued to be used. The Berminghams desecrated the abbey church in 1261, killing Cathal Ó hEadhra and five men of Leyny in it and, in reprisal, Domhnall Ó hEadhra killed Sefin Bermingham 'who had on his head the bell taken from the church in Ballysadare'. The abbey was plundered again in 1267 and 1291 *AFM*.[1]

St Mary's Abbey of Augustinian Canons, Ballysadare

In March 1423 Martin V (1417–31) ordered the appointment of a cleric, Conn Mac Searraidh, rector of Banada and Hy-Fiachrach 'if the defect which he has in his left eye be not so great as to give rise to scandal'. The same pope ordered Bishop Richard Belmer of Achonry and Canon Cormac O'Hara in October 1428 to have Mac Searraidh, then a priest, received as Augustinian Canon in Ballysadare. (Mac Searraidh had been dispensed on account of his defective eye in 1423 to allow him become a priest.) On the same day he ordered that Mac Searraidh be appointed abbot if the accusations he made against Abbot John (surname not given) were proven. He had accused him of dilapidation, simony and perjury, of being 'a notorious fornicator', celebrating Mass while excommunicated and absenting himself for long periods from the monastery. Bishop Belmer was to bless Mac Searraidh or allow him to be blessed by any Catholic bishop and to send his oath of fealty to the pope.

The One-eyed Abbot (Conn Mac Searraidh)

Conn must have been successful, as an Augustinian Canon from St Mary's Abbey in Inchmacnerin in Elphin, Cormac Mac Donnchadha, in turn accused him of allowing the abbey to fall into ruin, violating an interdict imposed on him by Bishop Maghnus Ruadh Ó hEadhra, by celebrating Mass 'in contempt of the Keys', and committing perjury. Cormac complained to Rome that because of Conn's power he had no hope of receiving justice in Achonry. For

1.   *CPL*, vii, 261 [see 46, 109 and 270].

this reason, Eugene IV in July 1435 ordered outsider Bishop Riocard Ó Fearghail of Ardagh (1425–44) to investigate the case and, if the accusations were proven, to remove Conn and replace him with Cormac, who could be blessed by any Catholic bishop without prejudice to the Bishop Ó hEadhra.

It would seem that Cormac failed to have Mac Searraidh removed because another Augustinian Canon, Ruaidhrí Mac Donnchadha, this time from St Mary's Monastery in Roscommon, accused Mac Searraidh of dilapidating the goods of the monastery in Ballysadare and of public perjury. Mac Donnchadha also complained that Mac Searraidh was blind in one eye which was not mentioned in his dispensation for a 'defective' eye. Eugene IV (1431–47) ordered the archdeacon and Canons Cormac Mac Donnchadha and Cormac Ó Mocháin in August 1444 to investigate. Ruaidhrí had gone to Rome in 1444 with Bishop Uilliam Ó hEideagáin (1429–49) of Elphin and many other religious, most of whom died. The Bishop of Elphin survived but the Abbot Tadhg Mac Diarmada of Boyle, Prior Uilliam Ó Flannagáin of Roscommon and Abbot Ruaidhrí Mac Donnchadha of Ballysadare died.[2]

In any event, Mac Searraidh was still *in situ* in 1456–7 when another member of the monastery and another Mac Searraidh, Uilliam, claimed that he had been provided to the abbacy by the pope and that Conn had been removed. The latter appealed to Rome against the decision but failed to prosecute his appeal within the required time. When Uilliam tried to assume the abbacy, Conn 'rebelliously opposing, stirred up a number of temporal lords, his friends, against Uilliam, and with their support, procured the violent expulsion from their homes of Uilliam, his father, brothers and friends'. He was compelled by intimidation and 'for the sake of the restoration of their homes of Uilliam and his said father etc., to surrender before witnesses all right in and to the monastery, to swear not to molest Conn about it and not to seek absolution from his oaths'. Because of Conn's power, Callixtus III (1455–7), instructed the abbot of the Premonstratensian Canons of Holy Trinity, Lough Key and two Killala Canons to investigate the case and if the charges of Uilliam were found to be true to remove Conn and induct Uilliam as the true abbot.

Conn Mac Searraidh appears to have survived and come to some financial arrangement with Uilliam which formed the basis of accusations against Uilliam by Domhnall Ó Clúmháin, an Augustinian Canon in the monastery of St John the Evangelist in Tuam but very likely a native of the Ballysadare region where the Ó Clúmháins were a prominent ecclesiastical family. He claimed that Uilliam Mac Searraidh was 'greatly defamed in those parts in these

2.   'Annals of Ireland 1443–68' in the *Miscellany of the of the Irish Archaeological Society* (Dublin, 1846) 205–6; *AFM.*

and divers other crimes'. Apart from perjury and simony, Ó Clúmháin claimed that Uilliam had 'consumed for evil uses the goods' of the monastery. Pius II (1458–64) ordered Canons Aodh Ó Mocháin and Alastar Ó Murchú on 11 July 1461 to examine the case and if required to remove Uilliam and appoint Ó Clúmháin.

Apart from disputes over the abbacy, other matters related to the Augustinian Canons were among the petitions to Rome during these years. One of the Ballysadare Canons, Seán Ó hArracháin (Orachin), priest and 'bachelor of degrees' was dispensed in January 1457 'to receive or retain one benefice only with or without cure, of any value, wont to be governed by secular clerks'. In other words, to be appointed parish vicar. Two Augustinians, Seán Ó Mithidhín (Omithian) and Domhnall Ó Dubhalcháin (Odulcnain), son of an Augustinian priest, seemed to have been accomplices in a theft of monastery property. At least they received stolen goods from those who carried out the theft, 'certain nobles' according to one and 'a certain number of sons of iniquity' according to the other. Later, they became scrupulous, fearing that they had incurred excommunication as a result of their actions, and in ignorance of the law. Paul II (1564–71) instructed the Abbot of Ballysadare, probably Domhnall Ó Clúmháin in March 1463–4, to absolve them after imposing a penance. Domhnall Ó Clúmháin occupied the abbacy after the death of Muirgheas Mac Donnchadha for seven or eight years without any right to it.

Sixtus IV (1471–84) ordered Bishop Brian Ó hEadhra (1463–84) at the end of November 1471 to appoint the Dominican Domhnall Mac Donnchadha as abbot. Mac Donnchadha was 'by both parents of noble race' and a native of Ballysadare and stated that he was 'desired by the greater part' of the monks in the monastery which was 'in great ruin'. Mac Donnchadha was to wear the habit worn in the monastery. *Dominican Abbot*

Over a dozen years later Conn Mac Searraidh was still abbot and had been for one to two years without any title. Sixtus IV ordered Archdeacon Tomás Mac Congaláin and Canons Aodh Ó Mocháin and Domhnall Ó Mionacháin (Ominachan) in May 1484 to remove Mac Searraidh and grant the abbacy *in commendam* for life to Abbot Maghnus Mac Donnchadha (Maccloneyd) of the Premonstratensian monastery of Holy Trinity, Lough Key. He was permitted to retain the abbacy of Lough Key as well. The newly-elected Bishop Tomás Ó Conghaláin of Achonry, appointed on 10 May, was still in Rome and pledged to the papal treasury for the *annates* on behalf of Mac Donnchadha.[3] *Premonstratensian Abbey of the Holy Trinity, Lough Key*

Little wonder that the annalist was lyrical in his praise of the generosity of Mac Donnachadha when he died in 1504 and was buried in Lough Key. He

3.   *CPL*, xiii, 179, 180; *Arch. Hib.*, v, 96–7.

could well afford to be generous with the revenue of two wealthy abbeys. Described as 'the preserving shrine and casket of the bounty and prowess of Erinn, and the man who, of all that had come down from Tomaltach-na-Cairge, had given and presented most to poets and musicians, and to men of every craft … and this death of Mac Donnachadha's son is a decapitating blow to the learned of Erinn.'[4]

The archdeacon and Canon Ó Mocháin together with Canon Diarmaid Ó hÉineacháin were instructed to appoint Augustinian Canon Domhnall Ó Clúmháin vicar of Kilbeagh (Kyllbayb) and remove Mathgamhain (Omichion) who had taken possession of the vicarage without any title.

Unbelievably, almost eighty-one years after his name first appeared in the papal records, the name Conn Mac Searraidh again reappeared and again as abbot in Ballysadare. If he was twenty when he was rector of Banada in 1423, he must have been over a hundred in 1504. More likely, this Conn was probably the son of the one-eyed abbot as the latter's death was recorded in a lost bull in the tenth year of the pontificate of Sixtus IV, sometime before August 1483 resulting in the abbacy being vacant. The Premonstratensian abbot of Lough Key was appointed the following May and while the papal mandate referred to Conn's removal, he was in all likelihood dead.

Tomás Ó Congaláin, one of the papal mandatories, in Rome and appointed bishop that May, was probably unaware that Mac Searraidh was dead.[5] Canon Feidhlim Mac an Bhreitheamhain (Macbrehun) informed Julius II (1503–13) in February 1504 that Abbot Conn Mac Searraidh of Ballysadare and Vicar Maghnus Ó Clúmháin of Kilvarnet had 'alienated and dissipated the immoveables of the monastery and the precious moveables of the vicarage and converted the price to their own uses'. He also alleged that Mac Searraidh had committed simony and Ó Clúmháin had celebrated Masses 'in the presence of excommunicated persons'. The canonry and prebend of Killoran had become vacant following the death of Ruaidhrí O'Hara but Pilib and Tadhg Ó Clúmháin held them for six years. Julius II commissioned Domhnall Ó Mocháin (Ommachan), Conn Mac Ceallaigh and Richard Barret to summon Conn, Maghnus, Pilib and Tadhg in February 1504 and if they found the foregoing to be true, to assign the monastery *in commendam*, the vicarage and the prebend to Feidhlim.[6]

St Mary's Cistercian Abbey, Boyle
The first Abbot, Muiris Ó Dubhthaig, died in 1174. Conchobhar Mac Diarmada, lord of Moylurg, became a monk there in 1198 and another lord

4.   ALC.
5.   *CPL*, xiii, no. 904.
6.   *CPL*, vii, 261, 270, viii, 52–3, 542, ix, 434, xi, 312–13, xii, 127–8, 219–20, 221, 487, 492, xiii, 179, 179–80, xviii, 14, 290.

of Moylurg, Maelruanaidh Mac Diarmada, resigned his lordship and became a monk in the abbey in 1331. The abbey church was consecrated sometime between 1218 and 1220 and affiliated to Clairvaux in 1228. Abbot Ó Maoilbhrénainn died in the monastery as a result of having been blooded in 1225 and five years later, Donsléibhe Ó Henmainen, 'chief master of the carpenters of the monastery of Boyle', died.

On the night of Trinity Sunday 1235, bands of Norman soldiers attacked the monastery, broke into the sacristy and took away chalices, vestments and other valuables. 'The English chiefs were highly disgusted at this and sent back everything they could find and paid for what they could not find.'

Abbot Eoghan Mac Donnchadha, deprived 'for his demerits' by Abbot Henry of Mellifont, acting on instructions from Abbot Matthew of Clairvaux, 'the father-abbot of Boyle', was replaced in April 1414 by Cormac Mac Dáibshí dispensed as son of a Cistercian abbot and unmarried woman.[7] He in turn was accused of leading an immodest life by one of his monks, Aodh Mac Diarmada, who replaced him in 1428.[8]

Abbot Domhnall Ó Mocháin, 'head of the wisdom, knowledge and instruction of Connacht', died in 1441. His successor, Tadhg Mac Donnchadha, died the same year on that ill-fated journey to Rome with the Bishop of Elphin. Seán Mac Dáibhsí, probably Abbot Cormac's son became abbot in 1444 and was succeeded by Conn Ó Mocháin, who became Bishop of Achonry in 1449.[9] One of the monks, Conn Mac Dáibhsí, accused Abbot Maeleachlainn Mac Donnchadha (Machdonnochayrmaich), of committing perjury and simony, dilapidating the goods of the monastery and 'openly keeping a concubine in his own house'. Conn was promised the abbacy if his accusations against Maeleachlainn were proven.[10]

Eoghan Mac Diarmada of Moylurg died in 1534 after a year in the lordship during which Moylurg was in a state of disturbance and commotion and Abbot Aodh Mac Diarmada of Boyle assumed the lordship. 'War and dissensions grew in the country through this.'[11] At the suppression in 1569, Tomaltach Mac Diarmada was abbot when the site contained the walls of church and belfry, cloister, hall, dormitory and some ruined buildings. It also owned about 1,700 acres, three castles, several granges and many cottages as well as many rectories and vicarages. It was leased to William Usher in 1589. Abbot Giolla Íosa Ó Cuileannáin was hanged in Dublin in 1584.

7.   *CPL*, vi, 435.
8.   *CPL*, vi, 435.
9.   *CPL*, ix, 418; x, 53–4.
10.   *CPL*, xi, 481.
11.   *ALC, AFM.*

CHAPTER SIX

Friars

Begging Friars

The Mendicant or Begging Friars, Dominicans and Franciscans, arrived in Ireland early in the thirteenth century, not long after they were founded. Dominic Guzman gathered a small group of followers around him in a house in Toulouse in 1215 and received official approval from Honorius III (1216–27) at the end of the following year. The aim of the new order was preaching and hence the title, Order of Preachers. Study is the first requisite of a preacher and every convent with at least twelve members ruled by a prior had a house of studies and with a doctor of theology. By 1248 there were five *studia generalia* in the five university cities of Paris, Oxford, Cologne, Montpellier and Bologna. The order grew rapidly and by the time of Dominic's death in 1221 there were sixty convents: France, Spain, Italy, England, Germany and Hungary.

Priory of the Holy Cross, Straide

The first foundation in Ireland was in Dublin in 1224 followed shortly by others in Waterford and Cork. Jordan de Exeter, Lord of Ballylahan, gave the Dominicans a site at Straide in 1252 where they established the Priory of the Holy Cross. *AFM* gives the foundation date as 1253. It is said that Franciscans were first on this site but Basilia de Bermingham from Athenry, where her family had founded the Dominican friary in 1241, was married to Jordan's son, Stephen, and refused to eat and drink unless it was given to the Dominicans. The Straide friary was burned down a year after it was founded but was rebuilt. Another Stephen born in 1246, probably the son of the above, became a friar at Straide on 25 March 1263. It is suggested that this Stephen was the author of the *Annals of Multyfarnham* compiled in Straide, because of the frequent references to the de Exeter family and the fact that they cover more fully the period 1245–74 roughly corresponding to his own lifetime. There are also frequent references to his own family from the year 1261, for example the death of Richard de Exeter's first wife Eva in 1262, and his second wife Mabel two years later.[1]

Most of its subsequent history is unrecorded and can only be guessed at from references in the annals to the de Exeter family and their castle in Ballylahon. King Feidhlimh Ó Conchobhar of Connacht mustered an army

1.   'Annals of Multyfarnham', in *Tracts relating to Ireland*, ii, v–vii, 1–16.

and marched to Ballylahon in 1316 where he burned the town and slew Slevin de Exeter, Lord of the town, together with de Cogan, 'the noblest baron of his time in Ireland'. Many other English were slain and Ó Conchobhar returned with much booty. The de Exeter family were also targeted by other Norman families. A battle took place in Ballylahon in 1380 between MacWilliam Burke and McWilliam Uachtrach where the lord of Ballylahon, MacJordan de Exeter and John de Exeter were slain. They were also victims of their own families. Another lord of Ballylahon, John MacJordan was murdered by his own kinsmen, the sons of John de Exeter. Ballylahon castle was only two miles from the friary in Straide and the friars must have suffered great anxiety during these violent incidents. The castle was breached by the Mac Donnchadha clan who took the castle gate with them to Ballymote.[2]

Pope Eugene IV (1431–47) conferred indulgences on the friary in 1434 for the purpose of raising funds to restore the building. However, with that exception, papal records refer only to the rectory and vicarage of Straide. Rectors and vicars must have had encounters with the friars and, perhaps, not always amicable as both were often competing for the same limited resources. Eoghan O'Hara was an eighteen-year-old cleric when Rome made him rector of Straide in 1404 if 'found fit in Latin', in succession to Pilib Ó Ceannabháin. A twenty-two-year-old scholar from Tuam, Tomás Mac Dhuarcháin, was promised the vicarage in 1418 after he had received tonsure. Worth only four marks, he would have had to employ a priest, possibly one of the Dominicans, for a year until he became a priest. His predecessor, John de Exeter, had to resign because he failed to be ordained within the required year.[3] Pluralism was rife in the church at this period and Straide was often sought after by outsiders like Mac Dhuarcáin. Vicar Domhnall Mac Dhuarcáin of Turlough in Tuam was granted the rectory and vicarage of Straide in 1418 for five years, after which he was to resign the vicarage. Canon Cormac Ó Dubhda, vicar of Kilglass in Killala, petitioned for and was granted the Straide rectory in 1423 at a considerable distance from Kilglass. Seán Ó Deirg (Odrich) unlawfully held the rectory in 1490 and Innocent VIII granted it to Canon Maolmhuire Ó Ceanndubháin of Tuam. Straide was also a prebend which was given in 1509 together to Vicar Domhnall Ó Banain (Ybenan) of Bohola.

Other references to Straide in the annals concern burials in the monastery of the renowned bardic Ó hUiginn family. Tadhg Óg, 'chief preceptor of the poets of Ireland and Scotland', described as 'the affablest and happiest that ever professed the Dán', died in Kilconly, County Galway and was buried in Straide

2.   *AFM.*
3.   *CPL*, v, 613, viii, 105.

in 1448.[4] Tuathal Ó hUiginn 'head of his nation and chiefe master of the Aesdana of Ireland died of a short disease' in 1450 and was succeeded by Ruaidhrí Óg Ó hUiginn. He too was probably buried in Straide though the annalist did not record it. However, Brian, 'head of his own tribe, superintendant of the schools of Ireland and preceptor in poetry', who died on Maundy Thursday 1476 was buried in Straide.[5]

St Thomas's Priory,
Urlaur

A Norman family, de Angulo, later Nangle or MacCostello, was lord of Costello barony and the priory was said to have been founded by Edmund MacCostello and his wife, Fionnuala. The friars settled here about 1430 and Eugene IV wrote on 15 April 1433 to the bishop, Maghnus Ruadh Ó hEadhra, on foot of a petition received from two Dominican friars, William de Angulo and Tomás Ó Gruagáin. Apparently, they had incurred the sentence of excommunication by acquiring houses or dwelling sites, one in Toombeola, County Galway and the other in Urlaur, where they spent some time without Rome's permission or that of the bishop. Boniface VIII (1294–1303) had decreed that mendicant orders were prohibited from acquiring new houses or sites anywhere whatsoever without Rome's special authorisation. Eugene IV ordered Maghnus to absolve William and Tomás and other friars from excommunication and any other irregularity they may have incurred from saying Mass while under that sentence and also gave them permission to build a church with bell and belfry and other necessary workshops. Each and every friar there was to enjoy all the 'privileges, indulgences, liberties and exemptions' usually conceded to such by the apostolic see.[6]

Cloonameehan

Following a petition from Eoghan Mac Donnachadha (and two other laymen, Baron of Norach and Edmund de Latin of Kildare and Meath), Innocent VIII (1484–92) gave permission in December 1488 to build a Dominican priory at Cloonameehan in Bunninadden, about three miles from Ballymote, dedicated to St Dominic and a cell of St Mary's, Sligo. Influenced by devotion to the order and its members, because of their exemplary lives and 'the rich fruits which they bear by continuous preaching of the word of God and by other good works among the people' they granted lands for dwelling houses for the friars. Brian Mac Donnachadha, lector of theology in the Dominican house in Sligo, was the first prior.[7]

Carmelites,
Knockmore

Carmelites settled sometime about 1320 at Knockmore near Gurteen in County Sligo, a few miles from Ballaghaderreen in the barony of Coolavin

4.   'Annals of Ireland'.
5.   'Annals of Ireland', 225; *AFM.*
6.   Full Latin text in de Burgo, 312–13.
7.   *CPL,* xv, 328; de Burgo, 327–8.

known as 'O'Gara's country' and were said to have been invited there by
Edmond, a member of that family. They were known as the 'black friars'.
Knockmore was one of four or five Carmelite monasteries still in existence in
the 1570s. The ruins of the rectangular church are located in the centre of
Knockmore graveyard with the external dimensions measuring 25.6m E–W,
8.65m N–S. The east window was said to be in perfect condition by a
correspondent for the Ordnance Survey in 1836. Four cross-slabs were found
on the site, each incised with a simple Greek cross. A short distance away there
is a holy well known locally as *tobar na mbráthair* or *tobar na mainistreach*, 'the
friars' well' or 'the well of the monastery'.[8]

Franciscans,
Ballymote

Francis was born in Assisi in 1182, the son of a wealthy merchant. As a
young man, after a profound spiritual experience in 1208, he decided to live
in absolute poverty, observing the most literal gospel message that has ever
been seen. Companions flocked to join him after Innocent III (1198–1216)
gave him permission in 1209 to found an order which experienced an
incredible expansion, reaching no less than five thousand members. A Second
Order for nuns was founded later by St Clare and a Third Order was for lay
people, men and women who took vows and lived in a community.

Eugene IV granted a licence in 1442 for the foundation of three monasteries
of the Franciscan Third Order, one of them in Ballymote founded by
Cúchoigcríche Mac Donnachadha. Building in Ballymote had already begun.
Another member of that clan, Donnachadha, together with a number of
accomplices burned the monastery, the house and 'seventeen stacks of corn',
as well as the town of Ballymote, drove the friars out and 'violently despoiled
them of their goods'. Donnachadha afterwards pretended to repent and
promised to make satisfaction but in fact, 'injured them as much more as he
could'. Another Mac Donnachadha, Brian, imposed 'unlawful cesses and
tributes' on the friars and their servants. All this information was contained in
a petition that the master, Domhnall Ó Dubhda, and the friars presented to
Sixtus IV (1471–84) on 13 December 1482. He ordered three bishops,
Raphoe, Clonfert and Achonry, to summon Donnachadha and Brian, and
compel them under pain of excommunication to make satisfaction to Ó
Dubhda and his friars. Oddly, there is no mention of 'sisters' in either the
petition of Ó Dubhda or the popes mandate.[9] It probably fell to Mathgamhain
Mac Craith of Clonfert (1463–87) to carry out the pope's instructions as

8.   O'Dwyer, *Irish Carmelites*, 27, 38, 94–5, 97, 131, 133–4, 136, 159, 170 no. 77; M.J.
     Connellan, 'Knockmore Carmelite Convent' in *Whitefriars* (Sept.–Oct. 1955), 10–11;
     Arch. Invent., 2664, 2689, 2760, 2879.
9.   *CPL*, xii.

Robert Wellys of Achonry was an absentee Englishman and the Bishop of Raphoe, Giovanni Rogerii, was an Italian from Rome.

Nicholas V (1447–55) instructed Bishop Conn Ó Mocháin in 1454 to confirm the grant of land made by Seán Ó hEadhra to Aindréas Ó Clúmháin and friars and sisters of the Third Order of Saint Francis, called the order of Penance. Ó hEadhra, 'lord of Campolagruin', had offered him and his community, with the consent of his brothers and children, 'a number of lands, namely, a half townland and the possessions called the cantred of Arduabair and the cantred of In[i]smaid and the place Ciurtw[i]lleag, in the said diocese, with all their appurtenances'. He was motivated by 'the welfare of his soul and the souls of his progenitors and to the praise of God and the Blessed Virgin Mary, and out of reverence for the said saint'.

Aindréas had already begun the building of a house or church for the friars and sisters there. The Pope asked Ó Mocháin to give permission to Aindréas, his friars and sisters, to complete the house or build another, with church, bell, bell-tower, cemetery, dormitory, refectory, etc. in Court, and 'to transfer themselves thither'. The latter phrase strongly suggests that the community had been formed some time previously and already had a number of friars and sisters.[10] Pilib Ó Clúmháin, probably a kinsman of Aindréas, who held a canonry in Achonry and the prebend of Kilmacteige, some time before July 1448, entered and made his profession as a friar of the Third Order of Saint Francis, 'called the order of Penance' in Rosserk, in Killala diocese.[11] Hadcock and Gwynn, 274, state that Rosserk 'had been fully established before December 1441 when Ó Clúmháin entered that friary which does not correspond with the date July 1448 given in *CPL*, x, 395.

The Augustinian Friars, the Order of Hermits of St Augustine, received a definitive constitution in 1256 but they existed long before then. The order was introduced into Ireland in the last decades of the thirteenth century with a foundation in Dublin in 1282. The monastery of Corpus Christi at Banada was founded in 1423 on land donated by local lord, Donnachadha O'Hara. A castle, sometime referred to as 'the seven towers of Banada' already existed and was converted into the friary with Cathal O'Hara as the first prior. By a decree of the prior general, Banada became a house of the Observance under the care of the general.

The Observant movement obliged friars to a stricter life, to observe as much as was humanly possible the vows of poverty, chastity and obedience as well as the Rule and constitutions of the order. It began in Italy towards the end of

10.   *CPL*, x, 713–14.
11.   *CPL*, x, 395–6.

the fourteenth century and later spread to France and Spain. In Ireland it was adopted in the fifteenth century largely among the Gaelic Irish in rural areas while the Anglo-Irish lived for the most part in towns. Observants often lived in small hermitages in remote places while others called 'conventuals' lived in larger convents or friaries situated largely in towns or urban centres. Banada had the distinction of being the first Observant friary in Ireland and spread from there some years later when it was also adopted by Franciscans.

A Banada friar, Aodh Ó Meallaigh (O'Malley), founded another monastery in 1453 in Murrisk at the foot of Croagh Patrick. Tadhg Ó Meallaigh, head of the O'Malley clan, gave Aodh a place called Murrisk (*Leathearmursge*) for a house, church, cloister, bell-tower, bell, refectory, dormitory and other necessary workshops. Aodh described Murrisk as a place 'far remote from cities, towns, castles, etc. and that the inhabitants of those parts, have not hitherto been instructed in the faith'. Callixtus III (1455–8) granted Aodh permission in February 1456–7 to build as above 'without requiring licence of anyone'. The friary, known as *Muirske Chruach Pádraig*, was dedicated to St Patrick and pilgrimages to the mountain were made from the friary.[12] Another Banada friar, Uilliam Ó Duibhidhir (Otedura), was accused by 'some of his enemies and other persons ignorant of the law' of being guilty of bigamy. He had secretly contracted marriage which he later consummated 'with certain virgin' unaware that they were related by marriage within forbidden degrees. After her death, he married another virgin unaware that she too was similarly related to him. Later, he entered and was professed in Corpus Christi in Banada. Eugene IV dispensed him in April 1445.[13]

Murrisk

When Nicholas V (1447–55) authorised the foundation of the friary in Moyne (Scurmore) in Killala in 1454, the papal document contained the following clause: 'As soon as the said friars of the province of Ireland learned the said papal provisions and the life and rule of their brethern of the Observance, they began to rule themselves in accordance therewith.' The Observant Augustinian friars of Ireland were given their own province and Meleachlainn Ó Clúmháin (Ocluban) was elected as vicar-provincial and this was confirmed on 7 August 1460.[14]

Twenty years after Banada was founded, the building of the church and house had only recently begun. Eugene IV granted in 1444–5 to all who visited Corpus Christi on the feast of St Patrick and gave alms for its repair and conservation, an indulgence of five years and five quarantines. The friars petitioned that the indulgence be increased in 1460.

12. *CPL*, xi, 294.
13. *CPL*, ix, 468–9.
14. *CPL*, xi, 583–4.

At the recent petition of the prior and friars of the said house, containing that it is situate in a desert and barren place and lacks choir, cloister, chalices, books and other things needful for divine worship, and that the friars therein are in want for their food etc. and if the said indulgence were extended to two other years, so that the faithful visiting the said house and giving alms there might gain an indulgence of seven years, they would visit it with greater devotion, and would give alms more frequently and more freely etc., the pope hereby extends the said indulgence of 5 years to 7 years and as many quarantines, granting to all the faithful being penitent and having confessed, who visit on the feast of St Patrick the church of the said house and give alms as above, a relaxation of 7 years and 7 quarantines of enjoined penance, these presents to last in perpetuity.

Because of the great poverty of the region, the Augustinian general in Rome gave the friars a special dispensation in 1476 allowing them to eat meat from All Saints Day until Advent and butter, eggs, cheese and milk products from Advent to Christmas Day.[15]

Ó hEadhra Family

The Ó hEadhra family dominated the monastery. Their original benefactor, Donnachadha Dubh Ó hEadhra, 'styled the O'Hara', resigned his lordship to his brother Cormac and entered Banada. Cormac's place in turn was taken by Seán Mac an easpaig Ó hEadhra. Cormac Ó Cathasaigh (Ykassy) complained to Rome that the prior and most of the community belonged to the Ó hEadhra family and 'do all capitular acts and utterly and entirely dispose at their pleasure, contrary to the regular observance, of all the goods belonging in common to the prior and convent without asking and rather in contempt of the other brethern who are not related, to the grave prejudice and hurt of the said other non-relatives'. Pius II (1458–64) instructed Bishop Brian Ó hEadhra on 25 June 1460 to investigate the matter and prevent the prior from disposing of anything which required the assent of the whole convent. Relations within the Ó hEadhra family were not always so cordial. Seán Óg Ó hEadhra and his son were treacherously slain in 1488 by Ruadhrí and Aodh, sons of his own brother, on Sunday in the monastery there.

Brian Ó hUiginn

Brian Ó hUiginn was one of the last friars in Banada prior to its suppression. Probably born in Kilmactigue he may well have been kinsman of the distinguished bardic poet, Tadgh Dall Ó hUiginn. While in Rome, Brian was appointed Bishop of Elphin on 5 May 1542 but failed to get control of the diocese due to local opposition. According to the Jesuit, David Wolfe, 'Bernard (Brian) was a good and religious man in himself but he was not acceptable to the people', particularly to the powerful merchant O'Crean family, who

15.   *CPL*, xi, 583–4, xii, 103; see *CPL*, ix, 455.

favoured their own Andrew O'Crean, a Dominican in Sligo Abbey. Crucially, Ó hUiginn failed to get control of the temporalities.[16] He left for the continent, spent some time in Lisbon and later in Spain. He resigned Elphin in 1561 and was succeeded by O'Crean, appointed at the same consistory on 28 January 1562 when Eoghan Ó hAirt became Bishop of Achonry. Ó hUiginn died in Villaviciosa, Spain in 1563 and was buried in the Augustinian friary there.

In 1586 the Governor of Connacht went through the province collecting forces and when he had the requisite number ready, he marched from the monastery in Banada at 'the beginning of a very dark night in autumn and stopped neither day or night, until he arrived at Ardnaree about noon the following day' where he inflicted a crushing defeat on the Scots mercenaries encamped there.[17]

16.   *ASV ARM.* LXIV 28, f118v–119f., *CSP*, Rome, Eliz., i, 49, Moran, *Archbishops of Dublin*,
        418.
17.   *AFM.*

CHAPTER SEVEN

Roman Tentacles

Roman Taxes   Rome spread its tentacles widely and relentlessly throughout Christendom, including Ireland, in the thirteenth century. In the early decades of that century the Pope appointed representatives in Ireland, mostly to collect taxes to fund the Crusades. These were levied at frequent intervals throughout the Christian world during that century. An Italian envoy organised a team of collectors and preachers, usually friars, who fanned out throughout the country to raise money. The *Annals of Loch Cé* recorded one of these envoys who came in 1221: 'Jacobus Penciail came to Erinn from Rome to settle and arrange ecclesiastical affairs; and he collected horse-loads of gold and silver from the clerics of Erinn through simony and departed from Erinn in the same year.' In other words, he sold church jobs all over the country.

Papal Fees   There were also all sorts of regular fees due to Rome for routine business. The dean and chapter of Tuam were given permission to contract a loan of 2,400 marks to meet expenses incurred in expediting their affairs at Rome. Penalties for non-payment were severe. Archbishop Tomás Ó Conchobhair of Tuam (1259–79) was ordered in 1266 to pay 500 marks within one month to Master Sinicius, clerk of the papal treasury 'sent on this and other business in England and Ireland'. If he did not pay, Sinicius was to excommunicate him.[1]

Coinage   The silver penny or denarius was introduced by Charlemagne in the eighth century and was the basic unit of commercial activity for at least four centuries. The pound and shilling were only monetary units for the purpose of accounting but not actual coins. The shilling became a circulating coin in the reign of Henry VII (1485–1509) and the pound was minted early in the modern era. For the purpose of accounting, though pennies and pounds were not in circulation, there were 12 pennies in a shilling or *solidus* and 20 shillings in a pound or *libra*. (£.s.d. survived in some countries like Ireland and England up to the twentieth century.) In the middle of the thirteenth century Genoa and Florence issued gold coins, a florin in the case of Florence which had a portrait of John the Baptist on one side and a lily on the other. Achonry was valued by Rome at 33 1/3 florins, one of the poorest dioceses in Ireland. Later in the thirteenth century Venice produced a gold coin, the ducat, and subsequently

---

1.   *CPL*, i, 3 May 1259 and 1266.

florins and ducats were circulating through hundreds of kingdoms, duchies and towns. A mark was worth 160 pennies or 13s 4d and was the unit by which all church benefices, including those of Achonry, were valued.

Innocent IV (1243–54) sent John de Frosinone to organise a tax on the incomes of the clergy for the relief of the Holy Land ordered by the Council of Lyons in 1245. It was alleged that he collected 40,000 marks, which included legacies, Holy Land subsidies, as well as jewels and annual payments from archbishops, bishops and other prelates. Some of the money was raised by releasing people from vows they had taken. John de Frosinone was also accused of appropriating 3,000 marks for himself which he deposited in the Cistercian abbeys in Dublin and Mellifont.[2]

John de Fronsinone

Maolruanaidh Ó Ruadháin (Ruane) attended the Synod of Kells in 1152 where Achonry was first included among the dioceses of the western province. It was then called Luighne, a *túath* or territory ruled by the O'Haras. The name survives in Leyney, a barony in County Sligo. Ó Ruadháin was chosen as its first bishop. He appears to have been a member of a family, probably natives of Cúil Neiridh in north Gallen, where Muintir Ruadháin were near neighbours of Muintir Duarcáin who held the lordship of Cúil Neiridh. No less than eight of that name served as bishops in the province of Tuam in the second half of the twelfth century and the first half of the following century, two in Kilmacduagh (Galway), two in Killala, three in Achonry, as well as Felix Ó Ruadháin, Archbishop of Tuam (1201–35). The *Annals of Loch Cé* record the murder of Meachair Ó Ruadháin by the Normans in the doorway of the church of Cill Seiscnén in the parish of Killasser in 1263. Early in the fifteenth century Aodh Ó Ruadháin was a casualty in a skirmish where Mac Duarcáin, lord of Cúil Neiridh, was also killed.[3]

Maolruanaidh Ó Ruadháin

The reign of Ó Ruadháin in Achonry coincided with meteoric rise of the Ó Conchobhair family in the Irish political world. Ruaidhrí succeeded his father as King of Connacht in 1156 and ten years later he had assumed the high-kingship of Ireland (1166–98). Ruaidhrí was a dominant figure at the Synod of Athboy in 1167 which was also attended by Archbishop Lorcán Ó Tuathail of Dublin and Archbishop Cadla Ó Dubthaigh of Tuam. In fact, Ruaidhrí appointed Lorcán as his emissary to Henry II and it was on this mission that he died in the little town of Eu in Normandy in 1180.

Rise of the Ó Conchobhair Family

2.   *CPL*, i (7 Feb. 1252).
3.   Nollaig Ó Muraíle argues convincingly in favour of the north Gallen location of the Ó Ruadháin family. I am indebted to Máirtín MacNiocláis for the Ó Muraíle reference. O'Donnell; *Killala*, 4, cites Kenneth Nichols on Kilmacduagh location of the Ó Ruadháin family. Kilmacduagh: Rugnad Ó Ruadháin, d. 1178 and Mac Giolla Ó Ruadháin, d. 1203, Killala: Imar Ó Ruadháin, d. 1179 and Giolla Kelly Ó Ruadháin, d. ante 1253.

About 1200 the King of Connacht, Cathal Cromhderg, wrote to Innocent III asking him what was the church teaching on the question of a freeman who takes refuge in a church. The Pope answered that he is not to be violently expelled or 'delivered up to death or punishment', no matter what he has done. The rectors of churches ought 'to obtain for him life and limbs, he making satisfaction for his crime, unless he be a public thief or highwayman'. If a slave takes refuge in a church, he is to be compelled to return to service, once his master swore to the clergy that he would not hurt him.[4]

Clemens Ó Sniadhaigh (Snee) (1214–19)

In January 1208, Cathal Cromhderg imprisoned Cathal, the grandson of Tadhg Mac Diarmada, King of Moylurg, in violation of the guarantees given by three bishops. One of these was Clemens Ó Sniadhaigh.[5] The other was the Bishop of Elphin, Ardghal Ó Conchobair, and the third was Muireadhach Ó Dubhthaigh. The diocese of the latter is not known but it was not in the province of Tuam. After some time the bishops secured the release of Cathal 'without pledge or hostage'. However, the story had a bad ending. Mac Diarmada was captured shortly afterwards in Moylurg by a 'great force' which included Ruaidhri Ó Gadhra, king of Sliabh-Lugha, and while his life was spared he was blinded as a punishment.[6]

Fourth Latern Council (1215–16)

Innocent III (1198–1216) wrote to the Irish archbishops on 4 April 1213 informing them that the Fourth Lateran Council would be convened on 1 November 1215.[7] They, in turn, were to inform the other bishops in their province. All were summoned to appear in person at the council. None would be excused except those unable to travel through sickness or ill-health and even these were expected to send a representative. No less than eighteen Irish bishops – six of whom were of Norman origin – and two bishops-elect travelled to Rome to participate in what became the greatest gathering of the whole Middle Ages. In all, there were 415 bishops and primates and 800 abbots and priors, as well as representatives of all secular rulers. Of the Irish bishops present, the largest contingent came from the western province. They were led by Archbishop Ó Ruadháin of Tuam (1201–35) and included the bishops of Elphin, Killala, Clonfert and the bishop-elect of Mayo. Achonry was represented by Clemens Ó Sniadhaigh.

Decrees

The decrees of the council condemned in a general way abuses then prevalent in the Irish church, such as storing household goods in churches,

4.   *CPL*, i, 9.
5.   The annalist describes Ó Sniadhaigh as a bishop, but only records the death of his predecessor in Achonry, Ó Ruaidháin, six years later in 1214.
6.   *ALC*.
7.   Dunning, 'Irish representatives and Irish ecclesiastical affairs at the Fourth Lateran Council', in *Medieval studies presented to Aubrey Gwynn*, 90–111.

nightly banquets after the celebration of the divine office and marriage within the forbidden degrees. The council limited the marriage impediments of affinity and consanguinity to the fourth degree. It also expressed disapproval at the frequency of episcopal resignations. One of the decrees of this council enjoined the observance of what became known as the 'Easter duty', i.e. that all Catholics were bound to confess their sins and receive Holy Communion at least once a year. Bishops were obliged upon their return to hold diocesan and provincial synods to insure the decrees were observed in their dioceses. In fact, Innocent III wrote to Cathal Crobhderg, King of Connacht, asking him to assist the Archbishop of Tuam and the other bishops in the province to enforce the decrees. He also asked him to allow freedom in ecclesiastical elections and to prevent those who tried to establish hereditary possession of 'the Lord's sanctuary'.

CHAPTER EIGHT

Matters Sexual

Marriage   There were widespread abuses in marriage and sexual morality in medieval Ireland. Reforms were undertaken in the twelfth century, not only in Ireland but in the church in general when the church defined its law on marriage in that and early in the following century.[1] Marriage is the result of the consent of the couple which ideally should be expressed in a public ceremony. After a public betrothal the banns were to be read in the parish church on three successive Sundays when parishioners could raise objections. Marriage took place at the door of the church when the couple expressed their willingness to marry and this may have been followed by a nuptial Mass.

Clandestine   But many marriages did not take place in public and the church accepted
Marriages   these 'clandestine' or secret unions as consent was the paramount element for the validity of the marriage. These marriages were common not only in Ireland but throughout western Europe and this remained the position until the *Tametsi* decree of the Council of Trent in the sixteenth century. Such marriages gave rise to many disputes. A partner could claim lack of consent at the original marriage and this, if proven, would lead to annulment. A husband could disown the marriage resulting in the loss of hereditary rights for his spouse and children. As society was largely based on a land economy, disputes and even armed conflicts over ownership rights were not infrequent.

Impediments   There was also a considerable number of impediments to contracting a valid marriage. Marriage was forbidden between couples who were related. This was intended to prevent sexual activity between people sharing the same dwelling places. But the prohibitions were far more wide-ranging than just preventing incest among family members. Children of the same great-great grandparents or third cousins could not be validly married. Not only were blood relations impediments but so were marriage relationships whether lawful or illicit, so that no one could marry a brother or sister, first, second or third cousin of someone with whom they had sexual intercourse.

The nuncio, Baptista de Padua, had power in 1444 to dispense men and women, aware that they were related in second and third degrees of affinity

1.   I am indebted to Art Cosgrove's 'Marriage in Medieval Ireland', in *Marriage in Ireland*, 25–50.

and third and forth of kindred after temporary separation and absolution, to contract marriage anew.[2] Spiritual relationships, such as godparents at baptism or sponsors at confirmation could not marry the widow or widower who was a parent of the child. Spiritual relationships or gossipred was particularly highly estimated in Ireland. The nuncio also had faculties to dispense to marry those related by spiritual affinity 'provided not between God-parent and God-child and between God-parent and God-child's mother'.[3] Boys under fourteen years and girls under twelve and priests or religious who had taken solemn vows were disbarred from marriage.

As the population was small – possibly just in excess of half a million – and society rigidly class-structured, people were very limited in their choice of spouses. This was particularly true for the aristocratic classes. A chieftain could often find no other woman of a similar status except within his own family. Bishop Ó hEadhra was requested by the pope in October 1405 to grant a dispensation to marry to Tadhg O'Hara and Úna Ní Dhonnchadha related 'by divers stocks' within forbidden degrees and committed fornication, and to legitimise their present and future offspring. Martin V (1417–31) authorised Bishop Brian Ó hEadhra in 1423 to dispense another Tadhg O'Hara and Fionuala Ní Dhonnachadha, to marry notwithstanding their being related within forbidden degrees 'arising from divers stocks', and to legitimise their past and future offspring. Similarly, he was to dispense Domhnall O'Hara as well as Úna Ní Chonchobhar and Ruaidhrí and Aoibheann (Avina) Ó hEadhra. Not only were Aoibheann and Ruaidhrí related on both sides in the forth degree, but there was also a spiritual affinity as the father of Aoibheann had confirmed Ruaidhrí.[4]

Bishop Richard Belmer was authorised to dispense Seán O'Hara and Dubhchoblaig (Dubelaid) Ní Chonchobhar to marry 'notwithstanding that they are related, from divers stocks' within the forbidden degrees and 'aware of which they have more than once committed fornication with one another and have had offspring'. Belmer was to absolve them for committing incest, having imposed a penance on them and to legitimise their offspring. Apparently, Belmer was then in Rome and probably facilitated the couple there.[5]

The same was true in the case of Uilliam and Beanmhumhan (Hennman) Ní hEadhra who were related in the 'simple third and simple fourth degrees of kindred' and Diarmaid Mac and Dubconlayg Ní Dhonnchadha related 'in the

Dispensations

2.   *CPL*, viii, 298.
3.   Ibid.
4.   *CPL*, vii, 254, 298–9.
5.   *CPL*, viii, 54, 55.

third and fourth and fifth degrees of kindred'. Conn Mac and Mór Ní Dhonnchadha, aware that they were related within forbidden degrees, committed fornication and the Pope authorised Bishop Maghnus Ó hEadhra in October 1433 to dispense them. The Bishop of Elphin was instructed in December 1441 to dispense 'after imposing penance', Diarmaid Mac Donnchadha and Dubconlayg Ní Dhonnchadha, living in Achonry, because, aware that they were related within forbidden degrees, 'committed fornication several times'. Their offspring were to be legitimised.[6]

The Ó hEadhra, Ó Conchobhar and Mac Donnchadha clans were the leading families of the region and had obviously frequently inter-married. Norman families, becoming 'more Irish than the Irish themselves', also sought dispensations. John de Exeter (de Uxonis), one of the Jordans of Ballylahan and Avelina de Burgo, were dispensed in 1443, 'after enjoining penance for incest', to marry even though related in the third degree of kindred and the third and triple fourth of affinity 'on divers sides'.[7] The nuncio in Ireland in 1444 was given power to dispense men and women to remain in marriages 'contracted wittingly or in ignorance, after fornication, provided it was private, committed with the wife's sister or another related to her by kindred or affinity'.[8]

Illegitimacy   Many children were born out of wedlock and a number of those were recorded in the Vatican archives because they later sought dispensations to become priests. Illegitimacy was then an impediment to ordination. Baptista de Padua, nuncio to England, Scotland, Ireland, Germany and Holland had among his faculties power to dispense illegitimate clerics after reaching the age of twenty-two to be ordained.[9] Muirgheas Mac Donnchadha, a Premonstratensian Canon, was appointed Abbot of Holy Trinity, Lough Key despite the fact that he was son of unmarried parents related in 'the double fourth degree of kindred and the fourth and third degrees of affinity'. Canon Tomás Mac an Bhreitheamhan, son of unmarried parents, was dispensed in 1443 to be promoted to all even holy orders. Vicar John Durkan of Straide was dispensed in 1447 as son of unmarried parents, as were the clerics, Tomaltagh Mac Donnchadha (Mycconchyd), in 1490 and Ruaidhrí Ó hEadhra (Chara) seven years later. Others similarly dispensed included Aindréas Mac an Bhreitheamhan (1402), Eoghan Ó hEadhra (1419), Vicar Seán Mac an Bhreitheamhan of Ballysadare (1425), Brian Mac Donnchadha (1443), Ruaidhrí Ó Mocháin (1441),

6.   *CPL*, ix, 179.
7.   *CPL*, vi, 69, ix, 179, 189, 361, x, 417–18.
8.   *CPL*, viii, 298.
9.   *CPL*, viii, 297–8.

Archdeacon Domhnall Ó hEadhra (1429), Vicar Mathghamhan Ó Callanáin of Ballysadare (1430), Archdeacon Seán Ó Duarcáin (1447), Muirgheas Ó Coimín (1470) and Vicar Ruaidhrí Ó hEadhra of Kilmacigue (1497).[10]

Calixtus III (1455–8) commissioned Bishop Ó Mocháin in July 1458 to absolve a cleric, Eoghan Omyged from the sentence of excommunication. He had married Felorsia Yngheagram, and had children by her, knowing that he was related to her within forbidden degrees of affinity. Felorsia did not know that he had 'committed fornication with another woman related to her in the same degrees of kindred'. After a temporary separation and imposing a penance on Eoghan, the bishop was to dispense them to remarry and to legitimise the children already born and those born in the future.[11]

Marriage in Gaelic Ireland had little or no regard for the Church's law. St Anselm complained to the Munster king, Muircertach Ua Briain, 'that in Ireland men exchange their wives with the wives of other men as if they might exchange their horse for a horse'. Irish Brehon law permitted divorce and remarriage and took no account of blood or marriage relationships. It also allowed a man to keep a number of concubines. Men and women of upper rank had a succession of partners. An O'Donnell of Tír Chonaill had eighteen children by ten different women and as late as the middle of the fourteenth century Maguire of Fermanagh had twenty by eight mothers. Aodh Dubh Ó Domhnall was married four times and had a number of other liaisons by whom, with his four wives, he had in total fourteen sons and probably several daughters, though only one, Róis, has been recorded. And yet by the standard of the times he was a religious man. He undertook a year-long pilgrimage to Rome in thanksgiving for surviving a battle. He died in the Franciscan friary in Donegal in 1537 and was buried there in a Franciscan habit. Ruaidhrí Ó Conchobhair, High-King of Ireland, had several wives and partners with the result that he had a large number of sons and several daughters. Monogamy was not obligatory in Gaelic Ireland.

Dissolute Living

Concubinage has been described as 'a stable but not indissoluble sexual liaison between a man and woman'. Inherited from Roman times, it enjoyed a peculiar status between marriage and fornication during the Middle Ages. The introduction of Christianity made little difference to the institution of concubinage and the Church oscillated between limited approval and a desire to eliminate it. The Council of Toledo in AD 400 expressly permitted Christians to keep concubines on condition that they were not married, while St Augustine was completely opposed to it. Church ambivalence continued from

Clerical Concubinage

10. *CPL*, v, 463, vii, 148, 201, x, 364–5, xii, 775–6, xv, 318, xvii, no. 731.
11. *CPL*, xi, 348–9.

the twelfth century on when canon law stated that the children of concubines were entitled to inherit their mother's legacy and their father's too, provided he had no children from a legitimate marriage. That attitude of the Church changed in the sixteenth century when the Council of Trent decreed that communion should be refused to those who were living in concubinage.[12]

Family-Oriented
Clerical concubinage was widespread throughout the church in general as well as in Ireland. Stable sexual relationships between clerics and women persisted after the twelfth century reform. Priests and monks continued to have sexual relationships with life partners called concubines rather than spouses. It was such a long-standing practice that it was widely regarded as the norm. Society was family-oriented. Not only were the ruling powers vested in families and transmitted through them but it was similar with other professions, like law, medicine and literature, which were held by specific families and handed on from generation to generation. Not surprisingly, a similar practice developed among the clergy. While it was not thought morally reprehensible for a priest to father a family, there were the undesirable consequences of the clergy becoming a hereditary caste. Married bishops, priests and abbots tried to transmit church positions and properties to their families.

Non-Celibate Clergy
To prevent this, the First Council of the Lateran in 1123 made it invalid for an ordained person to contract marriage. In real terms, it had little effect on the practice except that the partners of bishops and priests were regarded by the church as concubines rather than wives, but often enjoyed the same legal and social status as wives. Celibacy among the clergy was to remain little more than an aspiration for some centuries to come. As late as the middle of the seventeenth century, the vicar apostolic of Achonry complained that a Cistercian in Boyle was the son and grandson of monks in Boyle Abbey.

Episcopal Families
Many priests and at least two bishops in Achonry were fathers of families as were some abbots of Ballysadare and some of their children in turn became bishops, priests and monks.[13] He had a relationship with an unmarried woman to whom he was related in the third and fourth degrees of kindred and in the double third and in the third and fourth degrees of affinity.[14] One of his sons, Brian, later became bishop of the diocese (1463–73) and another, Diarmaid, was a Canon of the diocese.[15] The son of Bishop Ó Mocháin, Domhnall, became rector of Ballylahan in 1493.

12. *Dict. Mid. Ages*, 529–30.
13. *Annals of Loch Cé*. So prolific was the progeny of the red-headed Magnus O'Hara who died in 1435 that it was described in the sixteenth century as *Sloight an aspuick Ruoigh* (the sept of the red bishop).
14. *CPL*, x, 368–9.
15. *CPL*, xii, 194.

At least ten clerics in the diocese were recorded in Rome as sons of priests: *Mac an tSagairt*
Archdeacon Cormac Ó Coimín (1401), Rector Nioclás Ó Náradhaigh
(Grádaigh) of Sliabh Lugha (1411), Vicar Tadhg Ó hOireachtaigh (1422),
Vicar Conn Ó Mocháin of Killaraght (1435), Flaithrí Ó Branghaile (1435),
Vicar Mathghamhain Ó Callanáin (1480) and Conn Mac Ceallaigh of
Emlefad (1504) and Rector Tadhg Ó Clúmháin (1510). Cormac Ó
Connacháin (1489) was not only the son of a priest but also of a provost and
a married woman. She is the only such recorded as the mother of a priest. Vicar
Uilliam Ó Clúmháin of Killoran (1473) was the son of a cleric.[16]

An Achonry cleric, Nioclás Ó Náradhaigh (Ouradi/Onaraid), was not only *'Notorious*
dispensed as son of a priest, but in 1411 Rome assigned him the rectory of *Fornicators'*
Sliabh Lugha (Kilmovee).[17] Later, in 1432 he was accused of being 'a notorious
fornicator' who had begotten offspring 'by divers women'.[18] Abbot Seán of St
Mary's, Ballysadare was also accused of being 'a notorious fornicator' in 1428,[19]
as was Vicar Cathal Mac Cristín (Macaccristini) of Cloonoghill in 1435.[20]
Diarmaid O'Hara, himself son of a bishop, accused the provost Domhnall
McDonagh of being a 'notorious fornicator'.[21] The dean of Achonry, Seán
O'Hara, was alleged in 1431 to be leading 'a dissolute life'.[22] Abbot Uilliam
Mac Searraidh of St Mary's, Ballysadare, kept a concubine and was 'a notorious
fornicator'.[23] An illegitimate cleric, Conn Ó Gadhra, reported Vicar Muiris Ó
Coimín (Ocoymiean), of Cloynnahacglasse, to Rome in 1470 as 'an open
fornicator'.[24] Eoghan Ó Gadhra accused Rector Ruaidhrí Ó Mocháin of
Coolavin in 1447 of 'public fornication' and another Ó Mocháin, Vicar Éinrí
of Killaraght, was alleged to be a 'public and notorious fornicator'.[25]

Rome did not appear to be unduly perturbed by sexually-active priests or *Papal Tolerance*
bishops and gave dispensations liberally. Abbot Maghnus Mac Donnchadha
of Holy Trinity, Lough Key, was given the Abbacy of St Mary's, Ballysadare,
notwithstanding his birth as the son of unmarried parents. John XXIII
confirmed the appointment by the Abbot of Mellifont of Cormac Mac Dáibhsí

16. *CPL*, v, 342, 453, 463, 603, vii, 109, 148, 228, 270–1, viii, 12–14, 108–9, 201, 416,
     559, x, 364, xii, 775–6, xiii, 89, 189–90, 338, 729–30, xv, 308, 309, 310, xvi, 182, xix,
     187, 391–2, 701.
17. *CPL*, vi, 260.
18. *CPL*, viii, 416.
19. *CPL*, viii, 53.
20. *CPL*, viii, 558.
21. *CPL*, x, 381–2.
22. *CPL*, viii, 377.
23. *CPL*, xi, 487, 492–3.
24. *CPL*, xii, 775.
25. *CPL*, ix, 283, x, 727.

as Abbot of Boyle, even though he was known to be the son of a Cistercian abbot and an unmarried woman.[26] Another Mac Dáibhsí, a monk in the monastery, himself illegitimate, accused Abbot Maelaghlin Mac Donnchadha of openly keeping a concubine in his own house.[27] An Elphin cleric and a priest's son, Matthew O'Callanan, was appointed vicar of Emlefad in 1480.[28] Rector Seán Ó Clúmháin, rector of Kilmactigue and Killoran, son of a priest and cleric Tadhg Ó Clúmháin, was dispensed in 1510 as son of a priest.[29]

Ó Mocháin Clan

The Ó Mocháin clan was one of the leading, ecclesiastical families of the diocese, but not quite as aristocratic as Conn asserted when he claimed in a petition to Rome that 'he was of the stock of kings and dukes'. He was dispensed in 1444 as son of unmarried parents, to enter the Cistercians in Boyle 'to which by the favour of his parents and friends he could be of great service' and was appointed abbot in succession to another Ó Mocháin, Domhnall, lately deceased. Conn later became Bishop of Achonry (1448–63).[30] Another Ó Mocháin, Ruaidhrí, was dispensed by the bishop as son of 'an unmarried nobleman and an unmarried noblewoman related to the third and fourth degrees of affinity'. Describing himself as 'of noble race', Ó Mocháin seemed to regard class as a mitigating circumstance. He was appointed rector of Coolavin and Ranna in 1441 'notwithstanding the said defect', while another member of the family, Éinrí, also the son of unmarried parents, was appointed vicar of Killaraght in 1441. Given the three year time span of the dispensation, Ruaidhrí, Conn and Einrí were probably brothers, children of the same unmarried parents. The appointments of both Ruaidhrí and Éinrí were contested by another Ó Mocháin, Cathal, 'of noble race', who claimed that Rory had dilapidated a number of the goods of his rectory and had also committed simony and perjury, while Henry, who had been appointed vicar of Killaraght, entered into an agreement with his predecessor, Cormac, still another Ó Mocháin, allowing him to continue as vicar if he split the fruits with him for the rest of their lives. Because of the power of Ruaidhrí and Éinrí, Cathal could not safely meet them within the city or diocese of Achonry. The possession of the rectory of Coolavin (Killaraght) by Ruaidhrí was again disputed in 1447.

Ó Clúmháin Clan

Seán Ó Clúmháin (Coleman) dispensed in 1443 as a priest's son was appointed to the rural rectory of Hy-Fiachrach and Banada.[31] The Ó Clúmháin

26. *CPL*, vi, 435.
27. *CPL*, xi, 481.
28. *CPL*, xiii, 729, 730, 189–90.
29. *CPL*, x, 427–8, xix, 187.
30. *CPL*, xvi, 181.
31. *CPL*, ix, 403.

clan was also an important clerical family, while the cleric, Tomás Ó Comh-
dhain (Ochoan), alleged in 1447 that Vicar Domhnal Mac Ceallaigh of
Emlefad, had been 'duly excommunicated' but in spite of that had celebrated
Mass and other divine offices.[32]

32.   *CPL*, x, 281, 189, 200, 297, 358, 447–8, ix, 418, 552–3.

CHAPTER NINE

Crusading Knights

Pilgrimages   Pilgrimages were a popular religious phenomenon in medieval times. Sea transport remained virtually unchanged since the time of the Egyptian Pharaohs or perhaps long before. Sailing ships hugged the coast as they travelled from Ireland to England, then across land to the Channel where they embarked for St Malo. From there they could continue overland to Rome or to Santiago de Compostella in Spain.

At the end of the tenth century, pilgrimages were regarded as a means a sinner could use to lessen God's punishment and pilgrims expected that the saint whose shrine was visited would intercede for them. The beginning of the twelfth century experienced a remarkable growth, with Jerusalem regarded as the most meritorious destination as here they came closest to the relics of Jesus and his apostles. Medieval people were attracted to the tangible rather than to the theoretical and relics had huge attraction for them. Inevitably their credulousness was exploited by charlatans for financial gain. It was said that the number of relics of the True Cross treasured throughout christendom would have required a sizeable forest for their fabrication. It was claimed that they were brought back by Crusaders returning from the Holy Land.

Knights Templar   One of the more unusual institutions in Achonry was that of the Knights Templar at Templehouse (*Teach an Teampla*) near Ballymote. They were a military order originally founded to protect pilgrims to Jerusalem after it was recaptured during the First Crusade. That crusade was launched in the last years of the eleventh century to rescue the eastern empire of Constantinople and reconquer Jerusalem from Mohammedan rule. Following the fall of Jerusalem with the atrocious massacre of men, women and children by the crusaders, they set up their own kingdom there and established religious military orders to defend the Holy Places, one of which was the Order of the Temple founded in 1118.

The members consisted of knights, priests and lay-servants. The knights took vows of poverty, chastity and obedience, carried armour and wore white cloaks with a red cross. They lived in castles called preceptories with land attached. Templehouse, established sometime in the thirteenth century, was their only foundation in the west of Ireland and served as a recruiting and training centre for new members and a place of retirement for older members who had returned from the Crusades.[1]

Other crusades followed in the twelfth century (1146) and (1189) and again in the thirteenth century (1203), (1228–9) and (1247–54). Some natives of the diocese may well have gone on the crusades, while the diocese was expected to contribute towards these crusades. Gregory X ordered the Archbishop of Tuam and his provincial bishops on 1 April 1273 to attend the Second Council of Lyon which was to meet in 1274 to try to heal the Greek schism and promote the crusade. No Irish bishops attended the council. The pope wrote again in October of the following year urging the bishops to apply indulgences and protect those who took the cross. One hundredth of church revenues were to be collected and, together with legacies and other donations, were to be deposited with those charged with the Holy Land subsidy.[2]

Promoting Crusades

Nicholas IV wrote to the Archbishop of Tuam and the other bishops of the province in April 1291 'to warn and induce all persons not exempt to pay to the king the tenth ordered to be collected for the Holy Land during six years, using such compulsion as may be necessary'. They were to rectors who 'may be able without grave inconvenience to endure it'. He exhorted the faithful to take up the cross. 'Now is the time to strike a blow and as an inducement indulgences are granted to those who personally or by contributions assist the crusade.'[3] Rome wrote in August 1308 and again in February 1335 to the four archbishops and the other bishops of their provinces requesting them 'to induce their subjects to help in persons or property'.

One fifth of the tithes were to be paid into the war-chest and indulgences were granted to those who 'took the cross'.[4] Baptista de Padua, nuncio to Ireland in 1444, had faculties to grant indulgences of seven years and seven quarantines to those who contributed to the army and fleet against the Turks, and a plenary indulgence to those who went in person or sent a warrior and maintained him for six months. He also had powers to commute vows taken by people to undertake pilgrimages to the Holy Land, Rome or Compostella provided they gave the money they would have spent to the 'pope's fleet against the infidels'.[5]

1. O'Rorke states in *Ballysadare & Kilvarnet* that Templehouse was a preceptory but later in *Sligo* 73–80 changes his mind arguing at length that it was only a rectory. However, Gwynn and Hadcock, *Medieval Religious Houses in Ireland*, 330–1 does not accept O'Rorke's view.
2. *CPL*, i, 449.
3. *CPL*, i, 552, 553.
4. *CPL*, ii, 523 (1308).
5. *CPL*, viii, 297–8.

Suppression of
Templars

The Templars may have left Templehouse after the destruction of their castle in 1271 though they retained a church and property in the vicinity in the following century. They had become extremely rich and powerful and excited the envy of rulers in other countries. Philip the Fair of France informed Clement V (1305–14), the first Avignon pope, that he had received serious complaints against the Templars, that they denied Christ, spat on the crucifix and practised unnatural vice. The French king ordered the arrest of all Templars in his kingdom and extracted confessions from them under torture. As a result, the pope ordered all the princes of Christendom in November 1307 to arrest the Templars and confiscate their property. The Archbishop of Tuam received a commission from Rome in August 1308 to publish the bull ordering the Templars to restore their property to the bishop of the place where they were.

Accordingly, Bishop Benedict Ó Bragáin (1286–1312) should have become the proprietor of Templehouse, and he was also to summon members of the order and enquire into the charges made against them.[6] Together with the Archbishop of Tuam and other bishops of the province, Ó Bragán was invited in August 1308 to attend the Council of Vienne which met in 1311 but probably did not attend. The council decreed that the Templars be suppressed. In the taxation list of Achonry for 1306 the Templars are listed as rectors of the vicarage of Killecath or Kellecath. Their church was thought to be the old church of Kilvarnet, the parish where Templehouse is situated. It seems that Templehouse became a dependency of the Fratres Cruciferi of Rindoon in County Roscommon. The origin of the Fratres is obscure. They followed the Augustinian rule and were Hospitallers with connections with the Knights Hospitallers of St John of Jerusalem.[7]

Santiago de
Compostella

As a result of the Moslem conquest of the middle east and the bitterness left by the excesses of the crusaders, Jerusalem became a dangerous place for pilgrims. But other places emerged and pilgrimages continued unabated. A bishop restoring his church in Compostella in northern Spain in the middle of the ninth century claimed he had discovered the tomb of St James, the brother of the Lord. As news spread throughout Christendom, pilgrims flocked from everywhere to what became known as Santiago de Compostella. Cities all over Europe had streets named after James, 'Santiago', in Spanish-speaking cities, 'Jacobstrasse' in Ratisbon and other German-speaking towns and cities. Pilgrims in Paris gathered at Tour Saint Jacques in the centre of the city and made their way along rue Saint Jacques on their overland pilgrimage. Once

6.   *CPL*, ii, 48.
7.   Gwynn and Hadcock, 210, 216, 330–1; McKenna (ed.) *The Book of O'Hara*, xxx–xxxi; O'Rorke, *Ballysadare*, 311–17, *Sligo*, 73–80.

they had crossed the Pyrennees they followed the 'camino di Santiago' to Compostella.

Dublin too had it's James's Street where Irish pilgrims gathered before taking ship for La Corruna in Spain. The popularity of this pilgrimage gave a hugh impetus to international trade and led to the first fledgling seeds to what centuries later became modern tourism. Pilgrims were the first passengers to travel on boats other than galley-slaves, sailors or fishermen. Hostels were established along pilgrim routes to cater for their needs, leading to the establishment of hotels in later centuries. Fairs and markets were set up in honour of St James on his feastday and enterprising Spaniards travelled widely to pedal their wares abroad. A sixteenth century account describes the fair in Dublin:

Fair of St James

> S. James: his feast is celebrated the XXV of July, on which day in ancient time was there a worthy fayre kept at Dubline, continuing sixe dayes, unto which resorted divers merchantes as well from England as from France and Flanders. And they afourded their wares so doggecheape, in respect of the Citie merchantes, that the countrey was yere by yere sufficiently stored by estrangers, and the citie merchants … were very much empoverished: wherefore partly thorough the canvassing of the towne merchantes and partly by the wincking of the rest of the Citizens … that famous marte was suprest and all forreyne sale wholly abandoned.[8]

How many Irish pilgrims went to Compostella is not easily reckoned now, while the few mentioned in the annals are recorded often only because of their tragic deaths. Many perished at sea like an Ó Driosceól, and others in Spain like Gearóid FitzGerald and Eibhlín Ó Fearghail. Some deaths occurred immediately upon their return. Aodh Mag Uidhir died in Kinsale in 1428 and was buried in Cork while Finghin Ó hEidiresceoil died in 1472 in his own house and his son Tadhg, less than a month later 'after performing the pilgrimage of St James (San Seam)'. King Tomaltach Mac Diarmada of Moylurg was one of many Irish who went on pilgrimage to Santiago accompanied by 'many more noble and ignoble persons'. Mac Diarmada 'returned, safe and sound from Spaine after receiving the indulgences of Saint James'. Calvagh Ó Chonnobhar went to Compostella in 1451 'and returned in health after receiving indulgences in his sinns'. Afterwards, he married Caitríona Ní Cheallaigh, the widow of Ó Madaidhín.

Irish Pilgrims

Rome, however, became the destination of choice for many pilgrims. 1450 was a Jubilee Year and many Irish people went to Rome, including Tomás Óg mac Uidhir who returned home in 1451.

8.   *Holinshed's Chronicle*, 45.

CHAPTER TEN

Bishops (1219–1312)

Cormac
Ó Tarpaigh
(1219–25)

Cormac Ó Tarpaigh was Abbot of Mellifont when elected Bishop of Achonry in 1219. The Ó Tarpaigh family belonged to a sept which originated in County Sligo. Apparently, the chapter had not observed the usual protocol and had carried out the election without getting the royal licence. The Archbishop of Dublin, Henry of London (1212–28), informed Henry III of the illegality of the election in Achonry which he described as 'situated in the furthest parts of Connacht where the church was less informed and its clergy ignorant and unaccustomed to the manner and form to be observed in elections according to the statutes of other territories'.

After the election there were several objections to Ó Tarpaigh himself as well as to the manner of the election. The archbishop commented that 'no Englishman can stay or prosper in these parts up to now principally because of the poverty of the place and the hostility of a contrary people'.[1] However, it seems the election was allowed to stand and the king thanked the archbishop 'for his prudence in regard to the election'.[2]

War

Ó Tarpaigh resigned from Achonry in 1225, a year of great disturbances there. War broke out between two branches of the O'Connor clan over the succession to the kingship of Connacht after the death in May 1224 of the reigning king, Cathal Crobhderg. He was succeeded by his son, Aodh, and this was disputed by the sons of Ruaidhrí Ó Conchobhair, former High-King of Ireland. They were supported by Aodh Ó Néill who inaugurated Turlough, son of Ruaidhrí, as king. With the help of the Norman English Aodh confronted Turlough, forcing him to flee. He pursued him to Kilkelly and from there to Meelick where he remained three nights 'plundering Luighne on every side'. From there he continued his pursuit of Ruaidhrí who had fled to Attymass. When Aodh reached Attymass he plundered Coolcarney where he 'inflicted vengeance on cows and people'. At this point Ruaidhrí and his followers decided to disperse. But the war had wreaked havoc, particularly in

1. 'Unpublished Medieval Notitiae and Epistolae' in *Coll. Hib.*, nos 6 and 7, 15–16.
2. Ó Tarpa is also listed as Bishop of Killala at the same time. I agree with McDonnell who believed this was an error made by Ware and subsequently adopted by Eubel; *Killala*, 21 If the two dioceses were temporarily united there is no record of it.

the diocese which appears to have been the main theatre of war. 'Grievous indeed was the misfortune God permitted to fall on the best province in Erinn, east or west, south or north; for the young man would not spare his companion, in preying or in plundering, provided he was the stronger. Women and children, and young lords, and the mighty and the weak, were exposed to cold and famine through this war.'[3]

Giolla Íosa belonged to the well-known Gaelic literary family. Muintir Cléirigh were tenants of mensal church lands in Kilmactigue in the sixteenth century. The Ó Conchobhair family continued their internecine strife. In 1228 war broke out between two brothers Turlough and Aodh, the sons of Ruaidhrí and 'they desolated the region from Ballysadare southwards to the river of Moy, excepting only a small portion of Sliabh Lugha' (northern half of the barony of Costello in Mayo comprising the parishes of Kilbeagh, Kilmovee, Kilcolman and Castlemore in Achonry). 'An intolerable dearth prevailed in Connacht in consequence of the war. They plundered churches and territories; they banished its clergy and men of science into foreign and remote countries and others of them perished from cold and famine.'[4] The previous year Donnsleibhe O'Gara, lord of Sliabh Lugha, was slain by his nephew, Gillaruadh, after the latter had on the same night forcibly taken a house from him. Gillaruadh himself was afterwards put to death for this crime.[5] No record has come to light about the episcopacy of Giolla Íosa Ó Cléirigh except the notice of his death in 1230.[6]

Giolla Íosa Ó Cléirigh (1226–30)

Tomás Ó Ruadháin was commissioned on 21 July 1237 by Gregory IX (1227–41) together with the Bishop of Killaloe and the Abbot of St Thomas's, Dublin to enquire into a dispute between Giolla na Naoimh Ó Bragáin, Bishop of Clogher and the Archbishop of Armagh, and report their findings to him. He may have been dead then as his death was recorded in the annals for that year.[7] The *Annals of Ulster* mention that he was buried in his cathedral. The Archbishop of Tuam, Maelmuire Ó Lachtnain received his pallium from Rome that year and held his first synod in Athlone. His predecessor, Felix Ó Ruanadha, resigned and became a monk in Mary's Abbey, Dublin. According to the annals that year 'the barons of Erinn came into Connacht and began to build castles in it'.[8]

Tomás Ó Ruadháin (1230–7)

---

3. *ALC.* Whether or not this turbulence led to Ó Tarpaigh's resignation is not known. He returned to Mellifont where he died in January 1227.
4. *AFM, ALC.*
5. *AFM.*
6. *ALC.*
7. *ALC.*
8   *ALC.*

Aonghus
Ó Clúmháin
(1238–48)

Aonghus Ó Clúmháin was Abbot of Boyle when elected bishop in 1238 and was the second Cistercian to occupy the post. He took the extraordinary step together with Giolla Ceallach Ó Ruadháin, Bishop of Killala (1248–63), of excommunicating the papal envoy, John de Frosinone, which in fact was uncanonical since a papal envoy could not be excommunicated without the pope's express permission. It appears that they had been induced to take this drastic step by Hubert de Burgo, Bishop of Limerick (1222–72), who claimed to have obtained certain papal letters. Gregory IX (1227–41) had ordered an enquiry as Hubert was said to be illegitimate, lacking education and guilty of simony. The Archbishop and Archdeacon of Dublin were instructed on 13 April 1248 to publish the Pope's revocation of the sentence of suspension and excommunication passed by Ó Clúmháin.[9]

Aonghus Ó Clúmháin resigned because of old age and ill-health and the Pope instructed Maelmuire Ó Lachtnáin, Archbishop of Tuam, in November 1248 to accept his resignation and assign him a portion of the diocesan revenues for his support.[10] Ó Clúmháin retired to the monastery of Boyle where he lived for another sixteen years, dying there in 1264 just a year before his successor. A mounted party of young Normans attacked Sligo castle in 1249 and they were ambushed by the son of Fedhlim Ó Connchobhair, king of Connacht. Seven of them were killed and their bodies brought to Ballysadare for burial.[11]

Tomás Ó Maicín
(1249–65)

There is no record of any other priest or cleric in the diocese of the name Tomás Ó Maicin but the *Annals of Loch Cé* mentioned the death in 1225 of Maol Brighde Ó Maicín, Abbot of Ballintobber. The same annals recount an occurrence in 1256 when the 'Foreigners', i.e. the English, Mac William Burk and Mac Goisdelbh (Costello), 'assembled a very great host and proceeded to Ceis-Corainn, where they encamped, and where they remained the greater part of a week; and they plundered all the churches of the Corann'. After they returned home Bishop Ó Maicín 'was "drowning their candles" about nones, when it was equally dark in the field and wood'. In other words, he excommunicated them, which involved the ceremonial extinguishing of candles. The ceremony took place about 9 p.m. in mid-September when it was already dark.[12]

Ó Maicín petitioned the Pope to grant him a supplement, one-quarter of the diocesan tithes, because of the bishop's poverty. Alexander IV (1254–61)

9.   *CPL*, i, 253.
10.   *CPL*, i, 350.
11.   *ALC.*
12.   The next sentence refers to 'the night of the festival of the Cross', the feast of the 'Exaltation of the Cross', i.e. 14 September. Eubel, *ALC, A Conn, AU, AFM.*

replied to 'his venerable brother' of Achonry in March 1257 allowing him to take one-quarter of the tithes which his predecessors already had done, as did the other bishops of the Tuam province. It was 'an ancient approved custom which had been observed up to the present'.[13] The supplement to his predecessors would have reduced Ó Maicín's income and in addition, he was bound to remit the first year of his income to Rome. Tomás Ó Maicín died in April 1265.[14]

On Monday 1 June, the day after Trinity Sunday, the dean and chapter of Achonry requested the royal licence and assent to proceed with the election of his successor. King Aodh Ó Conchobhair of Connacht wrote to Henry III on their behalf urging Henry to give his assent to the chapter's messenger. 'The church having only 20 marks in rents, it ought not to suffer detriment in its temporalities or spiritualities by delay in granting the royal assent.'[15] Henry III (1207–72), who had the third largest reign in English history, was very protective of the royal right to the revenues of vacant bishoprics which between 1240–4 made up ten per cent of the royal income. The royal assent was granted in April 1266, just a year after the death of Ó Maicín and Archbishop Tomás Ó Conchobhair of Tuam (1259–79) was directed 'to do what depends on him in this matter'. There seems to have been no great delay on this occasion as Tomás (English documents call him Denis) O'Miadhacháin (Meehan), archdeacon of Achonry, was consecrated in Ardnaree on the last Sunday before Christmas in 1266.[16] A second bishop was consecrated on the same occasion. He was an Italian, named John, who was papal nuncio to Ireland and was made Bishop of Clonfert. He seems to have spent almost thirty years in Ireland as he was transferred to the diocese of Benevenuta in his homeland in 1296.

Tomás Ó Miadhacháin (1266–85)

The castles of Ballymote (Ath-Anggaile), of Sliabh Lugha and of Killcolman were demolished by Aedh Ó Conchobhair.[17] Ó Miadhacháin (he was still referred to as Denis in government documents) failed to appear when summoned and on 2 October 1285 was fined twenty shillings but he died in November and was buried in his own cathedral.[18] It was a year when Maghnus Ó Conchobhair inflicted a great defeat on Adam Cusack and his Norman followers at Ballysadare (Lec-Essa-dara) and a great many people were killed.

Castles Demolished

13. Theiner, *Vetera Monumenta*, 75, *CPL*, i, 343; Sheehy, *Pont. Hib.*, ii, 264, Potthast, 16783, De Loye and de Chenal, 1818.
14. *ALC.*
15. *Cal. Docs. Ire.* 1252–84. 774, 125, 787, 127, 794, 128 [Royal Letters, Nos 2458 and 2,460, Pat. 50 Hen. III, m.26] *Cal. Docs. Ire.* 1252–84. 774, 125, 787, 127, 794, 128 [Royal Letters, Nos 2458 and 2,460, Pat. 50 Hen. III, m.26].
16. *ALC, A Conn, AFM*; Flood, 475.
17. *AFM, ALC.*
18. *AC.*

Ó Conchobhair in turn was defeated by Pilip Mac Goisdelbh on the Ox Mountains 'where a great many recruits and inferior persons were slain. That year Ruaidhrí Ó Gadhra, king of Sliabh Lugha was killed on Lough Gara by Mac Feorais (Bermingham).

Benedict Ó Bragáin (1286–1312)

Peter Ó Braughill, chaplain, announced to the king on 29 April 1286 the death of the Bishop of Achonry and the dean and chapter asked for a licence to elect a successor. Edward I (1229–1307) granted his licence to them and instructed Bishop Stephen of Waterford and Justiciary of Ireland to exhort them to elect a bishop 'who shall be devout, fit for the rule of their church and useful and faithful to the King and Ireland.' Wishing to spare the chapter labour and expense he granted them 'of special grace and gives power to the justiciary on election made to give the royal assent in lieu of the king.'[19] Benedict Ó Bragáin was elected bishop and was the only one of that name who figures among the clergy of Achonry in the Middle Ages which suggests he may not have been a native. Two Ó Bragáin bishops occur in the list for the diocese of Clogher in this period, Giolla na Naoimh (1227–40) and Dáithí (1340–67). The name may be a form of Ó Brógáin which was an old Mayo surname and the family had estates in the barony of Carra in the county. Benedict was obliged to take an oath of fealty to the king in the presence of the Justiciary before the temporalities were restored. He also had to confirm by letter under his own seal and that of the dean and chapter that 'this election shall not tend to the king's prejudice, nor be drawn into a precedent'.

1306 Taxation

From 1302–7 jurors carried out a tax audit of every diocese in Ireland. The audit of Killala diocese took place on 29 August, the Saturday after the feast of St Bartholomew, 1306. As it appears in the records immediately before that of Achonry, it is reasonable to suppose that the audit of Achonry was made about the same time.[20] The value of the diocese was given as £35 6s. 9d. and the tax at one-tenth was 70s. 8d. There were only two dioceses in the country of lesser value, Kilmore and Clonmacnois. Surprisingly, the value of Killala was almost three times higher. There were thirty-three vicarages or parishes in Achonry, nineteen of which can be reconciled with the modern parishes. Three others, Killasser (Kellenalasscan), Kilconduff (Kilcormdilk), Killedan (Kelualydan), can be guessed at with some probability. Cluanmore may be Kilbeagh (Charlestown) called after the townland of Cloonmore located in that parish. It has been suggested that Kellecath is Kilvarnet (Collooney) as the rectors were Templars based in Templehouse nearby. Their church was thought to be the old church of Kilvarnet, the parish where Templehouse is situated. Coolavin

19.   *Cal. Docs. Ire.*, 1285–92, no. 227.
20.   *Cal. Docs. Ire.*, 1302–7, 217–9.

(Culonyn), while not a modern parish, is a half-barony in the diocese. Eight other parishes have not been identified. It was speculated that Kilcaochcrumyn *in rure*, is Keshcorran, i.e. Toomour. Clonbanna, Keltesguean Cill Seiscnén, Kilsheshnan in Killasser, Ratholuyn a church near Carrocastle in Bohola, Ardnach, Templerowuck in Carrowgallda townland in Straide, Kendoyn, Kinaffe in Swinford parish, Kekelcurn, Killoran. The vicarages of Kellosenyg, and Clonbanna as well as the single rectory, Mocrath and Thuamany remain unidentified.[21]

---

21. Knox, *Notes*, 372–4.

CHAPTER ELEVEN

The Avignon Exile (1308–78)

For seventy years popes left Rome and took up residency at Avignon in south-east France. The main reason was political, as Italy was then torn apart by the conflict between the Guelps and Ghibellines. The sudden arrest of the Templars by Philip IV also contributed to the general instability of the Church. Avignon was then a vassal of the Church and situated close to Italy, and Clement V (1305–14) intended to stay there only temporarily until conditions improved. He died two years later and his successor, John XXII (1316–34), despite his best intentions, did not manage to return. His successors, Benedict XII (1334–42), Clement VI (1342–52) and Innocent VI (1352–62), all had the idea of moving back to Italy but only Urban V (1362–70) did go back but left again because of the hostility of the Romans. Finally Gregory XI (1370–8), a Frenchman, ended the Avignon exile when he returned to Rome in 1378 where he died shortly afterwards.

In spite of being removed from Rome, the papacy managed to carry out many reforms particularly in administrative areas. Under John XXII, the financial department, the apostolic camera, was thoroughly overhauled. It controlled and supervised all financial transactions, especially those of papal tax collectors in Ireland and other countries and insured that taxes and other fees were rigorously collected. The apostolic penitentiary handled ecclesiastical censures, such as excommunication as well as dispensations from marriage impediments, many of them Irish. The chancery was the nerve centre and dealt with drafting and dispatching letters and decrees.

David of Kileany (1312–44)   The dean and chapter got the royal licence on 1 May to proceed with the election of a bishop. They elected David of Kileany (Kilkenny, Kilheny). His surname is unknown as is the place he came from. It was said that he held a benefice in the diocese of Kilmacduagh in 1306.[1] From Avignon John XXII (1316–32) commissioned David in June 1320 together with the Bishop of Lismore and William Payne, Cistercian Abbot of St Mary's, Dublin to protect the possessions of the master and brethren of the Augustinian hospital of St John the Baptist 'without the new gate of Dublin'.[2] Six years later the same

1. Cotton, *Fasti*, 100; O'Rorke ii, 99.
2. *CPL*, ii, 205–6.

pope wrote to the Archbishop of Tuam and the other bishops of the province requiring them to pay a subsidy for the crusade he had undertaken against heretics in Italy and they were to appoint fit persons to collect the subsidy.[3] Apparently, the western bishops ignored the Pope's request as his successor, Pope Benedict XII (1334–42), wrote again in February 1335 about it and instructed the bishops to carry out his predecessor's instructions.[4]

The Avignon administration would have dealt with Benedict Ó Bragáin, David of Kileany and Nicolás Ó hEadhra during that period, but no records of such dealings have come to light. But during the episcopacy of David of Kileany (1312–44) moves were afoot to unite Achonry to Tuam. Andrew Sapiti, agent for the Avignon administration, negotiated for Archbishop Maeleachlainn Mac Aodha (Malachy McHugh) of Tuam (1312–48) a bull issued on 31 July 1327 uniting the dioceses of Annaghdown, Kilmacduagh and Achonry to Tuam. The union was to take place on the deaths of the incumbents. Mac Aodha had already got King Edward III to petition John XXII in Avignon in 1327 for the union.[5]

Unification with Tuam

As a result the Pope instructed the Bishop of Killaloe, the Augustinian Abbot of Rattoo and the guardian of the Friars Minor in Claregalway on 2 July 1330 to ascertain the value of the fruits, rents and profits of each of the four dioceses and their distance from one another and to report back to the Pope on whether, according to the late king's petition, they should be united.[6] Tomás Ó Meallaidh, Bishop of Annaghdown, stated in consistory that under pretext of such union he was deprived of his diocese by Archbishop MacAodha. Ó Meallaidh died in Rome in 1328 where he had gone to plead his case.[7]

The chapter of Achonry asked to have the said union dissolved since the distance between the two churches and 'the ungovernable character of the Irish', made it impossible for them to share in the election of the archbishop. The archbishop and chapter were willing to agree to this separation. The Pope sent a mandate from Avignon in September 1346 to Bishops Eoghan Ó Fearghaile of Ardagh, Seán Ó Finachty of Elphin and Tomás Ó Ceallaigh of Clonfert requesting them to summon Archbishop Tomás Ó Cearbhaill of Tuam and his chapter and inform themselves regarding the union with Tuam of the suffragan churches of Annaghdown, Achonry and Kilmacduagh.[8]

3. *CPL*, ii, 478–9, Theiner, 233.
4. *CPL*, ii, 523.
5. Theiner, 239, *CPL*, ii, 263.
6. *CPL*, ii, 263, 318.
7. *ALC, CPL*, ii, 248, 407, iii, f.237.
8. *CPL*, iii, 227.

Ballylathan
Burned

At home in the diocese there were the usual disturbances. Felim Ó Conchobhair who became king of Connacht in 1316, mustered an army, burned the town of Ballylathan and slew lord Slevin de Exeter (Jordan) of Ballylahan and many other English, including de Cogan. Together with other chieftains of the province, including lord Art Ó hEadhra of Luighne, he marched against the English of West Connacht but was defeated in a fierce engagement in Athenry where Ó hEadhra was slain.[9]

Epidemics

1327–8 were years of epidemics. An outbreak of smallpox (*galair breac*) in 1327 caused many deaths and the following year a disease called *slaidán*, a flu epidemic affecting 'for three or four days everybody who caught it', raged throughout the country. One of its victims may have been Gormlaith inghean Mic Diarmada, wife of Fearghail Ó hEadhra and 'queen of Luighne' who died that year and another, Muirgheas Ó Gioballáin (Giblin) 'high master of Erinn in new laws and old laws … a philosopher in wisdom and true knowledge, an eminent professor of poetry and of Ogham writing, and many other arts'. He was a Canon of Achonry as well as of all the other dioceses in the province including Tuam where he was the 'official and general judge of all the archbishopric'.[10] Lord Maelruanaidh Mac Diarmada of Moylurg resigned his lordship in 1331 and assumed the habit of a monk in the abbey of Boyle.[11]

Political Changes

Politically the diocese underwent a major change in 1338 described by the annalist: 'Luighne and Corran were laid waste and wrested from the English and the chieftainship of them assumed by the hereditary Irish chieftains after the expulsion of the English.'[12]

David of Kileany died in 1344.[13]

Nioclás Ó
hEadhra
(1348–73)

Four years elapsed after the death of David before the appointment of his successor, Nioclás Ó hEadhra. This delay may be explained by the ongoing debate about the union of Achonry with Tuam. It may also explain the haste with which they elected Abbot Murchadh Ó hEadhra of Boyle, the son of Maolmhuaidh, which must have taken place within months or even weeks of the death of David because the union with Tuam was to become operational with the death of the incumbent.

Nioclás Ó hEadhra was a Cistercian monk in the Abbey of Assaroe in County Donegal, a daughter house of Boyle, his name suggesting that he was a native of Achonry. With the unexpected death of Murchadh, Nioclás made haste to Avignon to get dispensed from his illegitimacy 'so as to hold any dignity

9.   *AFM.*
10. *ALC, A. Conn.*
11. *AFM.*
12. *AFM.*
13. Eubel gives David's death as 1348.

including the abbatical or episcopal' thus advancing his claim to the diocese. Clement VI (1342–52) nominated him bishop on 22 October 1348 and the usual letters were sent to the chapter, the people of the city and diocese and to King Edward (1327–77).[14] The chapter accepted the Pope's nomination and Nioclás was consecrated in Avignon by Bishop Talairand of Albano.[15] Flood, who describes Nicholas as the Abbot of Assaroe, states that the consecration took place in Rome. It is difficult to understand why Nioclás would have to undertake that journey while the seat of the papacy was in Avignon.[16]

The appointment of Nioclás took place prior to the dissolution of the union with Tuam. Three years later the matter was still not resolved as Clement VI asked the bishops of Killala, Kilfenora and the Abbot of Boyle in 1351 to summon the archbishop and others and inform themselves touching the proposed dissolution of the union of the sees of Annaghdown, Kilmacduagh and Achonry to that of Tuam and to send a clear statement of the matter, under seal, to the pope.[17] Canon Robert Elliot from Waterford was in Avignon, when he was appointed Bishop of Killala on 8 June 1351. *Unification Still*

Nioclás Ó hEadhra began his reign in Achonry the year the Black Death raged throughout the country. The annals for 1349 record 'a great plague in Moylurg and in all Érinn in this year'. The clergy must have suffered severe casualties. One of the victims was Archbishop Maeleachlainn Mac Aodha of Tuam: even before the plague there was a dearth of clergy in Ireland. The Archdeacon of Cashel visited Avignon in 1346 and petitioned the Pope to grant him dispensations for twelve persons of illegitimate birth that they may be ordained because in Ireland 'there are found hardly any persons for the service of God and the church'.[18] *Death of Clergy*

Benedict Ó Mocháin, 'erenagh of Killaraght' may have been a victim of a new phase of the plague when he died in 1361. A petitioner asked Urban V (1362–70) in 1363 for the faculty to grant a plenary indulgence at the hour of death because 'of the great mortality in Ireland and especially in Connacht'. Two Augustinian Canons in Nenagh said the death rate was so high 'that hardly two persons remain in their house', presumably themselves.[19] Provost Gregory Ó Mocháin of Killala was nominated in 1353 Bishop of Down. Subsequently, the incumbent was found to be alive and Gregory had to withdraw. The pope instructed Nioclás Ó hEadhra together with Eoghan Ó Fearghail of Ardagh *1361 Plague*

14. *CPL*, iii, 279.
15. *CPL*, iii, 279.
16. Flood, 477.
17. *CPL*, iii, 388.
18. *Calendar of Papal Registers: Petitions 1342–1419*, 119.
19. *CPR: Petitions 1342–1419*, 511.

and the Abbot of Boyle to restore to Gregory the benefices he previously held, such as the provostship of Killala as well as canonries and prebends in Achonry and Elphin and other benefices.[20] However, shortly afterwards Elphin became vacant and Innocent VI (1352–62) nominated Gregory as bishop there in 1357. He was transferred to Tuam in 1372 where he died in 1384.[21] In my opinion, Achonry's claims on that extraordinary ecclesiastical family are stronger. Benedict O'Mohan was described as 'Erenagh of Killaraght' or 'archdeacon of Kill Athrachta' when he died in 1361.[22] King Toirdhelbhach Ó Conchobhar of Connacht was killed in 1356 by Donnchadha Carrach Ó Ceallaigh because Ó Conchobhar's son 'carried off privately and clandestinely' the wife of Ó Ceallaigh. He was succeeded by Aodh Ó Conchobhar. Domhnall O'Hara, 'king of Luighne', died in 1358 and two other 'royal' deaths occurred the following year, Maghnus Ó Dubhda, the son of the king of Hy-Fiachrach and Brian Mac Donnchadha 'the royal heir of Tirerrill' who was killed by one of the Ó Gadhra sept. The bridge across the river in Ballysadare was built with lime and stone by Cathal Óg Ó Conchobhar in 1360. Tensions continued in the diocese between Gaelic families and English settlers. An attack was made in 1365 by the Clann-Costello upon the people of Luighne and Cormac Ó hEadhra and 'six sons of kings' were slain.[23]

20.   *CPL*, iii, 540.
21.   McDonnell states that Gregory was a member of the O'Mohan family of Tireragh who gave their name to Ballymochany, *Killala*, 43.
22.   *AFM, ALC.*
23.   *AFM, ALC.*

CHAPTER TWELVE

The Black Death (1348–9)

'On all sides is sorrow; everywhere is fear. Would my brother that I had never been born, or at least had died before these times. In what annals has it ever been read that houses were left vacant, cities deserted, the countryside neglected, the fields too small for the dead and universal solitude spread over the whole earth? Will posterity ever believe these things when we, who see, can scarcely credit them?' Thus the great Italian poet and humanist, Francesco Petrarch (1304–74), described the Black Death. His wife and the love of his life, Laura, fell victim to the plague in 1348.[1]

Francesco Petrarch

The first instance of the plague was recorded at the Sicilian port of Messina in October 1347, spread rapidly throughout the island and then moved to the mainland. It reached Florence in the winter of 1348 where Giovanni Boccaccio had just begun writing his masterpiece, the *Decameron*. It recounts how seven young ladies and three young men fled from Florence to the neighbouring hills and passed the time each one telling a story each day for ten days. The *Decameron* also contains an eyewitness account of the effects of the plague itself.

Giovanni Boccaccio

> At the onset of the disease both men and women were affected by a sort of swelling in the groin or under the armpits which sometimes attained the size of a common apple or egg. Some of these swellings were smaller and all were commonly called boils. From these two starting points the boils in a little while began to spread and appear generally all over the body. Afterwards the manifestations of the disease changed into black or lurid spots on the arms, the thighs and the whole person. In many ways these blotches had the same meaning for everyone on whom they appeared …

Ireland was struck by the greatest plague ever recorded in world history in the winter of 1348–9. The Black Death was a bubonic plague which had already swept through Europe killing more than one-third of the population before reaching Ireland in the autumn of 1348. Germ-carriers reached Ireland through Howth and Dalkey at the beginning of August, probably on a boat

Drogheda Sermon

---

1. Qtd Poulet-Raemers, *Church History*, i, 676–7.

from Bristol whose crowded population had already been ravaged. Archbishop Richard FitzRalph of Armagh arrived in Ireland just a few months before the outbreak of the plague. He preached a sermon in Drogheda where he told the well-known tale of a necromancer in Toledo who asked the devil what country sent most people to hell. 'Ireland,' the devil answered, 'because all men rob one another there'. FitzRalph was preaching in English to the English colony in Drogheda, but his comments about the hatred between the English and Irish could be equally well applied to conflicts between the Irish themselves where war was almost endemic.

Centres of population were particularly affected by the plague, with Dublin and Drogheda almost completely depopulated within weeks. Twenty-five friars died in Drogheda during the same period. Norman settlements suffered most with many unwisely fleeing their homes in country districts into towns or to England where it was estimated that up to half the population perished.

Friar Clyn's
Account

A Franciscan friar in Kilkenny wrote an account of its ravages there. Rarely did it carry off one member of a family 'but as a rule man and wife with their children and all the family went the common way of death'. Friar Clyn claimed that fourteen thousand people perished in Dublin between the beginning of August and Christmas Day. Friar Clyn's account agrees with the observations elsewhere in Europe:

> This pestilence was so contagious that those who touched the dead or persons sick of the plague were straightway infected themselves and died so that the confessor and penitent were carried to the same grave. And from the very fear and horror men were seldom brave enough to perform the works of piety and mercy, such as visiting the sick and burying the dead. For many died from boils and ulcers and running sores which grew on the legs and beneath the arm-pits, while others suffered pains in the head and went almost into a frenzy, while others spat blood.

It was at its height in Kilkenny during Lent 1349 when six Dominicans died there on 6 March alone. The Kilkenny Franciscan concluded his chronicle thus:

> And I, Friar John Clyn, of the order of Friars Minor, and of the convent of Kilkenny, have written down these deeds that were worthy of note as I have learned them either as an eye-witness or else from trustworthy narratives, lest noteworthy deeds might perish with time and pass from men's memory; seeing these many ills, and how the whole world is as it were in an ill plight; among

the dead expecting deaths coming, I have set them down in writing, truthfully as I have learned them and tested them; and lest the writing should perish with the writer and the work fail with the worker, I leave parchment to carry on the work, if perchance any man survives or any of the race of Adam may be able to escape this pestilence and continue the work I have begun.

His premonition came true and his account came to a sudden end when he fell victim himself to the plague.

It is difficult to estimate casualties in a remote diocese like Achonry. The *Moylurg* Annals of Loch Cé have only a short single-line reference to the plague in 1349: 'A great plague in Magh-Luirg and in all Erinn *in hoc anno*', with an addition from the *Annals of Ulster* 'so that a great number of people were destroyed in it'. Why Moylurg was chosen for special mention is not clear. It may be that the plague was particlarly virulent there or it may just be that the chronicler of the *Annals of Loch Cé* was a native and eyewitness of the ravages of the plague there. The castle on the island of Loch Cé was the chief residence of Lord Mac Diarmada of Moylurg. Other Irish annals simply copied this entry. If this was true it is strange that there is no mention of the fate of the Premonstratensian Canons on Trinity Island in Lough Key, the Cistercian monks in nearby Boyle Abbey and Mac Diarmada and his retainers on the Rock. Elsewhere in Ireland and abroad monasteries suffered huge casualties but no record survives of the fate of the Augustinian Canons in Ballysadare or the Dominicans in Straide.

The plague had already struck Avignon in southern France in the early weeks *Avignon* of 1348, where popes were then resident, arriving up the mouth of the Rhone from Marseilles where it killed two-thirds of the population in a month. Avignon lost half its population during the seven months it raged in the city. Clement VI (1342–52) had a huge pit dug outside the city to accommodate the dead as all the city cemeteries were full to capacity. Nioclás Ó hEadhra may have been in Avignon during the plague as he was appointed bishop by Clement in the last months of 1348.

Back in Florence Boccaccio continues his story:

It was the common practice by most of the neighbours, moved no less by fear of contamination by the putrefaction of the bodies than by charity towards the deceased, to drag the corpses out of the houses with their own hands and to lay them in front of the doors where anyone who made the rounds might see them especially in the mornings … afterwards they would have biers brought up. Nor was it once or twice that one and the same bier carried two or three corpses at one. And times without number it happened as two priests were on their way to perform the last office for someone, three or four biers were brought up by the porters in the rear of them so that whereas the priests supposed they had but one corpse to bury, there were six to eight or sometimes more, a dead man was then of no more account than a dead goat today.

Boccaccio estimated that between March and July, 100,000 human beings lost their lives within the walls of Florence, which was probably an exaggeration as the entire population was less than that.

Children's Ditties   People were seized with a terrible panic, many believing the end of the world had come. They were gripped with despair which sometimes manifested itself in outbreaks of licentiousness. The memory of these wild parties appears to have survived in the popular ditty:

> *Sur les ponts d'Avignon, on y dansait, on y dansait.*
> *Sur les ponts d'Avignon, on y dansait tout en rond.*

A children's game in Ireland is generally believed to have its origin in the Black Death:

> A ring, a ring of rosies, a pocket full of poesies,
> Attisshoo, attisshoo, we all fall down.

Ballymote Burned   The MacDermots of Moylurg waged 'a great war' against the O'Connors in 1348 just prior to the onslaught of the plague and pursued Ruaidhrí O'Connor to Ballymote where they burned the town and all its stone and wooden buildings and took with them all the captives that were in the town which may have been a blessing in disguise as it was a main centre of population and may have been uninhabited. The 'great war' continued the following year when Ruaidhrí took his revenge when 'he burned and plundered the greater part of Magh-Luirg'. The brief entry about the 'great plague' follows immediately this account. Matthew O'Rourke was the only person mentioned who died of the plague.

Other Plagues   The plague gradually wore itself out through the winter of 1349–50 but there was a second wave some ten years later. About 17,000 people died in Avignon including a third of the cardinals in three months in 1361. This plague was called *pestis puerum* because of the large number of young people who died from it and reached Ireland in 1363. In that year the pope granted an Irish bishop the faculty to grant 'a plenary remission at the hour of death'. 'Whereas

THE BLACK DEATH (1348–9)   75

there is great mortality in Ireland and especially in Connacht', the bishop pleaded 'for power to absolve at the hour of death all those who labour in the said lands so long as the mortality lasts'.

The plague returned again in 1369 and from then on it entered a cycle, coming ever more frequently: 1375, 1379, 1381–2, 1383, 1387, 1390, 1399–1400, 1405–6, 1410–14, 1426, and 1428–9. It reoccurred once every four years in the 1430s. There were eleven plagues between 1442–59 and then another in 1463–4, 1471 and all over England in 1479–80. There was a respite with no plague at all for twenty years and then plagues again roughly every ten years in the sixteenth century. Most plagues were regional, rather than national or international and how many of them reached Ireland is difficult to determine apart from the occasional annal references.

CHAPTER THIRTEEN

The Great Western Schism
(1378–1417)

One of the results of the Avignon Exile was that the cardinals assumed ever greater powers and hoped to consolidate their position on the return of Gregory XI to Rome in 1378 where he died in March. Urban VI (1387–9) was elected in April, the last pope chosen who was not a cardinal. He was domineering and showed signs of insanity and most cardinals withdrew their support from him and elected Robert of Geneva, Clement VII (1378–94), who returned to Avignon. There were now two popes, one in Rome and the other in Avignon, both elected by the same set of cardinals. Both had their followers. France and Spain, as well as Scotland and Sicily, gave their allegiance to Clement while Urban was supported by the Holy Roman Empire, Hungary, Scandinavia, most of Italy, as well as England and their dependencies, which included Ireland. But the Irish church was already divided into Norman English and Gaelic areas.

Division in Ireland   The Norman-Irish church followed England and supported Urban. There is some evidence that Gaelic Ireland gave their allegiance to Clement. The Archbishop of Tuam, Gréagóir Ó Mocháin, openly favoured Clement in Avignon and it is likely that most suffragan bishops followed his lead. Clement wrote to Prior Tomás Mac Aodhgáin of St Coman's in Roscommon requesting him to assemble his adherents in Connacht and have his letters published by the Archbishop and his suffragans in their dioceses. Mac Aodhagáin convened a meeting of the archbishop and the other bishops in Roscommon.[1] However, Bishop Robert Elliot of Killala (1351–81), an Englishman from Waterford, was strongly committed to the Roman pope, Urban VI, and did not attend but sent the Archdeacon John Mac Geraghty of Killala to represent him. The archdeacon in the name of Bishop Robert refused his obedience to Clement and asserted that Urban VI was the only true pope.

The Archbishop of Tuam ordered Robert to desist from his rebellion and 'return to the unity of the Catholic church'. But Robert persevered and the archbishop declared that he was to be deposed as bishop. Robert retaliated with the backing of Urban and publicly declared the archbishop excommunicated.

1.   *CPL*, iv 245–6; see also McDonnell, *Killala*, 43.

76

Prior Mac Aodhagáin summoned Robert to appear at Avignon and when he refused to do so an enquiry was established and following their report, Robert was suspended and the administration of Killala was given to Canon Conn O'Connell, of Tuam. Among those listed as present in Roscommon with Archbishop Ó Mocháin, and the bishops of Kilmacduagh and Clonfert was the Bishop of Achonry. The Roscommon meeting took place sometime before February 1383 and the Bishop of Achonry then was an absentee Englishman who was certainly not present.

Gregory XI (1370–8) appointed English Dominican William Andrew(s) Achonry's first absentee bishop on 17 October 1373. He was then in Avignon where he continued to live. A master of theology, he was appointed by the Pope in February 1374 to examine, with six other masters in the faculty of theology in Avignon, another Dominican seeking to gain a mastership. If they found him suitable he was to be awarded the degree and given a licence to teach in the faculty. Andrews was transferred by Urban VI to Meath in 1380 and acted as auxiliary in Canterbury that year. Described as a 'prudent and erudite man, who after the manner of Socrates, wished to publish nothing'.[2] He died on the vigil of St Michael the Archangel, 28 September 1385.

William Andrews OP (1373–87)

The majority of the clergy probably supported Clement (1378–94) and possibly later Benedict XIII (1394–1423) in whose time the schism came to an end. Some of them later paid for their allegiance to the Avignon popes. The deceased Mathgamhan Ó Branghaile (Obrangaly), one time vicar of St Columba's, Emlefad supported Clement VII of the Avignon line during the Great Western Schism. He was probably appointed vicar by the latter during his pontificate before the death of Urban VI in 1389, as the appointment to the vicarage was reserved to but not disposed by him during his lifetime, and also to Boniface IX who died in 1404 without disposing of it. It was now left to Innocent VII, informed about this on 2 September 1405 by Priest Seán Mac an Bhreitheamhan, to make the appointment. He ordered Ó hEadhra to appoint Mac an Bhreitheamhan vicar.

Achonry Casualties

Vicar Nioclás Ó Clúmháin of Killoran, also an adherent of Clement VII, was removed on 10 October 1505 by the dean at the request of Julius II. Another Ó Clúmháin, Vicar Pádraig of Kilvarnet ('St Barnnrata's in the land of Luigne'), supported Clement VII too and Gregory XII (1406–15) instructed the archdeacon on 10 December 1408 to remove him and give the post to Domhnall Ó (Oseguaid). Vicar More Ó Giollagáin of Killaspugbrone (Strandhill) was removed because he had supported Clement VII and the Abbot of Boyle was ordered by the Pope on 17 November 1408 to appoint Priest Pilib Macgillabygi (Kilbeg) of Achonry, in his place.[3]

Connacht Excommunications

2.   De Burgo, *Hib. Dom.*, 465.
3.   *CPL*, vi, 63, 68–9, 1431.

Simon O. Cist.   Simon (his surname is unknown) was an English Cistercian appointed
(1385–95)   bishop by Urban VI (1378–89)[4] when the Great Western Schism had already
begun. He must have been consecrated before 1385 as he was acting then as
auxiliary in the diocese of London. He assisted the Bishop of London at the
consecration of William de Cordeberghe as Bishop of Tournai in Belgium on
9 July 1385. His co-assistant on that occasion was Robert Hyntlesham, the
Bishop of Sebastopol in the Thracian peninsula. Ireland was not the only
country that had absentee English bishops thrust upon them. Simon was
auxiliary in Canterbury in 1386, Conventry-Lichfield in 1387 and at the end
of that year, auxiliary in Ely. 'On 15 December 1387 Thomas Arundel, Bishop
of Ely, gave leave for the venerable father, brother Simon, *Dei gratias Achadensis
Episcopus*, to reconcile the church of Gamlingay, in Cambridgeshire, which has
been polluted by the effusion of blood.'[5] At the request of the founder, Bishop
William Longe of Winchester (1367–1404), he consecrated the chapel and
cemetery of Winchester College on 7 July 1395. He spent his last years in
Winchester from 1387 until his death in 1395.[6]

Tomás   Simon was succeeded by Tomás Mac Donnchadha. Eubel does not mention
Mac Donnchadha   Mac Donnchadha but records a certain 'Johannes' cited in a papal document
(1396–8)   under the date 13 September 1396.[7] He was the son of Muirgheas Mac
Donnchadha, who died in 1350, and grandson of Donnchadh from whom
Clann Donnchaidh was descended. Tomás was the second youngest of four
boys, Chonchobhar, Maolseachlain, himself and Tadhg. He was the first to be
described in the annals as Bishop of Achadh-Conaire (Achonry). For almost
two hundred years since its creation the diocese was called Luighne. The Latin
term 'Achadensis' had been at least fifty years in use in both papal and English
documents.

Book of Lecan   His niece, Caitherfhina, daughter of his older brother Maeleachlainn and
wife of Giolla Íosa Mac Firbisigh was 'drowned by a rushing flood whilst going
to Sunday Mass from her own house' in 1412. Giolla Íosa belonged to a very
distinguished literary family whose home was in Lackan. The *Yellow Book of
Lecan* containing a complete version of the *Táin Bó Cuailgne*, was largely the
work of his hand while other works he compiled included *An Leabhar Breac,
Annals of Tighernach* and above all, the *Book of Lecan*.

4.   *CPL*, iv, 437; *Gams.* 204.
5.   Qtd in Cotton, *Fasti*, 101 and in O'Rorke, ii, 100.
6.   Kivly, *Annals of Winchester College*, App. xiv, 530; Eubel i, 49 nos 10, 441; Gam dates his
      death ante 27 March 1398.
7.   Bon. IX Obl. 48 f191.

His nephew, Tomaltach, had also some literary credentials. He was the patron of the scribal team who compiled the *Book of Ballymote,* part of which was written in his house in Ballymote. The principal scribe was Maghnus Ó Duibhgeannáin. It was acquired by Clann Donnchaidh and remained in their possession until 1522 when it was sold to Aodh Óg Ó Domhnall for 140 milch cows. Tomás died in 1398 predeceasing his nephew Tomaltach described as 'lord of Corann and Tír Oilealla' who died in 1397. Tomás was described in the *Annals of Lecan* as 'a learned liberal prelate'.

Book of Ballymote

Canon Brian Ó Eadhra, 'son of great nobles', accused Dean Seán Ó hEadhra, who was 'by his lack of learning unfit to be dean and has led and leads a dissolute life' and guilty of perjury and neglecting the deanery possessions. Eugene IV (1431–47) ordered the prior of St Mary's, Inchmacnerin on 3 October 1431 'seeing that on account of John's power he cannot safely meet him within the city or diocese of Achonry, to summon Seán and investigate the case and if he finds the accusations to be true to deprive Seán and replace him with Brian'.[8]

Brian Ó hEadhra (1399–1409)

Canon Tomás Mac an Bhreitheamhan alleged that Dean Conn Ó hEadhra had publicly committed perjury, dilapidated and withdrawn goods from the deanery and permitted his subjects to traffic in his church. He was also 'of insufficient learning'. Eugene IV (1431–47) on 14 November 1443 authorised the provost and official of Achonry and Canon Niall Ó hÉanagáin, to enquire into the allegations and if proven to remove Ó hEadhra and assign the deanery to Mac an Bhreitheamhan who undertook to pay the annates at St Peter's in Rome on 20 November 1443.[9]

Rector Brian Ó hEadhra of Ballymote was appointed dean following accusations he made against Dean Tomás Mac an Bhreitheamhan, including allowing several of the faithful to die without the sacraments even though he had the care of souls. He also accused the dean of neglecting deanery property. Nicholas V nominated the official as well as Canons Uilliam Ó Connacháin (Ocommochan) and Seán Ó Clúmhain in April 1447 to investigate the charges and if found to be true to remove Mac an Bhreitheamhan and replace him with Ó hEadhra, which he did.

Climbing up the Ranks

Ó hEadhra claimed that the church in Achonry was 'threatened with ruin and in need of very great repairs'. Nicholas dispensed Ó hEadhra to hold together for life the rectory and deanery 'notwithstanding the pope's late ordinance forbidding holding together of a major cathedral dignity and a parish

---

8.   *CPL*, viii, 377.
9.   *CPL*, ix, 358–9; *Arch. Hib.*, v, XXVI.

church'. However, he entered a proviso that half the fruits of the rectory be used for the said repairs. Ó hEadhra was a cleric and not yet ordained and as the rectory had the care of souls, presumably he employed an ordained priest to carry out the functions of parish priest in Ballymote.[10] Brian Ó hEadhra, whose daughter Aoibheann (Aiuna)[11] was wife of Ruaidhrí Ó hEadhra, confirmed by Bishop Brian, resulting in the couple seeking a dispensation on account of spiritual affinity. Brian succeeded Tomás Mac Donnchadha as bishop and appointed Benedict Ó Mocháin vicar of Killaraght, vacant because Uilliam Ó Mocháin had failed to be ordained for more than a year. Benedict had doubts whether his appointment held good and hence his petition to Rome. Boniface IX (1389–1404) instructed Archbishop Muirgheas Ó Ceallaigh of Tuam on 5 November 1399 together with the abbots of Cong and Boyle to have Benedict validly appointed.[12] Brian O'Hara's death in 1409 is recorded in the annals 'after the victory of Unction and Penance'.[13]

Deaths   Two deaths were recorded during the early years of his episcopacy, both the offspring of Tadhg Mac Donnchadha, his daughter, Sadhbh in 1400 and his son Maelruanaidh, king of Tirerrill, who died in 1406 'after the victory of unction and penitence' and who was buried in Boyle Abbey. The castle of Cuil-Maoile (Colloony) was erected by Murchadh, son of Cormac Mac Donnachadha.

Maghnus   Canon Maghnus was mentioned in Roman documents of the pontificate
Ó hEadhra   of Alexander V (1409–10), a Greek from the island of Crete, the first of the
(1410–14?) two popes of the Pisan line during the Great Western Schism. He was seventy years old when elected pope by the Council of Pisa in 1409 and his reign lasted less than a year. John XXIII has been airbrushed out of history when Cardinal Roncalli chose that name when he was elected pope on 28 October 1958. It was hoped that the other two claimants to the papal throne would resign or be deposed but this happened only in 1417 when the Council of Constance elected Martin V (1417–31), the first pope in forty years recognised by all Catholics.[14] Maghnus Ó hEadhra was instructed in 1412 to conduct an enquiry concerning the Bishop of Kilmore.

Gallen Plundered   An attack was made in 1411 by Edmond Burke on the clan of Seán Ó hEadhra and one of them was killed by an arrow. Two other deaths were recorded

10. *CPL*, ix, 403, x, 319–20, 368–9.
11. *CPL*, vii, 298–9.
12. *CPL*, v, 283.
13. *AFM, ALC.*
14. Some authors list Laurence Peter Jacopini as appointed to Achonry by John XXIII in 1414 but it is based on a misreading of Achaden for Acharen. Ware, 660; Gams, 660, de Burgo, 470–1.

that year, Taichlech Buidhe, the son of Seán Ó hEadhra as well as Benmumhan Ó Conchobhar, wife of Murchadh Mac Donnachadha. The following year Brian Ó Conchobhar held a hosting in Gallen and the people of Gallen including the Costellos (Coisdelb) assembled against him 'but they gave him neither conflict nor battle'. He burned the district, destroying all their cornfields. Also in Gallen, Richard Barrett went on an expedition to Coolcarney where he was overtaken by 'the principal men of the country' who drove him to the Moy where he and a great number of his followers were drowned. Fearghal Ó hEadhra 'intended king of Luighne', died also that year.[15]

No record survives of Donatus except notice of his death in 1424.[16] He was said to be Donnchadh Ó hEadhra, bishop from 1414 to 1424. He probably died in 1423 because his successor was appointed in the beginning of April 1424.

Donnchadha (Donatus) Ó hEadhra (1414–24)

A war broke out among the people of Leyny in 1415. They gave battle to each other and the inhabitants of the eastern part were defeated and some of them killed. Art Ó hEadhra was taken prisoner and hanged by them at their own house. The following year Leyny was once more a theatre of war. Mac Jordan de Exeter and his kinsmen launched an attack upon the son of Seán Ó hEadhra who together with Toirdealbhach Carragh Ó Conchobhar and the cavalry of Carbery, met the van of the army of Mac Jordan. Ó hEadhra was killed and Maghnus Ó Conchobhar and Toirdealbhach Carragh were wounded. 'After this Mac Jordan plundered the country but the people of the whole territory assembled together and went in pursuit of him.' Mac Jordan was defeated and killed together with Aodh Ó Robhacháin and Ó Robhacháin himself, the two sons of Tomás Mac Maoilir, Mac Duarcán, lord of Culneiridh and many others. Ferchert Ó hUiginn, an eminent poet and a man who kept a general house of hospitality for the men of Éirinn died in 1419.[17]

War

15. *ALC.*
16. Martin V a, 7 Lat. I. pr. f71.
17. *AFM, ALC.*

CHAPTER FOURTEEN

'All Roads lead to Rome'

Annates   Besides collecting for the crusades, Rome had its agents criss-crossing the country collecting various dues and negotiating with Rome for bishops and other ecclesiastics. *Annates* was the term commonly used to describe payments made to the Papal Treasury by certain benefice-holders. They were first demanded in 1306 when Clement V (1303–14) reserved to his own use the first fruits of all benefices becoming vacant in England, Scotland, Wales and Ireland during the proceeding three years. John XXII (1316–34) imposed the payment of annates in 1426 on all minor benefices that became vacant by the death of the previous occupant in Rome or because the holder renounced the benefice resulting from pluralism, in which case the appointment was reserved to the pope. Some Achonry clerics did in fact die in Rome, such as Brian Ó Coinín (Oconnean), one-time dean, and the pope appointed his successor.[1]

First Fruits   This tax was expressly intended to help Rome in its government of the church and especially for organising crusades against the Turks who were threatening to overrun Europe. For most of the fourteenth century 'first fruits' amounted to all of the first year's revenue, paid in three annual instalments. Though papal appointments were made in Ireland during that century, it was not affected by the tax until the fifteenth century. Boniface IX (1389–1404) reduced it to half the first year's revenue which was not to be paid until a certain time after the person appointed took up his post. Petitions were signed by the Pope and submitted to officials who examined the petitioner regarding his suitability. Following this it was approved by the Pope and written on parchment with the papal seal called a *bulla* or bull. The appointee made a promise to the Papal Treasury to pay the tax to the regional collector usually within six or ten months, to be calculated from the day he was installed. Only then after payment did he receive the bull conferring his appointment. Failure to pay entailed the withdrawal of the bulls of appointment.

Exemptions   The petitioner had to pay fees and the cost of registering the bull unless he was too poor to pay. Benefices of an annual value of six marks of silver or ten pounds tournois (twenty-four gold florins of the Papal Treasury) or less were

1.   *Arch. Hib.*, xxvi, 90–1.

exempt from payment. Bulls were granted free of charge to Rector Ruaidhrí Ó Gadhra of Coolavin and Ranna (5 July 1428), Vicar Eoghan Macadruyth (Mac an Druaidh, Drury) of Kilmorgan (15 December 1428), Archdeacon Domhnall Ó hEadhra (14 February 1429), Vicar Diarmaid Ó Cléirigh of Bohola (15 May 1430) and Vicar Cathal Ó Mocháin of Killaraght (10 July 1444).[2] Later that century, the exemption was applied to benefices of higher value, such as the rectory of Banada and Hy-Fiachrach, worth sixteen marks when the bull was freely granted to Tatianus Ó Cearnaigh (17 October 1446) *gratis pro Deo*, as well the rectory of Kilmactigue worth eight marks, to Canon Brian Ó Coinín (29 April 1465) *gratis pro Ibernico paupere*. Surprisingly, the abbacy of Ballysadare, worth thirty marks was granted free to Domhnall Mac Donnchadha OP (31 January 1472), to Seán Ó hEadhra (28 February 1478) and to Maghnus Mac Donnchadha (26 May 1484) *quia pro Hibernico*.

The same formula was applied to exemptions for the prebend of Killedan, worth sixteen marks, as well as the rectory of Killoran and Hy-Fiachrach, eight marks, to Tatheus Ó hEadhra (13 February 1477), for the deanery, ten marks, to Tomás Ó Conghaláin (26 February 1477) to Cormac Ó hEadhra (27 February, 1478), and to Ruaidhrí Ó hEadhra (10 November 1494) *pro Hibernico,* for the vicarage and rectory of Kilmactigue, in total worth eight marks *quia non ascendit summam.* In fact it seemed that no annates were paid by twenty-one out of a total of forty-five Achonry clerics who received papal appointments.[3]

Tithes

The annate entries in the papal registers give the name of the rector or vicar appointed, the date of the appointment, the name of his predecessor or predecessors and the estimated income of the rectory or vicarage. The value of each benefice was computed by the value of the tithes. The people were obliged to pay tithes, i.e. one-tenth of all agricultural produce including butter, cheese, fowl or cattle. These were paid in kind while priests paid their subventions to the bishop in coin. There were heavier taxes known as 'common services', paid by those appointed bishops.

Papal Centralisation

There was an enormous, though gradual, growth in church centralisation through the thirteenth, fourteenth and fifteenth centuries up to the Reformation when the papacy busied itself with the smallest detail, making itself felt in the remotest villages and even the lowest ranks of society. Nothing illustrates this better than the expansion of the *curia* and ever increasing numbers of papal provisions. Papal provisions or appointments to church benefices became

2.   *CPL*, xxvi, 58–9, 65, 66–7, 83, 87, 91, 91–2.
3.   *CPL*, xxvi, 58, 59, 62, 63, 65, 66–7, 68, 69, 72, 74, 77, 78, 79, 80, 82, 83, 87, 90, 91–2, 96–7, 108, 109, 113.

frequent only in the thirteenth century, and became normal for all major and many minor benefices during the Avignon Exile in the fourteenth century, with an enormous increase during the fifteenth century.

The first entry for the Achonry annates is dated 9 January 1423 and concerns the appointment of Cormac Mac Donnchadha as vicar of Ballysadare, and the last entry on 23 May 1548 refers to a Dominican, Turlough Ó Conchobhar, who held the rectory of Killaraght among other benefices. Between these two dates no less than forty-five entries dealt with the diocese providing, together with the *Papal Letters*, a wealth of information, particularly the names of deans, archdeacons, provosts, canons, rectors and vicars as well as abbots of Ballysadare and Boyle.

Value of Benefices   Such benefices were defined by their yearly value, their location and whether or not they involved the care of souls. The annual value of a benefice depended on the amount of tithes paid to the occupant and was computed in marks, each mark worth six shillings and eight pence. They varied from one mark for the vicarage of Attymass to twenty-five marks for the rectory of Dá Chorann and Mota (Ballymote). The dean received ten marks, the provost eight and the archdeacon six but this was augmented by his income from the vicarage of Kilturra which went with the job. Rectors' incomes varied between eight and twenty-six marks.[4]

Vicars or parish priests, the only clerics who ministered to the people providing Sunday Mass, administering sacraments and burying parishioners, were poorly remunerated. Their incomes ranged from one to five marks, while the average was four marks. Their revenue then often reveals the changed status of several parishes compared with their modern counterparts. At the lower end, Kilconduff (Swinford) was worth only two marks, just one above Attymass. The only clerics rated below vicars were canons whose incomes were based on prebends worth annually two to four marks. But they were largely young men in their late teens, tonsured clerics still pursuing their studies.

4.   The following benefices and their value are recorded in the Vatican Archives. *Rectories:* Dá Chorann & Mota (Ballymote), 25 marks, Banada & Hy-Fiacrach, 16 marks, Sliabh Lugha (Kilmovee), 16 marks, Coolavin & Ranna, 15 marks?, Ballylahan (Straide), 12–15 marks. Bohola, 8 marks. *Vicarages:* Attymass, 1 mark, Ballylahan (Straide), 4 marks, Ballysadare, 4 marks, Cloonoghill (Bunninadden), 3–6 marks, Emlefad (Ballymote), 5–6 marks, Kilbeagh (Charlestown), 4 marks, Killaraght (Gurteen), 5 marks, Killasser, 4 marks, Killoran (Coolany), 4–5 marks, Kilmactigue (Tourlestrane), 6 marks. Kilmorgan (Ballymote), 4 marks, Kilshalvey (Bunninadden), 3 marks, Kilvarnet, 4 marks, Templemore (Straide), 3 marks. Toomour (Keash) 4 marks. *Prebends:* Doheran & Moymlough, 2 marks, Killaraght, 4–5 marks, Killedan (Kiltimagh), 2 marks, Killoran, 3–4 marks, Kilmactigue, 2 marks, Toomour & Drumrat (Keash), 1 mark.

Accusations made in these petitions should be treated with extreme caution. *Accusations*
Every fact alleged by a petitioner should not be taken as an objective account
of the local reality. At best these allegations represented only one side, the
petitioners', who had vested interests in making the accusations. Usually they
consisted of perjury, simony, 'dilapidation' or neglect of the upkeep of church
property, not attending to the care of souls, celebrating Mass or other
sacraments while under the sentence of excommunication and, most
controversial of all, fornication. Many medieval clergy in Ireland and elsewhere
did not practice celibacy, engaging in sexual activity deemed 'fornication' in
church law. Most sexual liaisons were with the same woman, a life partner,
called a concubine. Couples married within forbidden degrees were also
deemed 'fornicators'. Some clerics were accused of being 'notorious' fornicators, i.e. sexual relations with several women. The expression occurs so
frequently in different petitions that it appears almost formulaic. The Roman
scribes who drafted these petitions often tended to fit them into the legal
categories best suited to advance the cause of the petitioners.

Nioclás Ó Náradhaigh was appointed rector of Sliabh Lugha in 1423.[5] Pilib   *Accused*
Mac Éinrí informed the Pope in 1424 that Ó Náradhaigh was a 'notorious
fornicator, who has begotten offspring still alive by divers women'. He also
alleged that he allowed the property of the rectory to fall into ruin, neglected
Mass and other divine offices and the care of souls, engaged in secular business
and 'led a dissolute life in the houses of laymen'.[6] Rector Ruaidhrí Ó Mocháin
of Coolavin and Ranna was accused in 1444 of 'dilapidating a number of the
goods belonging to the said benefice' and committing perjury and simony.
Ruaidhrí was accused again in 1447 of neglecting rectory property and the
care of souls and publicly committing fornication.[7] Ó Mocháin had studied
canon law for several years and was appointed rector in 1441.

Seán Ó Clúmháin accused Priest Tatianus Ó Cearnaigh and cleric Brian Ó
hEadhra in 1443 of using false papal letters to get the rectory of Banada and
take fruits from it. Ó Clúmháin appears to have been successful as he
undertook to pay the annates on 4 November 1443. Later, Ó Cearnaigh in
turn accused Ó Clúmháin of dilapidating rectory property and committing
simony.[8] Paul II (1464–71) was informed by Canon Brian Ó Coinín in
1464–5 that Rector Seán Ó hEadhra of Kilmactigue was 'a wilful murderer,
and takes part like a layman in warlike acts in which death, mutilation and

5.   *CPL*, vii, 270–1, 350–1.
6.   *CPL*, viii, 416, 445–6.
7.   *CPL*, x, 282.
8.   *CPL*, ix, 552–3; *Arch. Hib.*, xxvi, 78–9.

bloodshed have taken place'. Tomás Ó Comhdhain (Ochoan) alleged in 1447 that Vicar Domhnall Mac Ceallaigh (Mackellayd) of Emlefad neglected the upkeep of the vicarage and while publicly excommunicated 'had in contempt of the Keys celebrated Masses and other divine offices and taken part therein'.[9]

Other accusations were made against vicars in Cloonoghill (Clunocoll, Cloynnahacglasse). Canon Uilliam Ó Connacháin accused Vicar Seán Ó Connacháin (Obcanhuchan) in 1443 of having 'recently seized violently and lacerated certain papal letters' against the wish of Cathal Mac Cristín, who obtained them, and having also committed perjury and simony. Uilliam studied canon and civil law for several years in a *studium particulare* and held the provostship.[10] Conn Ó Gadhra informed Paul II in 1470 that Vicar Muirgheas Ó Coimín (Ocoymiean) was 'an open fornicator', committed simony, and 'alienated or dilapidated the immoveable goods of the said vicarage'.[11] Canon Dáibhí Ó Con Learga (Ocoyulerga) informed Rome in 1454 that Vicar Éinrí Ó Mochan of Killaraght, 'a public and notorious fornicator' 'dilapidated, alienated and uselessly consumed a number of the possessions of the said vicarage' and while publicly excommunicated by Bishop Conn Ó Mochain 'celebrated or rather profaned Masses etc in contempt of the Keys, incurring irregularity to the shame of the priestly order'.[12]

Others Accused: Priest Tadhg Ó Cearnaidh of Hy Fiachrach and Banada (1443), Vicar Éinrí Ó Mocháin of Killaraght (1454), Vicar Muirgheas Ó Coimín (1417), Vicar Seán Ó Connacháin, Vicar Cathal Mac Cristín of Cloonoghill, Vicar Domhnall Mac Ceallaigh (1477) and Vicar Maghnus Ó Clúmháin of Kilvarnet (1504).

Petitioners   The vast majority of these provisions were granted to clerics who petitioned the Pope for them either in person or through an agent, specifying the benefice requested. Most were clerics, often in their late teens or early twenties. Eoghan Ó hEadhra was eighteen years old when he was appointed rector of Ballylahon in 1404 while Tomás Mac Dhuarcháin was a twenty-two-year-old scholar from Tuam in 1418 when he became rector. Cathal Ó Floinn was the same age when he became vicar of Killaraght in 1424. Aindréas Mac an Bhreitheamhan succeeded as vicar of Ballysadare in 1402 when his father, Aindréas, resigned in his favour. Another cleric, Maghnus Ó Ruadhán, became vicar of Kilvarnet in 1435. Vicarages had the care of souls thus requiring the services of a priest and when a cleric was appointed he was obliged to employ a priest. He himself

9.   *CPL*, x, 281.
10. *CPL*, ix, 395.
11. *CPL*, xii, 775–6.
12. *CPL*, x, 727.

was expected to become ordained within a specified time, usually a year, and unless he received a special dispensation he forfeited the vicarage, which explains the high turnover of vicars. Many benefices, such as rectories, did not involve the care of souls and thus did not require the services of a priest but even so occupants were sometimes obliged to become ordained. Ruaidhrí Ó Gadhra was rector of Coolavin for more than a year without being ordained.[13]

Some appointed to other benefices such as provosts were also clerics. Eoghan Ó hEadhra was provost sometime before 1419 after studying canon and civil law for several years. However, he failed to 'have himself promoted to the order required by the provostship' and as a result another cleric also Ó hEadhra, Cormac, 'in his twenty-third year or thereabouts', was appointed provost on 13 June 1420.[14] Cormac Ó Connacháin, a tonsured cleric and son of a former provost, became provost in 1489. Twenty-two-year-old cleric Domhnall Ó hEadhra was appointed archdeacon on 14 February 1429.[15]

If the purpose of these young clerics seeking these appointments was to secure an income for themselves they were not always successful. When Maeleachlainn Ó Clúmháin resigned as vicar of Killoran, Bishop Conn Ó Mocháin then appointed a cleric, Uilliam Ó Clúmháin (Oelnam) to replace him. Uilliam was vicar for between two or three years without becoming a priest and the first year he paid Bishop Ó Mocháin the first fruits and used the income the second year to restore the fabric of the church. The third year he received little or nothing and was deprived by the bishop. However, he was rehabilitated by the Pope in 1473.[16]

One particular cleric, twenty-three-year-old Brian Mac Donnchadha 'of kingly and princely race', was exceptionally ambitious. He boasted to Rome that he was 'so powerful that he can have at will 300 men for the defence of the church'. Brian had studied canon and civil law for eight years and was dispensed in 1408 'at the end of three more years to be promoted to the episcopal dignity, provided that it be in Ireland only'. It does not appear that he ever achieved his ambition.[17]

Brian Mac Donnchadha

Other clerics who received papal appointments included Cormac Ó Callanáin (1410), Pilib Mac Éinrí, Cormac Mac Donnchadha (1422), Eoghan Macadruch (1428), Conn Ó Mocháin (1435), Seán Ó Clúmháin (1443), Cathal O Mocháin, cleric (1444, 1447), Conn Ó Gadhra (1470), Uilliam Ó

13. *CPL*, ix, 189.
14. *CPL*, vii, 148.
15. *CPL*, viii, 108.
16. *CPL*, xiii, 338.
17. *CPL*, vi, 63, 68–9, 141–2.

Clumháin (1473), Tomás Ó Comdhain (1477), Maeleachlainn Ó Clúmháin (1491), Ruaidhrí Ó hEadhra (1497), Seán Ó Beannacháin. Some petitioners were Canons: Brian Ó Coinín (1464), Uilliam Ó Connacháin, Dáibhí Ó Con Learga (1454), Feidhlim Mac an Bhreitheamhan (1504).

Investigations   Where petitioners made accusations against an incumbent, the pope mandated or ordered a number of clerics within or without the diocese to investigate the situation and if the accusations or enough of them proved to be true to remove the accused and replace him with the petitioner. No records of these investigations in the dioceses have survived and therefore there is no evidence of how many petitioners were successful, except where later entries record the petitioner as the incumbent in that specific benefice. It has been estimated that in the wider church only half of the petitions led to the issue of papal letters and only about half of these letters resulted in the actual obtainment of a benefice.[18] In the final result only fifty per cent of papal letters were actually effective. Often it seems that orders from Rome were no match for the power of locals.

Intimidation   Some petitioners complained about intimidation by the powers that be, alleging that they could not get 'justice within the city or diocese of Achonry'. Cormac Mac Donnchadha alleged that he was intimidated by Rector Domhnall Mac Donnchadha of Ballymote in 1428 while that year a similar allegation was made against Rector Ruaidhrí of Coolavin. They were also made by Vicar Diarmaid Ó Cléirigh of Bohola in 1430 against Tomás Ó Murchú and by Brian Mac Donnchadha in 1443. Ruaidhrí Ó Mocháin of Killaraght claimed in 1490 that he was 'terrified' of the power of Conn Ó Gadhra. Incumbents often had powerful friends who protected them and when petitioners complained that they were intimidated, the pope nominated outsiders to judge these cases.

Appeal   One of the very few cases recorded, where the investigation ordered by the Pope was carried out in the diocese, occurred in 1497 when an appeal was made to Rome against the decision. Canon Tadhg Ó Tomhnair (Ythonit) was rector of Kilmactigue and Banada but Tadhg Ó Floinn (Ofloynd) falsely asserted that the rectory was rightfully his and had him summoned before Canon Domhnall Ó Cuinn who found in favour of Ó Floinn, which Ó Tomhnair appealed to Rome. While the appeal was pending, Ó Floinn was appointed by Canon Domhnall. To remain in the rectory in peace and not be molested further, Ó Tomhnair paid 'a certain of money' incurring simony and the consequent censure. Furthermore, he celebrated Mass while under censure,

18. Barraclough, *Papal Provisions*, 35, 37.

thus incurring irregularity. Ó Tomhnair asked the pope to absolve him from simony and dispense him from the irregularity in question. On 29 December 1497, Alexander VI ordered the absolution of Ó Tomhnair from simony after a 'salutary penance'. The adjudicators were to hear the appeal and if they found in favour of Ó Tomhnair, to appoint him rector.[19]

Simony – trafficking in church goods, whether temporal or spiritual – was regarded by the medieval church as the most heinous of clerical crimes and entailed the sentence of automatic excommunication which could only be lifted by the pope himself. Martin V (1417–31) had made a general reservation to himself and his successors of absolution from sentences of excommunication against simoniacs. Later that century, Paul II left little doubt about the Church's abhorrence of simony when he renewed 'all papal sentences of excommunication, suspension, interdict, deprivation and other ecclesiastical sentences, censures, pains against simoniacs (his will being that every simoniac, manifest or occult, should incur them automatically) and his reservation of their absolution to himself and his successors alone'.

Simony

Several cases of simony were reported to Rome from the diocese, particularly in the later decades of the fifteenth century. The earliest recorded case – though not specifically referred to as simony – involved lay people as well as clerics. St Attracta 'during her lifetime was divinely decorated with certain gifts, commonly called the Cross and Cup of Attracta'. Vicar Tadhg Mac Diarmada of Killaraght complained to John XXIII that these relics were very often 'by virtue of a certain ancient custom' or abuse, taken out of the church without consent of the vicar, to 'profane and perilous places by certain clerks and laymen … for the purpose of gain, handing over no part of their gains to the vicar, but converting the same to the use of themselves and their friends'. The Pope ordered Bishop Maghnus O'Hara (1410–14) on 15 November 1411 to decree 'that the said gifts (*munera*) shall henceforth be kept by Tadhg in the said church only and for its utility only'.[20] Brian Mac Donnchadha from Elphin was appointed rector by the Pope following the death of Domhnall Mac Donnchadha. He claimed that he was intimidated into swearing that he would give Conn Mac Ceallaigh a once-off portion of the tithes and another portion annually to Canon Cormac Mac Donnchadha which he subsequently did. He was thus guilty of simony and incurred the sentence of excommunication. On 3 November 1443, Eugene IV ordered Canon Conn Ó Mocháin and two others to absolve Brian after he resigned the rectory and did penance.[21]

Relics of
St Attracta

19. *CPL*, xvii, part 2, 72–3, no. 66.
20. *CPL*, vi, 260–1, 451.
21. *CPL*, ix, 360–1.

Mathghamhain Ó Callanáin, a vicar from Elphin, informed Sixtus IV that Emlefad vicarage was vacant following the death of Seán Ó Duarcáin (Ygartan). Subsequently (6 October 1460), a priest, Ruaidhrí Ó Siadhail (Oscluayd)[22] made a bargain with Bishop Conn Ó Mocháin that if he appointed him vicar he would give him 'moveable goods to the value of five marks sterling, and did so, thereby incurring simony and sentence of excommunication'. Ó Callanáin was appointed in December 1480.[23] The pope ordered an investigation into the allegation in January 1480 and if true to deprive Ruaidhrí and appoint Ó Callanáin.[24]

Bishops Implicated   Notwithstanding his absenteeism, Bishop Blakedon (1442–53) appears to have carried out some profitable transactions in the diocese. He accepted the resignation of Vicar Muirgheas Ó Clúmháin of Killoran and it was alleged that Seán Ó Clúmháin made a bargain with Blakedon to appoint him vicar in return for a sum of money and a horse.[25] Local bishops were also accused of simony. Fearghal Ó Mocháin accused Tomaltach Ó Gadhra of paying Bishop Conn Ó Mocháin (1449–63?) a certain sum of money for making him rector of Coolavin and Ranna. Innocent VIII ordered an investigation by three outsiders on 20 February 1486–7 and 'if they find the foregoing, or two of them sufficient for the purpose, to be true, to declare his institution to have been and to be null and void', to deprive Tomaltach and appoint Fearghal rector.[26] The same bishop was accused of appointing the vicar of Emlefad in return for 'moveable goods to the value of 5 marks sterling'.[27] *CPL*, xii, 113. A similar accusation was made against Bishop Ó Conghaláin (1484–1508) by Seán Ó Murchú, that if he was made rector of Bohola he would give him 'certain goods', which he did. The Pope ordered an investigation on 2 January 1491 and to remove Ó Murchú if the accusation was true.[28] Ó Conghaláin was involved in another incident of simony though the finger is not pointed directly at him. Canon Brian Mac (Macmyrythyn), 'aspiring by unorthodox means' to become provost, came to an arrangement with Tadhg Ó hEadhra in return for money to resign in his favour. Subsequently, Tadhg did resign 'spontaneously and freely' to Bishop Ó Conghaláin, which he accepted 'unaware perhaps of the above arrangement' and appointed Brian provost. Brian petitioned Julius II (1503–13) to absolve him and on 13 January 1504 the Pope ordered his absolution and reappointment.[29]

22.   Ruaidhrí Oseluit, *CPL*, xii, 113.
23.   *CPL*, xiii, 89.
24.   *CPL*, xiii, 729–30; re Ó Duarcáin see *CPL* xii, 113; x, 364, 427–8, 446–7.
25.   *CPL*, x, 432.
26.   *CPL*, xiv, 167.
27.   *CPL*, xii, 113.
28.   *CPL*, xv, 308, 309–10.
29.   *CPL*, xviii, 23.

Tadhg Ó hEadhra accused Provost Cathal Mac (Maconhanne) of simony, handing over 'a certain sum of money counted out' to Tadhg Ó Tomhnair, and as a result Ó hEadhra was appointed provost on 11 February 1495. On that day, Alexander VI ordered three Canons to summon Cathal and Tadhg and if they found the accusation to be true, to remove Cathal and appoint Tadhg Ó hEadhra provost.[30]

Cathal Ó Mocháin complained that Rector Ruaidhrí Ó Mocháin of Coolavin and Ranna had committed simony and the pope ordered an investigation in July 1444. At the same time Cathal also accused Vicar Éinrí Ó Mocháin of Killaraght of making a 'simoniacal agreement' with Cormac Ó Mocháin under oath to the effect that he Éinrí, 'should have possession, that Cormac should not molest him, and that the fruits etc should be divided equally between them for their lives'.[31]

Considerable numbers of clerics travelled from Achonry to Rome, particularly during the fifteenth century, to present their petitions personally, though on a number of occasions, pledges to pay annates were undertaken on their behalf by others. Vicar Simon Ó hOireachtaigh of Cloonoghill pledged in the name of Vicar Cormac Mac Donnchadha of Ballysadare in January 1423. Abbot Conn Mac Searraigh of Ballysadare made a similar pledge in December 1428 for Cormac Ó hEadhra who succeeded him as rector of Banada and Hy-Fiachrach. An Elphin vicar did the same the following year for Vicar Cormac Ó Cuinn (Ocuynn) of Bohola and another one from the same diocese for Dean Brian Ó hEadhra in 1431.[32] The bishop-elect of Achonry, Tomás Ó Conghaláin, gave an undertaking in the name of the Abbot of Ballysadare on 26 May 1484.[33]

Proxies

Recourse to Rome by clerics in search of benefices – 'Rome running' – particularly from Gaelic parts, was as striking a feature of the Church in Ireland as elsewhere in the fifteenth century. It was also a troublesome and expensive undertaking from which there must have been some return. The majority of petitioners presented their petitions personally and probably travelled together in sizeable groups. One such group was led by Bishop Uilliam Ó hEidhigheáin of Elphin in 1444 included Abbot Tadhg Mac Diarmada of Boyle, the prior of Roscommon, and the Abbot of Ballysadare and most of them, including the latter, died in Rome. 1450 was a Jubilee Year and many Irish people went to Rome[34] and while there were numerous Achonry clerics in Rome,

'Rome running'

30.   *CPL*, xvii, 44–5, no. 40.
31.   *CPL*, ix, 447, 448.
32.   *Arch. Hib.*, xxvi, 58–9, 63, 65, 68.
33.   Ibid., xxvi, 58–9, 65, 96–7.
34.   'Annals of Ireland', 203, 205–6, 211–12, 225; *ALC.*

particularly 1448–9, there are no indications in the papal records that any were there during the Jubilee year.

Provost Cathal Mac Conaonaigh (Mycconhane) was there between November 1490 and January 1491 as indicated by the papal mandates he received, not only to inquire into matters in his own diocese but in others such as Ardagh, Elphin, Tuam and as far away as Clogher. Others with him included the dean and Canons Gilbert de Exeter (Jordan), Seán Ó Deirg and Alastar Ó Murchú (Omurconda). Again Canons Brian Mac (Macinyrherryin) and Brian Ó hEadhra received several papal mandates between January and February 1510.[35]

Papal Mandatories   Those nominated as papal mandatories to carry out investigations in the diocese included the bishop, dean, archdeacon, provost, and official but their names were never given – understandably, as there was only one of each. However, canons were mentioned by both christian name and surname. Rome could hardly have known the individual names of the dozen or so canons in the diocese and those nominated must have been actually present in Rome then. They probably travelled there together. Four were named in 1428 and 1508, five in 1443 and 1448, six in 1435, 1440, 1449, 1484, 1495 and 1503, seven in 1447 and eight in 1509. Sizeable clusters occurred in other years in close proximity to the years mentioned above with the same names as those mentioned then. It is unlikely that they travelled so frequently to Rome and more likely that the Roman Curia kept their names on file.

Canons, like clerics, were young men and their nomination as canons was a first step on the clerical ladder. A relatively small number, the Ó Mocháin, Ó Clúmháin, MacDonnchadha, etc. clans, controlled the chapter with almost complete class exclusiveness and their names occur again and again with inexhaustible frequency. Tomaltach Mac Donnchadha informed Rome in 1490 that immediately after he became a cleric, having been tonsured by Bishop Tomás Ó Conghaláin, he was received by the bishop and chapter as a canon and given a prebend worth one mark sterling.[36]

35. *CPL*, xv, 309–10, nos 578, 311, nos 600, 311–12, nos 601, 313–14, nos 603, 315–16, nos 605, 317, nos 608, 318, nos 609, 320, nos 320, xix, 186, 187, 195, nos 319, 321, 322.
36. *CPL*, xvi, 318, no. 609.

CHAPTER FIFTEEN

Absentees et al

While records were extremely scarce on Bishop Donnchadh Ó hEadhra, on the contrary plenty of documents attest to the existence of Richard Belmer, an English Dominican from Hereford, who was named Bishop of Achonry on 2 April 1424. His appointment mentioned that Achonry had become vacant following 'the death of Donatus' (Donnchadh) during whose life the Pope specially reserved it. Martin V wrote to Henry to inform him, probably because he was an Englishman. Belmer, a bachelor of theology, was consecrated in Rome on 4 June 1424 by Thomas Polton, Bishop of Chichester, in the church attached to his dwelling 'at Saint James near the gate of Beatae Mariae de Populo de Urbe'. He was dispensed by Martin V to hold a benefice 'owing to the fact that the Irish are notoriously rebels against king Henry and enemies and adversaries of all Englishmen … (and) cannot reside in the said church and owing to the fact that the goods of the said church are dissipated and dilapidated, can get nothing from them'.[1] Blakedon and Belmer were two bishops of Achonry during the episcopacy of Maghnus Ruadh Ó hEadhra.

Belmer never visited Achonry but acted as auxiliary bishop in the dioceses of Hereford and Winchester. Bishop Bolton of Worcester petitioned the pope on behalf of Richard 'who was exercising pontifical offices for him in the city and diocese of Worcester' and Martin V dispensed him in August 1428 'to hold any benefice even with cure and wont to be held by secular clerks and to resign it, simply or for exchange, as often as he pleases'. He was transferred to the diocese of Meath in 1430 where he continued to be an absentee.[2]

Maghnus Ruadh Ó hEadhra belonged to the Riabhach Ó hEadhra branch of the Ó hEadhra family who were descended from Seán Óg, a nephew of Domhnall Cléireach who died in 1358.

The ruling Ó hEadhras split into two factions, Ó hEadhra Buidhe and Ó hEadhra Riabhach, leading to bitter conflict and war, and their dispute had important consequences on the diocesan structure. As the existing rector of the united rectory then, Seán Ó Clúmhain reported to Rome that 'such mortal enmities have arisen between the said lords that the said churches, which are

---

1.   *CPL*, vi, 513, the document is dated 9 July 1414 which probably should read 1424.
2.   *CPL*, viii, 55; Eubel i.

of lay patronage, cannot be peaceably and quietly ruled and governed by one rector'. Banada and Hy-Fiachrach rectory covered a large part of the Ó hEadhra territory of Luighne (Leyny) and the Ó hEadhra clan was patron with the right to nominate the rector for the bishop to appoint. Ó Clúmháin was joined by Priest Thatianus Ó Cearnaidh in his petition to have the rectory also split in two, and henceforth governed by two rectors, 'which would be to the great advantage of the said churches and their parishioners'. The united rectory was valued at sixteen marks and in order that the division of the revenue be equal they proposed that the townlands of Dougharne (Dubcarnd) be annexed to the church of Killoran. Nicholas V commissioned Archdeacon Seán Ó Duarcán in May 1448 to carry out the division and appoint Ó Cearnaidh and Ó Clúmhain, recently dispensed as the son of a priest and an unmarried woman, rectors.[3]

Ó Duarcán carried out the Pope's mandate and, without the consent of Ó Clúmháin, divided the rectory and appointed Ó Cearnaidh rector of Kilmactigue. Ó Clúmháin was worried that there was no mention in the archdeacon's proceedings that Ó Clúmháin held a canonry in the diocese and the prebend of Killoran valued at four marks, and consequently that the division did not hold good. Seán again petitioned to have the matter rectified and in December 1448 the Pope mandated Canons Muiris Ó Conchobhair, Maeleachlainn Ó Clúmháin, and Tomás Ó (Omathet) to assign the rectory of Killoran to Ó Clúmháin. The rectory was described as being located in Hy-Fiachrach.[4]

The Ó hEadhra split into two branches at the end of the fourteenth century or the beginning of the next. Ó hEadhra Buidhe had his castle at Coolany, and Ó hEadhra Riabhach was in the southern part of barony of Leyney with their seat at Ballyara (*Baile Í Eadhra*) near Tubbercurry. It was a bitter division. 'Mortal enmities' arose between Cormac Ó hEadhra and Seán Buidhe (John Flavus) Ó hEadhra and war broke out between them.

Bishop's sons   Maghnus fathered at least four sons, Brian, Uilliam, Diarmaid and Seán (John), and presumably some daughters as well, probably by the same woman who was related to him both by blood and marriage. One of his sons, Brian, at least was born when his father was the bishop. Uilliam, who later became the Ó hEadhra Riabhach died in 1477. Seán Mac-an-Easpuig Ó hEadhra took Cormac's place after he became chief.[5]

3. *CPL*, x, 427–8.
4. *CPL*, x, 448–9; see ix, 403.
5. *AFM* Maghnus built a castle for himself and his family on church lands in the parish of Achonry, which he later leased to his sons for an annual rent. It was later seized from the bishop and Brian and his brothers by Seán Buidhe Ó hEadhra and his sons and 'detained for many years'.

The bishop was himself accused by a cleric, Cormac, as well as laymen, Seán *Bishop Accused*
and Tadhg Ó hEadhra, of imposing sentences of excommunication and
interdict against them 'without lawful cause' and publicly proclaiming them
excommunicated. The Pope instructed the Dean of Clonfert to summon Bishop
Maghnus 'with the assent of proctors of both sides', to absolve the plaintiffs
conditionally, to hear both sides and decide what is just.[6]

There was a famine in the summer of 1434, called for a very long time *Famine*
afterwards, *Samhra na mear aithne* (the summer of slight acquaintance) because
no one used to recognise friend or relative because of the severity of the
famine.[7] In 1435 O'Gara was killed by his own kinsmen on Inis Bolg an island
in Lough Gara.[8]

The Four Masters record the death of Maghnus in 1435: 'The red Bishop
Ó hEadhra, Bishop of Achonry, died.' His descendants – *slioght an aspuick
ruadh* (sept of the red bishop) – were tenants on church lands in Tullyhugh in
the sixteenth century.

The Pope authorised the provost and Canons Diarmaid Mac Aodhagáin *Killoran*
and Seán Ó Cearnaigh that August to appoint cleric Tadhg Ó Clúmháin to
the 'perpetual benefice without cure' of Killoran, dispensed as the son of
unmarried parents, following the death of Flann Ó Clúmháin or because Seán
Ó hEadhra contracted marriage *per verba legitime de presenti*. Canon Cormac
Mac Donnchadha held the benefice for about three years 'under pretext of
papal letters in no wise extending thereto'.[9]

Tadhg, dispensed because of his illegitimacy as the son of unmarried nobles, *Tadhg Ó Dálaigh*
was appointed Bishop of Achonry by Eugene IV on 3 September 1436 *OP (1436–42)*
following the death of Maghnus 'during whose life it was specially reserved to
the present pope'. Letters were sent announcing it to the chapter, clergy,
people of the city and diocese and vassals of the church and, lastly, to the
Archbishop of Tuam. There is no mention of the King of England either in
the licence for the election or the papal confirmation which indicates that the
king's writ no longer ran, at least in Achonry. He was a Dominican friar,
possibly a member of Straide Abbey or more probably its motherhouse, Holy
Cross Abbey in Sligo. He was described as 'a man distinguished for many
virtues'.[10]

---

6.   *CPL*, viii, 487.
7.   *AFM; ALC* gives 1433 as the year of this famine.
8.   *AFM*.
9.   *CPL*, viii, 557, 558–9, 564.
10.   *CPL*, viii, 584–5, 617.

Ó Dálaigh Charter

He made an agreement in the form of a charter in 1440 with the unanimous consent of the dean and chapter granting cleric Tadhg Ó Clúmháin, and his heirs in perpetuity certain lands belonging to the diocese 'with all their rights and appurtenances'.[11] They consisted of a quarter of land belonging to the church of Kilvarnet (*Cille' Margnata*) and half a quarter of Tromna. The areas specifically named do not appear to correspond to any modern townlands in Kilvarnet or Killoran. The Ó Clúmháin (Coleman) clan was an ecclesiastical family who provided many parish priests of Killoran (Coolaney) over the centuries. In return, Ó Clúmháin undertook to pay the bishop and his successors yearly half a mark of silver. The agreement, dated Wednesday after the feast of St John the Baptist (26 June) 1440, was drawn up in Kilmactigue and the witnesses were Canon Diarmaid Mac Aodhagáin, Vicar Niall Ó hÉanagáin of Kilmacteige, and Comedino Ó (Obingli), 'a devout layman' and many others.

It appears that this grant was disputed after the death of Tadhg Ó Dálaigh in 1442 and Ó Clúmháin petitioned Rome presenting the Ó Dálaigh charter. Eugenius IV instructed the Abbot of Ballysadare to investigate the matter and may have found in favour of Ó Clúmháin as the family were still tenants of church lands in Killoran down to the sixteenth century.

Peace

The Ó Dálaigh episcopacy may have coincided with a rare period of domestic peace in the diocese as there are no events recorded there by the *Annals of Loch Cé*. The annals do record in 1440 the death of Domhnall Ó Conchobhar, lord of Lower Connacht 'and it is doubtful if there was of the Gaeidhil of Éirinn a greater calamity than that'.[12]

James Blakedon OP (1442–53)

Gams, 205, includes Blakedon in his Achonry list of bishops but Eubel claims he was not Bishop of Achonry (Akadensis) but of Killala (Aladensis) during the same period but this view is not borne out by the *Calendar of Papal Letters* ix, 288, x, 417–18, 431.

James (John?) Blakedon was appointed on 4 October 1442 succeeding Tadhg Ó Dálaigh 'during whose life it was specially reserved' to Eugene IV and in December of that year the Pope granted him permission to retain the parish church of Hedle in the diocese of Winchester 'seeing that he cannot keep up his state on account of the slenderness of the fruits of the said church (Achonry) which is taxed at thirty-three gold florins of the camera'. Among

---

11. *CPL*, ix, 381–2.
12. *ALC.* Tadhg Ó Dálaigh died in Rome where he may have gone on pilgrimage prior to 15 October 1442 when his successor was appointed. ob. Thaddei a.s.a. (apud sedem apostolicam.), Eubel; however *CPL*, ix, 299 mentions 'death of Thady (Tadhg) without the Roman court'.

the papal letters notifying his appointment, one was sent to King Henry probably because, like Belmer, he was an Englishman. James appears to have taken his surname from Blakedon in Somersetshire where he was born. He never visited Achonry and did not speak Irish. A measure of chaos reigned in Achonry during his six year rule there when some laymen and clerics took possession of 'divers of its goods and rights'.[13]

Blakedon was auxiliary bishop in Worcester in 1443, in Salisbury from 1443–9 and auxiliary to Bishop de Beckington of Bath and Wells from 1443–51. He was also Master of St Catherine's Hospital at Badminister near Bristol. On 7 August 1450, Nicholas V permitted him to hold an additional benefice in the diocese of Salisbury as well as the churches of Achonry and Stockton. He was a pluralist of considerable stature. He was transferred to Bangor diocese on 7 November 1453 and died on 24 October 1465.[14]

English Auxiliary

In 1444, the clergy of Ireland were involved in a controversy regarding the date of Easter Sunday which was to take place on 6 April that year which the annalist thought to be 'erroneous'. They finally decided on 12 April 'and that is the truth according to the common opinion'.[15] This controversy was not recorded by the *Annals of the Four Masters*.

Easter Controversy

The decade 1440–50 apparently had more than the normal number of bad years weather-wise. 1443, according to the annalist, was 'a rainy tempestuous year after May, so that many fishes multiplied in all the rivers of Ireland, and much hurted both bees and sheepe'. The following year was not any better with a wet summer and autumn 'which made all the corne maltish'. There were eclipses of both the sun and the moon that year. There was 'a great mortalitie' of the cattle of Ireland, both want of victuals and dearth of corn in 1445 and the annalist's terse comment on 1446 said it all: 'A hard year was this.' There was a 'greate pestilence' in Lower Connacht that year and among those who died were a number of the Mac Donnachadha clan including Maolruanaidh, Toirdealbhach, Maeleachlainn, with his wife and son, and the daughter of Cormac Ballagh, 'and many others both noble and ignoble'. There was a great famine in the spring of 1447 throughout all Ireland 'so that men were wont to eat all maner of hearbes for the most part' and this was followed by a great plague in the summer, autumn and winter when many died. 'It is difficult to get an account of the innumerable multitudes that died in Dublin by that

Bad Years

13. *CPL,* ix, 288, 299; Fryde, 344 gives date of appointment as 15 Oct. 1442.
14. *CPL,* ix, 288, 299, 358–9, 403, x, 78, 234–5, 381–2, 417–18, 431, xi, 237–8; Eubel, ii, 275; Cotton, *Fasti,* 101–2; *Arch. Hib.,* v, 72, 77, 78.
15. 'Annals of Ireland', 203.

plague.' 1450 was 'a hard warlike year, with many storms and great loss of cattle'.[16]

Conflict

Despite famine, plague and extreme weather conditions, internecine conflicts continued unabated. The son of Taithlech Buidhe Ó hEadhra was killed in his own house by his own son, East Ó hEadhra, in 1443 and that same year the son of King Tadhg of Fiachrach-muaidh was killed with a spear by his own brother, and five years later, Seán Boy Ó hEadhra, son of the King of Leyny, was 'slaine by one cast of a spear' by a Mac Maol Ruanaidh Fionn from Corran following a cattle raid. Ó hEadhra Riabhach was also killed the same year.[17] Fiachrach-muaidh, i.e. Fiachrach of the Moy which is in the barony of Tireragh which is bounded on the west by the Moy.

Mac Donnchadha
Clan Divisions

The Abbot of Muirgeas, son of Abbot Mac Donnchadha was killed by his own kinsman 'for taking from them certain hereditarie lands'. Tomaltach Óg Mac Donnachadha, King of Tirerrill, was killed near Sligo by an Ulster army in 1445 and his kingdom was divided between two kings, Seán and Tadhg Mac Donnachadha, 'so that great confusion and wars were raised betwixt them'. The clan later joined Seán and abandoned Tadhg who allied himself with O'Conchobhar Ruadh and 'received meanes of him'. That same year Maeleachlainn, son of Cormac Mac Donnchadha, and his brothers, together with the men from Carbury made a raid into Breifni and took large numbers of cattle. They were pursued by a 'greate multitude' and Maeleachlainn was slain and drowned in the River Bonnet as well as many of his followers. The following year Tadhg Mac Donnachadha joined together with the followers of Feidhlim Mac Diarmada and attacked Tomaltach Óg Mac Donnachadha and burned Ballymote. The latter's son, Aodh Buidhe, was killed. The attackers made off with large numbers of cows and horses. An attempt was made that year to reconcile the two warring groups of Clann Mac Donnachadha. They attended a meeting together with Toirdealbhach Ó Conchobhar and Ó Conchobhar Donn, hosted by Mac William of Clanrickard, 'to ye end they might make one Mac Donnchadha but so it was they returned as two Mac Donnchadha and their dominions shared into two moyties between them'. In 1447 Tadhg Mac Donnchadha and his followers submitted himself to Toirdhealbhach Mac Diarmada, King of Moylurg, who undertook to defend them against the followers of Cormac Mac Donnchadha.[18]

16. Annals of Ireland', in *Miscellany of the Irish Archaeological Society*, 202, 207, 213, 215–16, 218, 225.
17. 'Annals of Ireland', 200, 264.
18. 'Annals of Ireland', 202, 212, 213, 218, 219, 222.

Tadhg Óg Ó hUiginn 'a most eminent poet and head of the schools of Éirinn in his own time' died in 1447.[19]

Eugene IV ordered Bishop Uilliam Ó hEideagáin of Elphin (1429–49) and two of his clergy in October 1444 to receive Conn 'of the stock of kings and dukes' as a Cistercian monk in St Mary's Abbey, Boyle and receive his profession. Eugene, himself a former monk, followed the Augustinian rule and continued as pope to live a simple, regular and abstemious life, dispensing charity to the poor and needy. He thought that Conn 'by the favours of his parents and friends could be of great service' to the abbey. After his profession and already dispensed as son of unmarried parents related by blood within forbidden degrees, he became abbot following the death of Domhnall Ó Mocháin, probably a relative. It had been occupied for more than two years by an intruder, Cormac Mac Dáibhí.[20] This may have been the reason that he was now described as an 'intruder'.[21]

Conn Ó Mocháin (1449–63?)

Conn was nominated bishop by Nicholas V (1447–55) on 1 October 1449 and consecrated that year in the church of St Pudenziana in Rome by Cardinal-priest John[22] Fryde, 344, gives the date of appointment as 15 October 1449 and date of confirmation as 5 April 1452.

A problem arose after Conn's return from Rome to take possession of the diocese. He spent his first year trying to recover the goods of the diocese, seized by laymen and clerics during the episcopacy of his absentee predecessor but they refused to return them, claiming he was not canonically appointed as Blakedon was still the bishop when he was appointed. He feared that by ordaining priests he had 'incurred sentences of excommunication, suspension and interdict and become disabled' to rule the diocese. Nicholas absolved him *ad cautelam* on 12 February 1451 from all sentences of excommunication and rehabilitated him, his appointment holding good.[23]

Episcopacy Disputed

Ó hEadhra, 'half king of the west part of Leyny', died in 1449 and Tuathal Ó hUiginn 'who was the head of his nation and chiefe master of the Aesdána of Ireland' died the following year after a short disease. Brian Mac Donnachadha took sole control of Tirerrill in 1453 and Tadhg was abandoned by his own followers. Brian's rule was shortlived as he died the following year, and the annalist commented 'sure the year charged her due unlookyly, through

Deaths

19. 'Annals of Ireland', 203, 205–6, 211–12, 225, 230; *ALC.*
20. Mac Dáibhí, dispensed as son of a Cistercian abbot was nominated abbot by the Pisan pope, John XXIII (1410–15) during the Great Western Schism in 1414.
21. *CPL*, ix, 432.
22. *CPL*, x, 53.
23. *CPL*, x, 234–5.

the decease of the only most hospital and valiantest man, that had best command, law and rule in all Connaught'. He was buried in Sligo Abbey 'after extreame unction and due penance to God and to the Catholick Church'.

On the feastday of St Bartholomew 1458 the King of Moylurg and Corran, Tomaltach Mac Diarmada, died, 'a lord worthy of ye kingdome of Connaght' according to the annalist, 'through his greate expences in almsdeeds, hospitalitie, wages or meanes to all manner of men'. His son, Cathal, died a few days before him and they were both buried in Boyle Abbey. He was succeeded by Aodh Mac Diarmada. There were violent deaths as well. Fearghal Ó Gadhra of Coolavin was killed in 1461 by Mac Coisdealbh and the Bishop Brian Ó Connaill of Killala (1431–61) by the son of Archdeacon Maghnus Ó Dubhda who was elected bishop but did not obtain possession of the diocese.[24] Cormac Ballagh Mac Donnchadha died in 1463 and the annalist waxed eloquent in his obituary. 'The only man (of his own ranke) that most merited and gott note and fame and that had the best insight and knowledge in all arts, greatest goodnesse and familie and was the best warrior and preyer (against his enemies) in Lower Connacht.' Mac Donnchadha Riabhach too died that year as well as a certain Tomaltach Mac Maolruanaidh, who 'was a good man and died by too much drinking of *aqua vitae*'. 1463 was also probably the year that Bishop Conn Ó Mocháin died.[25]

Unseasonable There were also some bad years weather-wise. The very year, 1450, that Ó
Weather Mocháin returned as bishop from Rome, was 'a hard warrlike yeare … with many storms and great losse of cattle'. There was 'great dearth in 1461 and a great freeze in 1462 which lasted from the beginning of winter until the middle of February and flocks of birds died'. There was 'a great dearth' also the following summer. An eclipse of the sun occurred on the last day of November.

1450 was a Jubilee year and many pilgrims went to Rome, including Redmond Bermingham, who died on his way back after being appointed Archbishop of Tuam. 1462 was a 'year of grace' in Santiago de Compostella and great numbers went from Ireland on pilgrimage there.[26]

Brian Ó hEadhra Belonging to the Ó hEadhra Riabhach clan, of which his brother Uilliam
(1463–1484) was the chief, he studied canon law for several years 'at a place which was not a university'. As a cleric, he was alleged in 1443 to have taken certain revenues from the rectory of Banada 'falsely asserting that it was void' and claiming that it had been granted to him under 'pretext of other papal letters'. In fact, he

24. Domhnall Ó Conchobhar OP succeeded a bishop called Mylerus on 2 December 1461. No surname is given. It is more likely that he was Myler de Exeter who died in Rome after his appointment and consecration there.
25. 'Annals of Ireland', 222, 225, 236–7, 240, 242–3, 249–50.
26. 'Annals of Ireland', 225, 236, 246, 249.

must have been appointed by papal authority as he undertook to pay the annates for the rectory. He was deprived in 1443 for failing to be ordained within a year as required for rector with care of souls. Nicholas V instructed Canons Pilib Mac Éinri (Machenagh), Gormac Ó (Ocuynn) and Tomás Mac an Bhreitheamhan (Macabrethim) on 17 June 1447 to appoint him rector of the two Corrans and Ballymote (Dachorann and Mota).

His brother, Canon Diarmaid, was also advancing his own career. He made *Bishop's Brother* allegations against Provost Domhnall Mac Donnchadha that he had 'dilapidated the goods of the provostship and was a notorious fornicator and ignorant of letters'. Nicholas V nominated the Archdeacon and Canons Pilib Mac Éinrí and Brian Ó Cearnaigh on 31 August 1448 to investigate the allegations. Ó hEadhra was to accuse Mac Donnchadha before the above three and 'if they find the above or enough thereof to be true', to remove Mac Donnchadha and appoint Ó hEadhra who already held the canonry and prebend of Toomour and Drumrat.[27]

Brian attempted to recover by force the castle built by his father Bishop *Battle for the* Maghnus.[28] *Castle*

> (He) gathered together a number of men-at-arms for the purpose of capturing Ruaidhrí Ó hEadhra (Brian), in order to recover the said castle, expressly forbidding them to mutilate or kill the said Ruaidhrí or any of his servants; that going with the said men-of-arms to capture Ruaidhrí, and holding his unsheathed sword in his hand, in a fight between them and the said servants two laymen were killed in his presence and the said Ruaidhrí taken prisoner; that he handed over Ruaidhrí and begged and invited them with gifts to keep him safe from the kinsmen and friends of Ruaidhrí; that, after the disputes and wars had broken out between his kinsmen and those of Ruaidhrí and manslaughter had taken place, and after peace had been made war broke out again, and Ruaidhrí repaired with his kinsmen and friends to destroy and capture the said castle, and was trying to do so when one of his men at arms was killed by one of the said dean's (Brian's) friends in the dean's presence.

The chronology of the account dated 1463 is not entirely clear. The seizure of the castle from the bishop must have taken place before his death *c.*1435. It was probably held by Seán Buidhe Ó hEadhra up to the mid-1440s when these violent incidents took place. Brian Ó hEadhra became dean in 1447 but it is not certain that he was already dean then. This account appeared in a petition presented by Brian Ó hEadhra to Pius II in July 1463. He ordered

27. *CPL*, x, 381–2.
28. The date is uncertain – mid to late 1440s seems to be the most likely.

Archbishop Domhnall Ó Muirighthe (1450–85) of Tuam to provide for him 'seeing that … he had expressly forbidden, as stated, his men-at-arms to mutilate or kill anybody and that he himself mutilated or killed nobody with his own hand'.

Dean Brian O hEadhra, dispensed as son of a bishop, was nominated bishop by Pius II on 2 September 1463 almost thirty years after the death of his father, Bishop Maghnus Ruadh Ó hEadhra. He paid *servitium commune solvendum*, the papal tax amounting to one-third of the first fruits, levied on newly-appointed bishops on 2 November 1463.[29] Brian was sufficiently versed in canon law to realise that such violence might have raised problems about his becoming bishop. Hence his presence in Rome in the summer of 1463.[30]

Sixtus IV (1471–84)

The pontificate of Sixtus IV has been described as 'one of the saddest in papal history', his chief interest being the aggrandisement of his family.[31] He made two of his nephews cardinals, one of them the future Julius II. Despite his attempt to create new sources of revenue, the papal finances fell during his pontificate. His bad influence on Achonry can be discerned from his appointments, many of them pluralistic, with individual clergy occupying more than one position at the same time.

Robert Wellys (1473–?)

Sixtus IV appointed an English Franciscan, Robert Wellys, Bishop of Achonry in July 1473 while the incumbent, Brian Ó hEadhra, was still alive and would be for more than another ten years. The papal act of provision stated that Achonry became vacant following the death of Conn Ó Mocháin who in fact had died more than ten years previously. Wellys, supported by King Edward of England, petitioned the Pope on 24 July 1473 that he 'may, even after he has obtained possession thereof (Achonry) and had been consecrated, receive and retain for life *in commendam* with the said church, any two benefices with cure or otherwise incompatible, wont to be held by secular clerks, even if they be parish churches etc, and resign them simply for exchange, as often as he pleases'.[32]

Wellys was consecrated bishop in the church of the English Hospital in Rome by the Archbishop of Malta. Just over two years later, in October 1475, a papal document refers to Brian Ó hEadhra as 'the present bishop of Achonry'. Wellys may have been the bishop of Achonry mandated by Innocent VIII on 9 July 1487 together with the bishop of Worcester and the precentor of Salisbury to investigate a case in the diocese of Coventry and Lichfield. Whether his

29.   *CPL*, xii, 194.
30.   *CPL*, xi, 646–7, xii, 194.
31.   *Cath. Encyclopedia.*
32.   *CPL*, xiii, 232.

appointment was annulled or some other solution was found, there is no other record of Wellys and, unlike the other English bishops of Achonry, his name does not occur among the English auxiliaries of the period.[33]

The chronicler of the 'Annals of Ireland' completed his work in 1467 just four years after Brian Ó hEadhrí became bishop. Tadhg and Ruaidhrí Mac Donnchadha of Tirerrill died in 1463 and 1467 respectively. One interesting obituary was recorded in 1464. Tadhg Ó Conchobhar, 'half king of Connaght', died on Saturday after the Assumption of Our Blessed Lady Mary and 'it was difficult to account how many offerings, both cows, horses and moneys was bestowed to God's honour for his soule'. The annalist's comment may have been inspired by the generous funeral offerings. 'It was reported that he saw himself weighed and that Saint Mary and Saint Michael defended his soule through God's grace and mercy and so he was saved, it is thought.' The Lord of Coolavin, Eoghan Ó Gadhra, died 'between the festivals of the two Marys' in autumn 1469 and his son, also called Eoghan, soon afterwards of a short illness. His other son, Diarmaid, assumed the lordship.

Deaths

Some violent deaths in the diocese were also recorded. Tomaltach Óg Ó Gadhra was killed in a night-time skirmish in 1464 on Sliabh Lugha by Muirgheas Mac Diarmada and three years later Dáibhí Mac Coisdealbh was killed by Thomas Bermingham. That year too, Cormac Ballagh Mac Donnchadha seized Colloony castle from the clan of Cormac Mac Donnchadha. Brian Mac Donnchadha of Corran was killed in 1470 by Tadhg Mac Donnchadha of Tirerrill. Giolla Dubh Ó hEadhra was killed by his own brother, Eoghan, in 1474.[34]

Ó Domhnaill of Tír Connaill crossed the Eirne with a large army in 1468 and invaded Lower Connacht. 'He seized great spoils in the east of Tír-Fiach-rach, Cuil-Cnamha and Coillte-Luighne which spoils he afterwards carried home.' Eight years later, MacWilliam Burke led an army into Lower Connacht and advanced as far as Coillte Luighne, where he was joined by Mac Diarmada and Mac Donnchadha. They were opposed by Ó Domhnaill of Tír Connail. Eventually, they reached an agreement to divide Lower Connacht between them. MacWilliam got O'Dowda's country as well as Leyny and half Carbury, while Ó Domhnall got the rest.[35]

Lower Connacht Divided

33. *CPL*, xiii, 232, 331; xv, 37–8; Eubel ii, 275; Gams, 205, Ware, 660, Cotton, 102, Brady, 64, O'Rorke, *Sligo*, ii, 103, Flood, *IER*, 480 lists Wellys as Bishop of Achonry and, all except Flood, wrongly in succession to Conn Ó Mocháin.
34. 'Annals of Ireland', 262.
35. *AFM*.

Famine   Extreme weather was experienced in 1465.

> An exceeding great frost and foule weather that hindered the growth of all hearbs
> and leaves of the woods, so that no such was seen or growen afore the feast of
> Saint Brendan (14 May), which occasioned great famine in Sil Muireadhaigh
> (Co Roscommon), so that neither saints nor reverend persons were privileged
> in such misery in Sil Muireadhaigh, in that the priest was rescued for victuals,
> though he had been at the altar, with the holy Eucharist between his two hands
> and he invested in Masse vestiments.

The following year Holy Trinity monastery, Lough Key was burned down
by 'a candle and a woman'.[36]

First Camel   On the wider front, a strange animal was seen for the first time in Ireland
in Ireland   in 1472. The *Annals of the Four Masters* record its arrival:

> A wonderful animal was sent to Ireland by the King of England. She resembled a
> mare and was of a yellow colour, with the hoofs of a cow, a long neck, a large tail
> which was ugly and scant of hair. She had a saddle of her own. Wheat and salt
> were her food. She used to draw the largest sled-burden by her tail. She used to
> kneel when passing under a doorway, however high and also to let her rider mount.

Ireland had seen its first camel.

Ó hEadhra Deaths   Brian Ó hEadhra probably died sometime in 1483 as his successor was
appointed in May 1484. He was predeceased by his brother, Uilliam, the
O'Hara Riabhach, who died in 1478 and the latter's son, Diarmaid, killed in
1482 by the clan of O'Hara Buidhe.[37]

---

36. 'Annals of Ireland', 255–7, 259–60, 262.
37. *ALC.* Apparently, the conflict between the two O'Hara clans continued all through the
    episcopacy of Brian.

CHAPTER SIXTEEN

Achonry's 'Western Schism'

The Pope sent a mandate to the chapter, clergy, people and vassals of Achonry to receive him as bishop.[1] Eubel and Gams make no mention of him in their succession of Achonry bishops while another authority claimed that Thomas fitzRichard was appointed on 10 May 1484 and died before October 1495. Richard may have been the father of Tomás Ó Congaláin and 'fitz' is often used in the 'Annals of Ireland' in reference to Irish families.

Tomás
Ó Conghaláin
(1484–1508)

Innocent VIII (1484–92), who fathered three children when he was a youth, was elected pope at the end of August 1484, continued the decline in standards of his predecessor and did nothing to rectify the moral and political disorders of his time. Involving the papacy in several wars, he plunged it into debt and created numerous posts which he sold to the highest bidder.

Innocent VIII
(1484–92)

Innocent VIII appointed a Spaniard, John de Bustamente, Bishop of Achonry on 23 September 1489. The act of appointment mentioned the death of 'Bernard (Brian Ó hEadhra) late bishop' during whose lifetime it was specially reserved to the pope's disposition. What was astonishing about this appointment was that Brian Ó hEadhra had died six years earlier and the present incumbent, Tomás Ó Conghaláin, was to live for another nineteen years.

John
de Bustamente
(1489–?)

De Bustamente, was preceptor of the house of St Catherine in Toledo and belonged to the order of St Mary for the Ransom of Captives. He was absolved 'from any ecclesiastical sentences or censures in which he may be involved' and was allowed to retain the preceptorship, valued one hundred gold florins, even after his consecration as bishop. On the following day he requested and was granted the right to be consecrated by any Catholic bishop of his choice 'without prejudice being engendered hereby to the Archbishop of Tuam, to whom as metropolitan the said church is known to be subject'. There must have been considerable surprise in Achonry when the papal letters arrived to the chapter, the clergy, the people of the city and diocese informing them of the Spaniard's appointment. There is no mention of de Bustamente as auxiliary in any Spanish diocese during the period. He may well have resigned or more likely died.[2]

1.   *CPL*, xiii, 179.
2.   *CPL*, xv, 182–3, 302.

Alexander VI
(1492–1503)

Innocent VIII died on 25 July 1492 and it was said that on his deathbed he implored the cardinals to elect as successor a pope better than himself, 'a plea that proved as futile as his reign'. His successor, the Spaniard Rodrigo Borgia, who took the name Alexander VI (1492–1503) is widely regarded as the most notorious pope in the history of the papacy. He fathered four children, three boys and a girl, Lucrezia. Her older brother, Cesare, was made a cardinal by his father while still in his teens but later resigned his cardinalate, married and settled into a military career earning a reputation for exceptional cruelty.

Ó Conghaláin was still alive and indeed had another eighteen years to live, and during that time Achonry was to experience its own 'western schism' once more. Alexander VI, like his predecessor, appointed a successor in Achonry to 'the late bishop Thomas' and this was the second time such an appointment was made within three years. It was an uncharacteristically shoddy performance by the papal bureaucracy. The Pope claimed that churches like Achonry that had been reserved and not disposed of by his predecessor, Innocent VIII, remained reserved to himself.

Thomas Ffort
(1492–1508)

It must have come as some surprise to the chapter, clergy and people of the city and diocese when they received the papal letters informing them of their new bishop. The new bishop-elect chosen on 8 October 1492 was Englishman, Thomas Ffort, an Augustinian Canon of the monastery of Sts Mary and Petroc in Bodmin in the Exeter diocese. Five days later, Ffort petitioned the pope to dispense him to receive *in commendam* for life together with Achonry any three benefices with or without the care of souls, as he gets no fruits from Achonry and 'is unable to keep up his position in accordance with pontifical dignity'. The Pope duly granted his request with the proviso that the care of souls was not neglected. Ffort never came to Achonry. He was Prior of Huntington in 1496 and between 1496 and 1504 acted as auxiliary in Lichfield and Lincoln and died in 1508.[3]

St Mary's,
Inchmacnerin

Canon Ruaidhrí Mac Muircheartaigh (Macmaygierthasynd) informed the pope that Theoderic Ó Conchobhair (Oconcuir), who holds *in commendam* the monastery of St Mary, Inchmacnerin, publicly kept a concubine, dissipated the immoveable goods of the priory, converted the price of them to his own uses and committed simony. Ruaidhrí had a canonry only, the fruits of which were nil and wished to enter the said monastery under the regular habit. Julius II ordered three Elphin Canons on 29 July 1507 to hold an enquiry and if

3.   *CPL*, xvi, nos 39, 68; Fryde, 344.

they find the above to be true, to receive Ruaidhrí as a Canon of the priory and after his profession, to appoint him prior whereupon he is to resign the canonry of Achonry which the pope decreed vacant.[4]

An earthquake occurred in 1490 in the Ox Mountains killing one hundred people, among whom was the son of Maghnus Crossagh Ó hEadhra. 'Many horses and cows were also killed by it and much putrid fish was thrown up and a lake in which fish is now caught sprang up in the place.' This was in the townland of Moymlagh or Meemlough (which means 'erupted lake') in the parish of Killoran where the Ó hEadhra had a castle.[5]

Earthquake

The feuds of Clann Mac Donnchadha continued unabated. Maeleachlainn and Ruaidhrí, sons of Mac Donnachadha of Tirerrill, were slain in 1486 by Domhnall Cam Mac Donnchadha. Tadhg Mac Donnachadha of Tirerrill was killed in a battle in 1495 by Aodh Ruadh Ó Domhnall at Ballindrehid near Ballysadare, and Eoghan Caech Ó Dubhda and Brian Caech Ó Conchobhar were also killed while Diarmaid Ó Gadhra was taken prisoner. 'A great many besides of the nobles of Lower Connacht were killed and drowned there.' MacWilliam of Clanrickard also made an incursion into the region 'and all that Ó Domhnall had not previously destroyed was entirely destroyed by him'. Two years later another battle took place at the Curlews (*Corr-shliabh*) when Tadhg Mac Diarmada and his allies from Lower Connacht defeated Aodh Ruadh Ó Domhnall. Tadhg, 'the guardian of the fame of his own high family for nobility and hospitality and dignity and the protector of Sil-Muiredhaigh and men of Connacht died after triumphing over the world and the devil'. There was a great famine in Ireland that year and Brian Mac Donnchadha of Corran died. The *Annals of Loch Cé* also record the death of Tomás Ó Conghaláin bishop of Achadh-Conaire in 1508.

Battles and Deaths

Ó Flannagáin was a Dominican described as a bachelor in theology in his bull of appointment, and the Pope was assured by testimony worthy of belief that he was 'zealous in religion, knowledgeable in letters, purity of life, honourable in morals, circumspect in temporalities and many other gifts (*ac aliis multiplicium virtutem donis*)'. He was absolved from all irregularities and censures that he might have incurred, and before leaving Rome the Pope gave him a letter commending him to King Henry VII of England. O'Flannagáin may have died within a year of arriving home from Rome but more than likely neither he, nor news of his appointment, had reached Achonry by the beginning of February 1510. The appointment of Pilib Ó Clúmháin as vicar

*Eoghan
Ó Flannagáin
(1508–9?)*

4. *CPL*, xviii, 777.
5. *AFM*.

Deaths

of Killoran by the chapter on 5 February 1510 'while the see was void' was declared invalid.[6]

Eoghan Ó hUiginn, 'preceptor of the Gaeidhil in poetry', died in 1510. The following year Seán Mac Donnchadha of Tirerrill, 'torch of valour and bravery … and general sustaining patron of poets and men of learning of Leth-Chuinn, died in his own fortress in Baile-an-duin'. Archbishop Muirgheas Ó Fithcheallaigh of Tuam, 'the most distinguished man abroad or at home, for piety and clerkship', died in 1513.

Plague

A great number of people died, particularly in Dublin, during a great plague in 1519. 'A rainy, truly wet summer and harvest this year; it was a hard, tormenting year and a year of suffering and sickness.' The plague continued into the beginning of the following year.

Cormac
Ó Sniadhaigh
(1522?–47)

Cormac is something of a mystery. Only Archdeacon John Lynch gives his surname and even he admitted that he did not know when he was consecrated or when he died.[7] Two different dates have been given for his appointment, 15 June and 31 August 1522; the former is probably correct.[8] It was stated that he did not get possession. A signatory to the will of Doctor Dominick Lynch in Galway on 27 March 1523, but even here there is discrepancy between his first signature as *Cormacus Akadensis* (Achonry) and a second one as *Cormacus episcopus Aladensis* (Killala), though a certain Padinus signed as procurator for Richard Barret of Killala (1513–45).[9] Almost all authorities accept that Cormac was Bishop of Achonry. The exceptions are Konrad Eubel who lists Eoghan Ó Flannagáin as bishop from 22 December 1508 until his successor was appointed in 1547 and Grattan Flood (481–2) who was aware of the above signature but regarded the mention of the death Ó Flannagáin in the appointment of his successor in 1547 as decisive. 'Unless there were two prelates named Owen O'Flanagan, both of them Dominican Friars in succession, there is nothing improbable in assuming that Owen's episcopacy really lasted from 1509 (*rectius* 1508) to 1546.' The last published volume of the *Calendar of Papal Letters* covered the pontificate of Leo X (1513–21) and

---

6.   *CPL*, xix, 187, no. 321. Full text of papal appointment of Ó Flannagáin in de Burgo, *Hib. Dom.*, 480–1, see Moran, *IER*, i, 209–10; 1508 *Eugenius Oghlannagan* (Ó Flannagáin), *electus Achadensis Ecclesia per obitum.*; cf. *Handbook of British Chronology*, 329; Lost Registers. Indice 349, f253, *CPL*, xix, no. 1927; Flood dates Eoghan's appointment as 21 January 1509.
      The pope [granted] Priest Pilib Ó Clúmháin, [expectation to] one or two benefices, even if one of them have the care of souls, whose annual value [shall not exceed] 25 marks sterling if with care of souls or 18 if without care. [n.d. 1506] *CPL*, xix, 176, 302.

7.   *De Praes. Hib.*, 339.

8.   Maziere Brady, *Episcopal Succession*, 64; Fryde, 344.

9.   *Miscellany of the Irish Archaeological Society*, i, 76, 81.

the mystery of Cormac Ó Sniadhaigh may not be solved until subsequent volumes become available.[10]

Politically, the diocese as part of Lower Connacht was subject to the overlordship of Aodh Ó Domhnaill (1505–37) of Tyrconnell and from his castle in Donegal he dominated the north-west for thirty-two years. He demanded annual rents and tributes from local chiefs in Leyny, Corran, Costello and Gallen. To keep those chiefs in line he raided these areas almost every summer and carried off large herds of cattle and occasional hostages. Many of these raids involved the siege and capture of castles of those he claimed to be his vassals.

Overlordship of Aodh Ó Domhnaill

Aodh Ó Domhnaill came from Derry in 1512 with a small band and captured Aclare castle and left warders in it. Two years later he was back again in Gallen burning and plundering the country 'as far as Cruacha Gaileng' in Killasser and killed Ó Ruadháin with 'a great many more along with him'.

Sligo castle was captured by Ó Domhnall in 1516 after a long siege 'and this is the way in which it was taken: a French knight came on his pilgrimage to Patrick's purgatory and O'Domhnaill gave him great honour and presents. And the knight sent to O'Domhnaill a ship filled with ordinance and containing a large castle-breaking gun. And he sits down before the castle and demolishes the town before he obtained it and he gave protection to the warders'.

Capturing Sligo Castle

He went from there to Tirerrill and captured Collooney castle and the castle of Loch-Dergan (place now called Castledargan near Collooney and remains of castle are still observeable overlooking Loch-Dergan). Mac Donnachadha of Corran was killed on his way to join Ó Domhnaill.

Ruaidhrí Mac Donnchadha died in 1524 'and a great war occurred amongst the Clann-Donnchadha regarding the sovereignty of the country'. Cormac became chief and two years later, on his way back from an expedition into Tyrawley, Ó Domhnaill camped in front of Collooney castle 'and exacted peace and hostages from Cormac Mac Donnchadha'. That year Ó Domhnaill was back in Lower Connacht and this time he besieged Castlemore in Costello:

Clann-Donnchadha Conflict

This was an impregnable fortress, for it contained provisions and every kind of engines, cannon and all sorts of weapons. These chieftains proceeded to besiege the castle and they placed their army … all around it, so that they did not permit any person to pass from it or towards it, until at last they took it.

On this expedition they also took Banada castle.[11]

10.   See also Ware, 660, de Burgo, 480, Gams, 205, Cotton, 102, Moran, *IER* i, 210–11, O'Rorke, ii, 104.
11.   *AFM.*

He put down a revolt in 1526 against his over-lordship in Lower Connacht defeating the army besieging Sligo in a battle fought in Ballydrehid (Ballysadare). Returning from a raid into Tyrawley, he camped in front of Collooney castle and took hostages from Cormac Mac Donnchadha and his clan. Cormac died in 1527 and war broke out among the clan of Mac Donnachadha over the chieftainship. Eoghan Mac Donnchadha was finally proclaimed the Mac Donnchadha but peace between the Mac Donnchadha clan was shortlived. The castle was seized from Cormac by Muircheartach, his own brother, and Mac Donnchadha himself and his son, Murchadh, were soon afterwards taken prisoners by O'Dowda and Muircheartach and another of his sons, Donnchadh, was slain at that time.

Ó hEadhra
Subjection

Ó Domhnall had to force Ó hEadhra Buidhe into subjection and in 1533 raided his land between the two rivers, the Owenmore and the Coolany river, which meets at Annaghmore, and carried off a large amount of prey. It was the turn of Ó hEadhra Riabhach four years later when Maghnus Ó Domhnaill, the eldest of the sons of Aodh, held a hosting in September in Lower Connacht, including Tír Fiachrach, the two Luighne, Corran and Tirerrill. He burned much of Lower Connacht including the two Leynys and Corran. On this occasion he took Ballyara, the town of Ó hEadhra Riabhach, offering him protection in return for submitting to him and carried him off into captivity. People had to contend with other misfortunes in addition to those inflicted on them continuously by Ó Domhnaill.

Plague

There was a general plague in 1536, 'a sickly unhealthy year' with smallpox, a flux plague, and bed distemper (fever). One of its victims may well have been Aodh Ó Domhnaill who died in 1537.[12]

Tomás Ó
Fithcheallaigh
(15 June 1547–30
August 1555)

Tomás was an Augustinian Canon and Abbot of St Michael's in Mayo (near Claremorris) when appointed in Rome on 15 June 1547. Paul III (1534–49), a member of the Farnese family, was said to have owed his advancement in the church to the fact that his sister, Giula, was Alexander VI's mistress. His main claim to fame was that he summoned the Council of Trent in 1545 at the prompting of the Emperor Charles V. The early sessions continued until the autumn of 1548 and it is not impossible, though there is no record of it, that Tomás may have attended the Council briefly on his way home. In fact, the cardinals made him a gift of twenty-five gold ducats from the papal treasury on 5 December so that he could return home 'more fittingly'.[13] He was also permitted to retain St Michael's abbacy *in commendam* which had become an Augustinian abbey towards the end of the fourteenth century and an

12. *AFM.*
13. Eubel; Mss Barberini Latini, 2880 f24v [mf pos. 871 NLI].

inquisition of 1569 found that it had a church, cloister and conventual buildings on a half-acre site with other possessions, including 440 acres, four rectories and tithes valued at £6 4s 0d. He was also rector of Delgany in Dublin.[14]

He became bishop the year Henry VIII died, an event described thus: 'The prince of the Saxons and of Eirinn, i.e. King Henry died; and it is certain that there came not in later times a better king than this king.' Ó Fithcheallaigh governed Achonry for eight years until his translation to Leighlin and Kildare on 30 August 1555, and he must have been a person of some stature as his transference to Kildare was requested by no less personages than King Philip and Queen Mary.

The usual inter-clan wars continued. Ruaidhrí Mac Diarmada succeeded Abbot Aodh Mac Diarmada of Boyle as King of Moylurg. The latter died in January 1549 'after communion and sacrifice, after suffering numerous dangers from his own tribe and from other enemies'. Ruaidhrí subjected many of the neighbouring territories and exacted tribute, one hundred cows from Cairbre Mac Donnchadha of Corran and sixty cows from Ó Gadhra. His sons committed 'great depredations' in Corran, and Tadhg, son of Cairbre Mac Donnchadha, had to pay them one hundred marks. Things were no better within the Mac Donnchadha clan. The only incident recorded by the *Annals of Four Masters* occurred in the barony of Gallen in 1553 and involved the Burkes. Richard-an-Iarainn MacWilliam Burke was defeated by sons of Thomas Bacagh Burke and the people of Gallen, where Richard himself was taken prisoner and 150 of his army slain.[15]

Clan Wars

There is some doubt about his religious order as he was said to be the Franciscan Guardian of Galway who signed the decrees of the provincial synod in 1523. Cormac Ó Cuinn must have died sometime in 1561 as his successor and nephew, Eoghan Ó hAirt, was appointed in January 1562 and his bull of appointment explicitly mentions the death of 'Cormac Ocoyn of happy memory'.[16]

Cormac Ó Cuinn (O'Coyne) OP (1556–61)

Toirdealbhach Tuadh Ó Connchobhair died in 1559 and was succeeded by his son Cathal Ruadh. Mac Donnchadha of Corran was attacked by Mac Diarmada and son, Brian, 'and the country was burned by them and *Tech-a-templa* (Templehouse) was plundered.' Again in 1661 'enormous depredations' were committed by Ruaidhrí Mac Diarmada on Mac Donnchadha of Corran and Brian Mac Diarmada attacked Ballymote where one of his clan 'was killed withe one cast of a spear'.

Templehouse Plundered

14.   Moran, 211, Flood, 482; Gwynn and Hadcock, 186.
15.   *AFM*.
16.   Moran, 211 (see *IAS Miscell.* i, 81).

CHAPTER SEVENTEEN

'Cometh the Hour,
Cometh the Man'

Eoghan Ó hAirt (1503–1603)

Overseas Discoveries   Eoghan Ó hAirt's long life spanned one of the most momentous periods in world history, perhaps unparalleled previously or even up to recent times. A little over ten years before he was born, the known world grew by almost one-third in extent and population with the discovery of America by Christopher Columbus in 1492, followed quickly by the other overseas discoveries, with Spanish *conquistadores* fanning out through South America, looting the ancient Aztec and Inca kingdoms of huge amounts of gold. Pedro Álvares Cabral claimed Brazil in the name of Portugal in 1500, just three years before Ó hAirt was born. Shortly before that Bartholumew Diaz (1450–1500), also from Portugal, sailed around the southern tip of Africa while another Portuguese, Vasco da Gama (*c.*1469–1525) sailed around the Cape of Good Hope and discovered a sea route to India (1497–9). It was well into the sixteenth century when Copernicus published his *De Revolutiones Orbium Caelestium* in 1542, proving the earth's rotation around the sun, ominously only a year after the establishment of the Holy Office and the Inquisition where that other great astronomer, Galileo, was to be tried and condemned.

Renaissance   The sixteenth century, closely coinciding with Ó hAirt's own lifespan, was the beginning of the modern era. Culturally, it was the period of the Renaissance, of the great Italian painters: Leonardo da Vinci, Michelangelo and Raphael. Leonardo da Vinci (1457–1519) had painted his famous 'Last Supper' (1498) a few years before Ó hAirt was born and the 'Mona Lisa' (1504) the year after that happy event. Raphael (1483–1520) was only twenty years older than Ó hAirt and painted his 'The Holy Family' (1507) when O'Hairt was a child and his famous 'Transfiguration' (1520) when he was in his early teens. Michelangelo (1475–1564) was painting the ceiling of the Sistine Chapel (1508–12) while Ó hAirt was still a young boy (1504–8) and the 'Last Judgement' (1535–41) when he was a young Dominican in his thirties. He was still alive when Ó hAirt went to Rome and later to the Council of Trent.

There were other epoch-making cultural and literary events during that period. The great humanist scholar Erasmus of Rotterdam published his *In Praise of Folly* in 1509 and seven years later his *Institutio Principis Christiani*, the same year that Thomas More wrote his *Utopia*.

It was also a period of huge political changes, notably the growth of the modern national states, particularly Spain, beginning with the marriage of Ferdinand of Arragon and Isabella of Castile in 1569. Nearer to home the Tudors emerged victorious from the War of the Roses in England, establishing themselves as absolute monarchs on the English throne. Eoghan was five years old when Henry VIII, then eighteen years old, became King of England. The Tudors were to seal the fate of Ireland for several centuries to come. Ireland was an easy target for the Tudors, locked as she was into a medieval tribal system with its incessant wars and internecine strife. Henry VIII published an attack on Luther in 1521, when Ó hAirt was nineteen, earning him the papal title of Defender of the Faith, which belied his future intentions. His later actions and those of his daughter, Elizabeth, were to wreak havoc on the life and religion of Ó hAirt.

National States

There were other revolutionary changes too during that century with far-reaching consequences. Ó hAirt was a fourteen-year-old boy when an obscure Augustinian friar in Germany, Martin Luther, on the eve of All Saints in 1517, posted the 95 Theses on the door of the university church in Wittenburg. This act started a debate which ultimately led to the break up of Christianity in Europe. In the previous century, Johannes Gutenberg (1400–68) had invented the printing press (1436), making books speedily, widely and cheaply available, which contributed enormously to the rapid spread of Lutheranism. Luther's theses were in print within a month and in his own language, German, by December. Early in the new year, 1518, they were circulating everywhere. Copies went out to France, Spain, England and other countries, making Luther not only a national but also an international figure. Even in Rome students were spreading his tracts under the very shadow of the Vatican. Pope Leo X issued the bull *Exsurge Domine* in 1520 condemning the writings of Martin Luther and giving him sixty days to recant his errors. News of Luther's revolt may not have reached the Ó hAirt home in Grange for some time yet but its consequences were to play a major part in his future life. They also figured prominently in the life of Charles V, who became Holy Roman Emperor at the age of nineteen, only three years older than Ó hAirt, and now Luther's sovereign and responsible for reining in this turbulent friar. Other famous Protestant reformers, Ulrich Zwingli (1484–1531) in Zurich and Jean Calvin

Martin Luther

(1509–64) in Geneva, both lived and died during the lifetime of Ó hAirt. The Frenchman, Calvin, was only five years older than him.

First Jesuits   Another contemporary of Ó hAirt was Ignatius Loyola (1491–1556), a Basque who later founded the Jesuits. He was some ten years older than Eoghan but their paths may well have crossed in Paris where Eoghan spent about eight years, most likely in the 1520s, and where Loyola arrived in 1528, both of them to study at the prestigious Sorbonne. Also in Paris at that time was Francis Xavier (1506–52), only three years older than Ó hAirt one of the first seven Jesuits who took their vows in Paris in 1534 and later brought Christianity to India and the Far East. One of the early Irish Jesuits, David Wolf from Limerick, first recommended to Rome in 1561 Ó hAirt, then provincial of the Irish Dominicans, as eminently *episcopabilis*.

Alexander VI   Nothing better illustrates the transformation the Catholic Church underwent in the course of the sixteenth century than the lives and morals of the popes who reigned during that period. Alexander VI (1492–1503), who died the year Eoghan was born, was a member of the Borgias, a Spanish family. He led a dissipated life both as cardinal and pope, fathering at least eight children, all after he became a cardinal and one at least after he became pope. Three were by different mothers and another four to a woman who was married successively to three different employees of the Roman Curia. Clerical morals at home were not dissimilar.

Julius II   Julius II (1503–13) was notoriously violent and self-willed and spent much of his pontificate on military expeditions, leading the papal army himself. He often mixed with the soldiers round camp fires using the same blunt, coarse language common among them. After one successful expedition, he returned on the eve of Holy Week to a magnificent triumphal procession in Rome not witnessed since the time of the Caesars. It was Julius who commissioned the frescoes painted by Michelangelo on the ceiling of the Sistine Chapel, began the building of St Peter's and helped in the foundation of the Vatican Library.

Leo X   Leo X (1513–21) was only thirty-seven when he succeeded Julius II and the eldest surviving son of the Medici ruler of Florence, Lorenzo the Magnificent. According to the great historian of the papacy 'an insatiable thirst for pleasure was his leading characteristic.'[1] Perhaps Leo's greatest claim to fame or folly was the plenary indulgence he proclaimed in 1517 to raise money to rebuild the basilica over St Peter's tomb, leading directly to Luther's protest and the Protestant Reformation. Such were the popes who occupied the throne of St Peter during the childhood and adolescence of Eoghan Ó hAirt.

---

1.   Pastor, viii, 77.

Pius V (1566–72), pope during the first years of Ó hAirt's episcopacy, was the first one canonised in centuries. Clement VIII (1592–1605), pope during the last decade of the long life of Ó hAirt, was known for his high moral integrity and devout character, his kindness, charity and care of the poor, sick and imprisoned. He helped St Francis de Sales, was a lifelong friend of St Philip Neri, and one of the last of the Counter-Reformation popes.

Clement VIII and St Pius V

Eoghan Ó hAirt was born in 1503 into one of the ruling families of County Sligo. O'Connor Sligo was the chief lord of the five baronies in the county and the Ó hAirt clan, together with those of Ó Dubhda, two Ó hEadhra, two Mac Donnchadha and Ó Gadhra were the principal men under him.[2] Ó hAirt clan was a military family, described as 'the cavalry of the O'Connors' – sometimes referred to in official documentation as 'kern' or mercenary soldiers – who inhabited the mountainous region in north Carbury close to the border of Ó Ruairc's country in modern Leitrim.[3] However, out of some sixty-seven of the clan, including Eoghan himself, named in two general pardons granted by James I in 1603, only six of them were described as kerne. The vast majority were listed as yeomen, with one husbandman and three labourers.[4]

Ó hAirt Family

The term 'yeoman' had variable meanings, a gentleman serving in a noble household, but after the fifteenth century, a class of small farmers often serving as footsoldiers. The Ó hAirt family seat was at Grange, north of Sligo town in the parish of Ahamlish, the most northerly parish in Elphin, which includes also the villages of Cliffoney and Mullaghmore. It is bounded on the north by County Leitrim. The family also held small portions of land in the barony of Tireragh and Leyny in the diocese of Achonry.

O'Conor Sligo himself was subject to Ó Domhnaill of Tír Chonail. Sligo, especially the castle and town, were strategically important, and whoever had control of them was the dominant military power in the province. It was fought over frequently, particularly in the second half of the fifteenth century by Ó Domhnaill and the Burkes of Lower Connacht. Early in the sixteenth century Ó Domhnaill emerged as the superior power and by the time Aodh Ó Domhnaill died in 1537 his family claimed jurisdiction over a large section of Lower Connacht from Moylurg to Kilmaine, including Leyny, Costello and Gallen.[5] Their chief made annual visits to the region to collect tribute, which included horsemen for military service as well as victuals and money. Those

Ó Domhnaill Overlordship

2. *CSP Ire.*, 1586–8, 236–7.
3. O'Dowd, 'Landownership in the Sligo area', 229–30 (unpublished PhD thesis, UCD, 1979).
4. *Cal. Pat. Rolls. I James I*, 20–4 and 29, 1–32.
5. *AFM.*

who refused were ruthlessly punished, with their crops and lands burned and
destroyed.

Regional Politics   The following year Ó Domhnaill came into Connacht again ravaging the
country as he went. This time he besieged Castlemore. 'This was an
impregnable fortress, for it contained provisions and every kind of engines,
canon and all sort of weapons.'[6] Nobody was allowed to pass in or out of it
until it surrendered. Banada Castle was also taken. Ó hEadhra also fell victim
to Ó Domhnaill, Ó hEadhra Buidhe suffered 'a great depredation' in 1533
because he 'had been disobedient' and four years later, Balliary, the town of Ó
hEadhra Riabhach, was taken by Maghnus Ó Domhnaill and Ó hEadhra
carried off into captivity. War was also endemic among the subject septs
themselves and even between members of the same sept. When Cormac Mac
Donnchadha died in 1527 'a great war' ensued among the Mac Donnchadha
before his successor was chosen. Such was the political world into which
Eoghan Ó hAirt was born in the early decades of the sixteenth century.

Holy Cross,   Most likely, Ó hAirt got his early education at the Holy Cross Priory in
Sligo   Sligo. Founded in 1252, it was among the first dozen or so founded by the
Dominicans who originally came to Ireland in 1224. Here he would have
received his early training, particularly in the Classics, Latin and Greek. At
Holy Cross, he became attracted to the Dominican Order and found his voc-
ation. It was by no means a foregone conclusion as his uncle on his mother's
side, Cormac Ó Cuinn, was a Franciscan and probably guardian of the friary
in Galway in 1523, about the same time or shortly before Eoghan joined the
Sligo Dominicans.[7] Conn Ó hUiginn, then prior in Sligo, belonged to the
famous Gaelic literary family in Kilmactigue described by Lynch as
Tearmuinihiggin or *Tarmanballam O Higginorum ditionem.*[8] One of his fellow
novices was Aindréas Ó Criocháin (O'Crean), a member of a prominent
merchant family in Sligo.

Salamanca   Having completed his novitiate and other studies, he so impressed his superiors that he was sent abroad for further studies, first to Salamanca. The
university there originated as a *studium generale* in the thirteenth century and
by the fifteenth it was numbered with Paris, Bologna and Oxford among the
four greatest universities in Europe. During the reigns of Charles V and his son,
Philip II, it reached the highest peak of its development with over 6,000 students

6.   *AFM.*
7.   There is some doubt as to whether Ó Cuinn was a Franciscan or a Dominican. Moran
     accepted the assertion of David Wolf SJ in his letter of 12 October 1561 that he was a
     Franciscan, while Eubel, following Roman documents makes him a Dominican. See *IER*,
     i, 211–12 and *Hierarchia Catholica*, ii, 106.
8.   *De Praes. Hib.*, i, 246; ii, 242.

in its eleven faculties of philosophy and logic, ten in canon law and seven in theology. Francisco de Vitoria introduced the study of the *Summa Theologiae* of the great thirteenth-century Dominican, Thomas Aquinas, in 1526 just shortly before Eoghan arrived there and which he probably studied.

In the sixteenth century the theology faculty of Salamanca was to produce many of the theological champions of the Counter-Reformation, many of whom Eoghan would later meet at the Council of Trent. Ó hAirt probably stayed at the Dominican convent of San Esteban in Salamanca which was founded in the thirteenth century, which was just then undergoing a Renaissance makeover and is now considered to be one of the finest achievements of the Spanish plateresque style. About this time, Ignatius Loyola also spent some days at San Estaban but it is not likely that their paths crossed as Loyola spent less than two months in Salamanca.[9]

After some time Eoghan went from there to Paris where he spent about eight   *Paris* years.[10] The Dominican connection with the university of Paris goes all the way back to St Dominic himself when he sent three of his Order to found a house in Paris in 1217 and establish a school incorporated into the university. The Dominicans obtained their first chair of theology there in 1229. St Thomas Aquinas both studied and taught in Paris in the middle of the thirteenth century and even though he died before he was fifty, the Paris edition of his complete works runs to thirty-five volumes quarto.

Eoghan probably stayed in the Dominican priory of Saint-Jacques in the famous street of that name, where the friars were popularly known as the Jacobins, a name that was later adopted by one of the factions who used the priory as their meeting house, and played a major role during the French Revolution. The university had four faculties, Arts, Medicine, Canon Law and Theology and was made up of a large number of colleges which provided student accommodation, the most famous of which was College de Sorbonne, founded by Robert de Sorbon in the thirteenth century to accommodate poor scholars who were already Masters of Arts but who were studying in the faculty of theology.

In the late 1520s and the early 1530s when Eoghan was in Paris, he would have become very familiar with all the new ideas, which were to constitute the Reformation, in free circulation in the university. John Calvin himself had studied there in College de Montaigu until 1528, and fifty years later an Irish

---

9.   Purcell, Mary, *The First Jesuit*, 158–61.
10.   David Wolfe SJ to Cardinal Morone, 12 Oct. 1561, *Calendar of State Papers*, Rome, 1658–1571, i, 50; Moran, P. F., *History of the Catholic Archbishops of Dublin*, 86ff. 'The See of Achonry in the Sixteenth Century', *The Irish Ecclesiastical Record*, i, 212.

community was formed in the same college under John Lee to which the Irish College in Paris was to trace its origin. 1528 was the year that Ignatius Loyola came to Paris when he was housed in the College des Lombards as was Francis Xavier later, which a century and a half later was to become the first Irish college in Paris.[11]

Episcopal Succession in Elphin

Bearing the title of professor of theology, Eoghan Ó hAirt returned to Ireland and taught theology in Sligo Abbey where he was later elected prior for three years and was probably subsequently elected for a second term. The episcopal succession in the sixteenth century in Elphin, native diocese of Ó hAirt, was rather exotic to say the least.[12] The bishop, when Eoghan was born, was a Greek, a native of Athens, but never visited the diocese. Neither did his successor, Christopher Fisher, an Englishman, appointed at the end of 1508. The next bishop, another Englishman, John Maxey was appointed in 1525 and though he never left England, he had the distinction of being the first Anglican Bishop of Elphin as he accepted the Supremacy Act in 1534. Four appointments were made in 1539, one an Irishman and three Frenchmen, who never came to the diocese. Nor did the next, Brian Ó Domhnaill OFM, who died shortly after his appointment.

Brian Ó hUiginn OSA

His successor, Brian Ó hUiginn, seemed the best prospect for Elphin in almost half a century. An Augustinian Observant friar, most probably from the Corpus Christi friary in Banada, he probably also was a member of the Gaelic literary family whose home was in the same parish.[13] Brian was in Rome in March 1542 to deal with Irish Augustinian matters with Girolamo Seripando, general of his order. He was appointed, in April, vicar of the province in Ireland for six months during which he was to summon a synod to elect someone to act in the name of the Augustinian General there. But by September he had been appointed Bishop of Elphin.[14]

On returning to Ireland he seems to have spent some time in 1543 carrying out his Augustinian mission before making his way to Elphin. He failed to get control of the diocese because of local opposition, perhaps, and lost a great part of the temporalities which had been appropriated by laymen for decades, due to the absentee bishops. He returned to the continent and died in Villaviciosa in Portugal about 1564 'with a reputation for sanctity'. Previously, in 1561, he had resigned his bishopric in favour of Aindréas Ó Criocháin.[15]

11. Boyle, P., *The Irish College in Paris* (Dublin 1901), 26.
12. Beirne, ed., *The Diocese of Elphin*, 65–6.
13. F.X. Martin and A.D. Medijer, 'Irish Material in the Augustinian General Archives, Rome 1954–1634' in *Arch. Hib.*, xix, 81n.
14. F.X. Martin, 112–13.
15. *CSP*, Rome, i, 49; Brady, ii, 135–6, 199–200; Moran, 212, *Abps. of Dublin*, 85, 418.

Thus, in effect, there was no bishop in Elphin, not only when Eoghan Ó hAirt was a child and a youth but during all the period he spent in the friary of the Holy Cross in Sligo as a novice, friar and later as prior. During the latter period he was probably himself one of the leading churchmen of the area.

Henry VIII drifted into schism beginning in 1527 when the thirty-five-year-old Henry began his divorce proceedings against Catherine of Aragon, his wife of eighteen years. Catherine had been married to his brother, Arthur, who died and the Pope granted a dispensation in 1503 – the year Eoghan was born – to marry her. Henry now claimed that the dispensation was invalid as the Bible expressly prohibited a man marrying his brother's wife. While the matter was being investigated in Rome, Henry went ahead and married Anne Boleyn in January 1533. A little over a year later the Pope issued his judgement declaring Henry's marriage to Catherine truly valid and that he should restore her to her rightful place.

By the end of that year Henry had secured from the English parliament the Act of Supremacy by which he was declared to be the supreme head of the English Church, *Ecclesia Anglicana,* and later an Act for the Dissolution of the Monasteries was passed. Similar acts were passed by the Irish parliament and by 1537 a state church independent of Rome had been legally enacted. The king 'of this said land of Ireland, shall be accepted, taken, and reputed the only supreme head in earth of the whole church of Ireland'. Steps were taken from 1538 onwards to implement the Act of Supremacy but progress was very gradual and almost confined to the Pale.

Henry had to be content with the most nominal conformity by accepting the surrender of papal bulls of bishops who had been appointed by Rome, and in return he secured them legally in their dioceses by royal grant. Rome regarded this as no more than the formal gestures that had always been made by bishops to get their temporalities from their temporal ruler. Apart from his attempts to get bishops to surrender their bulls, his policy was one of non-interference with existing bishops. In the case of new appointments, Rome took a much stronger line and ignored those appointed by the king and provided their own bishops, which ultimately developed into the parallel systems of an illegal Catholic bishop and a legal Protestant one. But it was only in the last decade of the sixteenth century that such became the case in Achonry diocese. Elsewhere in Connacht Henry made a couple of unsuccessful attempts to impose his own candidate. Richard Nangle was ousted from Clonfert by the papal nominee, de Burgo, who was supported by the local lord, Burke of Clanrickard. The state also enjoyed some measure of cooperation from Richard Bodkin of Kilmacduagh.

Six Articles

After Henry's breach with Rome there was no attempt to change the traditional Catholic doctrine either in England or in Ireland. *Au contraire*, Henry was particularly fearsome in his treatment of those who departed from the traditional church practices and beliefs. He introduced the statute known as the Six Articles which came into force on 28 June 1539, the day of his forty-eighth birthday. It decreed that all who henceforward denied Transubstantiation (i.e. that the bread and wine became the body and blood of Christ at the consecration of the Mass) were liable to be burned as heretics and to lose all their property as traitors. Those who taught that it was necessary to receive communion under both species to receive the sacrament of the eucharist, or that private Masses were contrary to God's law, or that it was not necessary to actually confess sins to a priest in the sacrament of penance, as well as priests who married, or men or women who violated their vows of chastity, were all to be hanged as guilty of grave crimes.

In England, Lutherans were sent to the stake in 1543 and 1546, under the Six Articles Act and in that latter year there was a great official burning of heretical books. When he died on 28 January 1547, Henry's will showed in a striking way, his firm belief in the doctrine that the souls in purgatory can be helped by the offering of Masses. All this was to change as the education of his two younger children, Elizabeth, then over thirteen years old and Edward, just four years younger, had been left in the hands of Lutherans.

A Dominican, Eoghan Ó Flanagáin, who was then in Rome was appointed to Achonry by Julius II on 22 December 1508. Before leaving Rome the Pope gave him commendatory letters to King Henry VII stating that by his apostolic authority he had appointed Eugene Bishop of Achonry.[16]

Eoghan Ó Flanagáin was appointed on 22 December 1508 but he may have died before February 1509. Among the signatures to the acts of a provincial synod held in Galway on 27 March 1523 was that of *Cormacus Episcopus Akadensis mau propria*.[17] A bishop of Achonry paid the first fruits on 22 August 1526.[18] This Cormac is said to have died before the end of 1529 and was succeeded the following year by a Dominican, Eoghan, whose surname is not recorded. He died in 1546 and was succeeded on 15 January (June?) (a week before Henry VIII himself died) by Tomás Ó Fithcheallaigh (O'Figillay).[19]

16. De Burgo, 480, qtd Moran, *IER*, i, 210. [Since thus Most Beloved Son, it be a virtuous act, I have treated with kind favour God's ministers and to have them honoured in words and deeds for the glory of the eternal king, we ask and implore attentively Your Serene Royalty as far as the same Eugene chosen and appointed head of the church of his ministry, having, more disposed by reverence for Our Apostolic See, committed to your care, in fulfilling and conserving his rights thus would carry them out with the help of kind favour.]
17. Moran, 10.
18. *Sch. Ind.*, 475, Eubel, iii, 106.
19. Eubel, 106; Barb. Lat. 2880, f.24 who began as bishop the year Henry VIII died and Ó Fithcheallaigh, and his three predecessors in Achonry, may well have surrendered their papal bulls to Henry though there is no explicit evidence of it.

CHAPTER EIGHTEEN

Jesuit Missions

Rome was becoming increasingly concerned by the plight of the Irish church. *First Mission*
Conn O'Neill had sent the Bishop Rámonn Ó Gallchobhair of Killala to Rome
in 1541 to report to the pope on the situation. The first Jesuit mission came
to Ireland in 1542 consisting of two Jesuits, a Frenchman, Pascal Broet and a
Spaniard, Alfonso Salmeron, as well as a nobleman, Francis Zapata who offered
to pay their expenses. Salmeron was one of the first to join Ignatius and the
fledgling Jesuit community in Paris. The Jesuits had become the stormtroopers
of the Counter-Reformation Church, offering by their famous fourth vow to
go wherever the Pope might send them, no matter how dangerous it might be.
Paul III (1534–49) was happy to take them at their word.

Ignatius Loyola himself gave the missioners their instructions. They were to *Instructions*
visit the four most important chiefs, praising them for 'their constancy and
zeal for the Catholic religion and encouraging them to persevere'. They came
via Scotland, exchanging their gowns in Glasgow for Irish kilts, and arrived
somewhere in Ulster at the beginning of Lent. By now most chieftains had
taken the Oath of Supremacy, including Conn O'Neill who had crossed over
to London earlier that year and returned with the title of Earl of Tyrone. The
Jesuits spent little more than a month in Ulster and were not received by any
of the chieftains. At the end of Lent, Paul III ordered them to return and they
took ship for Scotland. Coming as they did from Renaissance Europe, the
Jesuits were unimpressed by the life and customs of the Irish, considering them
barbarous and their church badly regulated.

Almost twenty years later, Pius IV sent another mission in the person of *David Wolfe SJ*
David Wolfe, a Limerick-born Jesuit. Wolfe made no effort to disguise his
presence in Ireland: '… there is no one either heretic or Catholic that knows
it not, seeing that I caused it to be published in every part of the country.'[1]
The Pope's legate in Ireland caused particular annoyance to Elizabeth and was
one of the reasons she mentioned to the papal ambassador for not sending
representatives to the Council of Trent.[2]

Wolfe travelled all over the country with the exception of Dublin and the *Meeting with*
Pale, and was accompanied by Domhnall Mac Conghaol, a priest from the *Ó hAirt*
diocese of Raphoe in Donegal. Mac Conghaol came with him to Connacht

1. Moran, *Archbishops of Dublin*, Appendix no. v, 417–19; *CSP*, Rome, i, 50.
2. Hogan, *Distinguished Irishmen of the sixteenth century*, 8.

where Wolfe met Eoghan Ó hAirt and Aindréas Ó Criocháin, probably at Holy Cross Priory in Sligo where Ó Criocháin was then prior. He was greatly impressed by both of them but particularly by Ó hAirt, 'a great preacher and a man of good life and zealous for the honour of God'. He recommended both as candidates for bishop, Ó Criocháin for Elphin and Ó hAirt for Achonry.

Achonry Cathedral   Wolfe almost certainly passed through the village of Achonry as his account of the situation there seems that of an eyewitness, 'The church of Achonry is at present garrisoned as a fortress and is entirely secularised.' '*Quella chiesa Accadense é adesso per fortezza in mani di gentil'uomini e non vi sia vestigia di Religione.*'[3] 'The Cathedral church of Achonry is at present used as a fortress by the gentry of the neighbourhood and does not retain one vestige of the semblance of religion.' (Moran's translation)[4] He hoped that Ó hAirt with the help of his friends would restore it 'to its proper uses'.

Council of Trent Reconvoked   Pius IV was elected pope on Christmas Day 1559 and the following November issued the bull *Ad Ecclesiae Regimen* convoking the final session of the Council of Trent for Easter, 6 April 1561. The first session was held almost eighteen years earlier in 1545 and lasted almost four years from 13 December 1545 to 17 September 1549. After a gap of almost a year and a half, it resumed on 1 May 1551 and continued almost twelve months until 28 April 1552. The final session lasted almost two years from 18 January 1562 to 4 December 1563.

Trent Delegate   Ó hAirt was chosen by his confrères to represent the Irish Dominicans at the council. There is a suggestion that he was chosen by the clergy of Connacht to be their representative. These roles were not mutually exclusive.[5] Ó hAirt and his two companions, Ó Criocháin and Mac Conghaol, set out for Italy, probably on 13 October 1561 or shortly thereafter. 'The ship is now ready to sail', Wolfe wrote the day before. He entrusted his account of the situation in Ireland and another letter recommending the three travellers to Cardinal Morone to Mac Conghaol, whom he said 'was as able as any man in Ireland to give account of all matters'. They may have left from Kylchuan, where Wolfe had post-marked his last letter.[6]

Journey   Possibly, they set sail for northern France and may have put in at Le Havre or St Malo, and made their way down through France and across the Alps. In any case, Mac Conghaol was familiar with the route as he had visited Rome

3.   Moran, *Archbishops of Dublin*, Appendix no. v, 419.
4.   *IER*, i, 212.
5.   *Totiusque Connaciae clerum movit ut suum ad Concilium Tridentinum procuratorem eum instituerit*, De Praes. Hib., ii, 339.
6.   *ASV., Arm.* lxiv, xxviii, f.94; see *CSP*, Rome, i, 50.

the previous year. The road to Rome had been well travelled for centuries by Irish clerics and just a few short weeks before no less than fourteen others had set out. Ó Criocháin became ill in France where he remained while the other two continued on. They bypassed Trent – to where they later had to retrace their steps – going all the way to Rome. Wolfe had given Mac Conghaol explicit instructions to report to Cardinal Morone. None of them were aware that the letter he carried had Wolfe's recommendation that they be appointed bishops. Wolfe wrote of Ó hAirt: 'I deem (though he goes not for that purpose or gives it a thought) that he would make a good bishop.'

Both of them were appointed bishops at a secret consistory in Rome on Wednesday, 28 January 1562, as was Aindréas Ó Criocháin and the consistorial acts specifically recorded David Wolfe's recommendations.[7] They were consecrated in Rome. *Roman Consecration*

Accompanied by Bishop Tomás Ó hIarfhlatha (Herlihy) of Ross – he had been appointed some ten days earlier – they arrived in Trent on 25 May 1562. They were recorded in a metrical catalogue of the bishops attending. *Arrival at Trent*

> Three youths whom cold Ireland sends as legates
> Good Eugene and Thomas and honest Donald
> The wide world has sent them all endowed with powers
> Now all clothed with consecrated mitres.
> To take away the scar and festering disease.
> *(Tres juvenes quos frigida Hibernia legat*
> *Eugenium, Thomamque bonos, justumque Donaldum*
> *Omnes ornatos ingens virtutibus orbis*
> *Misit ut hanc scabiem tollant, morbumque malignum*
> *sacratis omnes induti tempora mitris.)*

What poetic licence, describing Ó hAirt as a youth! Eoghan was then almost sixty years old and had already outlived many of his more famous contemporaries. Henry VIII died in 1547, his son and successor, Edward VI, who reigned for only six years, died at the tender age of sixteen and his daughter, Mary, by Catherine of Aragon, queen for only five years, was merely forty-six when she died in 1558. The emperor, Charles V, born exactly on the turn of the century, died four years earlier at the age of fifty-eight.

Trent was chosen as the venue for the council in the hope of tempting the Lutherans to attend, as it was roughly equidistant from Germany and Rome. *Trent*

---

7.   'Quem R. D. David presbyter Societatis Jesu in Hibernia commorans per suas litteras commendavit'. Miscellanea – Vaticano – Hibernica, *Arch. Hib.*, v, 169.

But the Lutherans were not for turning and Luther himself died in 1546 at the age of sixty-two, the year after the council opened. Situated in the valley of the Adige on the north–south Brenner route across the Alps, the mid-summer temperatures were less oppressive than other Italian cities like Verona, that were also considered. However, winters were severe and the icy tramontana was almost unbearable for southern bishops who had to provide themselves with fur coats. The population of Trent was 7–8,000 and the council caused a shortage of accommodation and rents rose steeply.

Expensive   While there were only about 180 bishops present there in July 1562, many of them came with large retinues which numbered 1,670 in total. Cardinal Gonzaga had 160, while others had 70, 60, 50 down to three. While there was an adequate supply of meat and fish, butter and cheese, fruit and wine, the supply of wheat for bread was unsatisfactory. Shortly before the opening of the final session in the autumn of 1561, one thousand loads of corn had to be imported from the Papal States at the expense of the papal treasury. While supply remained the same, the demand kept rising and consequently prices.

Borromeo to the   The cost of living was a particularly acute for the Irish bishops. Their poverty
Rescue   had already been noticed when the cost of drawing up of their letters of appointment as bishops had to be waived.[8] Pius IV had given them an allowance of twenty crowns each, with which they found it impossible to make ends meet. They approached the four papal legates who presided over the council at the beginning of December 1562 who wrote to Charles Borromeo to intervene with his uncle on their behalf.

> The three Irish bishops that are here with nothing to live on but the trifling allowance of twenty crowns a month a-piece granted by his Holiness, make great complaint that, living being so dear, they cannot subsist, and crave and supplicate that their allowance be raised to twenty-five crowns a month since many less needy than they have as much. Should it seem good to you to speak to his Holiness on this matter, we are of opinion that you will do that which is well-pleasing to God.

Borromeo replied nine days later that the pope had agreed to their request.[9]

8.   *Tribus denique episcopatibus in Hibernia Elphinensium, Accadensium, Rapotensium, prepositi sunt episcopi, Andreas, Eugenius et Donaldus Hiberni Homines de quibus omnibus retulit Joannes Moronus Cardinalis. quibus propter inopiam pecuniae, que pro confectione litterarum Contificiarum debebatur remissa est: [ante diem quintum Kal. februariy Pius Pontifex.]. Barberini Latini,* 2877, f.14v.
9.   Cardinals Mantua, Seripando, Ermland and Simonetta to Charles Borromeo, Archbishop of Milan, Trent, 3 December 1562, and Rome, 12 December 1562, Vat. Lib. Vat. Lat., 6691, f.332; *Concilio di Trento,* cli, ff.143, 166d, *CSP,* Rome, 1558–71, 114, 201.

When the third session opened on 18 January 1562, it was attended by 106 *Attendance*
bishops (mostly Italians), four abbots and four generals of orders, besides the
four legates. The numbers gradually increased with, among others, the arrival
of the three Irish and at the close there were over two hundred and seventy,
with six cardinals, three patriarchs, twenty-five archbishops, one hundred and
sixty-nine bishops, nineteen proxies for bishops and seven generals of religious
orders. The majority were Italians with just short of one hundred and ninety,
followed by the Spaniards with thirty-one and the French with twenty-six.
There were six Greeks and three each for Portugal, Illyria and Ireland, while
England had only one, like Croatia. Poland, Netherlands and Germany had
two each. Besides Ó hAirt, there were thirteen other Dominican bishops, again
most of them Italians, with one from Portugal, another from Spain, from Crete
and from Nisyros, an island in the Aegean Sea.

The solemn sessions of the council took place in a conciliar hall in the form *Council Hall*
of an amphitheatre constructed within the renaissance church, Santa Maria
Maggiore. A semicircle of seats was built along one of the long naves while the
cardinals and papal legates sat along the opposite wall facing the semicircle.
The secretary sat in the middle of the assembly between the bishops and the
cardinals. Most of the great Catholic powers sent envoys and some demanded
precedence over others, which led to frequent disputes. They received incense
and the kiss of peace at liturgical ceremonies and as those of France and Spain
demanded precedence over each other it was tacitly decided both of them were
never allowed to attend the same ceremony. Speakers delivered their addresses
from a raised pulpit situated in the envoy section.

CHAPTER NINETEEN

Ó hAirt Interventions

Chalice for the Laity?

There are twenty-two recorded interventions or votes by Ó hAirt in the general congregations of the council between Wednesday 3 June 1562 and Thursday 18 November 1563. On the question of whether the laity should be allowed receive Communion under both species, i.e. the chalice as well as the host – a practice already adopted by Lutherans – Ó hAirt proposed that the matter of the chalice being given to the laity should be left to the Pope to decide. The Council decreed on 16 July 1562 that the whole and undivided Christ is received in the host or in the chalice.[1]

Burning Question

It is hard to believe now but this was a burning question in large parts of Europe. The Bavarian ambassador informed the council that the refusal of the chalice to the laity had led numerous Catholics to join the Lutherans and that it might even lead to rebellion. It was the same story in Austria, Moravia and Silesia, while in Hungary many priests were compelled to give the chalice as the only way of retaining their flocks. The French ambassador said it touched on the king's privilege as French kings had received communion under both species at their consecration for over a thousand years. After the Council had finished, the Pope authorised the chalice for the laity in certain ecclesiastical provinces of Germany.

The Mass

All Protestant reformers had denied the sacrificial character of the Mass, reducing it to a mere commemorative act. The question was debated at the General Congregation on Wednesday, 26 August 1562, where Ó hAirt recorded his first intervention.[2] The central point was the propitiatory or expiatory nature of the Mass, i.e. an atoning sacrifice. Ó hAirt acknowledged that the doctrine had been laid down with the declaration of the Portuguese Archbishop of Braga, Bartolomeo de' Martiri Fernandes, himself also a Dominican, that Christ had offered himself in atonement. Ó hAirt explored the notion of atonement. 'Otherwise, how were the Old Testament sacrifices expiatory, if that of Christ himself in the Last Supper was not expiatory? And if these were expiatory in virtue of Christ's passion which they prefigured, how much more that of Christ himself.' A decree was published on 17 September

1.   Gen. Congreg. Sat., 5 Sept. 1562, *Conc. Trid.* viii, 865–6.
2.   *Conc. Trid.* viii, 785.

1562 declaring that the sacrifice of the Mass was instituted at the Last Supper, that it is truly propitiatory, being the sacrifice of the Cross offered in a different manner. It also declared that Mass should not be said in the vernacular but in Latin, which was to remain the norm until Vatican II. This was a direct counteraction to Protestant use of local languages in their liturgies. The vernacular and the use of the chalice by the laity were among the reforms put to the conciliar legates by the French ambassadors.

Ó hAirt made several interventions on the floor of the council but his most substantial and important contribution came on 30 November 1562 on the subject of episcopal orders, and more specifically from whence a bishop derived his authority.[3] This was, in a sense, the eye of the storm. Some of the council fathers, especially the Spaniards, favoured the notion that their power derived immediately from God himself. The Archbishop of Granada strongly contested that the Pope was a bishop by precisely the same title as every other bishop, who were his brothers and not his sons, and derived their commission from Christ and not from him, just as the apostles derived theirs from Christ and not from Peter. The Italians favoured the ultramontane doctrine that bishops are only so in virtue of a privilege conferred by the Pope.

Origin of Episcopal Authority

These views were hotly disputed, with the Italians and Spaniards freely calling each other heretics, and riots took place in the streets between their followers, in which blood was shed. A huge commotion was raised within the council chamber itself with bishops shouting 'Out with him!' 'Let him be excommunicated!' While the Archbishop of Granada turned on them shouting, 'Let you yourselves be excommunicated!'

Rowdy Scenes

Silence was barely restored, with many of the bishops still fuming, when Eoghan Ó hAirt rose to his feet. 'I protest, however, that what I am going to say is not in the spirit of contradicting anyone but in the spirit of declaring the contradictory proposition for the purpose of expressing the truth.' While he accepted that many held that bishops had their power immediately from God and that there were plenty of authorities to support this view, he himself adopted the Italian position that the office of bishop was mediated through the Pope.

Contribution of Ó hAirt

He gave three reasons for his opinion. Firstly, were this jurisdiction derived immediately from God, we would have innumerable independent sources of authority, which would lead to anarchy and confusion. Secondly, that such an opinion favours the Anglican position: 'In England the sovereign styles herself

Anglican Orders

3. *Sententia episcopi Achadensis Hibernici de doctrina et canonibus sacri ordinis.* [4 decembris 1562], *Barb. lat.* 817 (XVI, 24) f.272r–275v, N.L. microfilm, pos. 817 printed in Concilii Tridentini Actorum, pars sexta., 205–6, 61.

head of the church and creates bishops, who are consecrated by three bishops and say that they are true bishops and are from God but we deny it, because they are not approved by the Roman pontiff, and we say so rightly, and it is with this one reason and no other that we argue against them (for they prove that they have been called, elected, consecrated and given mission).'[4]

What made the contribution of Ó hAirt unique was that apart from his two Irish companions and the solitary English representative, none of the other fathers had practical experience of what their decision might mean. Thirdly, that if a bishop's authority derived immediately from God, then the Pope could not dismiss him which was contrary to the traditional prerogative practised by the papacy. The position of Ó hAirt was vigorously contested by the theologian Francis Torres, but according to the historian of the council, the Ó hAirt argument was accepted by the whole assembly.[5]

Greek Sources   Ó hAirt argued his case in a tight syllogistic method, from first and second syllogism to conclusion, strongly reminiscent of the style used by Thomas Aquinas in his *Summa Theologiae*. In the course of his argument he cited the Greek philosopher, Aristotle, 'the father of logic', particularly, his *First Book of Physics, Eleventh Book of Metaphysics*, chapter ten and his *Preface to Alexander* in his *Book of Rhetoric*. He was also familiar with Greek mythology, warning the council fathers that in their eagerness to avoid Scylla they risked falling into Charybdis.[6]

New Testament   Ó hAirt also quoted from the New Testament, particularly the Acts of the Apostles, chapter fifteen when Paul and Barnabas were rebuked for not insisting that Gentiles be circumcised and were obliged to return to Jerusalem to have the matter decided. After the subject was debated, 'Peter rose and said to them: "Brethren you know that in the early days, God made choice among you that by my mouth the gentiles should hear the word of God and believe ... (God) made no distinction between us and them ... we believe that we shall be saved through the grace of the Lord Jesus, just as they will".' He also quoted St Paul's Letter to the Galatians, chapter two, verse two: 'I went up by revelation: and I laid before them (but privately before these who were of repute) the gospel which I preach among the Gentiles, lest somehow I should be running or had

4.   Le Plat, v, 578, qtd in Moran, *IER*, i, 213–14 and in Jedin, *Crisis and Closure of the Council of Trent*, 97–8n. Jedin wrongly describes Ó hAirt as 'Bishop of Aghadoe'.
5.   '*Quae sententia omnibus placere maxime visa fuit,*' Le Plat. v, 578.
6.   Scylla was a six-headed monster who sat on a rock on the Italian side of the Medina Straits separating the toe of Italy from Sicily and seized and drowned passing sailors. Charybdis was another monster on the opposite side in Sicily, who swallowed and churned up the waters into a whirlpool which drowned sailors, 'lest ever, wishing to avoid the indirect consequences of heretics, we fall directly into their opinion'.

run in vain.' And Hebrews, chapter five, verse four: 'And one does not take the honour upon himself, but he is called by God, just as Aaron was.' In his contribution to the council Ó hAirt was perhaps the first to incidently raise the question of the validity of Anglican orders, i.e. whether Anglican bishops are validly consecrated as there was a break in the apostolic succession.

Cardinal Giovanni Morone was appointed one of the papal legates and later first president of the council which he finally brought to a successful conclusion. He was the cardinal protector of Ireland when David Wolfe sent him his account of the Irish church in 1560 and his name occurs in the consistorial act appointing Ó hAirt bishop. A skilled diplomat, he succeeded in reaching a compromise on the question of the origin of bishops' authority. There was no definitive decree, the council contenting itself with condemning the contention that bishops named by the Pope are not legal and true bishops.

Cardinal Morone

Ó hAirt also spoke on the question of the residency of bishops. The council decreed that all bishops must reside in their dioceses and could only absent themselves for grave reasons and only then with the written permission of the pope or their metropolitan archbishop. One of the great abuses in the church was absenteeism, for which Rome itself was largely to blame, particularly in Ireland, by appointing foreigners to Irish dioceses.

Residency of Bishops

Abroad, absenteeism led to pluralism, one man occupying several dioceses. Luther's own metropolitan bishop, the Archbishop of Magdeburg, was one striking example. Albert of Mainz, a prince of the Hohenzollern house, became at the age of twenty-two, Bishop of Magdeburg and also of Halberstadt, but it was his burning ambition to become Archbishop of Mainz, and thereby primate of Germany, which was to dramatically change the history of Christianity. Albert needed a lot of money, which he borrowed at enormous rates from the Fugger banking firm. In return the pope agreed to allow him keep half the takings from the indulgence preached in Germany for the restoration of St Peter's, which directly led to Luther's revolt.

Albert of Mainz

Ó hAirt spoke in favour of the residency of bishops at the General Congregation on Tuesday, 12 January 1563.[7] He did not wish it to be made a requirement *de jure divino*, i.e. required by divine law (unlike Mac Conghaol of Raphoe), because of the particularities of the Irish situation, citing examples which happened during the reigns of Mary and Elizabeth, where 'bishops were expelled by the laity on instructions from the government with maximum damage to the Christian religion'.

The situation was markedly different on the continent, where bishops commonly neglected their dioceses preferring to reside at court or elsewhere.

Continental Situation

7.   *Conc. Trid.* 351.

It was believed that only a law of God would compel them to reside in their dioceses. The Spanish bishops were strongly in favour of residency as a divine obligation while the Italians unanimously favoured the contrary. There was a split vote in the council and the question was referred to the Pope. He sent all the Italian bishops then in Rome to Trent to swell the Italian majority. The final decree was fudged, leaving the basis of bishops' residency unresolved, preferring instead to begin the decree with the words 'It is a divine precept that the pastor know his flock.' Ó hAirt also requested that faculties be given to someone in Ireland for absolving heretics, since there was no papal legate there.

Sacrament of Orders   The General Congregation on Wednesday 9 June 1563 lasted from 10 to 2 p.m. and dealt with abuses in the administration of the sacrament of orders. There was to be a formal enquiry into the life and character of those proposed as bishops. Bishops were to hold frequent visitations of parishes where they were to preach to the people. A diocesan synod was to be held every year and a provincial one every three years. Parish priests were to preach on Sundays and feastdays and three times a week during Lent and Advent. Ó hAirt was the last speaker and proposed that thirty years of age be required for ordination to the priesthood and that priests and deacons were not to preach or administer sacraments without authorisation by the bishop.[8]

Seminaries   Among the decrees for the reformation of the clergy was one requiring the establishment of seminaries for the education of candidates for the priesthood. 'Ignorance of the clergy' is frequently cited as one of the prime causes for the Protestant Reformation. Trent now, in session twenty-three, 15 July 1563, required that each diocese establish seminaries, minor, for those of twelve upwards, and major, for young men destined for ordination. Such establishments would prove impossible in Ireland for the next two centuries. Instead, some thirty Irish colleges were set up all over Europe from Lisbon in Portugal to Vilnius in Lithuania. They proved to be a blessing in disguise since most of these colleges were established in university cities, such as Paris, Louvain and Salamanca, so that Irish priests became among the best-educated in the Church. Another by-product of the introduction of seminaries was that clerical celibacy became the norm rather than the exception as up to then.

Clergy Exempt from Law   One of the thorny questions raised was that of secular interference in ecclesiastical matters, which was something the Council had to handle very cautiously to avoid disputes with the ambassadors present. The draft contained several clauses certain to cause serious dissatisfaction – clergy were not to be judged in any secular court, appeal to secular judges in any ecclesiastical case, to be punished by excommunication and clergy were to be exempt from tax.

8.   *Conc. Trid.*, 578.

This draft received a stinging attack from the French ambassadors and they and several French bishops showed their disapproval by withdrawing from the Council.

A decree (*Tametsi*) was passed on 11 November 1563 which declared that marriage was indissoluble. It condemned specifically a number of positions adopted by Protestants, such as priests or men who had taken vows of chastity could lawfully marry for adequate reasons. Charles IX, Catherine de Medici and other members of the French Council of State favoured the marriage of priests in countries which had separated from Rome. *Marriage*

The council declared that henceforth clandestine marriages would be null. Up to then marriages, in Ireland and elsewhere, were frequently conducted in secret or clandestinely, where a couple pledged their love and mutually exchanged vows without witnesses. In a world so widely based on property, especially land and succession rights, this practice frequently led to bitter family rows, sometimes culminating in war. The French bishops demanded that clandestine marriages should be declared null in line with French civil law. Mac Conghaol of Raphoe and Ó hIarfhlatha of Ross, both proposed that clandestine marriages be invalid. The Ó hAirt contribution was more nuanced, proposing certain changes here and there to the wording but finally followed the decision 'of the greater part of the fathers'.[9] From then on up to the present, Catholic marriages took place in the presence of the parish priest and two witnesses.

One of the subjects that came up for discussion was that commonly known as the 'forbidden degrees', i.e. couples related within certain degrees by blood or marriage (consanguinity or affinity) could not lawfully marry without a dispensation. This relationship extended to the fourth degree, i.e. to third cousins or any one descended from a great-great grandparent. This also applied to affinity which applied to any man or woman and the blood relations of anyone with whom he or she had sexual intercourse. Such a person could not marry the sister or brother, first, second or third cousin of that sexual partner. In a small country like Ireland, whose population probably never exceeded a million and whose society was narrowly class-structured, where marriages only took places within classes, they often occurred within forbidden degrees. *'Forbidden Degrees'*

The Archbishop of Armagh sought a dispensation from Rome for Henry O'Neill in the second half of the fifteenth century, pointing out that many of the leading men in Ireland 'are living in incestuous relationships, for they can rarely find their equals in nobility with whom they can fittingly contract

9.   *Conc. Trid.*, IX, 734.

marriage outside the forbidden degrees of consanguinity and affinity'.[10] Dispensations were required to legitimise the children of these unions and, as these were mostly reserved to Rome, it was a lengthy and costly process.

Spiritual
Relationships

Ó hAirt proposed at the General Congregation on Friday, 20 August 1563 that bishops be allowed dispense in fourth degree relationships, i.e. in marriages between third cousins.[11] All dispensations granted in Achonry in the fifteenth century were for such marriages. Forbidden degrees also applied to the spiritual bond between relations of persons who acted as sponsors of a child at baptisms or confirmations, so that for example a widower could not marry a woman who was godmother to a child by his first wife. Ó hAirt intervened especially on the proposal made by some for repealing the spiritual relationship, asserting that most in Ireland held greater account of this relationship than of consanguinity with the result that some would marry a blood relation to produce less damage to true religion (than) to violate the spiritual relationship (*ita ut nonnulli, damno consaguineum efficere minime veriti, patrinum violare religioni duxerint*).[12]

'There is no greater proof of friendship in Ireland than to become the gossip to any man.' A contemporary English observer commented on this custom called gossipred or compaternitie about which 'there was no nation under the sun, that ever made so Religious accompt thereof as the Irish'.[13] Eoghan really believed that more ties existed for binding men by mutual love, than the duties of charity usually practised by the human race (*eo sarctius charitatis officia ab humano genere coli solere*).[14] I have found no account of this intervention in the official acts of the Council.

Written
Contributions

To avoid unnecessary repetition by different speakers, the council devised a method by which later contributors simply indicated what propositions of others they agreed with or what emendations they wished to make. These contributions may well have been submitted in writing and recorded by the secretary. Ó hAirt, not surprisingly, as he had spent almost forty years of his life as a Dominican novice, friar, prior, and provincial, contributed to the debate on the reform of the religious lives of monks, nuns and friars.

Indulgences

Oddly enough, indulgences – the *raison d'être* for the Lutheran revolt and consequently the Council itself – was one of the last subjects to be discussed

10. Reg. Octavian, f.203a, TCD MS 557, xi, 778–80, qtd in Art Cosgrove, 'Marriage in Medieval Ireland' in *Marriage in Ireland*, 30.
11. This meeting was held from 7–11 p.m., probably to avoid the midday heat. *Conc. Trid.* ix, 734.
12. *CSP Eliz.* (1589), 254.
13. Sir John Davies, *Discovery of the true causes*, 180–1.
14. *De Praes. Hib.*, ii, 339–40.

and then only cursorily. The Council declared that the church has full power to grant indulgences – charging fees was strictly prohibited – that purgatory was a place of purification for the dead, who can be helped by the prayers of the faithful. It also declared that it was 'good and profitable' to invoke the saints and venerate their relics and to place them and their images and that of Christ in churches to be venerated. The latter probably proved decisive in the battle for the minds and hearts of the people whose knowledge of their religion came as much from the colourful and spectacular images of the new baroque style as from preaching or teaching.

The closing session began on 3 December 1563 and lasted two days when the decrees from all the previous sessions were read again, approved and signed. The signatories included six cardinals, three patriarchs, twenty-five archbishops, one hundred and sixty-nine bishops, nineteen proxies for absent bishops and seven generals of orders.

Closing Session

Ó hAirt signed himself *'Ego Eugenius oHairt, eps Achaden diffiniens subscrissi.'* (I, Eoghan Ó hAirt, Bishop of Achonry, openly signed.)

CHAPTER TWENTY

Home Again

Imprisoned English Bishops

A proposal had been made at Trent, between the twenty-second and the twenty-third sessions, to proclaim Queen Elizabeth a heretic and schismatic, but the danger of provoking reprisals on her part was judged too serious to be risked. Rome was to pursue a similar policy for the rest of Ó hAirt's, and indeed, Elizabeth's lifetime. Some of the council fathers were eager in April 1562 that an appeal should be made to Catholic princes to intervene on behalf of the Marian bishops imprisoned in England, but no action was taken. A year later in April 1563, the proposal was revised.

Memorandum of Ó hAirt

Ó hAirt, his two compatriots and the single English bishop, Goldwell, presented to the council legates, a memorandum, dated, 20 March 1563.[1] An act had been passed by the English parliament which came into force on 1 April which declared all those persons guilty of high treason – and therefore liable to the death penalty – who refused to acknowledge Elizabeth as supreme governor of the Church of England. Ó hAirt and the others insisted that the bishops and other Catholic prisoners had no hope of life unless the emperor and other Catholic princes should threaten to break off relations with Elizabeth and withdraw their ambassadors, unless she agreed to show them mercy. This time the legates decided to take action and appealed to the emperor, Ferdinand. He wrote to Elizabeth imploring her to spare men whose consciences forbade them to obey her laws. Elizabeth sent him a polite reply but made no promise, though she acknowledged that she attached great weight to his letter. His nephew, Philip II of Spain, wrote later begging Elizabeth as a great favour to him to spare the lives of the imprisoned bishops.[2] Her reply has not survived but it may have contributed to the relaxation of the imposition of the law which now took place. By September, all the Marian bishops had been released from the Tower.

Return to Ireland

Ó hAirt made his way back to Ireland and Achonry in 1564. Unlike England, the early years of Elizabeth passed quitely, particularly in Connacht

---

1. Imperial ambassadors at Trent to the emperor, 6 April 1563, Vienna, Kaiserlich un Konigliches, Haus-, Hof- und Staatsarchiv, Conciliacten, v: reproduced, C. G. Bayne, 'Anglo-Roman Relations 1558–1565', *Oxford Historical and Literary Studies*, ii, 299.
2. Philip II to Queen Elizabeth, Madrid, 15 June 1563, Simancas Archives. Secretaria de Estado, Legajo 819, f.182: reproduced Bayne, 304.

where her writ scarcely ran. According to one near-contemporary: 'Priests initiated during Mary's reign were allowed by Queen Elizabeth to remain at peace within their borders and to wear clothes appropriate to their Order. This liberty was the reason (*in causa*) why no interference was made with Eoghan.[3] More than likely, Ó hAirt also enjoyed the protection of the overlord of his diocese, Domhnall Ó Connchobhar Sliggeach (O'Connor Sligo), whose family were always patrons of his Dominican monastery, Holy Cross Abbey in Sligo.

He was taken, together with the Earl of Desmond, by Lord Deputy Sidney and confined in the Tower of London. He submitted himself in November 1567 to Elizabeth at her palace at Hampton Court, 'and there in his Irish tongue, by an interpreter, declared to her Majesty that the chief cause of his coming was to see and speak to the illustrious and powerful Princess, whom he recognised to be his sovereign Lady, acknowledging that both he and his ancestors had long lived in an uncivil, rude and barbarous fashion, destitute of the true knowledge of God, and ignorant of their duty to the Imperial Crown of England'. He surrendered to the Queen all his lands and goods, together with the captainship of his country and asked the Queen's pardonship and grace and to be henceforth 'reputed as an Englishman'. He asked to be granted his country and lands, to be held of her Majesty 'and that he may be exempted from subjugation and servitude and from all other burdens to be exacted by O'Donnell or any other'.[4] *O'Connor Sligo Submits*

He returned to Ireland in 1568 with a patent in his hand but he needed more than that to shake off the tyranny of O'Donnell.[5] He wrote to William Cecil in June 1569 complaining that the neighbouring Irish were oppressing his country 'with many hurts'. The situation remained unresolved for many years and in May 1580 Sir Nicholas Malbie, Governor of Connacht (1576–84) reported 'The matter depending between O'Donnell and O'Connor Slygo is the only thing that now is to disquiet this Province.'

The Gaelic world of Achonry was anything but peaceful. The annalist records a violent incident there in 1560: 'Teige Boy, son of Kian, son of Oilioll O'Hara, was slain by Cathal Oge, the son of Teige, son of Cathal Oge O'Conor.'[6] There appears to have been an almost constant feud between the Mac Diarmada of Moylurg and the Mac Donnchadha of Corran. Mac Diarmadaigh attacked Mac Donnchadha of Corran 'and the country was burned by them and *Tech-a-templa* (Templehouse) was plundered'. In 1561 *Clan Warfare*

3.   *De Praes. Hib.*, ii.
4,   *CSPI, Carew* 1568, 378 qtd Knott, xxvi–xxvi.
5.   *Annals of Loch Cé.*
6.   *AFM*, 1559.

they attacked them again, this time in Ballymote, where Cathal Mac Diarmada was killed by gunshot and Eoghan Mac Diarmada Ruadh (Dermottroe) was killed 'with one cast of a spear'. Brian Mac Diarmada attacked Bunninadden in 1564 'and the place was burned to the door by him and he brought two hundred cows out of it and committed homicides there'. Little had changed there for centuries.[7]

'Bishop O'Hart's Town'

Seemingly, Ó hAirt recovered his cathedral which had been used as a fortress by some of the local gentry, probably Ó hEadhra, thus fulfilling David Wolfe's prediction. 'I am convinced that the aforesaid Eugene, by his good example and holy life, and with the aid of his friends, would be able to take back that church.'[8] Achonry village, described as 'Bishop O'Hart's town' – a throwback to the early Roman custom of establishing episcopal seats in *cives* or cities – had probably not much more than half a dozen houses, considering that the archdiocesan town of Tuam had then only twenty to thirty.

Bishop's Entourage

There were fourteen Canons, including dean, chantor, chancellor and treasurer, whose chief function was to sing the divine office daily in the cathedral choir.[9] The dean, parish priest of Achonry, had a house there called *Teampaill Muire*, without a garden but he had two portions of land known as *Gort Sagart*, 'situated in the eastern part of Achonry on both sides of the King's Highway'. He also got a quarter of the tithes and the other usual parish fees. The chantor had two quarters of land, 'commonly called *Cill Easbaig*', probably surrounding the cathedral and a portion of the tithes in the parish. Layman Éinrí Ó hAirt, probably a kinsman, was a judge in the bishop's court (*officiale*).[10]

Diocesan Inhabitants

Other inhabitants included five members of the famous bardic family Ó hUiginn in Doughourne, including the son of Tadhg Dall and four Ó Fionáin, all harpers. Diocesan inhabitants extended from O'Connor Sligo, with two castles, one in Ballymote and the other in Colloony, several gentlemen, like Ó Gadhra of Moygara and Cormac Ó hEadhra Buidhe, in Templehouse and his wife, Úna Ní Gallchobhair, to kerne, yeomen, farmers and labourers. There were at least four surgeons and some artisans like carpenters, masons, smiths, shoemakers, and at least one miller, weaver and shoemaker.

7.   *AFM*.
8.   Moran, *IER*, i, 212.
9.   Swords, 'A sixteenth century Register of Achonry', in *Coll. Hib.*, nos 39 and 40 (1997–8), 17–18.
10. A Henry Hart was a teacher in Achonry in the early years of the seventeenth century, and translated Keating's *Foras Feasa* into English. Diarmaid Ó Catháin, *Eighteenth Century Ireland*, nos 2, 70; see S. Ni Sheaghdha, *Catalogue of the Irish Manuscripts in the National Library of Ireland*, Fasc. vii (1982) 13–14: M. J. O'Doherty, 'Irish College, Salamanca', in *Arch. Hib.*, ii (1913), 32; see iii (1914), 90. Another layman, John Henegan, was his revenue collector (*procuratore et quasi censore*).

Parish priests were given the first fruits from the land which consisted of *beart arrabh*, a sheaf of oats, which they got in the form of oat-flour at harvest time, *cuid Carghas*, Lenten dues, the first-born of livestock due in spring and *meascán príomh*, the first pat of butter after churning. The laity paid twopence at Christmas and Easter and a penny for the priest's houseboy who made his bed and looked after his horse.

Priests' Remuneration

Offerings were made for baptisms and marriages and also for the funerals of the better-off which were shared between the priests and friars and a portion reserved for the education of students in seminaries abroad. Collections were also taken up on the occasion of months minds.[11] From all this each priest was obliged to pay the bishop ten testilia and also provide him with the usual *cuid-oíche*, overnight accommodation for himself and an entourage. In parishes with monasteries precise lines of demarcation between the rights of the priest and the monastery were established. The diocese got a quarter of the funeral offerings, the parish another quarter and the monastery a half of the total.

Offerings

His first undertaking was to promulgate the decrees of Trent in his own diocese. Numerous marriages there had just been declared invalid by Trent because they were clandestine, celebrated secretly without the presence of a priest and two witnesses. For a few, possibly this afforded them the unexpected opportunity to escape from a loveless union but this was unlikely as whatever marriage in that time was, it had nothing to do with love. Parish priests must have worked overtime to regularise these marriages and render their offspring legitimate. Ó hAirt himself on his first annual visitation of the parishes must have been inundated with appeals for dispensations from couples of all ages.

Marriages Regularised

When exactly the marriages in Achonry were regularised is not known but it was certainly one of the first, if not the first, diocese in the country where this occurred. The decree against clandestinity had to be published in every parish on three consecutive Sundays before it came into effect. Whenever it was introduced, the impediment of clandestinity was admitted in Achonry, Elphin and Killala long before the Synod of Tuam in 1658 though not yet accepted in Tuam, Clonfert or Kilmacduagh. Archbishop Micheál Ó Gadhra of Tuam ordered on 9 April 1745 that the decree be published in every parish of the diocese on the first three Sundays of July and should be binding thirty days after the first promulgation. Galway did not make the change until 2 December 1827 when the law of clandestinity was published throughout every part of Ireland where it had not been received hitherto.

Elsewhere, Dublin clergy with few exceptions were against the decree because of the inconveniences arising in civil law, ratifying clandestine

11.   *Pat. Rolls, 16 Jas. I.* qtd in *Tracts relating to Ireland,* 49n.

marriages. Those few who favoured its promulgation were alarmed by the consequences of 'couple-begging', a thriving trade at the time of a few degraded priests who assisted at secret marriages. The 'Takum', as he was called, never refused and interposed no delays. The decree annulling clandestine marriages was finally published in all parishes in the Dublin province on 2 December 1827.

In Munster, the Synod of Cashel accepted all the decrees of Trent in 1665 'as far as the circumstances of the time allowed' but it did not include the law of clandestinity 'on account of the evils that would result'. Even in strongly Catholic dioceses like Kerry and Killaloe the law of clandestinity was not promulgated until December 1827. The greatest fear was that a considerable number of existing marriages would break up, bringing them into conflict with civil law which recognised them as valid.

The meeting of the bishops of Armagh province in Clogher in 1587, attended by Eoghan Ó hAirt, published the decree of Trent on marriage before a large number of the clergy, ordering that it be received in every parish but, because of the shortage of priests, they forbade parties of existing marriages to separate or seek divorce, resulting in frequent concubinage:

> If the unhappy times in which we live do not permit us to adopt all the improvements we would desire and to follow all the usages of the church with becoming obedience, let us not therefore omit what is within our reach; but rather ... let us affect what we can.[12]

Synod of Tuam 1566   He attended a provincial synod in 1566 together with Andréas Ó Criocháin of Elphin and Réamonn Ó Gallchobhair of Killala.[13] Ó Gallchobhair, as senior bishop, presided. It declared that the decrees of the council should be observed not only in their own dioceses but in the rest of the province as far as possible. The synod also declared the Archbishop Christopher Bodkin of Tuam, a schismatic. Bodkin, as well as Nangle of Clonfert, had taken the oath of supremacy during the reign of Henry VIII. David Wolfe had met Bodkin sometime in 1560 and, though Bodkin tried to convince him otherwise, he believed that he had seized the archbishopric 'by force of arms and royal authority' and had driven out the 'true and legitimate archbishop', Art Ó Frighil, who was then still alive. Bodkin also held the dioceses of Kilmacduagh, Annaghadune, and Mayo. Wolfe seemed to have a certain admiration for Bodkin who succeeded in getting possession of the cathedral in Tuam and

12.   'Promulgation of law of clandestinity', Renehan, *Collections*, 435–7, 438–9, 439–40, 452–3.
13.   Lynch, *De Praes. Hib.*, ii, 232, 249.

hoped that Ó hAirt would take a leaf out of his book by doing the same in Achonry.

> That church had been forcibly occupied by the gentry for 300 years, without Mass or other divine office and he took it back by force at great personal risk and where formerly there were horses and other animals, now Mass was said and sung there, and he himself was in choir every day though in the region of Tuam there were no more that twenty or thirty houses. He has a good reputation and is held in high regard by every one, even by his enemies who had occupied the cathedral in the past.[14]

Ó hAirt was highly regarded by Rome, which gave him several important commissions elsewhere in Ireland as many of the other bishops were in prison or in exile. When Archbishop Richard Creagh of Armagh wrote to Rome in 1568 from prison urging the appointment of a bishop to Clogher, Cardinal Morone recommended that 'the case be committed to the Bishop of Achonry and to other provincial bishops' (*Causa committi posset in partibus D. Episcopo Achadensi et aliquibus aliis comprovincialibue Episcopis*).

Roman Assignments for Ó hAirt

'The administration of the see of Armagh should be given to some prelate during the imprisonment of the archbishop and should the Holy Father so approve this prelate should be the Bishop of Achonry. In each province of Ireland one Catholic bishop should be chosen by the Apostolic See to give testimonials to those of the clergy who come to Rome, viz., in Ulster the Bishop of Achonry during the imprisonment of the metropolitan', in addition to his own province Connacht. A similar role was given to the Bishop of Limerick in Munster and Leinster.[15] Ó hAirt was given special faculties by Rome to give dispensations throughout the 'whole province of Tuam' and was mentioned third on a list of those actively engaged on the mission in Ireland in 1578.

14.   Moran, *Abps of Dublin*, app. v, 418.
15.   Morone Papers, ASV; Moran, *IER*, i, 214–15.

CHAPTER TWENTY-ONE

'Calamitous Times'

Elizabeth
Excommunicated

As the Tudor conquest of Connacht gradually advanced, the situation became increasingly difficult for Ó hAirt and his priests in Achonry. This deterioration was probably due in great measure to the excommunication of Elizabeth, pronounced on 25 February 1570 by Pius V. The Queen was declared to have forfeited her right to the English crown and her subjects were no longer bound by any oath of loyalty to her. Ó hAirt painted a very bleak picture of this 'calamitous time' in the summer of 1575, which he compared to the terrible upheaval suffered by the people of Jerusalem as described by Jeremias.[1]

Letter to Rome

For my clergy who refuse to accept this new English religion, their very lives are in danger and there is no safe way of leaving the kingdom, for sea-ports are carefully scrutinised. Spies are dispersed throughout the kingdom, to such an extent that if those wishing to leave contrary to the Queen's proclamation are apprehended, they are either condemned to death or, with the greatest leniency, to life imprisonment. At this time our older clergy are demoralised, refusing to show their faces in doorways or in the streets. Similarly the young have disappeared from the office in choir.

Maolmhuire
Ó hUiginn

Ó hAirt wrote these words in a letter of introduction provided to Maolmhuire Ó hUiginn, to Cardinal-Archbishop Tolomeo Galli of Como seeking a place in the Germanic College in Rome.[2] Bellesheim describes the state of the Ó hAirt letter as '*Die Handschrift mehrfach unleserlich*'. Appreciation is due to Thomas Filan, emeritus professor of Latin, Maynooth College for his comments on the text. Tolomeo Galli had become virtual secretary of state to Gregory XIII just three years earlier. Cardinal Morone was involved in the founding of Collegium Germanicum in Rome in 1552 which was entrusted to the Jesuits and in spite of its name was prepared to accept candidates from various other nations. Ó hUiginn belonged to the well-known bardic family whose considerable estates were situated in the townlands of Mointiagh and Coolrecuill in Kilmactigue and Doughourne in Achonry.

1. 23 July 1575, Eoghan Ó hAirt to Cardinal Como, Rome in favour of the entry Maolmhuire Ó hUiginn to the German College in Rome.
2. *ASV*, Fondo Borghese, serie III, 9c: reproduced in Bellesheim, *Geschicte der Katholischen Kirche in Irland*, xxxiv, 715.

The poet, Mathghamhain Ó hUiginn, who died in 1585 was the father of Maolmhuire and of his more famous brother, Tadhg Dall, whose patrons included Richard MacWilliam Burke, Brian Ó Ruadhraic and Cormac Ó hEadhra. Maolmhuire also pursued the ancestral studies of poetry 'where he earned more than moderate acclaim'. He was accomplished in philosophy and music and was a distinguished lyre-player and afterwards applied himself to canon law 'where he committed to memory most of the decrees and decretals' (lyricen).[3] Maolmhuire was a 'very obedient and learned priest and dean of my cathedral church' (*presbyter bene morigeratus atque literatus et ecclesiae meae cathedralis decanus*). In fact, he had been ordained a priest by Ó hAirt probably in the early 1560s but, taking into account the 'miserable state' of the country, opted to go to Rome with the permission of Ó hAirt and pursue there literary studies (*in studiis bonarum literarum*).

He met Séamus Ó Ealadhaigh (James Hely), and Dáibhí Ó Cuinneacháin, then a boy but afterwards parish priest, in the diocese of Mayo, at the Ó hUiginn estate, described as Tarmonballam, who were to accompany him on his journey. They took a boat in Sligo which brought them to Ulster and from there got a ship heading for St Malo.[4] Here Maolmhuire met Archbishop Nicholas Skerret of Tuam, a former student of the German College, where he had spent six years studying philosophy and theology. Skerret had been appointed to Tuam in October 1580 only six months after he had been ordained, at the age of thirty-four. He sailed from Lisbon to Ireland in 1581 when religious persecution was at its height and worked at first in Galway as a teacher. He just spent a year in Ireland 'most of it in prison' when he managed to escape and fled the country. From St Malo, he went to Lisbon where he died in 1583. Before they parted Skerret gave Maolmhuire a letter recommending Ó hUiginn as a man endowed with 'many and rare virtues', who had spent all his time teaching young people.[5] According to Lynch, he opened an elementary school in Trim.[6] His name is not recorded in the student register of the German College but that may be explained by paying his way there and not in receipt of a bursary.[7] That he had means is clear from the Ó hAirt letter where he mentioned that a 'part of his inheritance had been forcibly

Romeward Bound

3. On Tadhg Dall (1550–91) see Knott, Ní Murchú agus Breathnach, 151–3: Ó Macháin, Pádraig, 'Tadg Dall Ó Huiginn: Foinse dá Shaothar' in *An Dán Díreach, Léachtaí Cholm Cille*, xxiv, 77–113.
4. *De Praes. Hib.*, vol. i, 242.
5. St Malo, 4 September, Nicholas Skerret to P. Laurentius, from sixteenth-century letters preserved in the German College, Rome, reproduced in Belleisheim, 717.
6. *De Praes. Hib.*, i, 244.
7. Information given to the author by the archivist in Collegio Germanico-Ungarico.

seized by heretics'. Besides he may have been allowed retain a fourth of the tithes he had as dean to fund his studies.

Archbishop of Tuam (1583–90)

Maolmhuire earned a doctorate in canon and civil law and was nominated Archbishop of Tuam on 23 March 1583. He began his journey back to Ireland 'but learning that Ireland was in the throes of cruel and widespread persecution he was compelled to remain in Belgium'. Here he remained having been co-opted among a number of advisors to the King of Spain. It was probably here he penned two poems which he addressed to Bishop Réamon Ó Gallchobhair, of Derry but formerly of Killala, and Bishop Riostáird Mac Brádaigh of Kilmore, expressing his eagerness to return to Ireland. Donogh O'Connor Sligo wrote to him in 1588 recommending one of the O'Mores who wanted to enter the Spanish army.[8] This letter appears to be a forgery. Maolmuire, after seven years as archbishop, died in Antwerp in 1590 at the age of fifty.[9]

Landowning Bishop

The Bishop of Achonry was one of the larger, if not the largest landowner, in the Sligo part of his diocese. He owned over fifty quarters there comprising well in excess of 6,000 acres as the phrase went 'that bears either hoof or corn, that is, with tillage or cattle'.[10] A quarter was a measure of value and not of actual acreage, but equivalent to 120 acres of arable land or pasture. It was the fourth part of a townland or *baile*. He occupied over four quarters or 500 acres in his episcopal seat of Achonry, as well as two quarters in Kilmactigue, which were mensal lands and immune from royal and county tax.

Church Tenants

The other lands were scattered throughout the baronies of Leyny, Corran and Coolavin and occupied by fee-paying tenants, some large landowners themselves, like Donough O'Connor Sligo, Cormack Ó hEadhra, Maeleachlainn Mac Donnchadha of Coolany and Irial Ó Gadhra of Moygara. Other tenants included well-known sixteenth century Sligo families, Ó Cléirigh, Mac an Bheatha, Mac an Bhreitheamhain, Ó Clúmháin, Ó Fionáin, Mac Duibhidhir, Ó Maolruanaidh, Ó Connacháin, Ó Sealbhaigh, and Ó Mocháin. Tenants are described in the Register as either *coloni* or *vassali* but it is not clear what, if any, distinction there might be between them. The total annual income from all tenants amounted to over £20. Some tenants, like Mac Duibhidhir in Kilmorgan, were obliged in addition to the rent to give yearly twenty-four quarts of butter and twelve medder of wheat at eight quarts to the medder. And they and all the other tenants were bound to provide cuddy, i.e. *cuid-oíche*, food and accommodation for the bishop, his servants and horses which he probably availed of during the course of his annual visitation.

8.   *CSP Ire.* (1588–92), 410.
9.   *De Praes. Hib.*, ii, 244 re Maolmuire Ó hUiginn.
10. Swords, *Coll. Hib.*, nos 39 and 40, 8–13.

The first signs of a changing religious landscape was the confiscation of the monasteries. Their suppression had been decreed by Henry VIII but could not be put into effect until Connacht had been securely brought under effective English rule, achieved finally by the Composition of Connacht. Sir Henry Sidney (1575–8) completed the shiring of Connacht, dividing it into counties Galway, Mayo, Sligo and Roscommon. County Sligo had been carved out in the 1560s from the lordship of the O'Connor Sligo family. An inquisition was carried out into the revenues of the diocese, presided over by Daniel, Bishop of Derry and attended by twenty-three large landowners who signed the findings on 18 August 1585.

Composition of Connacht (1585)

The Composition of Connacht resulted from the work carried out in 1585 by commissioners who were authorised to summon the chiefs and lords of the province and impose a rent on every quarter of land. The commissioners made their way through the province, determining the extent of the major holdings in each area and made indentures with the occupants, including Bishop Ó hAirt, who undertook to pay a yearly rent of ten shillings a quarter to the crown. An inquiry was held in Sligo on 25 September 1585 before Sir Richard Bingham, chief commissioner and Sir Nicholas White, and those summoned to appear included, among others, Maeleachlainn Mac Donnchadha of Collooney and Feidhlimidh Ó hAirt of Ardtarmon, 'chiefe of his name', probably a kinsman of Eoghan's. The inquiry found that the Bishop of Achonry had thirty-one quarters of land in the barony of Leyny. A similar inquiry on County Mayo on 8 September found that the bishop had only six quarters there and these were in Kinaffe and Killedan.[11] The barony of Costello was not surveyed because it was almost inaccessible and 'a verie receptacle of Scotts and a harbour of other lowse and evill people'.[12] It was agreed that 'the Bishop of Aghconry shall have hold and possess and enjoy to him and his successors 6 qrs of land as a domaine to his house or towne of Aghconry aforesaid in the Barrony of Magherileyny freely exonerated and discharged of and from this compossicion together with all the goods and chattles of persons attainted of felony that shall hap or chance to dwell or inhabit within the said 6 qrs and all other casualties and amercements growing from time to time within the same.'[13] Achonry Register must have been drawn up after 25 September 1585 as it describes the bishop's mensal lands in the parish of Achonry as '*immunis a censu Regis et Comitatus*'.[14] Eoghan Ó hAirt was among the signatories to the indenture.

11. *Comp. Bke of Conought,* 103, 123–4, 130.
12. Ibid., ix.
13. Ibid., 136–7.
14. *Comp. Conn.,* 136–7.

Confiscation of the
Monasteries

Of eight monasteries in the diocese, three were Dominican: Straide, Urlaur and Cloonameehan; two Franciscan: Ballymote and Court; one Carmelite at Knockmore; one Augustinian at Banada and one Augustinian Canons in Ballysadare. Ballysadare Abbey had four parishes: Ballysadare, Kilgarvan (Bonniconlon), Drumrat (Keash) and Annagh.[15]

Those in Mayo are Stradin-Ballahane, Straide-Ballylahon, Owrelare, Urlaur, and Banyde, Banada and it stated that they 'are possessed by friars and rebels, so as her Majesty had no commodity by the same'.[16]

Ballysadare

By now the monasteries had been confiscated as the composition refers to their lands as 'belonging to her Matie'. Connach Ó Siaghail was abbot when Ballysadare Abbey was suppressed during the general suppression of the monasteries at the end of the sixteenth century. Cotton, 365, 'In 1546 the king made an order appointing one Con O'Siagall, O'Donnell's chaplain, to be bishop of Elphin. He was Abbot of Esdara and prior of Aughros.' The site of the priory was leased to Brian Fitzwilliams esq, on 26 August 1588 'with three small quarters and Truneballie (the third of a bally or *trian baile*), the tithes of the town of Ballysadare, a third of the tithes of the rectory of Ballysadare, called Templemore, with a third of the tithes belonging to the same from the towns called Termains, the vicarage of Evenaghe (Annagh) in the country of Tirrerell, the vicarage of Drumrat in the barony, the vicarage of Kilnagarvan in McJordan's country, and the possessions of the said priory,' which consisted of a partly thatched church, a dormitory, two ruined buildings, three cottages, cemetery, etc. about 220 acres and the four churches enumerated above. The rent was 53s 4d.[17]

After suppression the monks dispersed, some reverting to the lay state, others may have been absorbed into the diocesan clergy. In any event, there are no further references to the Augustinian Canons of Ballysadare.

Ballymote

The Franciscan friary in Ballymote had been totally ruined by the rebels according to an inquisition of 1584–6. The possessions including gardens, orchards, buildings and one and half quarters of land became the property of Sir William Taaffe, a Catholic, and Franciscans of the First Order were back

---

15. 'The Division of Connaught and Thomond', dated 27 March 1574, purporting to name the baronies and abbeys, names among those listed in County Sligo, as Ballinvote (by friars), Ballymote, Tetemple (by friars), probably Cloonameehan near Templehouse, Beallesedery (by friars), Ballysadare, and Cowrte, Court.

16. *CSP, Carew,* 1601–3, 471–6. This list was probably compiled in preparation for their confiscation.

17. Fiants Eliz., ii, 85, 5256; Gwynn and Hadcock, 160–1; Swords, *Coll. Hib.,* nos 39 and 40, 20 largely agrees with the possessions specified above.

in Ballymote by the first half of the seventeenth century. There exists a complete list of guardians from 1650–1826.[18]

The court friary consisted of a thatched church with cemetery, dormitory and two other thatched houses, according to the 1586–7 inquisition 'with two quarters of land near this monastery, one called Carron Ardawer and the other Carron in Tawny (Carrownata) containing 80 acres of land' and a quarter of land in Kilcummin. It was then in the possession of a priest, Ruaidhrí Ballagh Ó hEadhra. It was granted, like Ballymote, to William Taaffe in 1598. There were two priests there in 1603, Aodh Ó Denge and Art Mac Maghnusa. Their address was given as 'Cowrteroriballagh', an obvious reference to the Ó hEadhra priest mentioned above.[19] *Court*

Straide friary was suppressed on 6 August 1578 when the site of the house of friars of Straide was leased to James Garveye and two quarters of land at a rent of 45s. Ten years later it was leased with the two quarters of land to Sir Patrick Barnewall of County Dublin while the tithes on the two quarters were granted to Edmund Barett. About the same time the castle of Straide-Ballylahon was granted to William Bourke of Lough Mask. However, Dominican friars continued to minister in the vicinity. Walter Styphen was prior there in August 1654.[20] Patrick Albert Lyons, who was professed in Lisbon and returned to Ireland in 1834, was the last recorded member of this community. *Straide*

The Dominican priory in Cloonameehan was granted to Richard Kindlemershe in March 1588. Its motherhouse and the alma mater of Eoghan Ó hAirt, Holy Cross Priory in Sligo, became the headquarters of George Bingham, Richard's brother, in 1595.

Because of its remoteness, Urlaur escaped the general suppression in the sixteenth century. Confiscated in 1612, it was later granted to Lord Dillon, Viscount of Costello-Gallen, a Catholic. Dillons were an Anglo-Norman family who had settled in the barony of Costello. The 'great castle (Castlemore) of Mac Goisdelbh and half the lordship of the country were given to Tibbot Dillon by MacGoisdelbh, i.e. John, son of Gilla-dubh, son of Hubert' in 1586.[21] Novices were being instructed there by two friars in 1622, with a community of nine or ten in 1629. The novitiate was principally for Connacht but also received novices from other areas. A Dominican chapter was held in *Urlaur*

18. Cathaldus Giblin, Liber Lovaniensis; A Faulkner, *Liber Dublinsis*; see Swords, *A Hidden Church,* Appendix xviiii, 421–3.
19. *Cal. Pat. Rolls, Jas. I.,* 23–4.
20. *Fiants Eliz.,* i, 86, 3368, ii, 24, 4978, 83, 5250; De Burgo, *Dom. Hib.,* 437.
21. *AFM.*

Urlaur on 16 August 1654 when Uilliam Ó Moráin was *vicarius in capite* and Ambrós Ó hÉanagáin, master of studies.[22]

Cromwellian Martyr   Dominic Dillon, former prior of Urlaur, was martyred by the Cromwellians in Drogheda in 1649. Another prior, Tomás Mac Cosdeilbh took the habit and was professed in Louvain, where his father was captain in an infantry regiment of Charles II then in exile. Having completed his studies, he returned to Ireland where he served several times as prior of Urlaur and once as prior of St Mary's Priory in Ballindoon, Co. Sligo. Forced into exile, he went to Rome and later to Louvain where in died in 1702 after a long illness. Another friar, Domhnall Mac Domhnaill, died in prison in Galway about 1707.[23] Patrick Sharkey, the last Dominican friar in Urlaur, died in 1846, possibly as a result of a disease contracted during the Famine.

Knockmore   The Carmelite friary in Knockmore had only one quarter of land, valued at six shillings, when it was dissolved according to an inquisition in Ballymote. It was then styled *Cella dissoluta fratrum nigrorum vocat Carmelyte Fryars*.[24] It was granted to John Rawson and Henry Deane in 1594 and later came into the possession of Richard Boyle, Earl of Cork.

Return of Carmelites   Carmelites, living in dugouts, continued to minister in the vicinity. Pope Clement XII (1730–40) issued a Brief officially restoring the province of Irish Carmelites in October 1737. At that time Knockmore was one of the Carmelite friaries in Ireland inhabited and, apparently, the monastery was restored in 1735. Dominic of St Teresa, prior in 1740, received letters of obedience from the General in Rome, Fr Benzoni, who sent them to the prior of St Teresa convent in Naples. Dominic had returned to Ireland after completing his studies on the continent. Henry Prendergast was elected prior at the provincial chapter in 1741. He was still prior in 1743 when acting as parish priest in Killoran, a considerable distance from Knockmore. There were two other Carmelites with him, James Nangle and another called Hart. Henry may have been related to Peter Prendergast and, if so, was a native of the neighbourhood of Clonfert. Peter, who spent all his ministry as a parish priest in France, wrote to the General in Rome suggesting himself as successor to the Bishop of Achonry who had just died, though he would prefer Clonfert whose bishop was then a centenarian.[25] Knockmore was one of fourteen Carmelite monasteries in Ireland with a total of about fifty friars in 1766.[26]

22. de Burgo, 437.
23. de Burgo, 314.
24. *Fiants Eliz.* 5865; Morrin, *Cal. Patent Rolls* ii, 273.
25. de Burgo, 438.
26. O'Dwyer, *Irish Carmelites*, 27, 38, 94–5, 97, 131, 133–4, 136, 159, 170 n77; M.J. Connellan, 'Knockmore Carmelite Convent' in *Whitefriars* (Sept–Oct. 1955), 10–11; *Arch. Invent.*, 2664, 2689, 2760, 2879.

The *Compossicion Booke of Conought* stated that Banada abbey had two   *Banada*
quarters of land, while an inquisition of 1613–14 found the friary owned the
half quarter of Knockglasse with the tithes of the same. The sixteenth century
Register of Achonry probably reconciles both by stating that it had one and a
half quarters annexed to the friary and another parcel of land on the mountain
called *Mían na gCléireach.*[27] The Cistercian Abbey of Boyle, which owned land
in Templevanny, was granted to William Usher in 1589.

27.   Swords, *Coll. Hib.*, nos 39 and 40, 22; *CPL*, xii, 88.

CHAPTER TWENTY-TWO

'A man of sin sitteth at Rome'

Eoghan O'Connor

It was stated by Archdeacon Lynch that Eoghan O'Connor, brother of Domhnall O'Connor Sligo, was appointed Bishop of Achonry and Killala by Queen Elizabeth sometime before the autumn of 1585. His participation in the Indenture of Sligo on 5 September reads 'Oyen Elect Bishop of killalo' which usually signifies that he had been nominated for Killala but not yet consecrated. He had attended Oxford University for a number of years and was recommended by Richard Bingham and other prominent government figures.[1] At the time of his appointment, he was said to have been Dean of Achonry.[2] By paying 180 marks annually, Ó hAirt secured peace for himself and could perform his episcopal functions within the borders of his diocese. 'With every obstacle removed, Eugene conferred sacred orders on many, confirmation to many far and wide, dispensation to some couples from degrees of consanguinity.'[3] In his absence, Elizabeth had appointed a bishop to Achonry. He was Eoghan O'Connor, who was appointed Bishop of Killala and Achonry on 1 December 1591.[4]

Not only is Eoghan O'Connor not mentioned as Bishop of Achonry in the Indenture but another participant, 'Oyne Bishop of Aythkonry', almost certainly refers to Eoghan Ó hAirt.

Richard Bingham

Life had become increasingly difficult for Eoghan Ó hAirt even before the arrival of Richard Bingham into the diocese, residing in Ballymote castle. Appointed President of Connacht in 1584, he held a hosting in Lower Connacht, seized Ballymote, plundered Corran and carried off Cathal Óg, son of Cathal Dubh Mac Donnchadha as a hostage.[5] Described as a 'man eminent both for spirit and martial knowledge, but of very small stature' he followed a military career, probably taking part under Don John of Austria in the Battle of Lepanto against the Turks in 1572. Sent to Ireland in 1579 to assist in the suppression of the Desmond revolt, he was joined there by two of his brothers,

1. O'Dowd, *Early Modern Sligo*, 107.
2. Moran, *IER*, i, 216 gives the date of his appointment by letters patent as 1 December 1591 and 'connected by a close tie of friendship before changing religion' to Ó hAirt.
3. *De Praes. Hib.*, i, 340; *Comp. Book of Conought*, 99, 125.
4. *De Praes. Hib.*, ii, 340; *Moran, IER*, i, 216–17.
5. *AFM.*

George and John. He impressed on Lord Burghley at the end of 1584 the necessity of strict government 'as the people are not naturally inclined to civility'.[6]

Much of the Tudor reconquest of Connacht was justified in the eyes of Elizabethan adventurers, like the Binghams, on the plea that they were attempting to civilise the people. Theobald Dillon, informing the Lord Deputy of the remarkable gift he received of a castle and a large estate in Costello, remarked that he was 'content to inhabit that barbarous corner only to do good among the savage people'.[7] The chief in the barony, MacCostello of the old Norman Nangle family, invited Theobald Dillon from the English Pale and gave him 'a fair portion of land and Castle More for his friendship'. Dillon accepted this extraordinarily generous gift, 'contented to inhabit that barbarous corner only to do good among the savage people'. His kinsman, Robert, described him to Walsyngham as 'honest and valiant, a gentleman who hath done his duty'.[8]

'Civilising the Natives'

The arrest of Eoghan Ó hAirt in the summer of 1585 has been attributed to Bingham and it certainly coincided with his activities in that part of Connacht.[9] Ó hAirt was imprisoned in Dublin Castle and Lord Deputy John Perrot (1584–8) commissioned Archbishop John Long of Armagh to interrogate him in prison. His account of the interrogation, which he sent to Sir Francis Walsingham, in June 1585 is nothing short of astounding:

Arrest of Ó hAirt

Owen O'Hart, Bishop of Achamore, alias Achadensis [Achonry] committed unto me by his Lordship [Perrot] to be conferred with, who was at the Council of Trent, is brought by the Lord's good direction to acknowledge his blindness, to prostrate himself before Her Majesty, whom he afore agreed to accurse in religion; so persuaded, as I doubt not, of great goodness to ensue by his means. He has renounced his bishoprick, and no doubt, void of all temporising, is thoroughly persuaded that a man of sin sitteth in Rome, under pretence of the seat of God. And I assure your Honour, if we used not this people more for gain than for conscience, here would the Lord's work be mightily preferred.[10]

There is little reason to doubt the veracity of Long's version. He was appointed Archbishop of Armagh by Elizabeth on Perrot's recommendation

Archbishop John Long

6.   *CSP, Eliz.*, 543.
7.   *CSP, Eliz.*, 334.
8.   10 June 1580, Sir N. Malbie; 10 Dec. 1581, Deputy and Council to Privy Council, Robert Dillon to Burghley, *CSP Ire*, 1574–85, 227, 334.
9.   'Liberum autem hoc exercitium sub annum 1586 aut paulo secus Bingamorum in Connaciam adventus aliquandiu interrupit,' *De Praes. Hib.*, ii. 341.
10. 4 June 1585, John Long to Francis Walsingham, SP 63/117 f.7; *CSP Ire*, 1574–85, 566.

and was consecrated in July 1584. An ex-Etonian, he was a scholar at Cambridge but there is no record of him ever having taken a degree before he left after three years. A rigorous Protestant, he advocated a vigorous policy of enforcing the Reformation but with no great success. After his death in 1589, the Lord Deputy remarked to Bishop Lyon of Cork that he 'loved good cheer but too well'.[11] His interrogation was probably conducted through Latin. Bilingualism in sixteenth-century Ireland and long before was generally considered to be competency in Latin as well as Irish. There is no evidence to suggest that Ó hAirt spoke English. All his studies in Sligo, Salamanca and Paris were conducted through Latin as were his interventions at the Council of Trent. Long had learned Latin at Eton where he contributed four Latin epigrams to verses presented by Eton scholars to Queen Elizabeth at Windsor Castle.

'Not the Stuff of Martyrs'

His most damning allegation that Ó hAirt was 'thoroughly persuaded that a man of sin sitteth in Rome', was no more than expressing the Catholic truth that all men, including popes, were sinners (*peccatores*). But it was a far cry from Thomas More's martyrdom for his refusal to take the oath of supremacy and his last words on the scaffold, 'I die the King's good servant but God's first.' Or Luther's refusal to recant at the Diet of Worms in 1521, thus signing what he believed was his own death warrant, with the words 'Here I stand, I cannot do otherwise.' Bishop John Fisher was martyred in 1535 for his belief in the divine origin of the papacy. One of the last acts of Ó hAirt at the Council of Trent was to appeal to the Emperor to save the lives of the English bishops languishing in the Tower of London. A compatriot of his at the Council of Trent, Tomás Ó hIarfhlatha of Ross, had also been arrested by Sir John Perrot but refused to deny his allegiance to Rome and was imprisoned in the Tower of London for over three and a half years.[12] Ó hIarfhlatha died in 1580 a few years after his release. The octogenarian Bishop of Achonry was, it seems, made of less stern stuff.

What is certain is that he continued, as he always had, to practise as a Catholic bishop. He also seemed to have acquired government recognition with 'a licence under Sir John Perrot's hand'.[13]

Armagh Council

He must have returned to Achonry after his release, as he was among a number who attended the Indenture in Sligo on 27 September 1585. 'Where it hath pleased you to send hither Sir Nicholas White, master of the Rolls,

11.   *DNB*.
12.   Moran, *Apbs of Dublin*, 136–7.
13.   Cork, 27 July 1595, William Lyons to the Lord Deputy, SP 63/183 f.4.1.; *CSP Ire*, 1592–6, 396.

joined in commission with Sir Richard Bingham, our chief officer etc, the composition is now certainly and indifferently set down.'[14] He attended a council for the province of Armagh, held in the diocese of Clogher in 1587 where arrangements were made to implement Tridentine disciplinary Canons, with the Bishops Risteárd Ó Brádaigh of Kilmore and Conn Mac Árdghail of Clogher, as well as old acquaintances, Réamonn Ó Gallchobhair of Derry (formerly of Killala), and his old Tridentine companion, Domhnall Mac Conghaol of Raphoe. Also there was Éadbhárd Mac Garacháin (McGauran) who was translated to Armagh shortly afterwards and Conn Ó (Devaney?) who was martyred in 1612.[15]

At first Theobald Dillon enjoyed a good relationship with Richard Bingham who described him to Walsyngham as 'very serviceable to Her Majesty in the place he holdeth'.[16] But that relationship soon soured. Bingham was miffed that the Lord Deputy Perrot favoured Dillon over himself. One of Bingham's supporters, who described Dillon as 'a most lewd fellow', complained. 'Assuredly the Lord Deputy dealeth very hardly with Sir Richard and generally with us all who be English.' Matters came to a head when Bingham raided Costello to recover cattle that had been driven there and Dillon complained to the Deputy that his own cows had been seized. Bingham was acquitted early in 1587 of the 'sundry grievous article' which Dillon alleged against him and failed to prove but Bingham was unforgiving.

Dillon's Clash with Bingham

If Dillon had his right and no more than he ought to have, he should not have any one foot of land in all Clancostulo, for what he hath there, he hath gotten by practising and by very indirect ways, from the inhabitants there in the time of his collectorship … being well known that he is as dangerous a man and as great a dissembler as any can be, a great extortioner, a favourer of rebels and malefactors.[17]

'A Great Extortioner'

By now the shoe was on the other foot and Dillon found himself in prison in Dublin Castle early in 1589. He was charged with delaying for forty-eight hours a messenger carrying a letter to the Lord Deputy informing him that one of the ships of the Spanish Armada 'had fallen upon the coast' and 1,600 well-armed men had landed. Not unreasonable to suppose that Bingham's

---

14. The Lords and Chieftains of Connaught and Thomond to the Lord Deputy. *CSP Carew*, 27 Sept. 1585, 406.
15. Records of the Synod of Drogheda, 1614, *Renehan Collections*, i, 435.
16. *CSP Ire*, 1574–85, 555.
17. 31 May 1586 Wallop to Walsyngham, 8 July 1586, Wallop to Walsyngham, 19 Aug. 1586 Bingham to Lord Deputy Perrot, 20 Feb. 1587, Acquital of Sir Richard Bingham, *CSP Ire*, 1586–8, 66, 97, 140, 267, 481, 482–3, 486–7.

fingerprints were all over this allegation. But Dillon was once more at liberty by the end of April due to the intervention of Walsyngham.[18]

Dillon Arrested

By now Ulster and most of Connacht were in open rebellion and Walter Burke, with a large following, raided Costello and carried off Dillon's goods and cattle though Dillon himself managed to escape. By late July three of his castles in Mayo were razed to the ground by the rebels.[19] Dillon was arrested again in August and conveyed with other prisoners to London where he was lodged in the Tower. He had spent eleven months there when his wife, Eleanor, petitioned the Privy Council to put him on trial or release him. He appears to have been released a short time later.[20]

Bingham's Campaign against Scots

Ó hAirt was certainly not in Achonry when Richard Bingham and his army encamped in the 'see town of Bishop O'Hart's'.[21] Bingham had been informed that over two-thousand Scots gallowglasses had crossed the Erne and were heading towards Sligo with the intention of joining up with the Burkes who were in rebellion in Mayo. He learned in Sligo that the Scots had eluded him, crossed the bridge at an unknown ford on 14 September, having been prevented by the English from crossing the bridge at Collooney and marching through the barony of Gallen. They camped at the foot of the Ox Mts on 15 September while Bingham camped at Ballysadare. The next day Bingham camped at Ardglass and the Scots moved from the side of the mountain to Ballyara, Ó hEadhra Riabhach's town, and stayed there two days. Bingham crossed the mountains and camped at Achonry, 'Bishop O'Hart's town', on 17 September. In order to lull the Scots into a false sense of security, Bingham put out a report that the Scots were marching up through Gallen 'towards inner and civil countries', in particular, County Roscommon. To give countenance to this report, Bingham marched his army to Moygara castle on 19 September while the Scots crossed the Ox mountains and reached Coolcarney. 'On the news of his returning back they grew somewhat careless and supposed he had returned to Roscommon.' From Moygara he moved to Castlemore where he spent two days gathering reinforcements and victuals.

Massacre of Ardnaree

Bingham marched to Banada Abbey where his guide, Edmund Costello, found a priest who had escaped that day from the Scots. The priest told Bingham that the Scots were all encamped at Ardnaree but refused to guide him there. He agreed, however, to find him 'a couple of gentlemen' who would

18. Dublin Castle, 24 Feb. 1588–9. Theobald Dillon to Sir F. Walsyngham, 29 April 1589 Lord Deputy to Walsyngham. *CSP Ire*, 1588–92, 126, 129, 155.
19. Athlone, 30 May 1589 R. Bingham to Lord Deputy, *CSP Ire*, 1588–92, 196–7, 221.
20. 16 Aug. 1591 Hilbrey, Nathaniel Dillon to Burghley, July Theobald Dillon to Sir F. Walsyngham, 29 April 1589 Lord Deputy to Walsyngham. *CSP Ire*, 1588–92, 129.
21. *CSP Eliz.*, 177.

act as guides and shortly afterwards brought in two Ó hEadhras. Bingham himself takes up the story:

> About three of the clock in the morning we rose which was as soon as the moon gave light, and marched towards a castle called Belclare, four miles from thence in the way to the enemy. … Here the night forsook us, and we forsook the highway and took through the mountains, with horsemen, footmen and carriage, carrying all our whole forces as in a 'heyrse' together, keeping the bottoms and lowest passages, as near as we might in circumferend ways, and with as great a silence as was possible. This mountain was in breadth a four or five miles, which we passed with all our forces, about 9 of the clock, and after we had marched a mile into the hard ground, and were not above two miles from the enemy, we made a halt, to have all our forces and baggage to come in to us, and there gave order, and direction for the fight, leaving the footmen to follow me with a speedy march, and myself with the horsemen marched more speedier towards the enemy, and about 12 of the clock the same Thursday, being the 23rd of September, we came within view of the enemy's camp, having sent out before half a dozen horsemen to view the ground, and the place where they encamped. Upon the discovery of which horsemen the Scots issued out ranged themselves in order of battle, and marched towards us, not thinking our footmen had been near, for they came with great silence; whereupon I charged their forward with my horsemen, beat them back into their battle, killed many of them and drew them into a bog, and yet I still drew them backwards by little and little to draw them to a better ground and caused my shot a horseback to light, and keep them play until my loose shot came in, and my whole battle of footmen, and then we all charged them together, and overthrew and discomfited their whole force. They fled before us to the river side, which was not far from us, where we slew and drown them all, saving fourscore or thereabouts which stripped themselves and swam over the river into Tyrawly, leaving their weapons and apparel behind them. The number of their fighting men slain and drowned that day we estimated and numbered to be fourteen or fifteen hundred besides boys, women, churls and children, which could not be so few as so many more and upwards.

The above account has been construed from two slightly different sources: firstly, 'A discourse of the services done by Sir Richard Byngham in the county of Mayo within the province of Connaught, for the quieting of the said country, the suppression of the Burkes as revolted there, and the overthrow of the Scots who lately invaded the same province in July, August, and September 1586,'[22] and secondly, 'A letter from a Gentleman to his friend, of certain

22. *CSP Eliz.*, 169–79 [Irish Maps, vol. 1, no. 4].

services done by Sir Richard Bingham upon the rebels and the Scots in Connaught.'[23] Bingham later revised this figure upwards to over three thousand, including those killed by his brother George, sheriff of Sligo with his quarters in Ballymote castle, as they tried to make their way back to the north. Like Cromwell nearly a century later, he had no doubt as to whom he should attribute the Ardnaree massacre. 'The Lord God of Hosts, by whose mighty arm we obtained this happy victory, be blessed and praised for it.'[24]

Accusations of Cruelty

Not surprisingly, accusations of cruelty against the Bingham administration persisted. Those specifically made by Theobald Dillon were examined and rejected by the Dublin commission in February 1587. The barony of Costello was surveyed, all 272 quarters named. 'For every quarter of land had his several name long before we were born, and not in us to new name them now.'[25] The Bishop of Kilmore declared in 1589 that in County Sligo the Mac Donnchadha, Ó hEadhra, Ó hAirt and Ó Dubhda clans all alleged that they were provoked into disloyalty by the 'cruel and hard parts of sheriffs, sub sheriffs … and the daily extortion of soldiers and soldiers' boys exacting meat and money'.[26] Dáibhí, 'chief of his name', made written accusations in June 1589 against George Bingham and William Taaffe for oppressing the inhabitants of County Sligo while they were sheriffs there.[27] 'They maintained great numbers of men and boys and horses at the expense of the people, and travelled about extorting meat, drink and money from the inhabitants.' Ó Dubhda was afraid to return to his own country while Bingham and Taaffe still ruled there.

> No man there can say that anything that he hath is certainly his own, so long as the said parties hath the stroke over them, for there is neither horse, hackney, hawk, hound or mantle, tablecloth, or anything else which is worth the asking or having, but they must have it, yea if it be but a man's wife or daughter which Taaffe doth fancy he must have her at his will.

Taaffe summoned all the clergy in the winter of 1588 and compelled those who had wives or kept concubines to pay him twenty to forty shillings, claiming he was acting on Richard Bingham's instructions. Besides Ó Dubhda, many of the other inhabitants, including Ó hAirt, Mac Donnchadha, Ó Conchobhair and Ó Gadhra fled to Ó Ruairc country.

23.   [This letter is in Carew's hand] *CSP, Carew*, Sept. 1586, 433.
24.   Ardnaree, 23 September, Sir Richard Bingham to Loftus, *CSP Eliz.*, 164.
25.   6 March 1588, Richard Bingham to Burghley, *CSP Eliz.*, 486.
26.   10 May 1589, John Garvey to Burghley, *CSP Eliz.*, 167.
27.   *CSP Eliz.*, 207.

A commission of enquiry was held in Sligo where the accusations of Ó Dubhda were largely proved 'betraying a strange course of government which hath bred a wonderful terror in that people'. Bingham earned a reputation for harshness in his presidency of Connacht though he himself could never comprehend 'why I am termed crewell for doing her Majestie trewe service'.[28]

Commision of Enquiry

The Great Armada was launched in July 1588. The greatest flotilla ever launched on the high seas was assembled at La Coruna, consisting of 130 ships, with 8,000 seamen, 9,000 soldiers and with galley-slaves, chaplains – one Irish – surgeons, etc. at least 3,000 others. The appearance of the Armada off the English coast caused widespread panic. A great storm blew up on 5 August, hurling the flotilla up the North Sea, past Scotland and down round the coast of Ireland. The impact of the Armada on Ireland was slight, leaving a number of castaways washed up on the coast who were for the most part badly treated except in Ulster and north Connacht. O'Donnell bartered forty of the castaways to secure the release of his son, Red Hugh, from Dublin Castle.

The Great Armada

Elsewhere they received no quarter from the native Irish. Those cast away off Clare Island were ruthlessly murdered by the followers of the O'Malleys as they limped ashore. One estimate put at 3,000 the number of those who managed to swim to land who were slain. Richard Bingham claimed that his brother, George, executed seven or eight hundred which might explain why Ballymote castle was burned in October 1588 by the Ó Conchobhair, Ó hAirt and Ó Dubhda men 'who called themselves the Pope's and King Philip's men'. The Spaniards were expected then to arrive in Sligo in five days and there was 'expectation of a general revolt'. Three hundred were formally executed in Galway city.

Survivors Slaughtered

All this time Ó Ruairc of Leitrim was a law unto himself. George Bingham wrote from Ballymote to inform his brother Richard: 'Last night (Monday, 9 March) Brian Oge O'Rourke with 500 footmen and horsemen came into the barony of Maugherey Leynye where he took prey of all O'Hara Boy's country – 700 or 800 cows and garrans.'[29] Ó Ruairc employed twenty-four Spaniards to train his kerne with pikes and armour which had been retrieved from Armada wrecks. According to Donagh O'Connor Sligo, 'no hope remains, but in O'Rourke only'.[30]

Ó Ruairc of Leitrim

A 'warlike dissension' arose in the month of May 1593 between George Bingham of Ballymote and Brian Ó Ruairc. The Queen's rent had not been

Ballymote Burned

28. *PRO*, SP 63/170 no. 45. He himself was somewhat at a loss at what to do 'there hath been such hard constructions made of all his doings.' *CSP Ire*, 1588–92, 254.
29. *CSP Ire*, 1588–92, 324.
30. *CSP Ire*, 1588–92, 410.

received from Breifny on that festival, Ó Ruairc asserting that all the rents not paid were those for wastelands uninhabited and Bingham sent soldiers and seized Ó Ruairc's milch cows. Brian sent for mercenaries to Tyrone, Tirconnell and Fermanagh and when they came he set out without delay for Ballymote. On arrival in the neighbourhood of the town, he sent marauding parties through the lands of Mac Donnachadha in Corran and 'there was not much of that country which he did not plunder'. On that day he burned thirteen villages on every side of Ballymote and ravaged Ballymote itself, 'returning back to his own territory loaded with great preys and spoils'.[31]

Spanish Help   Surprisingly, from Ballymote George Bingham was able to keep his brother, Richard, up-to-date on ecclesiastical happenings in Ulster. Archbishop Edmund McGauran of Armagh had landed in Drogheda at the end of 1592 from Spain where he had been since 1590 trying to secure Spanish military help for Irish Catholics. George got his information from one James O'Crean, who 'came lately out of the north from Hugh Roe O'Donnell, where as he saith, he saw seven bishops'. Magauran had summoned them to a council for a couple of days and informed them that Philip II was willing to send an army to Ireland which would come by way of Scotland and land in the north, 'but their only want was to have some great man here to be (as it were) their leader or general, and have now thought, Hugh Roe O'Donnell to be "the most fittest" for the same'.

The bishops drew up letters to be sent to the Pope and Philip II and dispatched Bishop Ó hEaladhaigh (he succeeded Maolmuire O'Higgin as Archbishop of Tuam) to deliver them. George Bingham advised his brother to inform the Lord Deputy and get him to keep a close watch on Drogheda in the hope of apprehending Ó hEaladhaigh. Ballymote, 3 January 1593, George Bingham to Richard Bingham.[32] Ó hEaladhaigh, however, made it to Spain and the Pope expressed his willingness to support military action in Ireland, but it all came to nothing. Richard Bingham reported to Burghley on 6 June 1593 that Archbishop Magauran, 'who terms himself Primate, doth much mischief, riding on his chief horse, with his staff and shirt of mail'.[33] Magauran was killed in a foray into Connacht and Ó hEaladhaigh was drowned in the Bay of Biscay on his way back to Ireland in the spring of 1594.

Ó hAirt in   Eoghan Ó hAirt next turns up in the vicinity of Mallow, County Cork of
Mallow   all places, more than 200 miles from his native Sligo, in the summer of 1595. He had escaped Bingham's reign of terror in Sligo 'in 1586 or a little later' and

31. *AFM.*
32. *CSP Ire*, 1592–6, 71–2.
33. *CSP Ire*, 1592–6, 103.

fled into Munster.[34] Anglican Bishop William Lyon of Cork and Ross reported the activities of the ninety-two-year-old Ó hAirt to the Lord Deputy:

> Also there is a Romish bishop that confirmeth children through the country, his name is Owen O'Harte. Great resort is to him, he was at Meallo the XXIII of this month confirming children and the people did flock unto him with their children from all parts as the Chief Justice told me.[35]

Bishop Lyon, who was a ship's captain before his appointment, was informed by the Chief Justice in Cork that O'Hart 'took an oath to her Majesty' before the Chief Justice and Sir Thomas Norris, which the said Owen denied saying that he never 'took the oath of the Supremacy'. Sir Thomas Norris was appointed vice-president of Munster in 1585 and had served in the army under Sir William Pelham who was Lord Justice in 1576.

Not long afterwards Eoghan Ó hAirt returned to Achonry, Donatus Mooney, then a young soldier not yet twenty, met him there about 1597. Many years later, when he had become provincial of the Irish Franciscans, he recorded the meeting with Ó hAirt. 'He lived to a very old age but was nevertheless robust, when I saw him about the year of the Lord 1597.' '… *vixit grandevus, robustus tamen, circa annum Domini 1597, quo tempore ego illud vidi.*'[36]

Donatus Mooney
OFM 1597

---

34. *De Praes Hib*, ii, 341.
35. Cork, 27 July 1595, William Lyons to the Lord Deputy, SP 63/183 f.4.1.; *CSP Ire*, 1592–6, 396. I am indebted to John Donnellan, St Brigid's Park, Cornelscourt, for bringing this letter to my attention.
36. Brussels MS 3947, 9; *Anal. Hib.* (1934), 25.

CHAPTER TWENTY-THREE

Nine Years' War

Eoghan Ruadh in
Connacht

Meanwhile the situation in Connacht and particularly in Sligo was changing and the era of the Binghams was coming to an end, which probably explains why Ó hAirt had returned. Eoghan Ruadh Ó Domhnaill had rallied his Connacht supporters near Sligo castle in the summer of 1595, seized the castle during which George Bingham was slain. Bingham's nephews were captured and, to ransom them, Richard Bingham had to deliver the castle.[1] 'Some of the most assured of the mere Irish have taken arms and amongst them, O'Hara.'[2] Richard Bingham reported in August that Ó Domhnaill 'hath thrown the Scots and the Irish into Connaught to trouble us'.[3]

Again he reported in January 1596 to the Lord Deputy that all the castles– Sligo, Collooney, Ballymote, Castlebar, Boyle and Tulsk – were all likely to be lost unless relieved and that Ó Domhnaill had summoned his supporters to meet him at the bridge in Ballysadare 'with 15 days victuals'.[4] By the end of February Bingham was informed that most of the occupants of Ballymote castle had been murdered.[5] Ó Domhnaill had crossed the Curlews again and was at Ballysadare in August. 'He hath not left a piece of wood or timber about Sligo as big as my arm fearing it should be built up again,' John Bingham told his brother, Richard.[6]

O'Connor Sligo

That autumn, O'Connor Sligo returned from England with a great number of Englishmen, where he was joined by the Mac Donnachaidh and occupied Ballymote castle.[7] Ó Domhnaill sent messengers in October to O'Connor Sligo threatening him that if he did not accept his terms he would set up another one of the O'Connors as O'Connor Sligo.[8] O'Connor Sligo had joined the Earl of Essex in his tour of Munster and now returned to Connacht where he joined the governor, Sir Conyers Clifford. From there he went to the only castle

1.   *CSP Ire*, 1592–6, 336.
2.   27 June 1595, Sir J. Norreys to Burghley, *CSP Ire*, 1592–6, 351.
3.   20 Aug. 1595, R. Bingham to Burghley, *CSP Ire*, 1592–6, 371.
4.   3 Jan. 1596, R. Bingham to Lord Deputy, *CSP Ire*, 1592–6, 446.
5.   Boyle, 20 February 1595–96, Lt William Martin to R. Binghham, *CSP Ire*, 1592–6, 477.
6.   21 Aug. 1596 John Bingham to R. Bingham, *CSP Ire*, 1596–8, 91–2.
7.   *AFM*.
8.   *CSP Ire*, 1596–8, 146.

still remaining to him, Collooney on the banks of the Owenmore. O'Donnell ordered his cavalry to proceed to the castle and prevent O'Connor Sligo escaping. The *Annals of the Four Masters* take up the story:

> The castle was an impregnable stronghold. O'Donnell pitched his camp before a wood that lay on the other side of the river, in front of the castle … strong squadrons of his cavalry were mounted on their horses on guard from dusk … to daybreak, in order that O'Connor might not escape. The news spread throughout Ireland that O'Connor Sligo was thus blockaded by O'Donnell at Culmaoile (Collooney) and when the Earl of Essex heard of it, he despatched messengers to the Governor of Connaught, commanding him to come to meet him … Essex instructed the Governor to order Theobald-na-long O'Flaherty (son of Grace O'Malley) to convey in ships to Sligo harbour the viands & drinks and engines for constructing castles which had arrived from England to Galway. The Governor himself was to proceed by land by the most direct roads to Culmaoile (Collooney) to relieve and release O'Connor Sligo … The Governor repaired to Roscommon and assembled the English and Irish who were obedient to the Queen in the neighbourhood … and went from Roscommon to Tulsk … and then to Boyle Abbey.

Siege of Collooney

Twelve months later the Abbey of Boyle was also captured 'and most of the province revolting'.[9] By October 1599 Ó Domhnaill was in control of Sligo and, according to the informant of the Earl of Essex, 'it maketh our honestest neighbours draw back and to seek to make their peace with him'.[10]

Eoghan Ruadh left Niall Garbh Ó Domhnaill in command of the besiegers of the castle and proceeded with the main body of the army to the Curlew hills.

Battle of the Curlews

> From when he first heard the Governor was approaching he was waiting for 2 months until the 15th of August. His forces were dispersed, one division besieging the castle, another watching Theobald-na-long and others guarding passes from Lough Key to the east of the mountain to Lough Gara to the west. On 15 August he observed the fast in honour of the Blessed Virgin, as was his wont; and Mass was celebrated for him and the army in general; he received communion after making his confession and doing rigid penance for his sins. And he ordered his forces to pray fervently to God for the health of their souls and to save them … from the English. O'Donnell divided his forces into two parts … In one division he placed his swift and energetic youths and his nimble

9.   19 August 1599, Earl of Essex to Privy Council, *CSP Ire*, 1599–1600, 125.
10.   8 October 1599, Sir Arthur Savage to the Earl of Essex, *CSP Ire*, 1599–1600, 179.

and athletic men, and his shooting parties with their high-sounding and straight-shooting guns, and with their strong smooth-surface bows and with their bloody venomous javelins and other missile weapons … In the 2nd division he placed his nobles, chiefs and veteran soldiers with strong keen-edged swords, with polished thin-edged battle-axes and with large-headed lances … He converted his cavalry into pedestrians … While a party were reconnoitring Boyle Abbey … they saw the army raising their standards and sounding their trumpet … They sent news to O'Donnell … He sent troops to engage the English before they passed the rugged parts of the flat mountain. O'Donnell set out after them at a slow pace until he arrived at a place they were certain the English would pass … As they approached each other the Irish discharged terrible showers of beautifully ash-handled javelins and swarms of sharp arrows and volleys of red flashing flames and hot leaden balls … They closed round them on every side … so that they drove the wings of their army into the centre … the English at last turned their backs to the mighty men of the north … such was the precipitateness of their flight … that no one looked behind for a relative or a friend … They pursued them until they got inside the walls of Boyle Abbey.

Conyers Clifford
Slain   The Governor, Sir Conyers Clifford was slain with countless number of English and Irish that were with him. He was beheaded … his body was interned at Holy Trinity in Lough Key and his head was carried to Cul-Maoile (Collooney) … O'Donnell's people returned thanks to God and the Blessed Virgin Mary for their victory … they proceeded to the castle of Cul-Maoile (Collooney) where O'Connor Sligo was blockaded. They showed O'Connor the Governor's head, he gave up hope of being released and made a full submission to O'Donnell … O'Donnell placed him in the full power and chieftainship of his territory and made him many presents of horses, cattle etc … When Theobald-na-long heard the English were defeated, the Governor slain and O'Connor released, he decided not to oppose O'Donnell anymore and sailed back to Galway.[11]

Ballymote Castle
Changes Hands   Bingham informed the Privy Council 'that the greatest part of it (Connacht) is brought under the tyranny of O'Donnell and his faction. He is now possessed of the castle of Ballymote which was delivered to him by the McDonoghs'.[12] The annals give an interesting account of how Ballymote castle changed hands in 1598:

Ballymote, which had been in the possession of the Queen's people for the space of 13 years before this time, was taken in the summer of this year by the rightful inheritors, the Clann-Donough of Corann, namely Tomaltagh & Cathal Duv.

11.   *AFM.*
12.   *CSP Ire,* 1598–9, 308–9.

The Governor, Sir Conyers Clifford and Red Hugh O' Donnell were auctioning the castle against each other in offering to purchase it from the Clann-Donough. The close of the bargain was that the Clann-Donough gave up the castle to O'Donnell, for a purchase and a contract, in the middle month of the autumn of this year. Four hundred pounds (in money) and 300 cows was the price which O'Donnell gave the Clann-Donough for the castle.[13]

Meanwhile, the Nine Years' War had just begun. The English continued to encroach on Tyrone's neighbours and allies in Ulster. Hugh Maguire, his nephew-in-law, was forced into rebellion in 1594 to protect his interests and was helped by his cousin, Eoghan Ruadh. Tyrone himself kept his powder dry and continued his policy of remaining compliant to the queen, even to the point of assisting Marshall Bagenal against Maguire but at the same time making preparations for quite a different scenario. He bought arms and ammunition in Scotland and, together with Ó Domhnaill, he recruited Scots mercenaries from there. The latter's mother, Ineen Duv, originally Finnuala McDonald from the Isles, played a major role in these transactions. *Beginning of Nine Years' War*

The real struggle began in 1595. In February he sent his brother to capture and destroy the fort and bridge that Essex had built over the river Blackwater. In summer he attacked and defeated at Clontibret, close to Monaghan, a large force under Bagenal. In June he was proclaimed a traitor. That September O'Neill and O'Donnell wrote to Philip II looking for help and he sent the following year a ship with arms and ammunition. *Battle of Clontibret*

O'Neill and O'Donnell employed guerilla tactics in their war against the crown forces which were admirably suited to the terrain in Ulster with which they were very familiar and could exploit to maximum advantage. This was typified by the battle of the Yellow Ford in 1598. The English had garrisoned a fort on the river Blackwater within sight of the cathedral city of Armagh and O'Neill promptly blockaded it. Soon the garrison there were starving and Bagenal with a force of 4,000 men was sent to relieve it. On the march he was continually harassed by Red Hugh and Maguire and eventually defeated on 14 August, with the loss of nearly half his force and his own life. *Battle of the Yellow Ford*

The battle had a huge impact on the rest of the country, causing a virtual collapse of English authority in Connacht, Munster and even parts of Leinster. Eoghan Ruadh had total mastery in the greater part of Connaught. Scattered settlers in Munster fled in fear and sought shelter in Cork, Waterford, Limerick and other towns. Philip II was then dangerously ill in his palace of the Escorial and died a short time later on 13 September. There was some doubt whether

13. *AFM.*

Earl of Essex

Philip III would be as supportive of Tyrone, as he had other preoccupations which took precedence with him.

At this juncture in 1599 Robert Devereux, Earl of Essex, the Queen's favourite, was sent to Ireland as Lord Lieutenant. He spent twenty-one weeks achieving virtually nothing, except subduing Leinster and parts of Munster. The Queen's patience was running thin and she peremptorily ordered him to move northward. He did so with 4,000 men but was confronted by Tyrone, just south of Carrickmacross. He persuaded him to parley and the pair conversed privately for the best part of an hour, with Tyrone on horseback in a river while Essex stood on the bank. What passed between them is unknown but the result was an agreed cessation of hostilities. Queen Elizabeth was furious with Essex when she heard what had happened. 'To trust this traitor on his oath is to trust the devil upon religion.'

Ó hAirt's
Account

Later, there were rumours of a conspiracy being hatched between them and there were some credible believers in this conspiracy. Eoghan Ó hAirt told a Munster visitor to Achonry, Dermod McMorris, in the last week of March 1601 that he had recently attended a three-week conference held in Sligo with Eoghan Ruadh, Ó Ruairc, Mac Uilliam, O'Connor Sligo and others to discuss letters received from Tyrone 'and other directions for the maintenance of the wars'. There, Ó hAirt was shown a letter from the Earl of Essex to Tyrone which Eoghan Ruadh received at the beginning of Lent. Essex addressed Tyrone as the 'General of Ireland' and assured him that 'he and the rest of his confederates should be of good comfort, for that he would shortly draw the English forces from Ireland into England, whereby he should with better ease obtain his purpose there, and desired Tyrone to send him a thousand light men to play withal in England'.[14] The Spanish Franciscan, Mathew de Oviedo, later named Archbishop of Dublin, informed Philip III in April 1600 'that O'Neill had almost prevailed upon the Earl of Essex to desert the Queen's cause and join that of Your Majesty and surrender all the Realm to you'. After leaving Ó hAirt, McMorris went on to Ballymote 'to O'Connor Sligo's house' where the story was confirmed. Whatever the truth was, Essex suddenly left Ireland and returned to England against Elizabeth's express wishes. He was later imprisoned and beheaded in February 1601. At his trial for treason in 1601, it was alleged that Tyrone had urged him 'to stand for himself', promising that if he did 'he would join with him.

Spanish Rumours

McMorris went on to Donegal Abbey where he saw Eoghan Ruadh attending Mass on Easter Sunday 'in a fine English gown'. It was McMorris

14.   29 April 1601, examination of Dermod McMorris by Sir Francis Barkley, *CSP Ire*, 1600–
1, 296–9.

who first informed Ó Domhnaill that Essex had been beheaded 'for which they all seemed to be very sorrowful'. McMorris heard that four Spanish ships had arrived in Killybegs but he did not see them, though the story was later confirmed in Ballymote. He said 'that in all the border counties where he hath been, there is a general expectation of Spaniards before St James tide, and that they make no doubt of their coming'. McMorris called on Ó hAirt again on his return. The country was alive with rumours of a Spanish invasion and sightings of Spanish ships in western ports. Two Spanish ships arrived in Killala on their way to the north. One of them was chased by a Queen's ship into Sligo Bay and landed seventy men in Sligo. The captain went overland to O'Neill and swore that he was 'content to lose his head if there be not 20 ships out of Spain in 15 days'.[15] Carew believed that the ship was sent to announce that the others were on the way. He did not think the Spaniards would come to the north, but to Munster. 'Wherever the Spaniards land, their arrival will be a signal for a general distraction throughout the country. The loose sort will immediately grow to a head and commit outrages, and the best affected will but temporise in neutrality until a judgement be made "whether side will prevail".'

The man who succeeded Essex in February 1600 was a completely different *Lord Mountjoy* kettle of fish, as Tyrone would very soon learn, to his cost. Charles Blount, Lord Mountjoy, soldier and administrator, sought to maintain pressure on Tyrone and his allies all year round and not just during short summer campaigns, as had been the custom of his predecessors up to now. Tyrone and Ó Domhnall had to constantly watch their backs. 'In his life Tyrone was not broken by England but by Ireland; by its deep atavism and inbreeding, so characteristic of abortive and arrested cultures in all ages of the world's history.'[16] One setback and they would be deserted by their so-called allies in droves.

The most striking example of this was the behaviour of Eoghan Ruadh's own brother-in-law and second cousin, Niall Garbh Ó Domhnaill. Mountjoy encouraged Niall Garbh to claim Tyrconnell over the head of the existing chieftain, Eoghan Ruadh, with the result that Niall entered the war on the English side, personally killing Eoghan Ruadh's brother, Maghnus. He took Ballyshannon and occupied Donegal Abbey in August 1601 where there were some forty Franciscan friars, but Eoghan Ruadh could do nothing as he was otherwise pressingly engaged. News had come that the long-awaited Spanish help had finally arrived.

15.   14 August 1601, Sir George Carew to Privy Council, *CSP Ire*, 1601–3, 33–4, 38–9.
16.   Seán Ó Faoileán, *The Great O'Neill*, 279.

Spanish arrive at Kinsale

The Spanish force, about 4,000 strong, under the command of Juan del Áquila, put in at Kinsale on 21 September 1601. The fleet consisted of about twenty-five sailing ships, of which seventeen were men of war, six galleons and the rest small boats of a hundred to a hundred-and-fifty tonnes. Rumours had been rife all that year of the imminent arrival of the Spaniards and the English were just as well aware of that probability as were the Irish. As early as Easter there was 'a general expectation of Spanish before St James tide and that they make no doubt of their coming'. In July, two Spanish ships landed in Killala with money and munitions and the Spaniards assured O'Donnell 'that they should presently have aid'. But as the summer turned into autumn the threat had receded. In early September Mountjoy himself was 'rather of opinion since they have waited so long they will not come this winter'. Luckily for him he was in Kilkenny when the news arrived and, gathering all the men he could lay his hands on, he made hot-footed for the south.

O'Neill's disappointment at the choice of Kinsale, the furthest point away from his power base in Ulster, can only be guessed at. He had expected them to land at Donegal or Killybegs but would have been happy if they came in at Killala or Sligo. Not only was Kinsale the wrong place, but it was also the wrong time of the year, and the wrong-sized force. Tyrone always requested a minimum of 6,000 men if they were planning a Munster landing. Had they landed in Ulster or Connacht, 3,000 might well have sufficed with the numbers O'Neill and O'Donnell could then muster. His own choice of a landing place would have been Drogheda, but the Spaniards wisely rejected anywhere on the east coast as there they would have to run the gauntlet of an encounter with the English navy.

Eoghan Ruadh assembles forces in Ballymote

Tyrone and Ó Domhnaill were now in a quandary, unsure what to do. At first they sent word to del Áquila to re-embark and make for Sligo but the Spaniards were unwilling to undertake what could be a perilous voyage round the west coast. The Earls had no option but to head for Kinsale.

> O'Donnell ... assembled his forces to proceed into south Connacht ... He took with him on this hosting ... all those who were under his jurisdiction in Ulster; and the Connacians, from the River Suck to the Drowes and from the west of Tyrawly to Breifny O'Reilly, expecting and awaiting his arrival at Ballymote, whither they were gone at his summons ... When O'Donnell and his forces out of Ulster had joined these Connachtmen at Ballymote, he marched through Corran etc ... to Kiltartan, County Galway.[17]

17. *AFM.*

It was the first week of November when he began his march southwards through County Roscommon, east Galway to the Shannon and then on to Kinsale. By then the Spaniards were shut into Kinsale and preparations were being made for the reduction of the town. Tyrone followed and later described the journey. 'In mid-winter they had to march a distance of about one hundred leagues through enemy territory, passing many rivers and forced to make bridges.' It was a heroic march and by the time they reached Kinsale, they had a combined force of about 5500 and took up their position surrounding the English who in turn were surrounding the Spanish in Kinsale. *Battle of Kinsale*

Mountjoy, despite his position wedged in between the two opposition forces, was eager to fight. Contrary to all their previous engagements, it was the Irish who were the first to commit themselves. They moved forward early on Christmas Eve but finding the English on the alert they withdrew again. Mountjoy decided to gamble and with his superior cavalry strength decided to charge Tyrone's infantry, which quickly broke. The battle was over in a matter of hours and the Irish were scattered with heavy losses.

Two days after the battle of Kinsale, Eoghan Ruadh set out for Spain to seek further help, having already chosen his brother Ruaidhrí to succeed him as chieftain. He sailed from Castlehaven in the ship of a Spanish general who was reporting back to Philip III on the outcome, while del Áquila and his force remained in Kinsale awaiting instructions. He was accompanied by the Franciscan, Flann Conry, who had come to Kinsale with the Spanish force. *Eoghan Ruadh sets sail for Spain*

Immediately after his defeat at Kinsale, O'Neill began to march swiftly northwards. There were complaints afterwards that the English forces did nothing to impede his progress. It was suggested that O'Neill sent runners ahead to spread the rumour that he had won the battle of Kinsale which would explain the reluctance of his enemies to tangle with a returning victorious army. Meanwhile, once back in Ulster, O'Neill evaded his enemies while making peace overtures to Mountjoy. At the same time he sent a message to Philip III and Archduke Albert saying that if Spanish help did not arrive before May 1603, a ship should be sent to carry him and his followers away 'from the fury of their enemies'.

Elizabeth instructed Mountjoy in February that year to assure Tyrone 'of his life, liberty and pardon upon some conditions'. The following month O'Neill signed the Treaty of Mellifont, unaware that Elizabeth had died six days previously, and was conceded recognition of absolute ownership of his lordship. A short time later he accompanied Mountjoy to London where he was formally pardoned by James I. *Treaty of Mellifont*

General Pardon   The king issued a general pardon on 19 April 1603 to Donnough O'Connor
1603   Sligo, his wife Lady Eleanore, Countess of Desmond, and 3,230 persons in
County Sligo mentioned by name, including Mac Donnchaidh, Ó Eadhraí,
Ó hAirt and Ó hUiginn. Among them was 'Owen O'Hart of Accadensis,
bishop'.[18]

Death of Ó hAirt   Sometime later, Ó hAirt died after receiving the last sacraments. He was
one hundred years old and in the forty-third year of his episcopacy. He was
buried in his cathedral church in Achonry 'near the principal altar on the gospel
side'.[19] Lynch states that he had a long illness and was confined to bed for the
last fourteen years of his life 'only leaving it to consecrate the oil and confer
the sacraments of orders and confirmation'. As shown, the documentary
evidence does not support this. His passing coincided with the passing of the
old Gaelic world into which he had been born one hundred years before.

18. *Pat. 1 James I*, 20–4; Repertory of the inrolments of Patent Rolls of Chancery [Patent
Letters granting King's pardon to 3,230 persons mentioned by name, including Lady
Eleanore, Countess of Desmond, wife of Donogh O'Conor Sligo, Owen O'Hart, bishop
of Achonry, and Owen O'Connor of Killala, otherwise Aladens; also in Co. Sligo, 6
McDermots, 7 McDonoghs, 52 McDonnoughs, 9 McGowans, 10 McManus', 7
McMulroony Finn, 9 McSwines, 30 McSwinys, 16 O'Dowda's, 7 O'Flanellys, 25 O'Haras,
54 O'Harts, 20 O'Higgins, etc. The latter included Will. Twoholl (Tuathal), Cormack,
Gillenewf (Giolla na naoimh) and Tadhg Óg, the son of the famous Tadhg Dall, all bardic
poets (rymers), from Dwacharny in Tourlestrane. In Achonry there were harpers, including
Cormac Ó Connacháin and Gillepatrick, Shane Buidhe, Edmond Óg, and Brian Dorrogh
Ó Fionáinn. There were surgeons too like Donnogh Ultagh McShane and Ulline McEllay
of Ballymote, and Eoghan, Connor, Edward Keogh, and Thadeus McElea (Mac an Leagha,
MacAlea) of Bonanydanie? Repertory of the inrolments of Patent Rolls of Chancery –
James I, 72].
19 *De Praes. Hib.*, ii, 342.

CHAPTER TWENTY-FOUR

'Rógaire Easpaig'

By the time of the death of Ó hAirt, the battle for the religious minds and hearts of the people had been largely won. Ireland had uniquely chosen to follow a religion other than that of its monarch, while the rest of Europe followed the dictum laid down at the Diet of Worms in 1521, *cuius regio, eius religio*. For that the Irish people had to pay a terrible price. Their religion was proscribed, their priests were hunted and pursued, their places of worship driven underground and their children denied education. The result was that 'Irish' and 'Catholic' became synonymous and it was to remain so until very recently.

Persecution

What contributed to the survival of Catholicism and the failure of the Protestant Reformation in Ireland was the early return of seminary priests from Europe, particularly the Jesuits and other religious orders, and the disinterest of the government in making any real effort to convert the people. The few Protestant livings provided were 'usurped by either massing priests or by mere laical persons'.[1] Proposed reforms in 1604 included 'that prebends, parsonages, vicarages and ecclesiastical dignities be not bestowed on lay persons, children, Popish priests and unworthy ministers' and 'that every minister being detected and convicted of whoredom, drunkenness or other notorious crime be deprived *ipso facto*'.[2]

Few Ministers of Dubious Quality

By 1615, the year of the first visitation, there were only two resident clergy in Achonry and the quality of these ministers was questionable.[3] They were probably former priests, like Hugh Brehony, who was granted the vicarage of Kilmorgan (Ballymote) as well as four others in Elphin in 1620. Similarly with James McConmy who was made provost as well as rector and vicar of Kilmactigue the following year.[4] The Bishop of Elphin stated in 1613 that 'there are above 30 parishes without any minister to take cure of souls, owing to the farmers of the impropriate parsonages, having taken up the profits of the vicarages and that the temporal lands of the see are withheld by persons

Former Priests

---

1. *CSP Ire*, 1600, 297.
2. *CSP Ire*, 1603–6, 241.
3. O'Dowd, *Early Modern Sligo*, 107.
4. *Pat. Rolls 1 James I*, 476 and 510 18 May 1613 (1 James I).

who claim them as an inheritance'.[5] The same was true in the archdiocese of Tuam.[6]

Miler Magrath

The situation in the archdiocese of Cashel, where the notorious Miler (Maolmhuire) Magrath was the archbishop, was even worse. Miler himself held twenty-three parishes, while three of his sons, Turlough, Séamas and Marcas, got profits from three others. 'There be other livings in these two dioceses of Cashel and Emly, whereof some poor men carry the name, but they have little learning or sufficiency, and indeed are fitter to keep hogs than serve in the church.'[7]

Career

A Franciscan friar whose family were caretakers of St Patrick's Purgatory in Lough Derg, sometimes referred to as Termon Magrath, he was appointed Bishop of Down and Connor by Pius IV (1559–65) on 12 October 1565.[8] Shortly afterwards in 1567 he submitted to Sir Henry Sydney in Drogheda and accepted his bishopric from the queen. She appointed him Bishop of Clogher in 1570 and a year later Archbishop of Cashel, to which Waterford and Lismore was later added. Rome deprived him of Down and Connor on 14 March 1580.[9]

Family

Miler was in his early fifties when he married in 1575 Áine Ó Meára from near Toomyvara in north Tipperary where her family were chieftains. She was a good deal younger than him and bore him nine children, five boys and four girls, Turlough, Réamonn, Brian, Marcas, Séamas, Máire, Síle, Anna and Eilís. Tradition has it that Áine was a devout Catholic and raised their children as Catholics. Years later Miler was described to the Archbishop of Canterbury as 'old and unable, whose wife and children do not accompany him to the church'.[10]

Bishop of Achonry and Killala

When the queen's Bishop Eoghan O'Connor of Killala died, Lord Deputy Sir Arthur Chichester (1605–15) informed the Earl of Salisbury early in 1606 and suggested that it should be united to Achonry as they each were worth not more than £20 a year. On 14 January 1606, Sir Arthur Chichester to the Earl of Salisbury. There is a suggestion that Achonry was not united to Killala under Eoghan O'Connor as Lynch stated in his *Praesulibus Hiberniae*, as Chichester stated that Achonry 'hath lain longer void', i.e. with the death of Eoghan Ó hAirt in 1603. Miler was persuaded in February 1607 to resign Waterford and

5.   18 May 1613, *Pat. Rolls 1 James I*, 250.
6.   Ibid., 251.
7.   4 Aug. 1607, *CSP Ire*, 1606–8, 235–44.
8.   Vat. Lib. MSS Barberini Latini 2884 f.23r.
9.   Vat. Lib. MSS Barberini Latini 2874, 293–4.
10.   *CSP Ire*, 1611–14, 80.

Lismore[11] and in return he was granted a year later, 7 February 1608, 'the custody of the bishoprics of Killala and Achonry and of their temporalities and spiritualities'.

The Lord Deputy commented that 'no one of worth would accept them by reason of their small value'. Chichester informed Salisbury that Killala and Achonry 'are such poor things as few will seek after them unless it be some silly man who will content himself with a little without means to support it, and smally attend the advancement of the gospel or reformation of the people'.[12] He was also allowed to hold for life the rectories of Castleconnor and Skreen in Killala, Kilmacallan and *Inter Duos Pontes* in Elphin, the prebend of Doughorne and the prebend and rectory of Killoran in Achonry.[13] The Royal Visitation Book of 1615 stated that the bishop also held the prebends of Kilmactigue, Kilbeagh, Killedan, Kilmovee.[14] Miler still had not possession of Achonry and Killala by 1611 as it was stated then that 'they were long since promised by the Deputy and Council'. *'Such Poor Things'*

Chichester had a poor opinion of Miler, and his coadjutor in Cashel and thought it would 'be a hard matter to make them run their course for the good of religion'. He regarded Miler as 'stout and wilful' though 'his delivery in the pulpit is not to be commended'. He was of the opinion 'it were better not to discontent that heady Archbishop and leave him at his liberty, for he is a powerful man amongst the Irish of Ulster and able to do much hurt by underhand practices, in which he is well experienced'.[15] *'Stout and Wilful'*

A former Franciscan colleague of Miler, Eoghan Ó Dubhthaigh, composed a long poem two years after Miler's marriage, *An Chliar Ghliogair* (*The Chattering Clergy*), of over ninety verses addressed to three priests who became Protestant clergymen, one of whom was Miler. It was largely a diatribe against Protestant clerics who made little of the Virgin Mary and a satyric play on Miler's Irish Christian name, Maolmuire or 'servant of Mary'. *Satire on Miler*

> *A Mhaoil gan Mhuire, ataoi leamh,*
> *dul ar neamh ní hé do thriall;*
> *Maol gan Aifrionn, Maol gan ord,*
> *Maol go hIfrionn is borb pian …*
> Slave without Mary, fool that you are,
> The rapture of Heaven you will not gain;

'Slave of Áine'

11   *Pat. Rolls 1 James I*, 106.
12. *CSP Ire*, 1606–8, 78 see photocopy; *CSP Ire*, 1606–8, 421–2.
13. *Pat. Rolls 5 James I.*
14. Wood-Martin, Sligo ii, 33n i.
15. *CSP Ire*, 1611–14, 241.

Slave without Mass, slave without an Order
Slave down under in bitter pain …
A Mhaoil gan Chreidiomh, a Mhaoil gan Dia,
A Mhaoil gan Íosa is sia neart
rachair síos go lasair ghéir
's do bhean féin ar leath-láimh leat …
Slave without faith, slave without God,
Slave without Jesus, the all-powerful
You'll go down in consuming flames
and your wife in tow with you …
Bean is cosmhuil ré a céile
's fear ris nach cosmhuil daoine –
ní Maol Muire acht Maol Áine
tug a náire ar fheoil Aoine …
A woman like her husband
a tonsured man not like others
Not Mary's slave but slave of Annie
Shaming themselves for meat on Friday …

'Sorry for your Plight'   Another Franciscan, Bonabheantúra Ó hEodhasa, Guardian of St Anthony's Louvain, penned a gentler reproach to Miler in *Truagh liom, a chompáin, do chor.*[16]

Truagh liom, a chompáin, do chor,
Truagh an modh ar a bhfuil sibh;
ní léir dhíbh solas sa ngrein,
an dorchact féin ní léir libh.
I am sorry for your plight, my companion,
Pitiable is the work in which you are engaged;
You cannot see light in the sun,
Even darkness you cannot perceive.

Crown Appointees   The quality of early crown appointees as bishops, like Miler Magrath, was equally questionable, or at least their motives in accepting such appointments. His two biographers describe him as *'rógaire easpaig'* and 'the scoundrel of Cashel'.[17]

Miler Magrath was a hundred years old, like his near-contemporary, Eoghan Ó hAirt, when he died in 1622.

16.   Mág Craith, *Dán na mBráthar Mionúir*, poems 9 and 27, 38–51 and 127–51.
17.   Ó Duáin, *Rógaire Easpaig* and Wyse Jackson, *Archbishop Magrath – the scoundrel of Cashel CSP Ire*, 1611–14, 43.

In May 1623, the king appointed Archibald Hamilton – the younger *Scottish Bishops*
brother of Sir Claude Hamilton of Clones – as Bishop of Killala, with the
bishopric of Achonry *in commendam* with a clause restoring the temporalities.[18]
He was a Scotsman as indeed was his successor, Archibald Adair (1630–40).
Adair was suspected of sympathising with the Scottish Covenanters and
deprived of Achonry and Killala. All charges against him were later erased from
the file of the Court of High Commission and he was subsequently appointed
to Waterford and Lismore.[19] He was succeeded by the Bishop of Ross, John
Maxwell.[20]

Under the Scottish bishops the Protestant clergy 'were transformed from a *Calvinist*
wholly native clergy in 1615 to a largely Scottish ministry in 1534'.[21] These *Ministers*
clergymen were tainted with the strong Calvinist views of Scottish
Presbyterianism which they passed on to the growing settler community,
making them more intolerant of Catholics. William Oliphant, vicar of
Ballysadare and Enagh in the 1630s, was a Scotsman. Thomas Hutchinson
was made vicar of Kilcolman, Templemuury (Ballaghaderreen), Kilbeigh
(Charlestown) and Kilmovee at the beginning of 1621. Nathaniel Johnson was
appointed perpetual vicar of Keash (Toomour) and Ballymote (Emlifad) in
June 1622 and Erasmus Mathews was presented to the rectory of Kilfree in
Coolavin in June 1623.[22] The Irish language has no words for Catholic or
Protestant. Protestants were called *Albanaigh* or *Sasanaigh* while Catholics were
known as *Éireannaigh.*[23]

The greatest achievement of these crown-appointed bishops was their *Tithes*
recovery of the temporalities and their systematic collection of tithes which
made them and their church even more unpopular among the natives. In some
cases monasteries like Ballysadare and Boyle had taken over the function of
appointing parish priests and received their share of the tithes. When they were
suppressed their properties, including tithes, were granted to laymen.
Ballysadare tithes passed to the Crofton family and they were obliged to pay
Vicar Oliphant £30 annually.[24] Protestant vicars were dependant on these tithes

18.   *CSP Ire*, 1615–25, 403, 567.
19.   10 October 1639, Bp of Derry to Abp of Canterbury, 7 June 1641 King to Lord Justices
      for Archibald Adair, bishop designate of Waterford and Lismore, *CSP Ire*, 1633–47, 225,
      300.
20.   29 June 1640, King to John Maxwell, Bishop of Ross, *CSP Ire*, 1633–47, 243.
21.   Ford, 137: see also *Cal. Pat. Rolls Ire*, Charles I, 26, 111, 316, 436, 511, 585 and TCD
      MS. 1067.
22.   *Pat. Rolls James I*, 460, 549 and 564.
23.   *Caitlicigh* and *Protastúnaigh* are merely transliterations from the English terms and are of
      more recent origin.
24.   O'Dowd, 110.

for subsistence and their bishops made huge efforts to recover them and largely succeeded. They also gave up their right to one-quarter of the tithes. Tithes were the accepted way of supporting the clergy all over the Christian world, both in Catholic and Protestant lands. Ireland was exceptional in that the majority of the people were obliged to pay them for the support of a clergy other than their own.

Prosperous Clergy   William Browne, registrar of the combined dioceses of Killala and Achonry in the late 1630s, built a dwelling house, barn, kill-house, dairy, stable and cowhouse in Kilvarnet. He had 'thirteen stackes of wheate, beare, barly and oates and three great ricks of hay and three stacks of turfe, in and about his haggard'. As well as a garden and orchard, he had six hundred English sheep, thirty-six English milch cows and 'six score and sixteen beasts, viz. some draught oxen, dry cowes, steeres, bulls, heifers and yearelings of English breed', and saddle horses, geldings, mares and stud horses.[25] Such prosperity was bound to create huge hostility towards Protestants in general and its ministers in particular, who undertook the collection of the tithes. This bitterness continued for years, culminating only in the middle of the nineteenth century with the ending of the Tithe War.

25.   Deposition of William Browne, Wood-Martin, Sligo ii, 198–9.

CHAPTER TWENTY-FIVE

Seminaries

More importantly for the survival of Catholicism was the creation of semin- *Political Threat*
aries for Irish priests in Europe and the return of these Counter-Reformation
priests to the mission in Ireland. They were seen by the English authorities as
a major threat to political stability and the establishment of Protestantism. It
was reported in 1600 that 'seminaries have crept into the hearts of all the people
… and they hold their souls in such bondage as, whatsoever they command,
it is performed.'[1] As rumours circulated and fears grew of an imminent Spanish
invasion in 1601, reports increased of the activities of these 'traitorly priests
who are the chiefest firebrands of these unnatural treasons'.[2] 'There is a number
of seminary priests in this country who by their wicked and pestilent
persuasions stir all those that be evil affected and disposed to rebellion and
seduce the ignorant sort of people from coming to hear divine service.'[3]

From early in the seventeenth century, the seminary priests returned to *Huge Impact*
Ireland in great numbers and had a huge impact on the people. Chichester
described their return as the 'continual flocking of such locusts into the realm'
and estimated that there were 'more priests here than Her Majesty has soldiers'.[4]
Their influence was particularly marked over women. 'The priests prevail
mightily with the women, and they with their husbands.' Men who attended
Protestant services 'were hated as devils and hell-hounds … and their Catholic
wives will not eat or lie with their husbands if they be excommunicated for
heretics, as they presently are, by the priests'.[5]

The king issued a proclamation in 1605 ordering that *Priests Proclaimed*

all Jesuits, seminary priests or other priests whatsoever, made or ordained by any
authority derived or pretended to be derived from the See of Rome, shall before
the 10th of December next, depart out of the kingdom of Ireland. And that no
Jesuit, seminary priest or other priest ordained by foreign authority, shall from

1. Limerick, 21 June 1600, Justice James Gold to Sir Robert Cecil, *CSP Ire*, 1600, 257.
2. 2 November 1600, Sir George Carew to Privy Council, *CSP Ire*, 1600–1, 5.
3. 2 November 1600, Sir George Carew to Privy Council, *CSP Ire*, 1600–1, 5. 16 April 1601
   Capt David Hetherington to Sir Robert Cecil, *CSP Ire*, 1600–1, 280.
4. *CSP Ire*, 1606–8, 309–11; 608–10, 147, 309.
5. Concerning reformation of religion in Ireland. n.d. [1606] *CSP Ire*, 1603–6, 544.

and after the 10th of December, repair or return to that kingdom, upon the pain of his high displeasure, and upon such further pain and penalty as may be justly inflicted upon them by the laws and statutes of that realm. And upon the like pain, he expressly forbids all his subjects within that kingdom to receive or relieve any such Jesuit, seminary priest or other priest, who, after the said 10th of December, shall remain in that realm or return to the same or any part thereof.[6]

Diocesan Priests connived at Irish Continental Colleges

It appears that the royal proclamation had little or no effect as priests continued to arrive in droves and new proclamations were issued in 1614 and 1627.[7] In the latter year all the Jesuits, Franciscans and Dominicans were to be banished at once but that secular priests were to be 'connived at'. The members of religious orders were deemed to be 'unquiet spirits' while secular priests were thought to be loyal to the state though they differed in religion. Religious orders were to 'seduce no more of the sons of Irish gentlemen to go into their societies or to be taught in foreign schools'.[8]

Irish Continental Colleges

The earliest seminaries were founded by Jesuits, such as the German College in Rome where Maolmhuire Ó hUiginn became the first recorded Achonry priest to attend a seminary. The first Irish student communities were formed in established colleges such as Collège de Montaigu in Paris where John Lee brought a group of Irish students together in 1578. Irish Colleges were established in Spain and the Spanish Netherlands in the last decade of the sixteenth century.[9] The Irish College in Salamanca, 'Colegio de Nobles Irlandeses' (College of the Noble Irish), was founded by a Clonmel Jesuit named Thomas White in 1592. Another one was established in Lisbon the following year.

Achonry Students

The earliest Achonry student in Salamanca was James McDonagh from Ballymote who arrived there in the middle of May 1615. He was the son of Maeleachlainn Mac Donnchadha and Finuala Ní Ruairc which suggests he belonged to upper-class Gaelic society. He had studied for a number of years in Achonry parish under Master Henry Hart where he became proficient in Latin. The next Achonry student, Maurice Herbert, entered Salamanca in June 1625. A native of Sligo and son of Richard Herbert and Maria Keenan he received his early education in Skreen from Mark McConnell and Aeneas

6.   Westminster, 4 July 1605, Proclamation of King James against Toleration in Ireland. *CSP Ire*, 1603–6, 302–3.
7.   *CSP Ire*, 1611–14, 481.
8.   *CSP Ire*, 1625–32, 297; *CSP Ire*, 1625–60, 108–9.
9.   Cathaldus Giblin, 'The Irish Colleges on the Continent' in Swords, *The Irish-French Connection*, 9–20; John J. Silke, 'The Irish Abroad, 1534–1691' in *A New History of Ireland*, iii, 615–32.

McNemoy. After following a course in Dijon in Burgundy, he arrived in Salamanca at the age of twenty-nine. He was among a number of students who were examined by their professors in the presence of the rector in August 1626, 'who affirmed unanimously that they gave great proof of their talents and application to study,' and was still there in September 1628.[10] Dermitius Maynanel (McDaniel) was ordained priest in the Irish College in Rome in *via degli Ibernesi* on 11 March 1634 and Jacobus Brennan received all the minor orders there on 28 February 1665, subdeacon on 21 March and deacon on 4 April of the same year.[11]

The earliest recorded Achonry student in Paris was Bernard Cunleus (Cunlevy) in 1651 probably residing in Collège de Montaigu which then housed the main Irish community in the city. Also there at the same time was Maurice Durcan, whose name was listed among a group of Irish anti-Jansenists involved in a dispute in the university known as *L'affaire des Hibernois*. Durcan, who was credited with a doctorate in theology, later became vicar-apostolic of Achonry.[12] A handful of others were there during the rest of the seventeenth century including Risteárd Ó Conaill (1672), who is buried in Ballysadare, Dómhnall Ó Gullyvene (1674), Cathal Ó hEadhra (1695) and Brian Morvornagh (1687–96) who subsequently served as chaplain to the Irish Brigade in France and founded a scholarship for Achonry students in the Irish College, Paris.[13]

Irish College, Paris

Another student abroad, Pól Ó hUiginn (1628–1724), probably from the famous bardic family of Tadhg Dall, studied literature and rhetoric in Ireland, and spent thirteen months in the Irish College, Seville. For health reasons he changed to the Irish College, Rome on 29 October 1666, the first Connacht student there since 1635. He was ordained in 1668 and returned to Ireland where he was made vicar-general of Killala 1677–8 and there became acquainted with Thomas Otway, Protestant Bishop of Killala and Achonry. He became a Protestant minister in 1680 and subsequently Narcissus Marsh, provost of Trinity, appointed him to teach Irish and preach in Irish once a month in College Chapel. He also collaborated on the publication of Bedell's Old Testament in 1685. He held benefices in Templemore, County Tipperary where he died on 10 October 1724 aged ninety-six.[14]

10. *Arch. Hib.*, ii (1913), 32, iii (1914), 95, iv (1915), 13, 14.
11. Egan, Giblin, McGrath, 'Irish students ordained in Rome (1625–1710)' in *IER*, lxxxi (1943), 116–24.
12. His name is not recorded in the fairly comprehensive list compiled by Brockliss and Ferté of Irish students in the university.
13. Brockliss and Ferté, 'Prosopography of Irish Clerics who studied in France', 138–9.
14. Ní Mhurchú and Breathnach, 1560–1781 *Beathaisnéis*, 150–1, Ó Moghráin 'Pól Ó hUiginn' in *Béaloideas* XV (1945–6), 86–101, Ó Fiaich in *Ón Chreagán go Dubhrann*, aistí.

Spanish Netherlands   The first Irish college in the Netherlands was established in Douai in 1594 by a Meathman, Christopher Cusack, and this became the motherhouse of other colleges in Antwerp (1600), Lille (1610), and Tournai (1616). Colleges were founded in France from the beginning of the seventeenth century with the establishment of one in Bordeaux in 1603. Between 1592 and 1700 some thirty such colleges sprang up across Europe extending from Lisbon in Portugal to Vielun in Poland. Up to three colleges were founded in some centres. Louvain had St Anthony's Franciscan college (1607), the Pastoral College (1623) and the Irish Dominican College (1626). Not surprisingly, Rome had four: St Isidore's Franciscan college (1625), the Irish College, Rome (1628), Irish Augustinian college (1656) and Dominicans in San Clemente (1677). Dominicans also had a house, Corpo Santo, in Lisbon (1659).[15]

Achonry Founders: Two colleges were founded by natives of Achonry. Franciscan James Taaffe
James Taaffe   established a house for Irish priests in Paris in the middle of the seventeenth century. Some were members of Old English families like the Taaffes and Dillons who were firmly loyal to the crown while remaining attached to the old religion at least by affection. Presumably, his grandfather, William Taaffe as sheriff in Sligo and Theobald Dillon, his counterpart in Mayo, were obliged as office-holders to take the Oath of Supremacy, but a new oath of allegiance to the crown was introduced early in the seventeenth century with no reference to the king as head of the Church.

George Dillon   James Taaffe was related through his mother to George Dillon OFM of the Costello-Gallen family and his brother of Louis, the only bishop of Achonry appointed in the seventeenth century. George got a little house in the suburb of Saint Germain in Paris, with the Queen's permission. The Abbé of Saint Germain imposed rather strict conditions. There were to be only six religious, all priests, who could only say Mass behind closed doors without letting anybody in and without ringing the bell. Dillon was a chaplain in Paris to the Queen Mother, Henrietta Maria, who recommended him for Elphin in 1662.[16]

Taaffes of   Part of the large estates the Taaffes carved out for themselves came from
Ballymote   suppressed monasteries. William Taaffe was granted the Franciscan friary in Ballymote and though the friary itself was in ruins, he got whatever buildings still remained standing as well as gardens, orchards and almost two-hundred acres

---

15. Others included Rouen and Seville (1612), Charleville (1620), Prague Franciscan (1631), Capranica Franciscan (1656), Alcalá (1657), Toulouse (1659), Nantes (1689) and Boulay Franciscan (1700).
16. Sauval, *Histoire et Antiquités de la Ville de Paris*, Liv. IV, 494–5: *SOCG*, vol. 390, ff. 478r, 483v; Acta, vii, ff.180v, 181r; Fondo di Vienna, xiv, ff.285r, 286r, 287r, 288r; Nunziatura di Francia, vol. 117, f.562rv; xvi, ff.68rv, 71r; CP, xix, ff.132r, 135v; see Coll. Hib., no. 2, 112.

of land. He was also granted the order's friary in 1598 in Court with its possessions, becoming easily the most powerful landlord in Sligo while his son, John, became Baron of Ballymote and first Viscount Taaffe of Corren in 1628.

Other Catholic sheriffs of Old English background were James French and Jasper Brett. Brett's were among a group of Old English that Taaffe lured from his native Louth to live on his estate in Ballymote.[17] Another Catholic sheriff was Andrew O'Crean from the Sligo merchant family with Old English connections. A small number of Irish Catholics were appointed sheriffs, like Tadhg Ó hEadhra in the first decade of the seventeenth century and Tadhg Ó hUiginn, son of Tadhg Dall, early in the 1630s.

Catholic Sheriffs

Apparently, friars were allowed to continue to live in Court and Ballymote, or in the vicinity, and carry on their ministry in the neighbourhood. Probably, they were the first recruiting grounds for novices in their newly-found colleges on the continent, St Anthony's, Louvain, St Isidore's, Rome and Immaculate College, Prague, all of which housed about fifty students.

Almost certainly the first wave of continentally-trained Counter-Reformation priests in Achonry were religious, Franciscans and Dominicans, where the suppression of monasteries was slow and intermittent. As late as 1586 it was reported that 'friars held in peace their abbeys and houses throughout all Sligo and Mayo'.[18] They had been the most active group there during the Reformation, steadying the people against the introduction of the new reformed religion from England. The Dominican friary of the Holy Cross in Sligo had been given a reprieve by Queen Elizabeth at the request of O'Connor Sligo on condition that the friars lived as secular priests. Later, it was granted to William Taaffe by James I. In 1608 one of the O'Creans, a Dominican, arrived back from Spain and re-organised the community which grew to about ten by 1622.

Protected Friars

Catholics in the half-barony of Coolavin enjoyed the protection of Fearghal Ó Gadhra. His father, Irriell Ó Gadhra of Moygara, was pardoned by James I in April of 1603 as was a friar there, one Irriell Mac Maelrunaidh Ó hUiginn. He was probably a Carmelite friar in Knockmore, founded by the Ó Gadhra family in the fourteenth century. The Augustinian friars in Banada were probably protected by the Ó hEadhra family who founded them early in the fifteenth century. Friar Uilliam Ó hÉanagáin (Will O'Henigan) of Tullanaglug was named in the general pardon of 1603. In such an environment, Catholics and particularly priests and friars probably enjoyed a certain level of official protection and this continued until the middle of the seventeenth century and the arrival of Oliver Cromwell.

17.   7 June 1628, King to Lord Deputy, *CSP Ire*, 1625–32, 354.
18.   Moran, *IER*, i, 216.

Dillon
Protection

A similar protective environment existed in the Mayo section of the diocese, the barony of Costello-Gallen, where the Dillon family held sway, and comprised the parishes of Castlemore and Kilcolman (Ballaghaderreen), Kilbeagh (Charlestown) and Kilmovee. Theobald Dillon, a member of an old established family in County Meath, was created the first Viscount of Costello-Gallen in 1623 with his seat at Castlemore.

The Dominicans there, particularly in Urlaur, escaped suppression largely because of its remoteness. When finally confiscated in the seventeenth century, shortly afterwards it came into the possession of Catholic Viscount Theobald Dillon of Costello-Gallen. With his protection it continued to function as a friary, becoming a house of novices for Connacht. There were ten novices there in 1629 receiving instruction from two friars. The friars were dispersed or imprisoned in 1650 under the Cromwellian regime.[19] The other Dominican friary, at Straide in the barony of Gallen, was confiscated in 1578 when it was leased to James Garvey and later to Patrick Barnwall, evidently of Old English backgrounds and Catholics and probably friars continued in residence there or nearby.

19.   Fenning, 87–9.

CHAPTER TWENTY-SIX

Vicar Apostolic James Fallon

After the death of Eoghan Ó hAirt in 1603 Rome appointed no successor, and in fact more than a century was to elapse before another Catholic bishop was to take up his ministry in Achonry. The reason why Rome was reluctant to appoint bishops to some dioceses, like Achonry, was their unwillingness to provoke the anger of the English crown and avoid more intense persecution of Catholics there. There was always the hope that the Stuarts might revert to Catholicism, which they eventually did. It was not such a vague aspiration considering that James I was the son of Mary, Queen of Scots, who was imprisoned and martyred for her faith.

No Bishop

Moves were afoot in the 1630s to have a bishop appointed to Achonry. The dean, Dominic French, and thirteen parish priests in Achonry petitioned Rome in September 1630 to appoint Anthony Lynch as their bishop. His four brothers and many relations had the means 'to maintain his episcopal status'. Called Anthony de Santa Maria, Lynch was a Dominican and prior in Galway. He was then sixty years of age, which was deemed his sole disadvantage, and had lived a fairly eventful life. He was professed in 1605 in his order's house of Sao Domingos in Lisbon, after being some time in the city as a merchant. A master of theology, he had completed his studies in Lisbon and Salamanca and, according to the Dominican master-general, Nicholas Ridolfi, was fluent in Irish, English, French, Spanish and Portuguese and, presumably, Latin. A fine public speaker and controversialist, he had served on the Irish mission for about twenty-two years and by 'his almost Pauline courageous and vigorous style of preaching confirmed innumerable Catholics in their faith' and was instrumental in converting many heretics. On a voyage to Spain 'obediently following the orders of his superiors', about 1615, he was captured by Turkish pirates and imprisoned in Morroco where he suffered torture, squalor and hunger.

Anthony de Santa Maria OP

Many recommendations were made on his behalf to Rome, including by Archbishop Malachy O'Queally of Tuam, Bishops Richard Archer of Limerick, Maurice O'Hurley of Emly, Boetius MacEgan of Elphin, Ross MacGeoghegan OP of Kildare and the vicars-apostolic of Clonfert, Kilmacduagh and Killala as well as his confrère, Daniel of the Cross O'Crean, vicar provincial of the order.[1]

1.   APF, *SOCG*, vol. 14, ff.25r, 26r, 27v, 28v, 122r, 123r, 124r, 125r, 126r, 127r; vol. 135, ff.204rv; vol. 140, f.14r; vol. 295, ff.90rv, 91rv, 92rv.

Nicholas Lynch OP   Another Dominican, also from the Galway priory and also a member of the Lynch family, and a kinsman, Nicholas, was also proposed for Achonry.[2] It was Nicholas who had secured Anthony's release from his Moroccan jail when he paid his ransom in 1621. As provincial of the Irish Dominicans he was instrumental in the establishment of their college in Lisbon. The petitions in favour of his appointment to Achonry are undated but must pre-date July 1634 as he died in Rome during that month.[3] A Franciscan, Francis Farrell, then in their college in Prague was also proposed as bishop.[4]

James Fallon   There were about fifteen bishops in Ireland in 1634, five in the province of Armagh and a similar number in Cashel, while Dublin had three. Tuam had only two in spite of a recent decree by the Congregation of Propaganda which proposed that each province should have three plus the archbishop.[5] Most of the other dioceses had vicars-apostolic. Rome appointed one to administer Achonry on 13 January 1631 and the diocese was to be governed by such for the rest of the century. The first was James Fallon, a priest of the diocese of Tuam, who had studied at the Irish College in Lisbon where he was a colleague of Luke Wadding. Fallon took his doctorate in France.[6] Two of his brothers, Gregory and Cornelius, were also priests and both wrote to Rome on his behalf.

Fallon's Report   Boetius MacEgan informed Ludovico Ludovisi, cardinal-protector of Ireland in October 1630, that he was unable to make his *ad limina* visit to Rome because of the expense, as well as persecution. He nominated James Fallon, then vicar general of Achonry, on 20 October 1630 as his procurator and agent in Rome. Fallon acted in the same capacity two years later for Malachy O'Queally of Tuam as well as the vicars-apostolic of Clonfert and Kilmacduagh, but due 'to the different dangers of the time and the journey he could not get past Paris' and returned home.[7] However, he made a report dated 27 November 1630 on the unwieldy state of some of the 'anciently divided' parishes in Connacht. 'At present woods, mountains and swollen rivers, render the ministry of the sacraments to parishioners in cases of necessity, very difficult.'

He asked Rome to give the local ordinaries power to make new unions and divisions with the agreement of the clergy and temporal rulers. The matter was assigned to four cardinals and it was decided to write to the Archbishop of

2.   Ibid., vol. 14, ff.32r, 33rv, 34r, 35rv, 36v.
3.   Flynn, *Irish Dominicans*, 115.
4.   n.d. (*c*.1630–40), APF, *SOCG*, vol. 140, f.14r.
5.   APF, *SOCG*, vol. 14, ff.25r, 26r, 27v, 28v.
6.   *SOCG*, vol. 135, f.294rv. S. Br. 770 f.82, Eubel.
7.   Moran, *Spicilegium Ossoriense*, i, 170, 178.

Tuam and the Bishop of Elphin to convene a meeting with vicars general and vicars apostolic, barons and lords, as well as religious orders who have monasteries in these parishes, to seek their consent or at least non-opposition to the changes.[8]

Fallon attended the Synod of Tuam in Galway and signed the statutes together with O'Queally and MacEgan in December 1632.[9] There were forty-four statutes, mostly concerning priests. Those addicted to gambling on games of dice or cards were bound to give back their winnings to the losers. They should avoid taverns and markets (business houses), the company of women of dubious reputation, under pain of suspension, banquets with both sexes, carrying a woman with him on his horse, debates with Protestants or attending funerals uninvited outside the parish. Priests on their travels should not associate or dine with vagabonds and idlers and should only have one horse and two servants at most. They should not keep (hunting) dogs, nor have long hair or beards and should confess to a confrère every fortnight.

Synod of Tuam 1632

Every priest should have a missal, breviary, catechism, manual for sacraments, collection of cases of conscience, silver pyx and chalice, soutane, surplice and four-cornered biretta. They should not add to or subtract anything from the Mass and avoid exaggerated gestures during the consecration of the host and the chalice. They were to recite the litanies of the Blessed Virgin Mary or of the saints on feastdays for the successful government of the church and the health 'of our most serene king and queen'. They should keep three books in which the names of those baptised, married and dead were registered.

Parish priests moving from place to place in the parish should sprinkle with holy water all the family in the houses where they spend the night and teach them the Lord's Prayer, the Ten Commandments, the precepts of the Church and the Creed, and similarly the people on Sundays and feastdays. They should not seek or demand from parishioners more than a modest subsistence, not more than two shillings for administering the sacrament of matrimony and one shilling for baptism, fourpence a year from each couple and nothing from the poor. They should take care to support the poor in their parish, excluding outsiders, and all those seeking alms, feigning insanity or deformity should be driven out. Informers should be excluded from the sacraments.

Modest Subsistence

There was a certain amount of feuding between the parish clergy and friars, particularly over funeral offerings. Spontaneous offerings were made on the

Funeral Offerings

8.   *SOCG*, vol. 100, ff.322r, 328v, vol. 294, f.194r, vol. 390, ff.478r, 483v, *Acta*, vol. 7, ff.180v, 181r, 259v, 363v, 364r.
9.   APF, *SC Irlanda*, vol. 1, ff242r, 247v; *SOCG*, vol. 100, ff322r, 328v, vol. 294, ff174rv, 194r, 201r–206v, 208r–211v; Renehan, *Collections*, 491–506, Moran, *Archbishops of Dublin, Coll. Hib.*, nos 6–7, 50–1.

occasions of funerals and these formed a sizeable part of a priest's income. As people often chose to be buried in monasteries, the friars claimed at least a portion of these offerings. The Synod of Tuam, following a decision by Rome, decreed that parish clergy had a precedence over friars with regard to funerals even when the burial took place in a monastery. The offerings were to be split evenly between the friars and the parish priest, with a quarter to the bishop. Peace was to be preserved between the two clergies until Rome made a final decision about the offerings.

Clash with the Cistercians

Fallon had already clashed with the Cistercians in 1630 when he was still vicar-general of Achonry.[10] He complained to the vicar general of the Cistercians in Ireland about one of his monks, Edmund Creavy in Boyle Abbey who was 'illiterate and undisciplined, exercising quasi hereditary rights'. Creavy's father and grandfather had been monks in the monastery before him and he himself 'begot sixteen children by different women'. He administered sacraments without permission, divorcing those legitimately married and giving dispensations. The Archbishop of Dublin deputed a Cistercian, Dominican and Franciscan to examine the case and Creavy was suspended.

Conflict with Urlaur

The Dominicans in Urlaur claimed the right to act as parish priests within the four quarters belonging to the friary. This caused a conflict between the prior, Hugh Grogan, and James Fallon, now vicar apostolic. Fallon complained to Rome that Grogan was baptising and assisting at marriages even though forbidden by the parish priest of Kilmovee.[11] Grogan claimed that he had been given permission to do so by Daniel of the Cross O'Crean, provincial of the Dominicans and Fallon's complaints to O'Crean fell on deaf ears.[12]

Fast and Abstinence

Milk products were permitted during Lent except for Ash Wednesday, Spy Wednesday and Good Friday (1631). The Lenten fast and the Friday abstinence could be exchanged, as granted by a papal indult, for other good works of satisfactory value (1640). These good works were specified in 1658 as giving alms to prisoners or the invalid poor and in 1660 a further good work was added, public prayers 'in this calamitous time' for God's mercy for Charles II that he may be preserved safe'.

Feastdays

Apart from Sundays there were a considerable number of feastdays of obligation, when people were bound to attend Mass and avoid servile work. The latter insured that serfs and labourers were given each year a minimum number (eighty-two) of holidays, a word obviously derived from 'holy days'.

10. *SOCG*, vol. 390, ff.480rv.
11. *SOCG*, vol. 14, ff.6rv, 7v.
12. Fenning, 'The Dominicans and Propaganda Fide 1622–1668' in *Archivium Fratrum Praedicatorum*, 41, 284–5.

There were nine feasts of the Lord including the Circumcision, Epiphany (6 January), Easter Monday and Tuesday, finding of the Holy Cross, Ascension, Monday and Tuesday of Pentecost week, Corpus Christi (6 June), and Christmas day. Five feasts of Our Lady included Purification (2 February), Annunciation (25 March), Assumption (15 August), Birth of Blessed Virgin, and Immaculate Conception (9 December). Apart from the feasts of All Saints (1 November), the Holy Innocents (28 December) and the patrons of parochial churches, as well as the two Irish saints, Brigid and Patrick, there were sixteen feasts of individual saints including the apostles, Philip and James (2 May), Peter and Paul (29 June), Thomas (3 July), James (25 July), Bartholomew (24 August) and Andrew (30 November) and Simon and Jude (28 October), the four evangelists, Matthew (21 September), Mark, Luke (18 October), and John (27 December). Others included the Birth of John the Baptist (24 June), Laurence (10 August), Michael the Archangel, Martin (11 November) and Stephen (26 December).

Some picture of the conditions of Catholics in Achonry can be gleaned from the 1637 reports on Elphin and Tuam, two dioceses bordering Achonry.[13] Boetius MacEgan described parish priests in Elphin celebrating Mass 'in secret and wooded places' and teaching parishioners Christian doctrine, depending on their charity for the wherewithal to live. His own plight was similar, 'fleeing from home to home, from mountain to wood, following in the footsteps of our Saviour, led by his Spirit, having no permanent home to lay his head'. Bishops or priests could not turn to the laity for shelter and support for this would have exposed their hosts to too much risk. They lived in huts, in bogs, in woods or in the mountains. However, as a general rule the priests moved about by night, saying Mass in some guarded retreat at or before daybreak. It was certainly in this decade that the tradition of the 'Mass-rock' stamped itself on the Irish experience.[14]

Elphin Report 1637

Boetius urged the Pope not to promote anyone to the episcopal status unless reliable and trustworthy witnesses could assure that he had powerful lay friends 'to support, cherish and nourish him'. The laity were threatened with huge penalties if they did not conform and accept the king as the supreme head of the Church. All youths and scholars were to be educated by Protestant schoolmasters and all had to attend Protestant services on Sundays. Those who contracted marriage in the presence of a Catholic priest were fined at least one mark as were those whose children were baptised by a priest. In future, nobody could be buried in a monastery cemetery 'where almost all the graves

Pressure on Laity

---

13. J. Hagan, 'Miscellanea Vaticano-Hibernica', *Arch. Hib.*, v, 92–102.
14. Corish, *The Catholic Community*, 49.

of this country lie'. All the young have to be brought to Protestant 'pseudobishops' to be confirmed. In spite of this, MacEgan had confirmed 'many thousands of all ages' and ordained at least two hundred priests, both regulars and seculars. Probably, some of these were from Achonry.

Priest Numbers   There were eleven parish priests in Achonry in 1630, as well as a dean. There were, of course, religious priests as well: five Dominicans as well as four or five novices in Urlaur and probably a few other friars in Straide. A complete list of the guardians in the Franciscan friary in Ballymote in the second half of the seventeenth century exists, and they must have had a number of friars under their care.[15] According to MacEgan there were only thirteen parish priests in Elphin before he was appointed, now there were forty-two. (Bishops tended to blow their own horns in their reports to Rome.) There were no religious living there prior to MacEgan. Now there were two convents of religious, one Dominican and the other Franciscan 'living in caves and woods and labouring strenuously in the Lord's vineyard, as often as they could'. In Tuam there were fifty-seven parish priests compared to only thirty before Malachy O'Queally was appointed. He travelled throughout the diocese at least once a year and like MacEgan, as there were only two bishops in the province, he confirmed 'many thousands of all ages' in his own and other dioceses. Things grew steadily worse in the second half of the seventeenth century.

Dominic de Burgo   Petitions were sent in 1640 by Conte di S. Albano and the Marchioness of
OP   Winchester to Rome in favour of Dominic de Burgo OP, to be made Bishop of Achonry or Killala.[16] He was the Irish Dominican procurator in Rome and was sent to England in 1639 to resolve disputes among Dominicans there. He compiled a directory early in January 1637 of Connacht clergy actively involved in the mission there. Urlaur and Straide were among Dominican houses with resident communities.[17] This compiler may have been the same Dominick Burke who was prior of Athenry in 1642 and chaplain to the Earl of Clanrickard. He acted as envoy to the Confederation of Kilkenny where he dealt with the Supreme Council and the nuncio, Rinuccini.[18]

Louis Dillon   After a lapse of almost forty years Rome appointed a bishop to Achonry.
OFM   Louis Dillon, a member of the Friars Minor of St Francis of the Strict

15. Giblin, *Liber Lovaniensis, SOCG*, vol. 294, f.103v.
16. 5 Oct. 1640, Rossetti to Barberini, Mss Barberini Latini, 8648 (part 1) ff.218r–219v [mf pos. 876 NLI].
17. APF, *SOCG*, 135, ff204rv, 209rv, 140, ff1v–2rv. B. Jennings, 'Miscellaneous Documents, ii, 1625–1640 in *Arch. Hib.*, xiv (1949), 21–2, B. Millet, 'Catalogue of Irish Material in vols 132–9, 140–3 in SOCG in Propaganda Archives' in *Coll. Hib.*, no. 12 (1969) 30, 13 (1970) 22.
18. Flynn, *Irish Dominicans*, 237, 269–70, 285, 303.

Observance, was then about forty years old, a priest and a master of theology. Edward – Louis was his religious name – was born into the Dillon family of Costello-Gallen.[19] Eubel could not find this appointment in the Vatican register of consistorial acts or among the Apostolic briefs. *[Haec promotio nullibi invenitur in actis consistorialibus in Tabulario Vaticano asservatis neque eam invenire potui inter brevia apostolica. A tergo folii 282 inveni pro eccl. Achaden. in Hibernia a.1641: 12 Aug. praeconisatur et 16 Sept. expeditur. Post Dillon eccl. Achaden. regitur a vicariis sed nihil de eis usque ad an 1667 invenitur in brevibus Apostolicis. Eubel.]* He was a former definitor of the Irish Franciscans and in 1634 Guardian of St Anthony's College in Louvain.

In June of that year, some of his family, as well as Baron John Taaffe of Ballymote and Ulick Burke, wrote recommending Louis to Cardinal Barberini and a month later to the Pope himself. Achonry lacked the means for the decent support of a bishop. 'We are the top people of the diocese,' they informed him, 'with lands, properties and possessions and are well considered by the royal magistrates and governors and we promise to protect and defend him and maintain him as long as he lives.' At the same time the president, provincial and definitors of the Irish Augustinians, assembled in Ballyhaunis, wrote to Rome recommending Louis for a bishopric. Ballyhaunis was in the heart of Costello-Gallen territory of the Dillons, and not surprisingly, 'a postulation was submitted for their inspection'. *'Top People of the Diocese'*

Malachy O'Queally of Tuam and Boetius MacEgan of Elphin wrote from Galway in September and again in December 1639 to Cardinal Barberini, pointing out that they had written often for about eight years 'at the request and ardent desire of the nobles and people of Achonry'. They informed him that a great part of the diocese was possessed by his brothers, nephews and close relatives. They wrote again from Galway at the end of July of the following year, probably at the close of the Synod of Tuam and this time they were joined by the vicars apostolic of Kilmacduagh, Clonfert, Killala, and James Fallon of Achonry: *Supported by Tuam and Elphin*

> In time of persecution, Edward's father, sent his children at great inconvenience and expense to be educated in France and Flanders and also his daughters who with the priests founded a convent of Saint Clare where there are now sixty nuns. The sons entered the Franciscans and recovered many of the convents which had been suppressed and founded new ones. The family today has twelve religious.

19.   ASV, Mss Barberini Latini 2887, f.279r [mf pos 871 NLI].

Luke Wadding's Influence

By now certain people were working hard in London to secure Achonry for Dillon. An Irish missionary Dominican there complained to Francesco Ingoli, secretary of Propaganda, that the Irish church was controlled by the powerful Luke Wadding, himself a Franciscan, 'who supplies all information and makes all recommendations on provision to Irish dioceses'. Wadding, he believed, was not impartial, and 'the secular clergy and the Franciscans are trying to suppress the Dominicans in Ireland'. At a particular meeting on Irish affairs on 4 March 1641, the cardinals recommended Louis Dillon and he was appointed Bishop of Achonry the following September. He died about a month later, before he was consecrated and on 2 November recommendations for his successor were already being sent to Rome.[20]

Fallon Excommunicated

He and his counterpart in Killala, Andrew Lynch, were excommunicated because of a decision taken against the Warden of Galway, and the Archbishop of Tuam – Malachy O'Queally had been killed in 1645 – asked Rome to depose them but Cardinal Barberini recommended that nothing be done.[21] Two Dominicans setting out from Rome for Ireland *c*.1654 sought faculties to absolve ten clerics, including James Fallon, from the excommunication imposed by the Nuncio six years earlier.[22] The ten comprised three seculars, three Franciscans, and one Dominican, one Augustinian and one Jesuit.

New Dean

Following the death of Boetius MacEgan of Elphin, Cornelius and Gregory Fallon petitioned Rome in 1649 and 1650 to have James appointed to replace him as 'he has many relations and friends in that diocese'.[23] James wrote to Rome from Galway at the end of June 1650 asking Rome to appoint Daniel Nelly as dean to replace Brian Ó hUiginn.[24] The deanery was valued at one hundred ducats.[25]

Tuam and Kilfenora

James Fallon was still in charge of the diocese but also of Tuam and Kilfenora at the end of August 1655, where 'he has remained with his flock'. He sought from Rome 'in the current cruel persecution', the usual faculties to consecrate chalices, bless the holy oils and dispense those wishing to marry related within

20. *SOCG*, vol. 139, ff283rv, 284rv, 140, ff10rv, 52rv, 53v, 205rv, 206rv, 213v, 207r, 208r, 209rv, 210rv, 211v, 212v, 214v, 215rv, 218r, 216rv, 217v (see *Spicilegium Ossoriense*, i, 249–50): vol. 295, ff. 2rv, 3v; *Barberini Latini*, 2287; *Hierarchia Catholica*, iv, 66.
21. *SOCG*, vol. 403, ff494, 503, *Acta*, vol. 15, ff33v, 34r.
22. *SOCG*, vol. 298, ff287r, 298v.
23. *SOCG*, vol. 298, ff175r, 758r.
24. He may have been the same as Daniel Nellis, vicar of the church in Galway in July 1667, Millet, *Calendar of Scritture riferite nei congressi, Irlanda* f 268r in *Coll. Hib.*, nos 6 and 7, 87: Godfrey O'Donel, a Tuam priest, had been appointed by the Confederation on 23 Oct. 1649.
25. Brendan Jennings, 'Ecclesiastical appointments in Ireland, 1643–1649', in *Coll. Hib.*, no. 2, 56.

the second degrees of consanguinity and affinity. He asked for these faculties also for priests deported to the Barbados. This petition was probably presented in 1656 and came before a general meeting of Propaganda on 11 June 1657 where his request was granted.[26]

At the same time his brother, Cornelius,[27] wrote from Madrid on behalf of James 'who is labouring in that distressed vineyard', describing 'the miserable state of the poor little sheep and their priests'.[28] James was given care of the collegiate church of Galway, as well as Achonry and of Tuam itself when the archbishop was imprisoned and later exiled.

The lives of priests became extremely furtive and they could no longer move from house to house as it would expose these families to severe reprisals. They lived in huts in the bogs, in the wood, or in the mountains. A contemporary described Fallon's hideout: 'He lived day and night in the open-air in a little peasant's hut at the foot of a rock. The hut was covered with leaves intertwined with twigs but even from this refuge he was forced to fly when goats had eaten the leaves.'[29]

Fallon 'was captured by heretics in Iarchonnacht probably in 1658 and despoiled of his copious library so that not even his breviary was left to him'. By then he was paralysed and deputed two priests, Phelim O'Hara and Hilary Conry (Elphin) to replace him and they signed the statutes in January 1660 in place of the imprisoned Fallon. Both of them were described as 'not very learned'.[30] Not surprisingly, the statutes of the Synod of Tuam mentioned the 'calamitous experience' of the Irish church. 'Imprisoned priests should be ransomed or at least supported in prison and their sufferings alleviated.' Rome should be informed about the state of Ireland and 'the daily calamities and persecutions, so many and so serious that they can scarcely be comprehended in writing'. The synod instructed their agent in Rome to keep the Pope informed and exhort him to fill the vacancies caused by those abroad for studies or in exile to be filled by suitable candidates with a preference, other things being equal, for those who 'endured chains, imprisonment, and persecution, so that nobody can complain that new men were preferred over those who bore the burden of fire of the present day'.[31]

'Distressed Vineyard'

Fallon's Hut

Imprisoned

26. *Fondo di Vienna*, vol. 13, ff.261r, 262v; *Atti* (Acts), vol. 26, 97–8: see Benignus Millet, 'Calendar of vol. 13' in *Coll. Hib.*, no. 25 (1983), 40.
27. A Cornelius Fallon was appointed chantor or precepter of Achonry in November 1644 and of Killala in May of the following year; see Jennings, 22.
28. *SOCG*, vol. 298, ff.350r, 363v, 969r.
29. *De Praes. Hib.*, ii, 342–3.
30. *SC Irlanda*, vol. 5, f.289r, *Coll. Hib.*, nos 15, 27 and 28, 105–6.
31. *SC Irlanda*, vol. 1, ff.242r–247v; *Fondo di Vienna*, vol. 14, f.237rv.

Deported to Barbados

A determined effort was made to expel priests from Ireland under penalty of death and in 1653 over a thousand bishops, priests and nuns fled to the continent. Priests held in Galway were ordered in June 1655 to ship themselves from there at their own expense to some foreign parts friendly to England before 10 June. The only ones spared were priests who 'by reason of extream old age or other infirmities of body cannot be put to sea without peril of their lives'.

Imprisoned on Aran Islands

This is probably why James Fallon was not transported but confined in various prisons in Galway, then moved to Inishboffin in 1658 and finally to the Aran Islands where he spent some years. Between 1655 and 1657 the government shipped priests, friars and schoolteachers to Barbados, holding 'popish priests and other dangerous persons' as prisoners in Inishboffin and the Aran Islands. The authorities allotted sixpence a day in December 1658 to pay the priests for building cabins on Inishboffin and Aran to house themselves. Priests were not welcome in the West Indies because they were, like Fallon, old and in ill-health. Planters preferred African slaves and regarded Irish priests as troublemakers especially among Irish Catholics there. Four priests were ordered to leave the Barbados immediately on arrival. Not all the priests were transported to the Barbados. The governor of Galway was ordered in June 1655 to ship thirty priests to Spain, Portugal or Flanders. The Archbishop of Tuam and Bishop Francis Kirwan were freed on their own security provided that within two months they transported themselves to France 'and not returne againe into this Dominion'.[32] Finally he was released with other captured priests, 'long after' the inauguration of Charles II in 1660. James Fallon died on 12 August 1662.[33]

32. 'Commonwealth Records' in *Arch. Hib.*, vi, 179, 197–9; vii, vol. 7, 34, 38–9; Kevin MacGrath 'Irish Priests transported under the Commonwealth' in *Arch. Hib.*, 92–5: *De Praes. Hib.*, ii, 342–3; Giblin, *Liber Lovaniensis*, 39.
33. *De Praes. Hib.*, ii, 343.

CHAPTER TWENTY-SEVEN

1641 Rebellion

There was huge discontent among the Old Irish, particularly in Ulster, where *Irish Discontent*
they had lost a large part of their hereditary lands following the plantation
there. Hopes of undoing this plantation remained very much alive, fomented
largely by priests returning from the Continent as well as contacts with soldiers in the Spanish service, like Eoghan Ruadh Ó Néill, who carved out for
himself a substantial military reputation in Flanders. These hopes soon evolved
into a conspiracy and a rebellion was planned for 23 October 1641. Within
two days much of the centre of Ulster was in rebel hands and all over the north
groups were rising against the settlers.

Many murders were committed and these were greatly exaggerated by *Protestant*
Protestant propagandists into a massacre which became deeply embedded in *Propagandists*
the Protestant consciousness and was later the justification of vicious reprisals
against Catholics. The actual figures of those murdered vary between 4,000
and 8,000. The Ulster rebels captured Dundalk at the end of October and a
month later defeated a government force sent to relieve Drogheda. This was
decisive in drawing in the Old English of the Pale on the side of the insurg-
ents who had been teetering on the brink. This took place early in December
1641 and notice of it was posted in Connacht towns including Sligo.

The rising quickly spread to the neighbouring county of Leitrim and fears *The Friar and*
were growing that Sligo would be next. The first inkling of the storm about to *the Minister*
erupt came from Coolany. A Franciscan friar, Brian Mac (Kiggan?), Guardian
of the friary of Creevelea near Dromahair in County Leitrim, preached an
inflammatory sermon rousing Catholics to action. Word reached William
Browne in Kilvarnet, worried not least because he had a couple of hundred
sheep grazing there on the lower slopes of the Ox Mountains. Browne wrote
to the friar asking to meet him. McKiggen came to Kilvarnet on 2 November
1641 where he refused to retract and asserted that the blood spilt by the
Binghams in Connacht would soon be revenged. When Browne pointed out
that Catholics had fared badly in previous rebellions, the friar retorted: 'Ah!
Sir, it will not be so with you now as it was in those days.' Catholics were all
united now. Many settlers there, including William Oliphant's wife, Jane,
and their seven children, took refuge in the Crofton home in Templehouse
and other safe areas.

Preventative Measures

The first reaction of the landed gentry in County Sligo was to take steps to prevent a rising in their county. A meeting of the principal landowners in Ballysadare was called by Andrew O'Crean, the high sheriff, where they agreed to prevent outsiders, particularly from County Leitrim, fomenting trouble in the county, with a close watch on unemployed militia in their own areas. The Ballysadare meeting had little or no effect and soldiers continued to attack and plunder English settlers. Another meeting was held in Ballysadare early in December resulting in a new situation, with the principal gentlemen, such as the Taaffes, O'Connor Sligo and Mac Donnchadhas, partaking in the siege of Sligo.

Templehouse Captured

This was followed by the siege and capture after ten weeks of Templehouse, the home of William Crofton, and the Protestant refugees there, by among others, John O'Crean and members of the Taaffe, Ó hEadhra and Mac Donnchadha families. Protestant clergy were especially targeted. Vicar William Oliphant of Ballysadare and Enagh, a Scotsman, was stripped and hanged and afterwards 'they tyed him to a horse's tayle and draged him about the streets in a most inhumane and barbarous manner'. His widow, Christian Oliphant and her three small children 'were all stript naked, beinge a week before Candlemas, in the extremity of the winter, which so penetrated the infants that since they have all dyed'.[1] On the following day, another minister, George Wray, was stabbed while being conveyed to Ballymote where he died two days later. Jane Brown, wife of William of Kilvarnet, registrar of Killala and Achonry, was stripped before the gates of Templehouse and, covered with a few rags, went begging from door to door. Three of her seven children died, her eldest son Frederick, from drowning in the River Bonnet near Dromahair, Sarah and Roger from starvation and exposure. She 'did begg up and downe the Countie of Sligo a quarter of a year at least and had been starved and killed for not going to Mass had not ffarrell O'Gara esquire charitablie preserved and relieved this Deponent and her said children for a long tyme ...' Surprisingly, the name of Feargal Ó Gadhra of Coolavin was included among sixteen men in County Sligo who were to be arrested because allegedly they had committed 'massacres, outrages and roberies'. The Confederation of Kilkenny issued instructions early in 1643 to Brian MacDonagh and Luke Taaffe to carry out the arrests.[2]

Cruelty of Catholic Rebels

Ó Gadhra's humane action was in marked contrast to the vicious cruelty of the Catholic rebels, which their leaders made no effort to restrain. Most of the depositions named John O'Crean as the principal leader and others were Brian

1. Deposition of Mrs Christian Oliphant, 3 February 1645, in Wood-Martin, *Sligo* ii, 217; deposition of Jane Boswell in ibid., 232–4.
2. Order 12 march 1643, printed in *Another extract of several letters from Ireland*, 48–9.

Ó hEadhra and Aodh and Cormac Oge Mac Donnchadha. They swore that they would spare the lives and goods of William Crofton and other refugees in his house before he agreed to surrender and would convey them safely to Ballymote, nine days after the surrender. Crofton had specifically asked that Irriel alias Oliver Ó hEadhra of Tullyhugh, then about thirty years old, accept his surrender and wrote to him to come Templehouse. When he arrived he found that O'Crean, Ó hEadhra and Mac Donnchadha had seized and carried away Crofton's goods and despoiled Templehouse and left again taking no part in the affair.[3]

Sligo was besieged in December and among the leaders were members of the Taaffe, O'Connor Sligo and Mac Donnchadha families. Following the siege many settlers left town but some thirty-eight remained; they were put into Sligo jail, allegedly for their own safety. On the night of 13 January they were savagely attacked and most of them murdered 'save two or three, that in that hurley-burley gott out from among them and gott away'.[4] A meeting was held in Holy Cross Abbey that day attended by Tadhg O'Connor Sligo and members of his family as well as some of the O'Ruairc of Leitrim. Some remained on drinking afterwards and later that evening attacked the jail. They were named later as two brothers of O'Connor Sligo, members of the Ó hAirt and three or four butchers who lived in the town.

Sligo Murders

There was only one deposition made concerning an incident in the Mayo side of the diocese, probably because of the relative scarcity of Protestants in that region. Fifty-five-year-old John Borrell 'of the Abbey of Strade' alleged that he and his wife were stripped and robbed.[5]

By the beginning of 1642 Sligo was in rebellion. The Catholic Old English there, such as the Taaffes of Ballymote, played a leading role, following the lead taken a month earlier by their counterparts in the Pale. The Protestant New English lay low, barricading themselves in their castles, fearful of losing their newly acquired estates while some even sided with the rebels for the same reason. Others like O'Connor Sligo, Cormac Ó hEadhra and smaller landlords joined the rebellion because they had lost so much land in the previous decades. Some Old Irish families who had managed to hold on to their estates were slow to join, such as Fearghal Ó Gadhra of Coolavin and the Ó Dubhda. Fearghal Ó Gadhra had Old English connections, married to a daughter of Viscount John Taaffe and his wife, Anne Dillon.

Old English Involvement

3. Depositions of Oliver O'Hara, ibid., 237, Ann Loftus and Rose Ennis, 16 April 1653, ibid., 239–40 and 240–1; deposition of Jane Brown, 8 January 1644, ibid., 204–5.
4. Examination of John Harrison, 23 April 1644, Wood-Martin, *Sligo* ii, 210–11.
5. Depositions, Mayo, TCD.com.

*'For God, King
and Country'*

They only threw in their lot with the rebels after the Confederation of Kilkenny was established in October 1642. Prompted by the clergy, a central organisation was set up in Kilkenny to direct the war with the motto 'Ireland united for God, king and country.' By then Eoghan Ruadh Ó Néill, Thomas Preston and other professional Irish soldiers had returned from Flanders to offer their services. Civil war had finally erupted in England between Charles I and parliament. In the summer of that year a meeting of the principal landlords of Connacht was held in Ballinrobe where a provincial council was set up. County Sligo was represented there by Tadhg Óg Ó hUiginn and Tadhg Riabhach Ó Dubhda. Ó hUiginn, son of the famous poet, Tadhg Dall, was one of the ten largest Gaelic landlords in County Sligo where he served as sheriff in 1634. Patrick Plunkett of Markree, son of Sir Christopher Plunkett of County Meath, and Luke Taaffe, brother of Viscount Theobald of Corran, MP for County Sligo in 1639, who had gone to England to fight for Charles I, were chosen to represent County Sligo at Kilkenny. The king also maintained an army, mostly based in Dublin under the command of the Earl of Ormond while the English parliament also kept an army there though their main focus was on the defeat of the king in England.

Catholic Split

The situation was further confused by a split among the Catholic Confederates, despite their motto 'Ireland united for God, king and country'. The Old English were prepared to accept moderate terms with Charles while the Irish were determined to hold out for nothing less than full recognition of Catholicism and the restoration of confiscated lands. They were led by the clergy, Eoghan Ruadh and Archbishop Rinucinni, who was appointed papal nuncio to the Confederation in 1645. No agreement proved possible. Despite Eogan Ruadh's brilliant victory at Benburb in 1646, the war dragged on.

Meanwhile, Fallon continued to govern the diocese. He attended the Confederation of Kilkenny on 6 February 1646 when he signed, with thirteen bishops including the archbishops of Armagh, Dublin and Cashel and a number of other ecclesiastics, a statement supporting Rinuccini, and another on 30 August 1648 signed by Rinuccini and sixteen other ecclesiastics. He sent a letter, together with the Archbishop of Dublin, the Bishop of Clonfert and the Dean of Tuam, from Galway on 12 February 1651 to the nuncio. Again in Galway on 23 August 1650 he confirmed his consent to a declaration made by the Archbishop of Armagh and a large number of clergy at a meeting made at Jacobopolim (Jamestown) on the sixth of the same month and consented to their sentence of excommunication. He was the third named, after the Archbishop of Dublin and the Bishop of Clonfert, on a statement signed at a meeting in Loughrea.[6]

6.   *Commentarius Rinuccianus*, ii, 222; iii, 498, iv, 339–41, 425, 427–8, 444, 492, 493.

On his return from England, Theobald Taaffe attended the general assembly *Theobald Taaffe*
in Kilkenny where he sided with the Ormondist faction who had split with
the clericalists, one of whom described him as 'a seeming Catholicke'. The
supreme council appointed him commander of the army of Connacht in 1644
and after some early successes, he suffered several reverses and was replaced.
Back in Kilkenny, he kept in close contact with Ormond, Charles I's deputy
in Dublin and it was alleged that he kept him informed on 'all the intelligence
and secret intentions' of the confederate Catholics. When Ormond surrendered
Dublin and left Ireland, Taaffe with his kinsmen, Viscount Dillon and Sir
James Dillon, made up with the confederate Catholics and in 1647 was
appointed general of the army of Munster. This decision of the supreme council
was due to the leader of the Ormondist faction, Viscount Muskerry and
represented a defeat for Rinucinni. Taaffe's military incompetence was evident
in his defeat near Mallow by Lord Inchiquin, leader of the parliamentary forces
in 1647. The war dragged on for two more years and finally came to an end
with the end of the civil war in England and the trial and execution of Charles
I in 1649.

After the king's execution, the English parliament turned its attention to *Oliver Cromwell*
Ireland. Oliver Cromwell landed in Dublin in 1649 at the head of a formid-
able Puritan army of Ironsides, intent not only on conquest of the country but
also on revenge for Catholic massacres at Templehouse and Sligo and elsewhere.
'Cromwell came over, and like a lightning passed through the land.'[7] Rinuccini
published his excommunication against all members of the Supreme Council
of the Confederation of Kilkenny who supported a truce with Inchiquin.
Ultimately, twelve bishops out of twenty-five agreed with the truce. Rinucinni
retired to Galway from where he sailed back to Italy on 23 February 1649. By
now everything had changed.

Connacht experienced major changes as part of the Cromwellian settlement *Settlement*
and this included Achonry.[8] A system of new forts was constructed, one of
these in Bellahy called Fort Cromwell, built in 1555 while the existing garrison
at Ballymote was strengthened. Cromwellian soldiers were rewarded with
confiscated land in Connacht like those in the regiment of Charles Coote,
brother of Richard of Collooney, who got land in Sligo. Charles was made
president of Connacht, was one of the commissioners supervising the
transplantation scheme, and could look after his own soldiers.

---

7.   Bishop Nicholas French of Ferns, qtd in Corish, *The Catholic Community in the Seventeenth
      and Eighteenth Centuries*, 46.
8.   Much of this summary account has been gleaned from O'Dowd, *Power, Politics and Land*,
      131–48.

New Landlords   The baronies of Leyny, Corran and Coolavin were included in the general transplantation to Connacht. New landlords, the Gores, Ormsbys, Cootes, Kings, Jones and Nicholsons, were English and Scottish soldiers who had fought for Cromwell. They intermarried and consolidated their estates and insured that Sligo would become the most Protestant county in Connacht and one of the most sectarian counties outside Ulster. Catholic landlords, like Ó Gadhra of Coolavin, were dispossessed but seemed to have remained on as tenants.

CHAPTER TWENTY-EIGHT

Restoration

Another land settlement followed the restoration of Charles II in 1660 which left the situation in Connacht largely unchanged. Catholic landownership in the province fell from 80 per cent to 50 per cent. Charles rewarded Theobald Taaffe, his comrade in exile, for his loyalty by creating him Earl of Carlingford and restoring him about 11,000 acres, much of it around Ballymote, as well as the estates of his kinsmen in County Louth. The Taaffes remained staunchly Catholic and his father sent Francis, his son born in Ballymote in 1639, to a Jesuit college in Moravia. Later Francis followed a military career in the Austrian empire and was made a count, becoming a field marshal and was said to be 'probably the most prominent Irishman of his generation in mainland Europe'. Following his Franciscan connections, he was instrumental in the founding of the Irish Franciscan college at Boulay.[1] A descendant, Count Edward Taaffe, was the Austrian prime minister in the late nineteenth century. Francis Taaffe of Killedan House also belonged to the same family. His mother, Honoria Lynch of Galway, as Francis himself, were patrons of the blind poet, Anthony Raftery, and were recorded in a couplet in his *Cill Éadain*:

> *Sé deireadh na cainnte: saoghal fada ag Franc Taafe ann*
> *Sliocht Loinnsigh na féile nár choigil an fiadhach.*

Thanks to Máirtín Mac Nioclás for drawing my attention to the above.

Remonstrance

In Dublin in 1661, to prove their loyalty to the crown, a group of Catholic laymen drew up a document known as the Remonstrance in which they stated their grievances and sought for redress. They rejected the Pope's power to absolve Catholics from the king's authority and the doctrine that any subject might kill the monarch. Kings, whatever their religion, were declared to be God's lieutenants on earth. Rome condemned these terms. Nevertheless, pressure was put on Catholic clerics to support the Remonstrance. Peter Walsh, a Franciscan, drew up a remonstrance which was signed by a number of Catholic laity and some of the clergy. The first signature was that of George Dillon, founder of an Irish Franciscan house in Paris and a member of the

1. *DNB.*

Castlemore family. However, the majority of the clergy strongly opposed it, as did the Vatican.[2] About a hundred clerics met in Dublin in the summer of 1666 and rejected Walsh's proposal. An alternative was proposed and accepted. While it rejected the doctrine that the Pope could absolve subjects from their allegiance to the king or that a subject might kill him, it declared that the Pope had no authority in temporal matters over the king. The Duke of Ormond refused to accept it and Rome declared that it contained 'atrocious errors' contrary to Catholic teaching.

James Taaffe OFM

Franciscan James Taaffe was born in Ballymote, the eighth child of fifteen of Viscount John Taaffe and his wife, Anna Dillon, daughter of Viscount Theobald Dillon of Costello-Gallen.

The Vatican despatched him as a special envoy to impress on the clergy the gravity of their error. In his early forties, he had studied at St Isidore's and was superior of Irish Franciscans in Paris. He was recommended in 1664 to Cardinal Chigi (later Pope Alexander VII) by the Queen-Mother, Henrietta Maria, for the diocese of Elphin.[3] However, William Burgat, the agent of the Irish bishops in Rome, warned Propaganda that Taaffe 'was and is procurator, agent and solicitator of all those schismatics who subscribe to this infamous schism' (Walsh Remonstrance). He also sought approval for the Remonstrance from Jansenist theologians in the University of Paris. Rome was to ignore this warning to its cost.[4]

Taaffe's Arrogance

Taaffe went to Ireland via England, where his brother, Theobald Earl of Carlingford, a comrade in exile of Charles II, secured for him an audience with the king, to whom he showed his commission. The rumour was spread both by himself and his friends that his powers were greater than those of all previous papal legates or nuncios and he passed himself off as a vicar apostolic with power to appoint bishops and vicars apostolic. He appears to have acted with extraordinary arrogance, trying to make Jesuits subject to his authority, limiting the power of the provincial of Irish Dominicans, all under the threat of excommunication.

He appointed other friars as his delegates to carry out canonical visitation of Irish dioceses. John Reynolds OP, a follower of Peter Walsh, was delegated to visit Killala and Achonry where he conducted himself 'with the maximim violence', particularly against those who supported Rinuccini and opposed

2.   *Fondo di Vienna*, vol. 14, ff.285r, 286r, 287r, 288r.
3.   His cousin, George Dillon had been recommended for the same diocese, by the same queen to the same cardinal two years earlier. *Nunziatura di Francia*, vol. 117, f.562rv: *Coll. Hib.*, no. 2, 112.
4.   *Fondo di Vienna*, vol. 14, f.240rv; vol. 16, f.68rv, 71r.

Walsh's Remonstrance. Taaffe issued his delegates (*c.*May 1668) with no less than thirty specific directions, some of which bore no relationship to the world where Irish priests lived.[5] The eighth direction required them to investigate whether the 'sacred vestments were becoming, whether altar cloths, corporals and purificators were neat and clean and frequently changed'. Delegates were also to enquire how priests spent their time during the week and whether they visited hamlets or places in their parishes. They were to gather round them 'in private houses or in their own rooms a goodly number of young or old people to instruct them in Christian doctrine'. Taaffe family politics are clearly evident in his directions. Ecclesiastics were 'in communication with the Tories' (i.e. bandits in the woods or mountains), who were in fact dispossessed Gaelic families. It would seem that Taaffe, though born in Ballymote, had spent most of his life in France and Spain and had no experience of Irish church life in the seventeenth century.

Complaints were made to Claudio Agretti, in the internunciature in Brussels, that Taaffe was detested for his excesses and because his delegates were extorting money from the clergy under censure. Vicars had to pay a tax of twenty scudi and parish priests four scudi under threats of interdicts and suspensions.[6] Taaffe's delegates deposed vicars and parish priests who refused to submit to their authority. 'Priests, because they have suffered so much up to this for the church of God and the Holy See, tearfully complain that they are now being persecuted by the authority of the same Holy See, and they say that the Supreme Pontiff treats them as the king of England treats the Catholic nobles of this kingdom, who fought for him at home and abroad …' The Jesuit, Netterville, a relative of Taaffe's, believed he had 'gone too far' and was 'amazed and grieved that Taaffe did not adopt a more private method and one less likely to burden the unfortunate parish priests'.

Complaints

He complained that 'Taaffe himself is in such bad repute with prudent men because of his drinking bouts and dancing late at night.'

Riotous Behaviour

Taaffe 'came to them, not like John the Baptist, but clad in soft garments, eating and drinking; scarcely had he arrived when the city of Dublin echoed with his parties, which gave great scandal to all the Catholics and permanently injured his reputation; for he turned days into nights and nights into days, very frequently in the company of young women, so that those who lodged in the same house in Dublin could not sleep because of the music and the noise which he made dancing with Walsh and his companions; wherever he went after he left Dublin he followed the same course and as the writer learned from

5.   *Coll. Hib.*, nos 6 and 7, 123–8.
6.   4 scudi to a £1.

a cleric most worthy of credence who accompanied the commissary for nine days, during all that time the commissary (Taaffe) was never sober and never went to bed until after 2.00 or 3.00 a.m.'[7] The account of his behaviour is scarcely credible and it should be remembered that complaints to Rome were often laced with such accusations which had very little basis in reality and to which the Roman authorities gave little or no credence.

Taaffe left Ireland   Taaffe forbade the clergy, under penalty of excommunication, from sending representatives or letters to Rome without his permission. His papal bull had a clause declaring it was not lawful to regard it as a forgery but it was, and he was recalled immediately when the deceit was detected. Claude Agretti wrote from Brussels on 5 January 1669 that Taaffe was himself the author of the commission he claimed to have received from Rome while the internuncio suggested to Propaganda that to proceed against Taaffe might drive him to apostasy. Another Franciscan received a letter from Rome which he handed to Taaffe in the presence of witnesses and Taaffe promised to set out for Flanders as soon as possible. He did not publish the excommunication which he also received from Rome because he feared that to do so would be construed as an exercise of foreign jurisdiction. The internuncio in Brussels continued to hold the view that it was not necessary to excommunicate Taaffe as it might cause 'notable disturbances' in Ireland. To avoid excommunication, Taaffe left for London with his brother, the Earl of Carlingford, where he arrived on 26 March 1669. Archbishop Peter Talbot of Dublin offered him fifty florins to go to Flanders but he waited in London until he had the internuncio's protection. Meanwhile, Taaffe had his defenders in Ireland who asserted 'that many of the things attributed to him were false and unworthy of this upright'. Among about twenty signatories – all senior ecclesiastics – to a statement to that effect was Maurice Durcan, vicar general of Achonry.

From London Taaffe informed his agent in Rome that he wished to remain there until Cardinal Rospigliosi received a full report on the affair, and his brother, Theobald, at the same time wrote to Cardinal Spinola. Taaffe protested that he had been calumniated by false reports to Rome. No one, he asserted, had achieved more for religion and Ireland during the past hundred years, than he. He claimed that he was deceived by Cardinals Roberti and Rospigliosi. He had been persuaded to accept the mission under three conditions: that he would be given full power over both secular and regular clergy, that he would be paid £100 annually and that no report against him would be given credence until he himself had been heard. The reason for the latter was that he was only

7.   Millet, 'Calendar of Scritture riferite nei congressi, Irlanda,' vol. 1, ff508r–511v in *Coll. Hib.*, nos 6 and 7, 158–9.

too aware that there were many Irishmen who wished to blacken him and his family. He had refused to go to Ireland without such commitments in writing. Cardinal Roberti persuaded him to go first to England and as soon as he was accepted by the king he would forward the required letters. He personally compiled a document because he never doubted that he would receive from Rome the powers he had been promised. He admitted that the delegates he appointed exceeded the authority he gave them. Taaffe left Brussels for Paris on his way to Rome in November 1669. He wrote a letter from Ghent to the internuncio in Brussels, confirming his promise to go to Rome 'even if a thousand crosses and imprisonment await him there'. There Cardinal Spinola interceded with Propaganda for him. His brother, Theobald, petitioned Rome to appoint him Bishop of Killala. It was a forlorn hope. Cardinal Giulio Rospigliosi, whom James had blamed for his Irish debacle, went on to become Pope Clement IX.[8]

Some statutes concerned the laity. Certain customs associated with holy wells and wakes were the subject of specific statutes passed at the synod held on 8, 9, 10 and 11 January 1660 in *loco refugii* (place of refuge). The ululatus or cry of the keening women at wakes was originally forbidden in 1631 but persisted and was again targeted in 1660. The custom was to continue well into the twentieth century.[9] Excessive drinking, dancing, games, and 'similar profane corruptions' were also prohibited on these occasions as well as flute-playing and concerts at holy wells. Drunkenness, the 'root of many evils', and the 'depraved custom of swearing, blaspheming and cursing' were singled out in particular statutes as were witchcraft, magic, spells, pacts with the devil, consultations with witches or fortune tellers, and every kind of superstition such as crosses, images or collections of stones, superstitious prayers, herbal cures, collections of superstitious herbs, and users were to be severely punished with the incorrigible excluded from the communion of believers. Priests were to hide away sheelanagigs and keep a note of where they were hidden.

A report on the state of the church in Ireland in 1662 makes stark reading:[10]

Tuam Synod 1660

8. Millet, *Calendar of Scritture riferite nei congressi, Irlanda*, vol. 1, 512r–515v, 524r–525v, 526r–528v; vol. 2, ff23r–24r, 25r–26v, 39r–40r, 43r–44v, 47r–48v, 51rv, 54rv, 73r–74v, 110r–111v, 116r–117v, 118r–119v, 145r–146v, 149rv, 150rv, 151rv, 152rv, 240r–241v, 354r–354v, 364r–365v, in *Coll. Hib.*, nos 6 and 7, 100–1, 159–61, 166–9; nos 16, 10–25, 34–5, 44–6; *CP*, vol. 19, ff. 132r, 135v.
9. See Swords, *A Hidden Church*, 258–9.
10. Millet, 'Archbishop Edmund Reilly's Report on the state of the Irish Church', in *Coll. Hib.*, no. 2, 106–14.

Our clergy live in the height of suffering and misery in worldly terms. At night they visit the sick; they celebrate Mass before or at dawn in hideouts or caves, with lookouts posted, eyes and ears alert for the military. They fall into the style of those among whom and between whom they live. They are exposed and subject to the wickedness and hatred of any rascal whatsoever who can lay his hands on an ecclesiatic and bring him to prison, without any special order or authority and further to strip him of clothes, money, books and horse, if he happened to have one.

Only Two Bishops Left

The episcopal and parochial system had almost completely collapsed. There were only two bishops in the whole country, both in the province of Armagh: Bishop Anthony MacGeoghegan OFM of Meath, and the aged and infirm Bishop Eugene MacSweeney of Kilmore. He 'could barely stand on his feet, so that he could not say Mass once a month or carry out his episcopal functions, impotent in all except prayer'. Two bishops were in exile, the Bishop of Dromore in London and the Bishop of Ardagh in Normandy while Clogher and Derry had apostolic vicars. In Leinster, Dublin and Kildare had apostolic vicars while the Bishop of Ferns was in Spain. In Munster the Bishop of Cork and Cloyne and the Bishop of Kilfenora were in Brittany; Cashel, Killaloe and Emly had vicars-apostolic while Limerick, Ross and Kerry were vacant. Connacht was the worst; the Archbishop of Tuam was in France, the Bishop of Clonfert was in Germany and Killala and Kilmacduagh were vacant. Nobody in authority remained in the whole province except James Fallon and he was paralysed and in prison. The town of Galway, the territory of Iarchonnacht and, about the same time, the archdiocese of Tuam and the diocese of Kilfenorawere committed to the care of Fallon even though he was said to be '*incarceratus et senectute oppressus*' ('imprisoned and worn out with old age').

'Cruel Extirpation of Religion'

He described to Rome 'this cruel extirpation of religion' with priests prevented from saying Mass or administering the sacraments. Many women were forced to marry heretics without dowries. He asked for faculties to consecrate portable altars, to dispense in marriage cases and the usual faculties given to bishops to be communicated to suitable priests 'even in America'.[11] The church can function, at least for a time, without bishops but not without parish priests and these were at an all-time low. In many dioceses they could be counted in single figures. It was said that there was only one in Kilfenora. While Tuam and Elphin had a 'modest' number there were 'very few' in

11.   'Dún Mhuire, Miscellaneous Papers', in *Coll. Hib.*, nos 15, 38–9: n.d. *Fondo di Vienna*, vol. 13, f.261r.

Achonry, probably less than the eleven parish priests listed over thirty years earlier.

The state of Achonry diocese in the mid-1660s was the subject of a report made by a priest who spent two years as a pastor in a large parish there, though it was probably not Achonry, more likely it was Aghadoe or Kerry diocese. Millet misread Achadoensis (Aghadoe) for Achadensis (Achonry).[12] John Sullivan (a Kerry name), author of the report, described the diocese as 'mountainous'. However, Sullivan said 'the same holds good for other parts', presumably including Achonry. The people were 'completely ignorant of the very fundamentals of the faith'. When asked how many Gods there are, they replied three, while others said four, adding the Blessed Virgin Mary to the Father, Son and Holy Ghost. Their ignorance was such that he heard some swearing by the seven all-powerful Persons of the Trinity.

Religious Ignorance

Their ignorance was partly due to the shortage of priests. Many Irish priests who studied in Belgium and France and were bound by oath to return to the Irish ministry failed to do so, partly because the people were too poor to support them. 'There are many persons of both sexes', he concluded, 'who are pious, good and instructed in the faith; but there are many unlettered people who, however, would show themselves docile and of good will if they had a sufficient number of learned and zealous directors.'

Scarcity of Priests

The picture painted by the Roman agent of Connacht and Munster bishops, William Burgat, was particularly bleak:

Bleak Picture

> The church in Ireland has been almost wiped out; more than two hundred (ecclesiastics) (elsewhere, he puts the figure at 'more than three hundred, including three bishops) were put to death by the sword and torture; up to one thousand were driven into exile; besides these there were very many who died in prison and in hiding-places from hunger, thirst and lack of clothing.[13]

There was no bishop left in Ireland except the incapacitated Bishop of Kilmore. In Achonry the vicar apostolic, James Fallon, was still alive 'but old age and paralysis have rendered him incapable of functioning,' and he had deputed Feidhlim Ó hEadhra and Hilary Maolchonaire to take charge of the diocese. Burgat suggested that it was better to leave the affairs of the diocese in the hands of these two priests until Fallon died.[14]

12. 'Calendar of Scritture riferite nei congressi, Irlanda,' in *Coll. Hib.*, nos 6 and 7, 145–8, Corish, *The Catholic Community*, 56–7.
13. Millet, 'Calendar of Scritture riferite nei congressi, Irlanda', in *Coll. Hib*, nos 6 and 7, 69–71.
14. Millet, 'Calendar of Scritture riferite nei congressi, Irlanda', vol. 1, ff. in *Coll. Hib.*, nos 6 and 7, 78.

Temptation to
Abandon

With the shortage of priests, each had five or six parishes and it was impossible for one priest to administer the sacraments and preach to so many people. Many died without the sacrament of Extreme Unction and such was their attachment to this sacrament that 'at least the less educated believe that it is scarcely possible to die a Christian death without it'. In many dioceses no one under the age of twenty-one had been confirmed.

For, of the more than 200,000 Catholics who enjoyed an hereditary right to lands and moveable goods, all with the exception of thirty-six were excluded by royal mandate from pursuing their claims; these have now nothing intact but their faith, but this is in greater danger now than ever before, because it is greatly feared that in the hope of regaining their possessions they will conform to the erroneous beliefs of the ascendancy.

Friars Criticised

Burgat singled out the friars – 'very few of them remained there during the persecution' – for special criticism. The fact that no guardian was appointed to Ballymote friary in 1658 gives some credence to his criticism. Now many of them had returned and tried 'to entice the people from allegiance to their own proper pastors', resulting in dissensions and open quarrels between the two clergies. In spite of the ferocity of the persecution, the old 'split' was alive and well.

'Firmly in the
Breach'

Burgat implored the Pope to appoint 'prelates and pastors who are distinguished for learning, prudence, authority and upright living' with a preference for those 'who stood firmly in the breach during the persecution'. In a list of candidates suitable for promotion, Tuam priest Cornelius Fallon, a parish priest in Madrid and doctor of theology, was proposed as vicar apostolic for Achonry. He may have been the brother of James but unlike him, had no experience of persecution. The Archbishop of Armagh proposed John Lynch (Archdeacon of Tuam, now in France) or Dominick O'Kelly (OP) for Achonry.[15]

James Taaffe had appointed the vicar general of Clonmacnois to visit Elphin and he made his report in 1688. A similar visit was carried out by the Dominican John Reynolds of Achonry and, in the absence of his report, that of Elphin probably paints a picture of what happened also in Achonry. Of some thirty priests, one was captured five times and once was 'drawn tied to a horses tail'. Another was captured and 'left half-strangled hanging from a gibbet' and still another who refused to desert his parish was captured and robbed of his vestments.[16]

15. Millet, 'Calendar of Scritture riferite nei congressi, Irlanda,' vol. 1, in *Coll. Hib*, nos 6 and 7, 137 Elphin Report 1688.
16. Ibid., ff84r–87v in *Coll. Hib.*, no. 16, 16–18.

He was a priest and professor in the church of Achonry in November 1645 for which he received £40, and canon and student as well as *personatus* of St Delphinus[17] of Bohola in June 1648, for which he received twenty-four ducats. His predecessor had died six months previously. In that month Gulielmus du Val (a priest from Cashel) attested in Rome that Durcan was 'pious, virtuous and reputable, had devoted himself assiduously to theological studies and accordingly was worthy of a pastoral benefice and care of souls'.[18] These appointments were made by Luke Wadding, agent of the Confederation in Rome.

Maurice Durcan (Muirgheas Mac Dhuarcáin)

Three years later (1561) he was in Paris, already a doctor of theology, though it seems he had acquired it elsewhere, probably in Spain. He was the first in a list of Irish students in the University of Paris who signed a declaration against Jansenism.[19] A few months after he was appointed vicar-apostolic, the Internuncio in Brussels, following the recommendation of the cardinal-protector of Ireland that the number of bishops be increased in the province of Tuam, suggested that Durcan be made a bishop. He mentioned the important consideration that he had 'a sufficient personal income and would not have to depend for his livelihood on the charity of the faithful'.[20]

Paris

Maurice Durcan was nominated vicar-general of Achonry about 1662 by the Archbishop of Tuam shortly after he returned to Ireland having spent twenty-five years in France and Spain.

He signed an attestation in favour of James Lynch for Tuam in 1668 where he was described as vicar general of Achonry and 'apostolic missionary'. Durcan was sixth on a list of fifteen Connacht theologians (*c.*1668) who 'by reason of their conduct, scholarship and prudence are clearly suitable for the episcopal dignity'. He was recommended by the Archbishop of Tuam in 1669 for the post of vicar-apostolic of Achonry and by the Bishop of Ferns for some diocese in the Tuam province. The Archbishop of Armagh proposed him as vicar-apostolic of Killala. He was included in list of 117 suitable priests for appointment as bishops. Maurice Durcan signed an attestation in December 1675 by the bishops and prelates of Ireland for John Burke, vicar-general of Tuam, who was in prison in Ballinrobe. Oliver Plunkett, on a visit to the province of Tuam, spent some time with him in the spring of 1673 and

17. Bishop of Bordeaux who died in 404 and feastday is on 24 December.
18. Jennings, 'Ecclesiastical Appointments in Ireland, August 1643–December 1649', *Coll. Hib.*, no. 36, 47, 63.
19. Brockliss and Ferté, 1300.
20. *SC Irlanda*, vol. 4.

described him as 'a man of gravity'. He was appointed vicar-apostolic on 27 July 1677 and governed the diocese as such for fifteen years.[21]

Aodh
Mac Diarmada

On 21 May 1685 the internuncio informed Rome that he had heard that Maurice Durcan had died.[22] In fact, he had died some time before that in 1683 as his successor, Aodh, petitioned Rome for the post and was appointed vicar-apostolic on 12 January 1684.[23] Mac Diarmada, an Elphin priest, was then thirty-two years old, having been ordained in 1675. The following year he gained a scholarship to Paris and in October 1678 he registered in the faculty of law at the university of Paris.[24] Later, he moved to Bologna in Italy and continued his studies at the famous law school there. He acquired doctorates in theology and civil and canon law, 'having at different times publicly defended *con gran applauso* theological and legal theses'. Cardinal Buoncompagno of Bologna wrote to Rome recommending Mac Diarmada. Feidhlim Ó hEadhra, dean and vicar general, together with three canons and eleven parish priests petitioned the internuncio at Brussels for Mac Diarmada, as vicar apostolic. The petition also contained the names of fourteen lay people, including Baron William Taaffe and six other members of that family, two Ó hAirt, two Mac Donnchadhas, one Brett and one Ó hEadhra.[25]

21. *SOCG*, vol. 463, ff49r, 50r, *Acta*, vol. 47, ff78v, 79r, *Cong. Gen.* 4 May 1677, *Fondo di Vienna*, vol. 16, ff39v, 41v, 47v, 141r, 217v, 219r, 220v, 279r, 280v, *SC Irlanda*, vol. 1, ff106rv, 109rv, 112rv, 113rv, 129r, 269rv, 3 83r, 563r: vol. 2, ff149rv, 152rv, vol. 3, ff304rv, 305r, 457rv, 458rv, vol. 4, ff12r, 171r, 190rv, 191r, 313r, 314r, vol. 6, ff. 350r–369v, *Hierarchia Catholica*, v. 67, *Lettere*, vol. 66, ff66r, 68v, *Coll. Hib.*, nos 6 and 7, 31, 39, 88, 109, 137, Hanly, *The Letters of Oliver Plunkett*, 1625–81ff., 199rv, 200r; see vol. 1, f101v.
22. *SC Irlanda*, vol. 4 ff. 313 r, 314r.
23. *CP*, vol. 30, f223r: *SC Irlanda*, vol. 10, f29rv.
24. Boyle, *Irish College Paris*, 199, Brockliss and Ferté, 1072 and 1132.
25. *CP* xxx, ff197r, 223r, 242rv.

Appendices

Raths in South Sligo (Total: 580, 72 possible)

Achonry

Achonry, 12; Ballyara, 7; Ballyara-Falduff, 5; Ballyglass, 1; Carnyara, Carrowcarragh, 1 and 1 poss.; Carrowkeel, 1; Carrowntober, 2; Carrowreagh (Cooper), 3 and 2 poss.; Carrowreagh (Knox), 1; Carrowreilly, 8; Carrowwilkin, 2 and 1 poss.; Carrowmurray, 3; Carrowmore, 2; Carrownacreevy, 5; Carrownaleck, 1; Carrownaworan, 3; Carrownedin, 1; Cashel N., 5; Cashel S., 6 and 1 poss.; Castleroye, 1 poss.; Cloonacool, 3; Cloonaraher, 2; Cloonarara, 2; Cloonbaniff, 1; Clooncunny, 2; Clooningin, 3; Cloonaughil, 2; Coolrawer, 1; Cully, 1; Cunghill, 4 and 1 poss.; Curry, 1 poss.; Derreens, 2; Doomore, 3 and 1 poss.; Drumbaun, 3; Laughil, 2; Lavy, 3; Leitrim N., 6; Leitrim S., 2; Lisduff, 1; Lissaneagh, 1; Montiagh, 2; Mullaghanarry, 5 and 1 poss.; Mullanabreena, 1; Moylough, 10 and 1 poss.; Muckelty, 1; Mulraun, 3 and 1 poss.; Oghambaun, 2 and 2 poss.; Powellsborough, 2; Pullagh, 1; Rathscanlan, 2 and 3 poss.; Rinbaun, 10 and 1 poss.; Sandyhill, 2; Sessualcommon, 1; Sessualgarry, 2 and 1 poss.; Spurtown Lr., Tanagh, 1; Tobarscardan, 2; Tullyhugh, 3 and 1 poss.; Tullycusheen Beg, 1 and 1 poss.; Tullycusheen More, 2; Tullyvelia, 2; (Total, 168, 20 poss.).

Ballaghaderreen

(Kilcolman) Tawnymucklagh, 1.

Ballysadare

Abbeytown, 2; Ardcotton, 1; Bleachgreen, 1; Bunnacrannagh, 9 and 1 poss.; Carrickbanagher, 4; Carricknagat, 2; Carrowclare, 1; Cloonacurra, 2 and 1 poss.; Cloonamahon, 1 and 1 poss.; Cloonmacduff, 1 poss.; Corhawnagh, 1; Crockacullion, 1 and 1 poss.; Halfquarter, 1 poss.; Knockbeg E., 5; Knockbeg W., 4; Knockmullin, 3; Largan, 2; Larkhill, 4; Lisduff, 1 and 3 poss.; Lisruntagh, 2; Lissaneena, 1; Markree Demesne, 4 and 1 poss.; Rathrippen, 1; Spotfield, 2 and 1 poss.; Streamtown, 4; Tobarbride, Union, 1 poss. (total 58, 11 poss.).

Ballymote

Ardnaglass, 1; Ardrea, 3; Ballybrennan, 4; Cappagh (Kilmorgan), 3; Carrigans Lr, 3; Carrigans, Upr, 6 and 1 poss.; Carrownanty, 1; Carrownree, 1; Cloonagashel, 4,; Cloonamanagh, 1; Cloonkeevy (Emlefad), 2 and 1 poss.; Cloonlurg (Kilmorgan), 1; Cluid, 4; Carrowcauly or Earlsfield, 1 poss.; Carrowkeel, 3; Carrowcushcly, 2; Deerpark, 1; Derreen, 1; Doobeg, 3; Doorly, 1; Drumcormick, 4; Emlaghnaghtan, 4; Doomeegin, 4; Knockadalteen, 2; Knockmoynagh, 1; Lisdoogan, 4 (Total, 64, 2 poss.).

Bunninadden
Ardkeeran, Baghloonagh (Kilshalvy), Ballinvally, 5; Ballinvally East, 1; Ballinvally West, 2; Ballyfahy, 7; Ballynarraw N., 1 poss.; Ballynarraw S., 5; Brackloonagh 1; (Cloonoghill), Carrowloughlin (Cloonoghill), 2; Church Hill, 2 and 1 poss.; Cloonahinshin, 3; Clooncose, 1; Clooncunny, 1; Cloonena, 1; Coagh, 2; Deechomade, 1; Derrynagraug, 1; Doobeg, 3; Drumanaraher, 1; Drumrolla, 1; Everlaun, 1 and 1 poss.; Flower Hill, 4; Greyfield, 2; Killavil, 1; Killnaharry, 1; Killandy, 2; Kilshalvy, 1; Kilturra, 2; Knocknakillew or Woodville, 2; Lecarrow, 2; Lisnagore, 1; Knockalass, 2 and 1 poss.; Knockgrania, 2; Ogham, 2 poss.; Phaleesh, 1; Quarryfield, 8; Riverstown, 2; Rinn, 1; Rathbaun S., 2; Shancarrigeen or Oldrock, 1; Tunnagh, 4 and 1 poss (Total, 56, 7 poss.).

Collooney
Annagh, 2 poss.; Annagh More, 2 poss.; Ardcree, 3; Ballymurray, 3; Ballynacarrow N., 6 and 1 poss.; Ballynacarrow S., 1; Carrowntawy, Claragh (Irish), 3; Claragh (Scotch), 5 and 2 poss.; Finlough, 5; Glebe, 1; Kilvarnet N., 2; Rathbaun, 4; Rathbran, 5 and 1 poss.; Rathnarrow (Brett), 1; Rathnarrow (O'Hara), 2; Rockfinlough, 6 (Total, 53, 8 poss.).

Coolaney
Carrowgavneen, 4; Carrowdooneen, 5; Carrownacarrick, 2; Carrownacleigha, 1; Carrowmaglerach, 2; Carrownaskeagh, 1; Carrownateewaun, 1; Carrownleam, 3; Carrowloughan, 7; Coolaney, 3; Deenodes, 6; Gortakeeran, 5 and 1 poss.; half-Quarter or Curraghaniron, 1; Killoran N., 3; Killoran S., 1; Knockadoo, 9; Knockatotaun, 4; Lissalough, 2; Rathbarron, 1; Rathmactiernaw, 2; Rathmore, 1; Rathosey, 2 and 1 poss.; Shancough, 1; Sccvncss, 2 (Total, 69, 1 poss.).

Gurteen
Ardgallin, 1 poss.; Ardlona, 4; Ardmoyle, 2; Ardsoreen, 5; Cloocunny, 1; Cloonanure (Kilfree), 1; Clooneagh, 1; Cloonsillagh, 1; Cloontycarn, 2; Cuilmore, 2; Derrybeg, 1 and 1 poss.; Doon, 1; Emlagh, 3; Gortygara, 4; Greyfield, 2 and 1 poss.; Inch Island, 1; Kilfree, 1; Killaraght, 7; Knocknashammer, 1 poss.; Knocknaskeagh, 1; Lisbaleely, 3; Lisgullaun, 2; Lismerraun, 3 and 1 poss.; Lisserlough, 2; Lomcloon, 1; Moygara, 3; Mountirvine, 2; Moydough, 1; Mullaghroe, 1; Rathermon, 3; Ross, 1; Stoneparks, 2 (Total, 61, 5 poss.).

Keash
Ardsallagh, 1; Ballinvoher, 5; Battlefield, 1; Bellanascarrow E., 2; Bellanascarrow W., 1; Carrowcrory, 1; Carrickrathmullin (Drumrat), 5; Bunnamuck, 2; Templevanny, 2; Carrickmaclenany, 2; Carrownacreevy, 1; Carrowreagh, 1; Cletty, 1; Cloonacaltry, 1; Cloonagh, 2; Cloonshanbally, 2; Graniamore, 3; Graniaroe, 2; Greyfield, 1; Kingsfort, 1; Knockatelly 1; Knockgrania, 1 and1 poss; Knocklough, 1; Knocknawishoge, 1; Lavally, 2; Murhy/Treanmore, 1 and 1 poss.; Roscrib E., 3; Roscrib W., 1; Treanmore, 1 (Total, 44, 2 poss.).

Tourlestrane
Banada, 2 poss.; Belclare, 1 poss.; Carns, 2 and 1 poss.; Carraun, 7; Carrownlobaun, 1 and 1 poss.; Carrowreagh, 7 and 1 poss.; Castlerock or Castlecarragh, 1 poss.;

Cloonbarry, 1 poss.; Cloonydiveen, 1 and 2 poss.; Coolrecuill, 2 and 2 poss.; Corray, 1; Dawros, 1 poss.; Drummartin, 1; Eskragh, 3; Glenawoo, 2; Gortermone, 1; Kilmacteige, 6 and 2 poss.; Kinkillew, 3; Knockahoney, 1; Knockbrack, 2; Lislea, 1 poss.; Rue, 6; Toberroddy, 2; Tourlestraun, 1; Tullnaglug, 4 and 1 poss (Total, 53, 16 poss.).

Cashels (Total, 110, 7 poss.)
Achonry
Carrowcarragh, 1; Carrowmurray, 1; Carrowmore, 4; Carrownedin, 1; Cashel N., 1; Gortnagrass, 4; Kilcummin, 1; Leitrim, S., 2; Mullaun, 2; Muckelty, 2; Oghambaun, 3; Rinbaun, 3; Tubbercurry, 2; Tullyvelia, 1 (Total, 27).

Ballaghaderreen
(Kilcolman) 3; Monasteredan, 1 and 1 poss.; Tawnymucklagh, 2; Shroove, 8 and 2 poss.

Ballysadare
Bunnacrannagh, 1; Carrickbanagher, 1; Carricknagat, 2; Cloonmacduff, 4; Crockacullion, 2; Glen, 3; Lisduff, 1; Union, 1 poss. (Total, 28).

Ballymote
Carrigans, Upr, 1; Cappagh (Kilmorgan), 1; Lissananny More, 1 (Total, 3).

Collooney
Cladagh, 2; Kilvarnet N., 1 (Total, 3.).

Coolaney
Cabragh, 1; Carrownleam, 2 poss.; Rathosey, 6; Shancough, 1; Seevness, 1 (Total, 9).

Gurteen
Cashel, 1; Clooneagh, 1; Doon, 1; Inch Island, 1; Kilfree, 2; Moygara, 4 (Total, 10).

Keash
Brougher, 1; Templevanny, 2; Greenan, 1; Templevanny, 2; Treanmore, 3 and 1 poss (Total, 9).

Tourlestrane
Belclare, 1; Carrownlobaun, 2; Carrowreagh, 4; Culdaly, 1; Kincuillew, 2; Knockbrack, 5; Letterbrone, 1; Oughval, 1; Rue, 2 (Total, 21).

Ringforts, E. Mayo
Attymass, 1; Bunnafinglass, 2; Carrick, 1; Carrowdoogan, Carrowkerribly, 2; Cartron, 1; Corradrishy, 1; Corrower, 2; Mullaghawny, 1; Roosky, 2.

Ballaghaderreen
(Castlemore), Ardkill, 1; Barnaboy, 3; Cashelcolaun, 1; Drumnalassan, 5; Glebe, 2; Kilvanloon, 1.

Bohola
Ballinlag, 4; Carrowkeel, 4; Carrowmore, 7; Clooneen, 2; Gortnasillagh, 3; Lismiraun, 1; Lissaniska, 6; Shanaghy, 1; Treanfohanaun, 3.

Bonniconlon
Bunnyconnellan W, 4; Carrowcastle; Carrowconneen, 3; Carrowreagh, 1; Carrowcrom, 3; Craggera, 7; Graffy, 1; Lissardmore, 5; Loughnagore, 9; Rathreedaun, 6.

Foxford
Belgarrow, 2; Boherallagh, 3; Creggagh, 2; Rinnananny, 2; Shanwar.

Kilbeagh
(Charlestown) Bulcaun, 1; Ballyglass, 2; Barnacahoge, 3; Barnalyra, 1; Bellahy, Bracklagh, 1; Calveagh Upper, 1; Carna, 3; Carracastle, Cartron, 1; Cashel, 2; Cloonalison, 1; Cloonlyon, 1; Cloonfane, 2; Cloonmeen West, 2; Gortanure, 1; Fauleens, 1; Lavy More, 2; Lissymulgee, 2; Lurga Lower, 3; Mullenmadoge, 1; Shragh Upper, 1; Sonnagh, 3; Stripe, 6; Tomboholla, 2; Treanacally or Hagfield, 1; Trouthill or Knockbrack, 1.

Kilconduff
Ardlee, 1; Ballydrum, 2; Ballyglass, 3; Brackloon, 3; Carrowbaun, 3; Carrowbeg, 2; Carrowcanada, 8; Carrownaculla, 4; Castlebarnagh 3; Castlecrunnoge, 1; Castleroyan, 1; Cloonaghboy, 2; Cloonfinnaun, 4; Cloongulaun, 1; Cloonlara, 3; Cloonlumney, 3; Cloonacannana, 2; Cornaveagh, 3; Cuillaun, 2; Cuilmore, 1; Cuiltybo, 1; Curryaun, 3; Deerpark, 2; Derryronan, 6; Drumshinnagh, 1; Faheens, 5; Johnsfort, 1; Kilbride, 1; Kinaff, 2; Lagcurragh, 2; Liscottle, 2; Lisheenabrone, 5; Lissanumera, Midfield, 1; Newpark, 3; Rabaun, 3; Carrownaculla, 3; Rathscanlan, 5; Swinford, 3; Tawnaglass, 2; Tawnamullagh, 2; Tonroe, 1; Treanlaur, 3; Tullanacorra, 9 (Total, 139).

Killasser
Askillaun, 2; Attimachugh, 1; Attinaskolia, 2; Blackpatch, 2; Boleyboy, 1; Callow, 11; Carrowbeg, 2; Carrowliambeg, 1; Carrowliam More, 1; Carramore, 9; Carrowmoremoy, 3; Carrowneden, 7; Cartron, 4; Cartonmacmanus, 1; Cloonfinish, 1; Cloontubbrid, 1; Coolcashla, 6; Coolagagh, 3; Creggaballagh, 1; Creggaun, 5; Cuildoo, 8; Cuilllonaghtan, 6; Cullin, 6; Darhanagh, 1; Doonmaynor, 4; Doonty, 2; Dromada Duke, 2; Dromada Gore, 3; Dromada Joyce, 1; Drumagh, 5; Graffy, 5; Knockfadda, 3; Knockmullin, 1; Larganmore, 2; Lislaughna, 1; Lismoran, 5; Listernan, 2; Rubble, 2; Tiraninny, 3; Tooard, 5; Treanrevagh, 5; Tumgesh, 1.

Kiltimagh
Annagh Hill, 1; Ballynamona, 1; Brownespark, 3; Carrick, 2; Carrownageeragh, 1; Cordorragh, 2; Garryroe, 1; Lisduff, 2; Oxford, 2; Pollronahan Beg, 2; Pollronahan More, 4; Shanvally, 2; Gortgarve, 1; Killedan, 6.

Kilmovee
Carrownlacka, 2; Cashelahenny, 1; Cuilliaghn, 3; Kilcashel, 3; Kilmovee, 2; Magheraboy, 2; Ranagissaun, 6; Rusheens West, 1; Rusheens East, 1; Raherolus, 2; Tavraun, 3.

Meelick
Ballintemple, 1; Bothaul, 5; Carrownacross, 1; Carrowreagh, 5; Castlesheenaghan, 2; Cloonagalloon, 1; Clooneen, 1; Clooninshin, 1; Killeen, 1; Lisbaun, 4; Lisbrogan, 4; Meelick, 1; Oldcastle, 2; Pollsharvogue, 2; Rinbrack, 1.

Crannógs
Attymass: Ballymore Lough, 1; Glendaduff Lough, 1.
Killasser: Callow Lough Upper, 1; Callow Lough Lower, 1; Cuillonaghtan, Lough Muck, 1; Rubble Lough Ogirra, 1; Shanwar, Lough Muck, 1.
Kilmovee: Urlaur, Urlaur Lough, 1.
Kiltimagh: Canbrack, Carrick Lough, 1.
Kilmacteige: Lough Talt, 1.

APPENDIX TWO: BISHOPS

St Brocaidh, contemporary of St Patrick.
St Finnian of Clonard, founder of church of Achonry.
Maolruanaidh Ó Ruadháin (Ruane), 1152–70
Giolla na Naoimh Ó Ruadháin, d.1214
Clement Ó Sniadhaigh (Snee), 1214–19
Condmach Ó Tarpa (Tarpey) O Cist, 1219–25
Giolla Íosa Ó Cléirigh (O'Clery), 1226–30
Thomas Ó Ruadháin (Ruane), 1230–7
Aengus Ó Clúmháin (Coleman), 1238–48
Thomas Ó Maicín (Macken), 1249–65
Thomas Ó Miadhacháin (O'Meehan), 1266–85
Benedict Ó Bragán (Bragan), 1286–1312
David of Kileany, 1312–44
Nioclás Ó hEadhra O Cist, 1348–73
William Andrews OP, 1373–87
Simon O Cist., 1385–95
Tomás Mac Donnchadha (McDonagh), 1396–8
Brian Ó hEadhra, 1399–1409
Maghnus Ó hEadhra, 1410–14?
Donnchadha Ó hEadhra, 1414–24
Richard Belmer OP, 1424–30
Maghnus Ruadh Ó hEadhra, 1430–5
Tadhg Ó Dálaigh (O'Daly) OP, 1436–42
James Blakedon OP, 1442–53
Conn Ó Mocháin O Cist, 1440–63?
Brian Ó hEadhra, son of Bishop Manus Ruadh, 1463–73
Robert Wellys OFM, 1473–?
Tomás Ó Conghaláin, 1484–1508

John de Bustamente, 1489–?
Thomas Ffort OSA, 1492–1508
Eoghan Ó Flannagáin, 22 Dec. 1508–?
Cormac Ó Sniadhaigh, 1522–47
Tomás Ó Fithcheallaigh (O'Fihily) OSA, 15 June 1547–30 Aug. 1556
Cormac Ó Cuinn (O'Coyne) OFM, 1556–61
Eoghan Ó hAirt (O'Hart) OP, 1562–1603
Vacant, 1603–31
James Fallon (Séamus Ó Fallamhain), Vicar Apostolic, 1631–62
Louis Dillon OFM, 1641
Maurice Durcan (Muiris Mac Dhuarcáin), Vicar Apostolic, 1677–85
Hugh MacDermot (Aodh Mac Diarmada), Vicar Apostolic, 1685–1707
Hugh MacDermot (Aodh Mac Diarmada), Bishop, 1707–25

APPENDIX THREE: ARCHDEACONS, DEANS, PROVOSTS AND PREBENDS

Archdeacons (Elective dignity with cure, three marks)
Ante Feb. 1401, Aodh Mac Giolla an Aingeal (Odo Macguillichaenygel), alias Mac
    an Bhreitheamhan;
2 Feb. 1401, Cormac Ó Coimín (Ocoymiean);
1425–9, Cormac Ó Coimín (Ocoymiean);
1429, Domhnall Ó hEadhra (22 years old);
3 Apr. 1447–8, Seán Ó Duarcáin;
1476–7, Tomás Ó Conghaláin;
1484, Mathgamhain Ó Callanáin.

Deans (Major elective dignity with care of souls, eight to twelve marks)
Ante 1425, Domhnall Ó Raghaillaigh;
c.1425–8, Pilib Ó Clúmháin;
1428–31, Seán Ó hEadhra;
1431, Brian Ó hEadhra;
Ante 1440, Seán Ó hEadhra;
9 May 1440–4 Nov, 1443, Conn Ó hEadhra, Augustinian Canon;
Ante 1443, Pilib Ó Clúmháin;
14 Nov. 1443–7, Tomás Mac an Bhreitheamhan;
1447–63, Brian Ó hEadhra (son of Bishop Ó hEadhra);
Ante 1476, Aodh Ó Duibhidhir (Otedura), Brian Ó Coinín;
26 Feb. 1476–7, Tomás Ó Conghaláin;
27 Feb. 1478–3 June 1494, Cormac Ó hEadhra;
3 June 1494–?, Ruaidhrí Ó hEadhra;
1512, Aodh Mac Donnchadha.

Provosts (Non-major elective dignity with cure, eight marks)
1419, Eoghan Ó hEadhra;

1420, Cormac Ó hEadhra, Domhnall Mac Donnchadha;
1436–40, Cormac Ó hEadhra;
1440–?, Uilliam Ó Connacháin,
Ante 1448, Domhnall Mac Donnchadha;
1448, Diarmaid Ó hEadhra, son of Bishop Ó hEadhra;
Ante 1490, Diarmaid Ó hEadhra;
1489, Cormac Ó Connacháin, son of Uilliam above;
6 Dec. 1490–Feb. 1495?, Cathal Mac Cuinneáin? (Mycconhane);
Ante 1495, Tadhg Ó Tomhnair;
Feb. 1495–1503, Tadhg Ó hEadhra;
12 June 1505–12, Tomás Ó Conghaláin (Ochocolan),
1510, Brian Mac Muircheartaigh;
1512, Conn Mac Ceallaigh.

Prebends
Ante 1401 Brian Ó Gadhra, Lucás Ó Ciaragáin, Cormac Ó Coimín;
1430, Cormac Mac Donnchadha;
1442, Diarmaid Ó Cléirigh.
Cloonoghill (Cluncocoll), two marks.
Dá Corran (Dacorran and Mota), two marks.
?–1443, Uilliam Ó Connacháin;
1490, Cathal Mac Cuinneáin (Maconhanne).
Emlefad
1482–3, Domhnall Ó Branghaile (Ybrangale);
1482–3, Conn Ó Scannláin (Ystanlayn);
Kilmactigue
Ante 1419, Maghnus Ó hEadhra;
1419–?, Eoghan Ó hEadhra.
Killedan, two marks
1461–2, Uilliam Mac an Bhreitheamhan,
1477–?, Tadhg Ó hEadhra.
Killoran, three to four marks
1428, Seán Ó hEadhra,
Ante 1441, Pilib Ó Clúmháin), entered Rosserk OFMs.
1441, Conn Mac Ceallaigh (Killnathruid),
Ante 1440, Tadhg Ó Clúmháin (Killuathrend).
Toomour & Drumrat, two marks
1448, Diarmaid Ó hEadhra, son of Bishop Ó hEadhra

APPENDIX FOUR: PAPAL MANDATORIES — CANONS

1422, Domhnall Mac Donnchadha;
1428, Domhnall Mac Donnchadha, Diarmaid Mac Aodhagáin, Seán Ó Cearnaidh,
    Cormac Ó hEadhra;

1430, Domhnall Mac Donnchadha, Diarmaid Mac Aodhagáin, Domhnall Ó
hEadhra, Cormac Mac Donnchadha;
1435, Cormac Mac Donnchadha, Seán Ó Cearnaidh, Tadhg Mac Diarmada, Pilib
Mac Éinrí, Pilib Ó Clúmháin, Conn Ó Mocháin (6);
1440, Cormac Mac Donnchadha, Domhnall Mac Donnchadha, Diarmaid Mac
Aodhagáin, Conn Ó Mocháin, Uilliam Ó Mocháin, Elias Ó Murchú (6);
1441, Conn Ó Mocháin, Aodh Ó Mocháin, Ruaidhrí Ó Mocháin (2);
1443, Diarmaid Mac Aodhagáin, Conn Ó Mocháin, Elias Ó Murchú, Muirgheas Ó
Conchobhair, Niall Ó hEanagáin (5);
1444, Cormac Mac Donnchadha, Cormac Ó Mocháin (2);
1447, Pilib Mac Éinrí, Tomás Mac an Bhreitheamhan, Seán Ó Clúmháin, Uilliam Ó
Connacháin, Cormac Ó Cuinn, Diarmaid Ó hEadhra, Ruaidhri Ó hEadhra (7);
1448, Pilib Mac Éinrí, Diarmaid Ó hEadhra, Brian Ó Cearnaidh, Conn Ó Cearnaidh,
Milerus de Exetor (5);
1449, Tomás Mac an Bhreitheamhan, Diarmaid Mac Aodhagáin, Muirgheas Ó
Conchobhair, Maeleachlainn Ó Clúmháin, Ruaidhri Ó hEadhra, Tomás Ó
(Mathet?) (6);
1460, Conn Ó Cearnaidh, Seán Ó hEadhra (2);
1461, Aodh Ó Mocháin, Alastar Ó Murchú (2);
1462, Diarmaid Ó Floinn, Seán Ó hEadhra, Uilliam Mac an Bhreitheamhan (3);
1463, Brian Ó Cearnaidh (1);
1465, Uilliam Mac an Bhreitheamhan, Brian Ó Coimín, Maeleachlainn Ó Mocháin
(3);
1470, Uilliam Ó Clúmháin, Brian Ó Coimín (2);
1472, Domhnall Ó Mionacháin, Alastar Ó Murchú (2);
1473, Eoghan Mac Broinn, Muirgheas Ó hEadhra, Ruaidhrí Ó hEadhra (3);
1475, Domhnall Ó Mionacháin, Seán Ó hEadhra (2);
1480, Seán Ó Clúmháin, Ruaidhrí Ó hEadhra (2);
1484, Diarmaid Ó hEanagáin, Muirgheas Ó hEadhra, Ruaidhrí Ó hEadhra, Uilliam
Ó Clúmháin, Domhnall Ó Mionacháin, Aodh Ó Mocháin (6);
1489, Uilliam Ó Clúmháin, Éamonn Mac Éinrí, Ruaidhrí Ó hEadhra (Ohegea) (3);
1490, Seán Ó Derrig, Tomaltach Mac Donnchadha (2);
1493, Éinrí Mac Breandáin, Pilib Mac Éinrí, Domhnall Ó Cuinn (3);
1495, Brian Ó Conchobhair, Tadhg Ó Conchobhair, Seán Ó Domagáin, Pádhraic Ó
Flanghaile, Maghnus Mac (Maccultoihid?), Seán Mac Giolla (Macgyllahulyd
Gillhooley) (6);
1497, Mór (Marianus) Mac Duibhir, Eamonn Mac Éinrí, Pilib Mac Éinrí, Séán Ó
Clúmháin, Uilliam Ó Clúmháin, Tadhg Ó Coigligh, Domhnall Ó Cuinn, Conn
Ó Gadhra;
1504, Diarmaid Ó Mocháin, Ruaidhrí Ó Mocháin;
1508, Brian Ó hEadhra, Maeleachlainn Mac Donnchadha, Brian Mac Macmerbertrin,
Brian Machmyrherryn;
1509, Tomás Mac Iryllubne, Dáibhí Mac Cléirigh, Domhnall Olryn, Richard de
Burgo, Domhnall Ó Beirn, Tomás Mac Ceallaigh;
1510 (Machmurtahyn), Brian Ó hEadhra, Cathal Ó hEadhra, Dáibhí Mac Cléirigh;
1512, Maeleachlainn Ocerhury.

Canons

1419, Eoghan Ó hEadhra;

1422–35, Domhnall Mac Donnchadha;

1428, Cormac Ó hEadhra, Diarmaid Mac Aodhagáin (also Killala), Seán Ó hEadhra;

1428–35, Seán Ó Cearnnaigh;

1430, Domhnall Mac Donnchadha (Elphin), Cormac Mac Donnchadha;

1430–5, Cormac Mac Donnchadha, Diarmaid Ó Cléirigh;

1431, Brian Ó hEadhra, Brian Ó Cuinneáin (Ochonnean), Domhnall Ó Mocháin;

1432, Conn Ó Mocháin, Domhnall Ó Mocháin (entered Cistercians in Rome);

1435, Pilib Mac Éinrí, Pilib Ó Clúmháin, Diarmaid Mac Aodhagáin, Seán Ó Cearrnaigh, Cormac Ó hEadhra, Cormac Mac Donnchadha, Conn Ó Mocháin;

1440, Diarmaid Mac Aodhagáin, Elias Ó Murchú, Domhnall Mac Donnchadha, Uilliam Ó Connacháin, Cormac Mac Donnchadha, Conn Ó Mocháin;

1441, Aodh Ó Mocháin, Ruaidhrí Ó Mocháin;

1442, Cormac Mac Donnchadha, Diarmaid Ó Cléirigh, Conn Mac Ceallaigh;

1443, Muiris Ó Conchobhar (also Killala), Diarmaid Mac Aodhagáin (also Killala), Niall Ó hÉinacháin, Elias Ó Murchú, Uilliam Ó Connacháin, Conn Ó Mocháin, Tomás Mac an Bhreitheamhan;

1444, Cormac Mac Donnchadha, Cormac Ó Mocháin; Ante 1448, Pilib Ó Clúmháin;

1447, Uilliam Ó Connacháin, Seán Ó Clúmháin, Diarmaid Ó hEadhra, Cormac Ó Cuinn (Ochuinn), Tomás Mac an Bhreitheamhan, Pilib Mac Éinrí (Machenagh);

1448, Milerus de Exeter, Diarmaid Ó hEadhra, Conn Ó Cearnaigh, Tomás Ó Cearnaigh, Brian Ó Cearnaigh, Pilib Mac Éinrí;

1449, Conn Ó Conchobhar, Ruaidhrí O'Hara, Tomás Mac an Bhreitheamhan, Maeleachlain Ó Clúmháin, Tomás Ó (Omathet?), Seán Ó Clúmháin, Muiris Ó Conchobhar;

1454, Brian Ó Cearrnaigh, Dáithi Ó Con Lurga;

1460, Muiris Ó Cearnaigh, Aodh Ó Mocháin, Diarmaid Ó Cléirigh, Seán Ó hEadhra, Maeleachlainn Ó Mocháin;

July 1461, Aodh Ó Mocháin, Alastar Ó Murchú, Uilliam Mac an Bhreitheamhan, Milerus de Exeter;

1462, Seán Ó hEadhra, Diarmaid Ó Floinn;

1463, Tomás Mac an Bhreitheamhan;

1464–5, Uilliam Mac an Bhreitheamhan, Brian Ó Coineáin (Ochonnean);

1471, Brian (Ocoymiean), Uilliam Ó Clúmháin;

1473, Ruaidhrí O'Hara, Muiris O'Hara, Eoghan Mac (Macbrenn or MacBrenir?);

1475, Seán Ó hEadhra, Donnchadha Ó Miadhacháin, 1476–7, Tomás Ó Conghaláin, 28 February 1478, Seán Ó hEadhra;

1480–1, Ruaidhrí Ó hEadhra, Seán Ó Clúmháin;

1484, Aodh Ó Mocháin, Domhnall Ó Miadhacháin, Diarmaid Ó hÉineacháin (Onyaghan), Uilliam Ó Clúmháin;

1489, Ruaidhrí Ó hEadhra, Uilliam Ó Clúmháin, Eamon Mac Éinrí, Tomaltagh Ó Scannláin;

1490, Alastar Ó Murchú (Omurconda), Gilbert de Exeter, Tomaltach Mac Donnachadha (Mycconchyd), Donnchadha Ó Miadhacháin, Gilbert (Macemundduhyili) (Mycconchyd), Donnchadha Ó Miadhacháin (Omynachan);

1491, Felim Mac an Bhreiteamhan, Ruaidhrí Ó hEadhra (Ohona), Tomaltach Mac
Donnachadha;

1493, Pilib Mac Éinrí, Domhnall Ó Cuinn (Ocuyn), Éinrí Mac Brandáin
(Macbrandarn);

1495, Brian Ó Conchobhar, Padraig Ó Flanghaile (Offlagfmigale), Seán Ó Domagáin
(Odamagan);

1497, Uilliam Ó Clúmháin, Seán Ó Clúmháin, More Mac Dubhuidhir (Marianus
Macdayr), Domhnall Ó Cuinn (Ocuynd), Tadhg Ó Tomhnair (Ythonit), Pilib Mac
Éinrí, Eamonn Mac Éinrí, Conn Ó Gadhra;

1504, Ruaidhrí Ó Mocháin, Tomaltagh Ó Scannláin (Ascalanus?), Conn Mac Ceallaigh,
Felim Mac an Bhreitheamhan, Brian Mac Muircheartaigh (Macmyrythyn); 1505,
Tomás Ó Cocholáin (Ochocolan?);

1507, Ruaidhrí Mac Muircheartaigh (Macmayrgurthasynd), Gilbert de Angulo;

1508, Risteárd, Ó Grádaigh (Igrada), Pilib Ó Clúmháin, Oscar (Ochardius) Ó
hUiginn, Maghnus Mac Cléirigh, Maeleachlainn Mac Donnchadha;

1509, Niall Mac Neachtain, Domhnall Ó Banáin (Ybenan), Domhnall Ó Beirn
(Oberney), Tomás Mac Ceallaigh, Richard de Burgo, Domhnall Ó Cuinn (Okym);

1510, Aodh Mac Donnchadha, Domhnall Ó Miadhacháin (Omnyhan), Brian Mac
Muircheartaigh (Macnnrhuyton);

1512, Conn Mac Ceallaigh, Maeleachlainn Ó Cuirín (Ocerhury?), Dáithí Mac
Chléirig (Mackalerra);

Ante 1513, Muirgheasa Ó Connacháin (Oconnachayriz?), Gearóid (Gargallus) Ó
Dubhda, Seán Ó Fearghaile.

Julius II-Lost Registers, *Indice*, 349, ff.46, 53, 97, 105, *CPL*, xix, 587, nos 1911, 1912,
1913, 1914.

Barret, Richard, canon, 1504,

Bickar, Will. priest, 1603, Castleloghdargen?, (*Cal. Par. Rolls, I James I*, 20–4, 29),

de Angulo (Nangle), David,

de Angulo (Nangle), Gilbert, canon, 1500, 1507,

de Burgo, Richard, canon, Tuam, rector, Bohola, 1502, canon, Achonry, 1509,

de Exeter (Exonia, Uxonis), John Juvenis, rector, Straide, 1423, Bohola, removed,
1429, Ann. Milerus, sometime vicar, Killasser, canon, Killedan, 1441, 1448, made
bp of Killala but died, Rome, *c*.1461, Gilbert, canon, 1490, Macauvi?, Charles,
vicar, *c*.1503–13; *Mac an Bhreitheamhan* (Judge, Breheny or Brehony),
Macbrechim, Macaberchun, Macabrachim, Macabrecheman, Macabrechun,
Macabrethon, Macabrethim, Machambrecheim, Machabrethum, Machbrehun,
Meicabrechnyn, Meicabrechuyn, Macbrechim, Macbrehim, Macbrehuun,
Micbrechim, Andrew jr, Andrew, sr, Andrew, vicar, Ballysadare, resigned, *c*.1423,
Ann. Phelim (Felyno), canon, 1504,

Feynus, canon, 1504, Feynus, canon, 1491, 1504, vicar, Kilvarnet, abbot in
commendam, Ballysadare, prebend of Killoran, 1504, see Macbrenn.

Gavin (Gebhyno), canon, 1504, John, John, priest, John alias Micdannchayd, vicar,
Emlefad, Thady, clerk, Thady, priest, sometime vicar, Killasser, Thomas, canon,
1447, 1449, 1463, Thomas, dean, 1443, Ann., 1447, William, canon, Killedan,
1461[–2], 1464[–5]

Macbrenn, Macbrenir, Macbreynd, Macbreim, Macchbreun (Brennan?), Cornelius, canon, 1497, Eugenius, canon, 1473, Thomas, sometime, vicar, Cloonoghill, resigned it to bp Brian O'Hara, Feynus, canon, 1491, 1504, vicar, Kilvarnet, abbot in commendam, Ballysadare, prebend of Killoran, 1504 see Macbrehuun above. Clery, MacCleary, Macacleri, Macclery, Macachlerid, Machlery, Mackalerra, Macleri, Makaelery, Mauleri John, David, canon, 1512, Magonius, canon, 1508, vicar, Kilmorgan (& Drumcolym & Camuach, d, Elphin), 1508, removed, 1510, vicar, Killoran, deprived, 1512. Maurus *c.*1505–6, cleric, vicar, Kilmorgan, removed 1508, 1603, Henry McEclerie (Mac Cléirigh, MacCleary, Clarke), priest, Clony-Mahine (Cloonamahon or Cloonameehan, Cloonoghill) (*Cal. Par. Rolls, I James I*, 20–4, 29)

Mac Cristín, Macacristini, Micmcristin, McChristine Charles, priest, vicar, Rorie, priest, Ballyhara (*Cal. Par. Rolls, I James I*, 20–4, 29)

Macadruych, Macadruyth, Eugenius, Kilmorgan, 1428, Ann.

Macbrandayn (Mac Branain?, Brennan), Henry, canon, 1493

Maccamilii, Eugene, vicar, 1501–2

Maccannadan, Thomas

Maccloneyd, Macclonehyd, Magonius O. Prem., abbot of Holy Trinity, Lough Key, abbot in commendam of Ballysadare, 1484, Ann., rector, Emlefad, 1490

Maccultoihd, Magonius, canon, 1495

Macdair, Macdayr, Macdir (MacDyer), Marianus (Morianus), canon, Achonry, vicar, Achanat, d.Elphin, 1497, canon, 1510; Thaddeus, parochial vicar, 1521

Macdnachan, Nygelldus, canon, prebend of Athleathan, 1509

McDonagh, Macdonnchaid, Macdenchid, Macdoncayd, Macdonchaid, Macdonchayd, Macdondchayg, Macdonchid, Macdonchyd, Machdonchayd, Macdondchuyd, Macdonnchaid, Macdomichaid, Macdomidach, Mecdonchyg, Micdonchid, Bernard, sometime rector, Ballymote, died *c.*1460 Ann., Bernard, canon, 1465 Cormac, vicar, Ballysadare, 1423, removed, 1428, Ann., Cormac, rector, Ballymote, 1427, 1430 Ann., Cormac, canon, 1444 Donald, provost, 1448 Donald OP, abbot, Ballysadare, 1471, 1472, Ann., Malachy, canon, 1508 Magonius, vicar, Kilmorgan, 1458, Maurice OSA, abbot of Ballysadare, 1463, d.*c.*1472, Ann., d. ante 1484, Ann, Odo, canon, dean, rector, Killoran & Offichaire, prebends of Killoran, OSA, son of Melaghlin, son of Cormac, abbot, Ballysadare, d. in Rome, 1441, *AFM* Doheran & Cloonoghill, 1512 Rory OSA, abbot, Ballysadare, 1444 Ann., Tumultheus (Tomaltagh), canon, 1490, 1491, 1492, Melaghlin, priest, Emlefad, 1603 (*Cal. Par. Rolls, I James I*, 20–4, 29)

McDonnell, Mark, student, Ballymote, 1603 (*Cal. Par. Rolls, I James I*), 20–4 McEparson (Mac an Phearsúin, MacPharsons, Parsons), Turlough, student, Ballymote, 1603 (*Cal. Par. Rolls, I James I*, 20–4, 29), Durcan, Macduarchayn, Donald, Thomas, priest

McGowane, Brian McRorie (Mac Gobhann, MacGowan), priest, 1603, Ballymote (*Cal. Par. Rolls, I James I*, 20–4)

McKelly, Macealay, Maceally, Mackellayd, Makeallayg, Makealyg, Makeallyg, Micciallaid Cornelius, clerk, Cornelius, son of priest, canon, *c.*1503–13, 1504, 1512, provost, vicar, Killoran, Tuemenere (Toomour?) & Cloonoghill, 1512, David, vicar, Emlefad, 1447, Donald

Macemundduhyili, Gilbert, canon, 1489

Mac Aodhagain, MacEgan, Egan, Macgaedagan, Magaedagan Dermit, canon, 1443, d.1449

Macgillalnachrind, Murianus

Macgillibygi, Philip

Macguillichaenygel alias Macabrechim

Macgyllahulyd, John, canon, 1495

Machenri, Machenry, Machani, Machenei, Machenagh, Machenregi, Machenryg, MacHenry, Henry, Macquenry, Edmund, canon, 1489, 1497, Edmund, cleric, vicar, Chiluchach & Cloonmore, removed, 1508, Muritius, cleric, vicar, Kilmovee, removed, 1508, Philip, rector, Sliabloga, 1432, Ann., canon, 1447, Philip, canon, 1493, 1497

Machmerbertrin, Bernard, canon, 1508 see Macmirhuytn below.

McGilligan or Gilligan, Machyllichan, Murianus, vicar, Attymas, 1456

Mackyllayc, Thomas, canon, 1509

McLoughlin, Maclochlainn, Machloclaynd, Murianus

MacManus, Mac Maghnuis, priest, McManes, Arte (Art) 1603 (Cowrteroriballagh) (*Cal. Par. Rolls, I James I*, 20–4, 29)

Macmirhuytn, Macmurhytahyn, Macmyrthayn, Macmyrythyn, Machmyrherryn,

Macnnrhuyton, Bernard, canon, provost, 1504, 1508, 1510, vicar, Cloonoghill, 1510, deprived, 1512.

Maol Ruadháin, Irriell (Irial) McMoelrony O'Higgin, friar,

Maconhanne, Mycconhane, Charles, provost, prebend, Meemlough & Doheran, 1490, deprived of provostship, 1495, see Macrorehane, below.

Macrorchanc, Charles, cleric, rector, Benada, 1489

Macruern alias Ochara, Charles, rector, Benada, 1510. see above & also O'Hara

Macsearraith, Maccearryd, Macerry, Macscarri, Mactearryd (McSharry), Cornelius, rector, Benada, 1423, resigned, 1428, abbot, Ballysadare, 1428, abbot, Ballysadare, removed 1444, Ann., still in possession, 1556[–7], Cornelius, abbot, Ballysadare, 1484, removed, 1504 William OSA, abbot of Ballysadare, 1556[–7], deprived, 1461, Ann.

Mag Néill, McGrail, Magneill, Morianus, Geraghty, Mag Oireachtaigh, Magoreachtaid, Cornelius

McDermot, Micdiarmada, Thady

Mac Muircheartaigh?, perhaps MacMurty, Macmayrgurthasynd, Macmaygierthasynd Rory, canon, 1507, Elphin; prior, St Mary's, Inchmacnerin, 1507 Mycconchyd, Thomulteus, cleric, canon, prebend of Toomour, rector, Emlafada, 1490; Farrell, Fearill, Fearghal, Fergal, More, priest, 1603 (*Cal. Par. Rolls, I James I*, 20–4, 29); Banahan, Ó Beathnachain, Obeachnachan John, clerk, canon, vicar, Cloonoghill, 1443.

Obenan, Ybenan, Donald, canon, prebend of Athleathan, vicar, Bohola & Cornan, d.Tuam, 1509.

Obeollayn (Boland), Laurence

Oberney (O'Birn, O'Beirne, Byrne), Donald, canon, 1509

O'Branley, Obrangali, Obrangli, Ybrangale, Donald, prebend, Emlefad, d.c.1482, Florence, priest, Matthew

Ocaela, Cornelius, priest, Achonry, vicar, Maghrata, dioc., Cork, 1488.

Ocallanan, Ochalanam, Okallanayn (O'Callanain, Callanan), Cormac, Matthew, clerk, sometime vicar, Kilmorgan, died in Rome *c.*1452, Matthew, clerk, dioc. Elphin, 1480, priest, son of priest, vicar, Emlefad, 1482 & Emlefad & Toomour, archdeacon, 1484 Matthew, priest, vicar, Toomour, deprived, 1512

Canavan, Oceandubain, Ocennamayn, Philip, Miler, canon, Tuam, rector, Athleathan, 1490 1492 (described several times as canon, Tuam)

Carney, Kearney, Ocearrnaid, Ocernayd, Okcarnagh, Okearnaych, Okearnayd, Okearnaid, Okearrnaid, Okearnaind, Brian, canon 1448, 1454, 1463, sometime vicar, Kilmacteige, Brian, OSA, Inchmacnerin, abbot, Ballysadare, 1463, Conn, canon, 1448, sometime, vicar, Kilconduff, vicar, Killasser, 1448, canon, 1460, Dermit, vicar, 1460, John, canon, Maurus OSA, formerly vicar, Kilmacteige, *c.*1438, Tatianus, priest, 1443, 1446, rector, Kilmacteige, 1446, 1448, Thomas, canon, prebend of Kilmacteige, 1448

Ocerhury, Malachy, canon, 1512; Kerrigan, Ociaragan, Luke

O'Keane, Ochian, Thady, rector, Killoran, deprived, 1512; Coen, Coyne or Quinn, Ochoan, Ocuynn, Ochuinn, Cormac, Bohola, 1429, Cormac, canon, 1447, Thomas, clerk, 1447

Ochonayn, Ychonayn, Thomas, sometime vicar, Emlefad, d.*c.*1482

Ochonnean, Ochoneam, Ochonncam, Brian, canon, Kilmacteige & Benada, 1465

Ochuer, Thady, priest, rector, Benada, 1491; Clery, Oclerig, Ocleri, Dermit, vicar, Bohola, 1430, Ann., Dermit, canon, 1460, Denis, vicar, Toomore, removed, 1509

Oclonen, Philip, canon & prebend of Killoran, 1504 see Ocliman below, Thady, canon & prebend of Killoran, 1504 see Ocluman below

Coleman, Ocluman, Yclumain, Oclinan, Oclinnan, Oclinnhan, Oclauun, Oclonen, Ocluan, see above

Ocluayn, Ocluban, Oclunain, Oclunan, Oclwan, Ycluan, Andrew OFM, Donatus, OSA Tuam, abbot Ballysadare, 1461 (for 6 or 7 years), Donatus, OSA, canon, Ballysadate, vicar, Kilbeagh, 1484, John, clerk, 1443, son of priest, John, rector, 1446, rector, Kilmacteige & Killoran, 1443, deprived 1446, Ann., 1448, John, canon, 1447, John, canon, 1480[–1], John, canon, 1497, Magonius, vicar, Kilvarnet, 1504, d. vicar, Ballysadare, abbot in commendam, Ballysadare, canon & prebend of Killoran, 1504, Malachy, vicar, Killoran 1449, resigned *c.*1473, Malachy OFM, vicar-provincial, Malachy, cleric, rector, Benada, 1491, Maurice, sometime, vicar, Killoran, Nicholas, Patrick OFM, Philip OFM, Philip, canon & prebend of Killoran, 1504 see Oclonen above, Patrick, Philip, priest & canon, Philip, sometime dean, Philip, canon, 1508, priest, vicar, Killoran, 1510, Thady, clerk, rector, 1449, Thady, canon & prebend of Killoran, 1504 see Oclonen above, Thady, cleric, son of priest, rector, Ui Fiodhcuire & Benada, 1510. See above William, canon, 1470, 1472, 1484, 1489, William, cleric, vicar, Killoran, 1473, Ann. William, canon, 1497, vicar, Killoran, d.*c.*1510 see above, Donatus (O'Clawne, Ó Clúmháin, Coleman), priest Killwohrine (Killoran?), 1603 (*Cal. Par. Rolls, I James I*, 20–4, 29)

Ocogli, Thady, canon, 1497

Ocogolan, Ochocolan, Ochongulan (Coughlan?), Thomas, alias Omaygnay, *c.*1503–13, provost, rector, Clerandirach? & Culein? (Coolavin?), priest, prebend of

Doheran, deprived, 1512, deprived of provostship, 1512.

Ocongulain (O'Conghalain, Connellan, Conlon), Thomas, dean, archdeacon &
canon, 1476[–7], dean, 1477, bp elect 1484 Ann.

Oconiel (Conneely), Maurice

Ocoimean, Ochonnean, Oconnean, Ocoymiean (Cummins?), Cormac, Bernard,
canon, 1470, dean, d.c.1476[–7] in Rome, Maurice, vicar, Cloynahacglasse?, 1470;
Connington, Ó Connachain, Conaghan, Cunningham, Ocomnachan,
Ochonnochan, Ocommochan, Ycomnachan, Yc(h)onnochan, Oconnincham,
Conaghan, Cunningham, Oconnochan, Cormac, cleric, provost, vicar, Kilvarnet,
1489, son of priest, provost (William below) and married woman, Ludovicus,
priest, vicar Clunoghill, 1475, Ann. d.c.1510, Thomas, clerk, William, canon,
provost, vicar, Cloonoghill, 1443, 144?; Moriasse (Muirgheas, Maurice)
Cunningham), priest, 1603, Achonry (*Cal. Par. Rolls, I James I*, 20–4, 29)

Oconnachayriz, Maurice, canon, c.1503–13

O'Connor, O'Conchubhair, Oconchubar, Oconchubair, Ococonbar Bernard, canon,
1495, Maurice, canon, 1449, Odo, Odo, rector, Ballymote, d.c.1427, Terence OP
(Elphin), rector, Killaraght, 1548, Ann.

Ó Con Lurga, David, priest, canon, 1454, vicar, Killaraght; Counihan?, Ocunamhan
Maurice, cleric,, prebend of Cloonghill, deprived, 1512

O'Quinn, Ocuyn, Ocrun, Donat, canon, 1493, 1497, vicar Killasser, 1521; Durcan,
Odarcan, Odarchan, Odartan Bernard, priest, vicar, Kilmorgan (1452–8); Bernard,
clerk, sometime vicar, Toomour, 1484, Dermit, priest, vicar, Toomour, John,
archdeacon, 1449, 1460, vicar, Kilshalvy, 1460

O'Derrig, Oderich, Odrich John, canon, rector, Athleathan, 1490, Hugh (Ó Deirg,
Derrig), priest, Cowrtcroriballagh? (Court) (*Cal. Par. Rolls, I James I*, 20–4, 29)

Odomagan, John, canon, 1495

O'Donilly, Owen (Eoghan) Carragh (Ó Donnghalaigh, Donnelly), priest, 1603,
Inileaghefadda? (Emlafad) (*Cal. Par. Rolls, I James I*, 20–4, 29)

O'Dowd, Ó Dubhda, Odubda, Oduda, Cormac, rector, Straide, 1423, Cormac, priest,
vicar of Kilmacteige, 1442[–3], Donald OFM, prior, Ballymote, 1482, Eugenius,
c.1503–13, archdeacon, c.1503–13, Gargallus, vicar, canon, c.1503–13

Odulcnain, Donald OSA, Ballysadare, 1463[–4], son of ordained Augustinian Canon

Oegle, Thady, canon, 1510, see Ocogli

Oelnam?, William, clerk, son of clerk, vicar, Killoran, 1473

O'Farrell, O'Fearghail, Iffargaill, Offergayl, John, vicar, canon, c.1503–13, Maurice,
canon, 1495, Torroleus, vicar, c.1503–13

O'Ferries (Ó Fearghuis, Fergus, Ferris, etc.), Brian, priest, Rossonever?, priest, 1603
(*Cal. Par. Rolls, I James I*, 20–4, 29)

Oficeallaid, Oficillaid, Yficeallaid (O'Fihily), Charles, vicar, Toomour, 1441

O'Flannelly, O'Flannghaile, Offlagmigale, Offlangalle (O'Flannelly, Flannery), John,
prior, c.1503–13, Patrick, canon, 1495, James O'Flanelly, priest, Rathlie?, 1603
(*Cal. Par. Rolls, I James I*, 20–4, 29); Flynn, Ofloynd, Offuyn, Ofloynn Charles,
Dermit, canon, 1462, Thady, priest, rector, Kilmacteige & Benada, 1497

Ofynnachta (O'Finaghty), Thady

Ogamanayn, Miler, cleric, rector, Athleathan, 1493

O'Gara, Ogara, Cornelius, clerk, 1470, Cornelius, canon, 1497, Eugenius, clerk, 1447, Rory, rector, Coolavin, 1428 Ann., Thomolteus, priest, rector, Coolavin, deprived, 1486/7

Ogartan, Ygartan, sometime vicar, Kilshalvy, see Odarcan, John, sometime vicar, Emlefad, d.*c*.1480

O'Grady, Igrada, Richard, priest, canon, vicar, Chiluchach? & Cloonmore, & Kilmovee, 1508

O'Hara, Ohadra, Ochara, Oara, Ochegra, Ohacgra, Ohagra, Ohara, Ohcara, Oheadgra, Oheadra, Oheagra, Oheara, Ohegra, Ohera, Chara, Yagra, Yara, Yhegra, Bernard, canon, Bernard, clerk, 1443, Bernard (son of bishop), clerk, dean, 1431, Ann., 1447, 1463, bishop, 2 Sept. 1463, Bernard, *c*.1503–13, canon, 1510, Charles, canon, 1510, Cormac, canon, Cormac, rector, Benada, 1428, Ann., Cormac, cleric, dean, 1478, deprived, 1494, Ann, Cormac, dean, deprived, 1512, Cornelius, Cornelius, dean, Cornelius, rector, Coolavin, 1490, Dermit (son of bishop), canon, provost, prebend, Toomour & Drumrat, 1448, d.*c*.1490, Donald, canon, Donald, archdeacon, 1429 Ann., 1447, Donatus OSA, sometime abbot Ballysadare, Donough O'Hara Duv OSA, the O'Hara, son of John, entered Benada, 1439, Eugenius, John, canon & dean, 1428, deprived, 1431, Ann., John, canon, rector of Benada, 1456[–7], canon, 1460, 1462, rector, Kilmacteige, 1464[–5], deprived, 1465, Ann., canon, 1475, canon, vicar, Kilmactigue, 1478 Magonius, Maurice, canon, 1472[–3], 1473, rector & vicar, Kilmactigue, 1473, Rory, canon, 1449, Rory, sometime vicar, Killoran, resigned it to bp Cornelius Omochan, Rory, canon, 1472, 1473, 1480, 1489, cleric, dean, 1494, Ann., Rory, cleric, rector, Kilmactigue & Benada, 1497, Rory, canon & prebend of Killoran, d. ante 1504., Tacianus, sometime vicar, Killasser *c*.1448, Tatheus, cleric, canon & prebend of Killedan, rector, Wykare & Kalludrin (Offichaire & Killoran?), 1477, Ann., Thady, canon, provost, 1495, resigned *c*.1504; Henigan, Oheanagan, Ohacnagan, Oheaynhugan, Ohynangan, Ohynaga, Ohynhagan, Ohynnigan, Oynaghan, Dermit, canon, vicar, Kilmactigue, 1484, Neill (Nigel), canon, vicar, Kilmactigue, *c*.1348, Niall (probably same as above), vicar, Kilmactigue, died in Rome, *c*.1446, Odo, priest, vicar Killasser, 1521 1603, Will. O'Henygane (Ó hÉanacháin, friar, Tullynegloge (Tullynaglug, Tourlestane?) (*Cal. Par. Rolls, I James I*, 20–4, 29)

O'Hara?, Ohegea, Roderick, cleric, rector, Killoran, 1490; Heally or Hely, Ohely Yhely, John, sometime vicar, Emlefad, Malachy, sometime vicar, Emlefad

O'Higgin (Ó hUiginn), Irriell (Irial) McMoelrony (Maol Ruadháin) friar, 1603, Moygara (*Cal. Par. Rolls, I James I*, 20–4, 29), Pól (1628–1724), studied literature and rhetoric in Ireland, 13 months in Irish College, Seville, 29 Oct. 1666, Irish College, Rome, 1668, priest, returned to Ireland, PP, Achús, 1677–8 VG, Killala, became acquainted with Thomas Otway, Bp of Killala and Achonry, 1680 became Protestant minister, Narcissus Marsh, provost of Trinity, appointed him to teach Irish and preach in Irish once a month in College Chapel, collaborated on publication of Bedell's Old Testament, 1682, benefices in Templemore, Tipperary, 10 October 1724, died, aged ninety-six.

Ohona, Roger, canon, 1491; Heraghty?, Ohoreachtayg, Ohorachtaih, Ohorechti, Rory, clerk, Simon, vicar, Cloonoghill, 1423, Thady

O'Higgin, Ohuycgynd, Ohygyn, Malachy, cleric, Tuam, son of priest & unmarried relative, rector, Bohola, 1491, Ochuardius, canon, prebend of Doheran, 1508

Okassy (O'Casey), Cormac OSA, Benada, 1460

Okeanaid (Kenny?), Cornelius, canon, 1448, see Ocearnaid

Okygan (Keegan), Rory, vicar, Killasser, removed, 1509

Okerina, Malachy, vicar, c.1503–13

Okym, O'Quinn), Donat, canon, vicar, Killasser & Toomore, 1509

Omathet, Thomas, canon, 1449

Omaylli (O'Malley), Hugh, OSA, Benada, 1456

Omerimchan, Matthew, priest, vicar, Kilmorgan, 1510

Omiagaid, Omigard, Eugenius, vicar, Kilmacteige, Thady, rector, Benada, d.c.1423

Omichion, Matthew, sometime vicar, Kilbeagh, d. ante 1484

Ominachan, Omirachan, Donald, canon, 1484, Donatus, canon, 1475, 1490 see above

Omithian, John OSA, Ballysadare, 1463

Ommachan, Donat, canon, 1504 see Ominachan.

Omnyhan, Donat, canon, 1510; Mohan, Moon, Maughan, Omochan, Omocan, Omocham, Omachan, Omochon, Omokan, Omothan, Ymochan, Ó Mocháin, Benedict, Charles, clerk, 1444, vicar, Killaraght, 1444, Cormac, Cormac, canon, 1444, Cornelius, clerk, Cornelius, priest, canon, Cornelius, Achonry priest, O. Cist, abbot, Boyle 1444, bp Achonry, Donald, son of bishop (above), priest, rector, Athleathan, 1493, Donald, canon, Donald, abbot, Boyle, 1444, Fergal, cleric, 1486/7, rector, Coolavin, 1486/7, Henry, priest, vicar, 1444, vicar, Killaraght, 1454, John, Malachy, rector, Benada, 1456[–7], rector, Dacorran & Mota, 1460, canon, 1460, 1465, Achonry & Elphin, 1460, canon, 1465, Odo, Odo, priest, sometime rector, Benada, c.1456, canon, 1461, 1484, Odo O. Cist., Odo, canon, Odo, canon 1460, Patrick, Rory, clerk, 1441, Rory, priest, rector, Coolavin, 1441, Ann., 1447, Rory, vicar, Killaraght, rector, Coolavin, 1490, Rory, canon, 1504, William Shane (Ó Mocháin, Maughan), priest, Bonanysdanie?, 1603 (*Cal. Par. Rolls, I James I*, 20–4, 29)

Omoitani, Roger, canon, 1515 (see Rory Omochan); Murphy, Omurchu, Omurcheu, Omurchonda, Ymurchw, Alexander, canon, 1461, 1472, Alexander, canon, 1490 see above, David, Elias, canon, John, rector, Bohola, 1491, d. ante 1502, Thomas, priest

Omynachan, Donatus, Donat, canon, 1489, 1490

O'Mwllvihilly, Dermot Glasse, priest, Bonanydanie?, 1603 (*Cal. Par. Rolls, I James I*, 20–4, 29)

Onachon, Donaldus, priest, parish, Hanleon? Ann., see Omochan; Neary, Onaray, Ynaraid, Andrew Nicholas, priest, Sliablugha, Odo OSA, Ballysadare

Orachin, Orachnyn, Oracnaid, Oracuiad, John OSA, abbot, Ballysadare, 1446, Ann., 1457, John, vicar, Kilvarnet, 1489

O'Reilly, O'Rahily, Oraegaily Donaldus, dean, d.c.1428 Ann.

Ordartan, John, priest, vicar, Templemore, vicar, Kilshalvy, archdeacon, 1447, see Odarcan

Oruhan, Oruam (Ruane), Magonius, clerk, sometime vicar, Killasser

Oscluayd, Rory, priest, sometime, vicar, Emlefad, & Killimicallain?, 1480 see below

Oseluit, Rory, priest, vicar, Kilshalvy, 1460

O'Scanlan?, Oscanlayn, Ostanlayn, Ystanlayn, Cornelius, canon, prebend & vicar, Emlefad, 1482, Tomultheus, canon, 1489 (see below), Tomulteus, canon, prebend, vicar, Emlefad, 17 Feb. 1504

Osuegaid, Ysingaid, Donald, clerk; Dyer? O'Dyer?, Othedura, Otedura Odo, canon, 1460, sometime dean, Achonry, became a Hermit of St Augustine, in Holy Trinity, Skreen, dioc. Meath, William OSA, Benada, 1445

O'Toner, Othinir, Othonijr, Ochonyr, Othonir, Othonyr, Ochonir, Othomnayr, Ythonyr, Othanyr, Octonyr, Tonyr, Thady, vicar Kilmacteige, 1460, priest, 1462, 1484, rector, Kilmactigue & Benada, 1495, canon, 1497

Otonley, Thomas, cleric, canon & prebend of Doheran, removed, 1508

O'Grady?, Ouradi, Nicholas

APPENDIX SIX: RECTORS AND VICARS

Rectors

Athleathan (Ballylahan), twelve marks:

Ante 1405, Pilib Ó Ceanndubháin, Eoghan Ó hEadhra;

Ante 1418, John Juvenis de Exeter;

1418–?, Domhnall Mac Duarcán;

1423, Cormac Ó Dubhda;

1 July1492, Domhnall Ó Neachtain (Onachon).

Banada & Hy-Fiachra, lay patrons:

Ante 1410, Eoghan Ó hEadhra;

1410–17, Tadhg Ó (Omiagaid?), d. ante Dec., 1417, Maghnus or Cormac Ó hEadhra;

Dec. 1417, Tadhg Ó (Omiagaid);

Jan. 1419, Eoghan Ó hEadhra (d. in Rome);

1423–8, Conn Mac Searraidh (resigned to pope in Rome);

1428 Cormac Ó hEadhra;

10 May 1440, Tadhg Ó Clúmhán;

18 May 1440, Brian Ó hEadhra (son of Bishop Ó hEadhra);

Ante 1443, Tadhg (Tassianus?) Ó Cearnaigh, Brian Ó hEadhra;

1443–6, Seán Ó Clúmháin;

Ante 1446, Cormac Ó hEadhra, Tadhg Ó Clúmháin;

17 Oct. 1446, Tadhg (Tatianus) Ó Cearnaigh;

Ante 1448, Tadhg Ó Clúmháin;

1448, Seán Ó Clúmháin;

1465, Seán Ó hEadhra;

1465, Brian Ó Coinín (Ochoneam).

Bohola, ten marks:

Ante 1429, John de Exeter;

1429, Cormac Ó Coinne (Ocuynn);

Ante 1491, Seán Ó Murch;

1491, Maeleachlainn Ó hUiginn (Ohuycgynd).

Coolavin and Ranna, five to ten marks, of lay patronage, with care of souls:
1401, Cormac Ó Coimín;
1425, Cormac Ó Coimín;
1428, Ruaidhrí Ó Gadhra;
1428, Ruaidhrí Ó Mocháin;
1428, Eoghan Ó Gadhra;
Ante 1441, Ruaidhrí Ó Gadhra;
Dec. 1441–4, Ruaidhrí Ó Mocháin;
1444–?, Cathal Ó Mocháin;
Ante 1447, Eoghan Ó Gadhra,
15 December 1441–6, May 1447, Ruaidhrí Ó Mocháin;
Ante 1486–7, Tomaltach Ó Gadhra;
1486–7, Fearghal Ó Mocháin;
Ante 1490, Conn Ó Gadhra;
1490, Ruaidhrí Ó Mocháin;
1505–?, Tomás Ó Cochláin (Ochocolan).

Dá Chorann & Mota (Ballymote), twenty-five marks:
Ante 1410, Brian Mac Donnchadha;
Ante 1412, Aodh Ó Conchobhar;
25 May 1411–24, May 1412, Domhnall Mac Donnchadha, dean of Elphin;
1418, Cormac Mac Donnchadha;
1419–26, Domhnall Mac Donnchadha, dean of Elphin;
1426–30, Brian Mac Donnchadha (entered OP's Sligo);
1427–30, Cormac Mac Donnchadha;
1443, Domhnall Mac Donnchadha;
1443, Brian Mac Donnchadha (Elphin);
1447, Brian Ó hEadhra, son of Bishop Ó hEadhra,
Ante 1460, Brian Mac Donnchadha,
4 July 1460–?, Maeleachlainn Ó Mocháin,
Ante 1490, Maghnus Mac Donnchadha O. Prem,
1490, Tomaltach Mac Donnchadha (Mycconchyd).

Emlefad, six marks:
Ante 1447, Domhnall Mac Ceallaigh, Maeleachlainn Ó hEaladhaigh (Yhely), Seán
    Mac an Bhreitheamhan (alias Mac Donnchadha);
1447, Tomás Ó Cuinn (Ochoan);
1482, Tomás Ó Conáin (Ychonayn), Mathghamhain Ó Callanáin;
1482, Conn Ó Scannláin (Ystanlayn).

Killoran, eight marks:
1477, Tadhg Ó hEadhra;
Ante 1490, Ruaidhrí Ó hEadhra.

Kilmactigue, eight marks:
Ante 1454, Maeleachlainn Ó Mocháin;
*c.*1454–6[–7], Aodh Ó Mocháin;
1456[–7]–*c.*1478, Seán Ó hEadhra, 1489, Cathal Mac (Macrorehane?).

Sliabh Lugha, twelve marks:
Ante 1411, David de Angulo;
Nov. 1411, Nioclás Ó Grádaigh;
1423–32, Nioclás Ó Náradhaigh;
1432, Pilib Mac Éinrí.

Vicars
Athleathan (Straide), four marks:
Ante 1418, John de Exeter;
1418, Tomás Mac Duarcán,
Ante 1442, Dáithí Ó Murchú;
1442, Diarmaid Ó Cléirigh.

Attymass, one mark:
1426, Diarmaid Ó Conaill (Killala);
1456–7, More Mac Giollagáin (Murianus Machyllichan).

Ballysadare, seven marks:
Ante 1402, Aindréas Mac an Bhreitheamhan sr;
1402, Aindréas Mac an Bhreitheamha jr;
c.1425, Cormac Mac Donnchadha,
1426–8, Seán Mac an Bhreitheamhan;
Nov. 1428, Augustinian Canons.

Bohola, six marks:
Ante 1430 More (Morianus?) Mac Néill, Tomás Ó Murchú;
1429, Cormac Ó Coinne (Ocuynn);
1430, Diarmaid Ó Cléirigh.

Cloonoghill, three to six marks:
Ante 1435, Tomás Ó Comhdhain (Ycomnachan);
1435, Cathal Mac Cristín;
1435–43, Seán Ó Beathnacháin;
Ante 1443, Tomás Ó Connacháin;
1443–?, Uilliam Ó Connacháin;
Ante 1475, Tomás Mac an Bhreitheamhan (Macbreim);
29 November 1475–?, Lughaidh Ó Connacháin (Ludovico Oconnuochan);
Ante 1470, Muiris Ó Coimín (Ocoymiean);
1470, Conn Ó Gadhra.

Emlefad (Ballymote), eight marks:
c.1389, Mathgamhan Ó Branghaile;
1405, Seán Mac an Bhreitheamhan;
1422–5, Cormac Mac Donnchadha;
1425, Seán Mac an Bhreitheamhan;
Ante 1447, Seán Mac Donnchadha, Melaghlin Ó hEalaidhe, Domhnall Mac Ceallaigh;
1447, Tomás Ó Comhdhain;

Ante 1480–1, Seán Ó Duarcáin (Ygartan), Ruaidhrí Ó (Oscluayd?);
1480–1, Mathghamhan Ó Callanáin (Elphin).

Kilbeagh, four marks:
1429–32, Pilib Mac Éinrí;
Ante 1484, Mathghamhan Ó (Omichion?).

Kilconduff (Caylconduy):
Ante 1448, Conn Ó Cearnaigh.

Killaraght, four to five marks:
Ante 1411, Giollabranaynd Mac an Leagh;
1411, Tadhg Mac Diarmada (Elphin);
1413, Tadhg Mac Diarmada;
1424–35, Aodh Ó Mocháin (entered Cistercians in Rome);
1435, Conn Ó Mocháin;
Ante 1440, Domhnall Ó Mocháin (entered Cistercians in Rome);
1440, Cormac Ó Mocháin;
Nov. 1441, Éinrí Ó Mocháin;
10 July1444–?, Cathal Ó Mocháin;
1444, Padraig Ó Mocháin, Cormac Ó Mocháin;
1444–54, Éinrí Ó Mocháin;
1454, Dáithí Ó Collearaigh (Ocoyulerga).

Killasser, four marks:
Ante 1448, Tadhg (Tatiannus) Ó hEadhra, Maghnus Ó Ruadhán (Oruam), Milerus
    de Exeter, Tadhg Mac an Bhreitheamhan;
1448, Conn Ó Cearnaigh.

Killoran (Coolany), six marks:
*c.*1394, Nioclás Ó Clúmhain;
Ante 1405, Domhnall Ó Miadhacháin;
Ante 1435, Seán Ó hEadhra, Flann Ó Clúmhan, Cormac Ó hEadhra;
1435, Tadhg Ó Clúmháin (Killluathreand);
Ante 1449, Muiris Ó Clúmháin, Seán Ó Clúmháin;
1449, Maeleachlainn Ó Clúmháin;
1473, Ruaidhrí Ó hEadhra;
12 June 1473–?, Uilliam Ó Clúmháin (Oelnam, Killnaheind).

Kilmactigue, five to six marks:
Ante 1439, Muiris Ó Cearnaigh (entered Augustinians, Banada);
1439–43, Niall Ó hÉineacháin;
1443–, Cormac Ó Dubhda;
1446–60, Brian Ó Cearnaigh;
1460, 1462, Tadhg Ó Tomhnair (Othonir);
31 May1473–, Muirgheas Ó hEadhra;
28 Feb. 1478–, Seán Ó hEadhra;
Ante 1484, Tadhg Ó Tomhnair (Ochonir);
1484, Diarmaid Ó hÉineacháin.

Kilmorgan (Ballymote), four to five marks:
Ante 1405, Murchadh Mac Lachlainn, Murchadh Mac (Macgillanachrind?);
1410, Domhnall Ó Mocháin;
1410–?, Cormac Ó Callanáin;
1412, Seán Mac Cléirigh;
1428, Eoghan Mac (Macadruyth?);
Ante 1430, More (Murianus) Mac Lachlainn;
1427–30, Donnachadha Ó Miadhacháin,
1430–40, Mathghamhan Ó Callanáin (Killmur?), an Elphin cleric of the same name
    was vicar of Kilmacallan;
1440, Ruaidhrí Ó hOireachtaigh (Elphin);
1454–8, Brian Ó Duarcáin;
1458, Maghnus Mac Donnchadha.

Kilshalvey, three marks:
Ante 1447, Benedict Ó Duarcáin (Ygartan).

Kilturra (Bunninadden):
Ante 1401, Aodh Mac an Bhreitheamhan;
1401, Cormac Ó Coimín.

Kilvarnet (Collooney), four marks:
Ante 1435, Padhraig Ó Clúmháin, Domhnall Ó Scingín (Ysinguaid);
1435, Maghnus Ó Ruadhán (Oruhan);
*c.*1394, Padhraig Ó Clúmháin;
1408, Domhnall Oseguaid;
Ante 1435, Padraig Ó Clúmháin, Domhnall Ó Scingín (Ysingaid);
1435, Maghnus Ó Ruadháin;
Ante 1489, Seán Ó (Oracchnyn?);
1489, Cormac Ó Connacháin (Oconnincham).

Toomour (Keash):
1414, Domhnall Mac Ceallaigh;
1422, Tadhg Ó hOireachtaigh;
1424, Cathal Ó Floinn;
Ante 1435, Cathal Ó Fithcheallaigh, Domhnall Mac Ceallaigh;
1431–5, Diarmaid Ó Duarcán
1435, Flann O'Branghaile (Obrangaly);
1440, Brian Ó hEadhra, son of Bishop Ó hEadhra, together with those of Morachd
    & Drumrat;
1435, Flann Ó Branghaile;
1441, Diarmaid Ó Duarcán;
Ante 1484, Brian Ó Duarcáin;
1484, Mathghamhan Ó Callanáin.

Priests & Clerics
1408, Pilib Mac Gillabygi (priest);
1440, Tadhg Ó Clúmháin;
Ante 1513 Toirdealbhach Ó Fearghaile, vicar, Brian Ó hEadhra, Seán Ó Flannghaile, prior;
Julius II Lost Registers, *Indice* 349, ff.116, 117, 193, *CPL*, xix, nos 1915, 1916, 1917.

APPENDIX SEVEN: ABBOTS, MONKS AND FRIARS

St Mary's Augustinian Abbey, Ballysadare, 20–40 marks
Abbots
1428, Abbot Seán?, Oct. 1428, Conn Mac Searraigh, 1435, Cormac Mac Donnachadha 1435–44. Conn Mac Searraigh, 12 Aug. 1444, Ruaidhrí Mac Donnchadha, 1446, Conn Mac Searraigh, 3 June 1446, Seán Ó (Oracuaid or Oracniad), ante 1456–7, Conn Mac Searraigh, 1461, Uilliam Mac Searraigh, 24 Dec. 1461–71, Donnchadha Ó Clúmháin, 1463, Uilliam Mac Searraigh, 11 Aug. 1463–71, Muiris Mac Donnchadha, ante 1471, Donnchadha Ó Clúmháin, 31 Jan. 1472, Domhnall Mac Donnchadha OP, ante 1484, Muirgheas Mac Donnchadha, Conn Mac Searraigh, 1484–1504, *in commendam*, Maghnus Mac Donnchadha, O. Prem.

Augustinian Canons, Ballysadare
1503–4, Seán Ó Mithidhín (Omithian), 1503–4, Domhnall Ó Dubhalcháin (Odulcnain).

Cistercian Abbots of Boyle
d.1174, Muirgheas Ó Dubhthaig, d.1225, Ó Maoil Bhreanainn, ante 1238–48, Aonghus Ó Clúmháin (1248, Bishop of Achonry, resigned and d. in Boyle 1263), d.1263, Dáithí Ó Finn d.1280, Mathghamhan Ó Conchobhar, 1297, Maelseachlainn Mac Briain, More Ó (Marian Odonnover OP), d.c.1302, Maeleachlainn Ó Baoighil, c.1280, Luirint Ó Lachtnán (d.1307 as Bishop of Kilmacduagh), 1298–1303, Donnchad Ó Flannagán (1303–7), Bishop of Elphin d.1344, Murchadh O'Hara ('intended bishop of Luighne'), resigned 1350, Maeleachlainn?, 1350, Donnchadha?, 1414, Eoghan Mac Donnchadha, 1414–28, Cormac Mac Dáibhidh, 1428, Aodh Mac Diarmada, d.1441, Domhnall Ó Mocháin, 1441–4, Tadhg Mac Diarmada (d.1444 in Rome), 1444, Seán Mac Dáibhidh, 1444–9, Conn Ó Mocháin (1449, Bishop of Achonry), ante 1463, Maeleachlainn Mac Donnchadha, 1463, Conn Mac Dáibhidh, 1470, Cormac Mac Dáibhidh, 1534–49, Aodh Mac Diarmada 1539, 1555, Tomoltach Mac Diarmada 1569, d.1584, Giolla Íosa Ó Cuileannáin (hanged in Dublin).

Augustinian Friars, Banada
1439, Muiris Ó Cearrnaigh

Third Order, Franciscans, Ballymote
1441, Padhraig, Pilib and Aindréas Ó Clúmháin (founders).

16 Sept. 1630, postulation by Achonry clergy for Anthony Lynch OP (*SOCG*, vol. 14, ff, 126r, 126bisv: see *Coll. Hib.*, no. 10); postulation for Hugh MacDermott for vicar apostolic, 20 Aug. 1683, *CP*, vol. 30, f.242rv; 4 Sept. 1684, postulation by chapter and clergy of Achonry for Hugo MacDermott, vicar apostolic for Bishop of Achonry, 4 Sept. 1684, vol. 5 f.289r: see *Coll. Hib.*, nos 27 & 28, 105–6 (1630), Dominic Francus (French), dean, Eugene Kennanus (Kennan), *curatus*, Kilbeagh Patrick Heoig, *curatus*, Kilcolman, Hugh Martin, *curatus*, Bille (Kilvarnet) Columban Higgins, *curatus*, Templemore, Magonius (Mághnus, Manus) Laighnain, *curatus*, Pocola (Bohola), William Mac a Lea (Mac an Leagha, MacAlea), *curatus*, Kilmaghain (Kilmorgan) and Tuaim Over (Toomour), James Gnelius (Nelly, O'Neill) *curatus*, Imlecensis (Emlefad), Richard Donoghue (MacDonagh), *curatus*, Ballysadare, Patrick Brenan, *curatus*, Killasser, Fernal (Ferghal, Fergal) Kirain (1683), *parochus*, Kilturra, Arthur Bern, *parochus*, Kildarine, Phelimeas O'Hara, *vicarius generalis Achad. et decanus Acadensis*, Johanes Thogher, *canonicus Eccliae Cathedralis Achadensis*, Thadeus Higgins, *canonicus Eccliae Cathedr. Accadensis*, Galerus Costelloe, *canonicus Eccliae Cathedralis Achadensis*, Jacobus O'Connell, *parochus de Ballisdara in Dioesi Achadensi* (1684), Johanes Mc Donogh, *parochus de Killtora*, Thadeus Brynane, *parochus de Clunoghil*. Terentius Gara, *parochus de Castelmore*, Mauritius Frayne, *parochus de Kilcolman*, Bernardus Brynane, *parochus de Kilmacteig*, Milerus Mc Donogh, *parochus de Drumratt*, Petrus Nelly, *parochus de Killfry*, Rich. Cluan, *parochus de Killoran*, Patricius Henry *parochus de* Killvarnad, John McDonogh, *parochus*, Kilturra, James O'Connell, *parochus*, Ballysadare (see 1704 Registration Act) Richard Cluane, parochus, Killoran & Kilvarnet (see 1704 Registration Act), Thady Brenayne (Brennan), parochus, Clunoghil (see 1704 Registration Act), John Mortagh, parochus, Kilmactigue (see 1704 Registration Act), John Roddy, parochus, Kilconduff (see 1704 Registration Act), Phelim O'Hara, dean, Achonry (see 1704 Registration Act), Thady Higgins, praebendarius, Monlagh (Moymlough, Meemlough), Walter Costello, praebendarius, Kilmovee (see 1704 Registration Act), John Tougher, praebendarius, Dughern (Doheran) (see 1704 Registration Act), John Donough, parochus, Kill Carva, Miler Donough, parochus, Drumrat.

Irish Catholic Directory 1838, William J. Walsh, IER,
April–September 1876
James O'Hara, Templemore, Twomore, John Durkein (Durcan), Killedan & Boghola, John Roddy, Meelick, John Thogher, Killegarvan & Attymass, Johin Ruane, Killasser and half parish of Toomore, Morrish (Maurice) Frayne, Killconduffe, Walter Costello, Kilmovey, Dominick Berne, no parish, Chas. Hara (Charles O'Hara), Aconry, James Connell, Ballisadare, John Mortagh, Aconry, James Howly, Kill mac Teige, Patrick Kenry (Henry), Aconry, Rich. Cloane, Killoran, Will. Kenedy, Kill mac Teige, Bryan Brenane, Kill mac Teige, William macDonaugh, Killvarnett, Peter Nelly, Emlaghffad, Teige Davy, Killasalvy, Teague macDonagh, Killtorruffe (Kilturra), Edmonde Conane,

Kilmorhan (Kilmorgan), James Mullruniffin, Jewhmoure (Toomour), Teige Brenane, Cloonoghill, John mcDonnagh, Drumratt, John Maran, Killaraht, David Henery, Killffree, Terence Garra, Killcolman, Thady Higgin, Emlaghffad.

APPENDIX TEN: 1302–7 TAXATION OF ACHONRY

Church Value Tenth

The temporalities and spiritualities of the Bishop
of Achonry are taxed in the year at 25 marks 2 1/2 marks
The temporalities and spiritualities of the Abbots
and Convent of Monks de Buellio [of Boyle] 22s 2s. 2 1/4d
Temporalities and spiritualities of the Abbot and
convent of canons of Estdara [Ballysadare] … 2 marks. 40d. 3s.
Achagonny [Achonry] 2 marks 2s, 8d.
The community of the chapter in the sanctuary. 1/2 mark 8d.
Vicarage of the same 13s. 4d. 16d.
Kilmactarg [Kilmactigue] 5s. *in rure* 6d.
The same church in the sanctuary. 40d. 4d.
Vicarage of the same. 1/2 mark. 8d.
Kilcaochcrumyn *in rure* 5s. 6d.
And in the sanctuary 12d. 1 1/4d
Vicarage of the same. 3s. 3 1/2d
Estdara [Ballysadare] 40d. 4d.
Vicarage of the same. 20d 2d.
Athlechan [Straide]. 40s. 4s.
Vicarage of the same. 20s. 2s.
Clonbanna [?] 10s. 12d.
Vicarage of the same. 5s. 6d.
Milio [Meelick]. 13s. 4d. 16d.
Keltesguean [?] 1/2 mark 8d.
Vicarage of the same. 40d. 4d.
Kellenalasscan [?] 1/2 mark 8d.
Vicarage of the same. 40d. 4d.
Authigymnessik [Attymass] 5s. 6d.
Vicarage of the same 30d. 3d.
Kilnangarnan [Kilgarvan] 5s. 6d.
Vicarage of the same 30d. 3d.
Ratholuyn [?] 20d. 2d.
Vicarage of the same. 10d. 1d.
Ardnach [?] 12d. 1/4d.
Vicarage of the same. 6d. 1/2d.
Bothcomla [Bohola] 10s. 12d.
Vicarage of the same 5s. 6d.
Thuamore [Foxford]. 4s. 4 3/4d.
Vicarage of the same. 2s. 1/4d.

Kelcormdilk [Kilconduff?] 3s. 3 1/2d.
Vicarage of the same. 18d. 1 3/4d.
Kendoyn [?] 1/2 mark 8d.
Vicarage of the same. 40d. 4d.
Kelualydan [Killedan] 20d. 2d.
Vicarage of the same. 10d. 1d.
Clonochulli [Cloonoghill] 2s. 4d. 2 3/4d.
Vicarage of the same. 14d. 1 1/2d.
Kekelcurn 2s. 2 1/4d.
Vicarage of the same 12d 1 1/4d.
Kellosenyg 20d. 2d.
Vicarage of the same 10d. 1d.
Imelachfada [Emlaghfad] 40d. 4d.
Vicarage of the same. 20d. 2d.
Drumrathi [Drumrat] 2s. 4d. 2 3/4d.
Vicarage of the same. 14d. 1 1/2d.
Rectory of the churches de Mocrath and Thuamany. 20d. 2d.
Vicarage of the same. 10d. 1d.
Kellethratha [Killaraght] 40d. 4d.
Vicarage of the same 20d. 2d.
Culonyn [Coolavin] 40d. 4d.
Vicarage of the same. 20d. 2d.
Kelnafriych [Kilfree]. 2s. 2 1/4d.
Vicarage of the same. 12d, 1 1/4d.
Kellcalman [Kilcolman]. 5s. 6d.
Vicarage of the same. 30d. 3d.
De Castro Magno [Castlemore] 5s. 6d.
Vicarage of the same. 30d. 3d.
Kelmoby [Kilmovee]. 5s. 6d.
Vicarage of the same 18d. 1 3/4d.
Cluanmore [Clonmore Cloonmore in Kilbeagh parish]. 3s. 3 1/2d.
Vicarage of the same. 30d. 3d.
Vicarage of Kellcath, whose rectors are Templars. 30d.
Kelmorchun [Kilmorgan]. 2s.
Vicarage of the same. 12d.
Sum of taxation of the Diocese of Achonry. 35l. 6s. 9d. 70s. 8d.
(Q. R., Irish Exchequer, 533/9, Roll A., membr. 3 dors).

1423

16. Eadem die [9 Januarii], Symon Ohorachtaih, perpetuus vicarius de Cluaineocaill, Akadensis diocesis, tamquam principalis et privata persona, obligavit se camere nomine Cormati Macdomichaid super annata perpetue vicarie parrochialis ecclesie de Asdara, dicte diocesis, cuius fructus septem marcharum sterlingorum communi extimacione,

vacanti per resignacionem Andree Meicabrecuyn extra curiam, collate eidem Rome etc., iiij kal. Decembris, anno sexto. Item promisit producere mandatum ratificacionis infra x menses.

17. Eadem die [23 Marcii], Cormacus Odubda, principalis, obligavit se camere super annata rectorie de Athleathayn vulgariter noncupate, Akadensis diocesis, cuius fructus xij marcharum sterlingorum communi extimacione, vacantis per non promocionem Johannis juvenis de Exonia, collate eidem Rome etc., non., Marcii, anno sexto.

18. Die xxiiij mensis [Marcii], Cornelius Macsearraith, principalis, obligavit se camere super annata rectorie de Offhicari ac de Beannfada, Akadensis diocesis, cuius fructus xvj marcharum sterlingorum communi extimacione, vacantis per obitum Tathei Omiagard [vel Omiagaid] extra curiam, collate eidem Rome etc., ij non. Marcii, anno sexto.

1426

37. [Killala] Dicte die [13 Junii], una bulla pro Dermicio Oconaill pro Ardnariagh Sancte Marie virginis et de Attigymeassa, Aladensis et Akadensis diocesium perpetuis vicariis, quarum fructus quatuor Marcharum sterlingorum communi extimacione, fuit restituta sine obligacione. Ita est N. de Nica.

1427

39. Eadem die [29 Octobris] Cormacus Macdonnchaid [vel Macdomichaid], principalis, obligavit se camere super annata perpetui beneficii rectorie de Dacorand et Mota noncupati, Akadensis diocesis, cuius fructus vingentiquinque marcharum sterlingorum communi extimacione, vacantis per obitum Odonis Oconchubair extra curiam, collati eidem Rome etc., xij kal. Novembris anno decimo.

1428

47. Die x dicti mensis [Novembris], Cornelius Macsearaid, principalis, obligavit se camere super annata monasterii beate Marie de Asdara, ordinis S. A[ugustini], Akadensis diocesis, cuius fructus vigenti marcharum sterlingorum communi extimacione, vacaturi per privacionem Johannis abbatis etc., faciendam, collati eidem Rome etc., v non Octobris, anno undecimo.

48. Die prima dicti mensis [Decembris], Johannes Oheara, principalis, obligavit se camere super annata decanatus ecclesie Akadensis, cuius fructus octo marcharum sterlingorum communi extimactione, vacantis per obitum Donaldi Oraegaily, extra curiam, collati eidem Rome etc., vj kal. Novembris, anno undecimo.

49. Eadem die [10 Decembris] Cornelius Macsearaid, abbas monasterii beate Marie de Esdara, ordinis S. A[ugustini], Akadensis diocesis, ut principalis et privata persona, obligavit se camere nomine Cormachi Oheadra super annata rectorie terrarum ruralium de Offichaire et Beanfada, Akadensis diocesis, cuius fructus quatuordecim marcharum sterlingorum communi extimacione, vacantis per resignacionem Cornelii Micserrayd in curia, collate eidem Rome etc., xiij kal. Decembris, anno undecimo. Item promisit producere mandatum ratificacionis infra decem menses.

[20. Diocesis Elphinensis] Die dicti mensis Decembris, Johannes Oheara, canonicus ecclesie Akadensis, ut principalis et privata persona, obligavit se Camere, nomine abbatis et conventus monasterii Sancte Trinitatis de Lochque, Premonstratensis ordinis, Elphinensis dioc., super annata rectorie parrochialis in terris ruralibus inter duos pontes ecclesie de Minbrisgh alias castri de Sligeach noncupate, Elphinensis dioc., cuius fructus vigenti marcharum sterlingorum communi extimatione, vacantis per ingressum religionis Bernardi Macdoncayd, ad domum de Sligeach ordinis (et dioc. [sic]) Predic[a]torum, prefato monasterio uniende; collate eisdem Rome etc., ii kal. Novembris, anno undecimo. Item promisit producere mandatum ratificacionis infra decem menses.

50. Eadem die [17 Decembris], Cornelius Macsearaid, abbas beate Marie de Easdara, ordinis S. Augustini, Akadensis diocesis, principalis, obligavit se camere proprio nomine ac eciam nomine conventus dicti monasterii super annata perpetue parrochialis ecclesie de Easdara, Akadensis diocesis, cujus fructus septem marcharum sterlingorum communi extimatione, prefato monasterio uniende, vacantis per non promotionem Cormaci Macdonchaid, collate eidem Rome etc., vj Novembris, anno undecimo.

1429

62. Eadem die [25 Maii], Edmundus Dihedi, vicarius perpetuus ecclesie Sti. Nicolay, Elfinensis diocesis, ut provincialis et privata persona, obligavit se camere nomine Cormaci Ocuynn super annata parrochialis ecclesie de Botcomla, Akadensis diocesis, cuius fructus sex marcharum communi extimacione, vacantis per non promotionem Johannis de Exonia et per devolucionem, collate eidem Rome apud Sanctos Apostolos, vj non. Maii, anno duodecimo. Item promisit producere mandatum ratificacionis infra sex menses. [In margine: Non fuit sortita effectum, quia est infra taxam, et fuit [bulla] die xxij predicti mensis restituta sine obligacione.]

72. Dicta die [4 Maii] Cormacus Macdomidach, principalis, obligavit se camere super annata perpetui ecclesiastici beneficii sine cura, rectorie terrarum ruralium de Dachorand et Muta noncupati, Akadensis diocesis, cuius fructus xxv marcharum sterlingorum, vacantis per obitum Odonis Oconchubar extra curiam defuncti, collate eidem Rome etc., viij kal. Aprilis, anno terciodecimo.

73. Die dicta [5 Julii 1428], una bulla pro Ruarico Ogara pro perpetuo beneficio, rectoria de Cuilobinn et Ranna nocupato, Akadensis diocesis, cuius fructus sex marcharum sterlingorum communi extimacione, fuit restituta sine obligacione. Ita est, Alfonsus.

74. Die dicta [15 Decembris 1428], una bulla pro Eugenio Macadruyth, super parrochiali ecclesia de Kyllemirchan, Akadensis diocesis, cuius fructus quinque marcharum sterlingorum communi extimacione, fuit restituta sine obligacione. Ita est, B. dellante.

75. Die xiiij dicti mensis [Februarii 1429], una bulla pro Donaldo Oheara super archiadiaconatu ecclesie Akadensis, cuius fructus sex marcharum sterlingorum commune extimacione, fuit restituta sine obligacione. Ita est, Bertranus [vel Bertram] Roberti.

76. Dicta die [27 Maii 1429], una bulla pro Cormaco Ocuynn, super parrochiali ecclesia de Betcomla, Akadensis diocesis, cuius fructus sex marcharum sterlingorum, fuit restituta sine obligacione. Ita est, Alfonsus.

77. Dicta die [15 Maii 1430], j bulla pro Dermico Oclerig super perpetua vicaria parrochialis ecclesie de Bothcamla, Akadensis diocesis, cuius fructus etc., iiij marcharum sterlingorum communi extimacione, restituta sine obligacione.

1431

89. Dicta die [2 Januarii] una bulla pro Matheo Ocallanain, super perpetua vicaria parochialis ecclesie de Killmur, Akadensis diocesis, cuius fructus etc., iiij marcharum sterlingorum communi extimacione, restituta fuit sine obligacione.

90. Dicta die [31 Octobris], Johannes Macbrecchunim, vicarius de Keysinnablan, Elphinensis diocesis, ut principalis et privata persona, obligavit se camere nomine Bernardi Oheadra super annata decanatus ecclesie Akadensis, cuius fructus etc., octo marcharum sterlingorum communi extimacione, vacaturi per privacionem Johannis Oheadra extra Romam curiam faciendam, collati eidem Rome etc., ut supra [anno incarnacionis dominice mcccxxxj], iij kal. Octobris anno primo.

1432

99. Dicta die [16 Octobris], Philippus Machenregi, principalis, obligavit se camere super annata rectorie parrochialium ecclesiarum terrarum ruralium de Sliabhloga, Akadensis diocesis, cuius fructus etc., duodecim marcharum sterlingorum communi extimacione, vacature per privacionem Nicolai Onaraid faciendam, collate eidem Rome etc., anno incarnacionis dominice mcccxxxj, v non Octobris, anno secundo.

1440

116. Dicta die [10 Maii]. Tatheus Ocluman, principalis, obligavit se camere super annata rectorie terrarum ruralium de Officaire de Beanfada, Akadensis diocesis, cuius fructus etc., quidecim marcharum sterlingorum communi extimacione, vacantis per devolucionem, collate eidem Florencie, anno ut supra [1440], xvj kal. Maii, anno decimo.

117. Dicta die [18 Maii], Bernardus Ohagra, principalis, obligavit se camere super annata rectorie terrarum ruralium de Ofychary de Bennfada, Akadensis diocesis, cuius fructus etc., sexdecim marcharum sterlingorum communi extimacione, vacantis per devolucionem, collate eidem Florencie, anno etc., mccc[c]xl, viiij kal Maii, annodecimo

1441

132 Die xv eiusdem [Decembris] Ruadricus Omochan, principalis, obligavit se camere super annata rectorie terrarum de Cuilofind et Rama, Akadensis diocesis, cuius fructus etc., decem marcharum sterlingorum communis extimacione, vacantis per non promocionem ad sacerdocium, collate eidem Florencie, anno etc., mccc[c] xlj, v id. Decembris, anno undecimo.

1443

153. Dicta die [4 Novembris], Joannes Ocluman, principalis, obligavit se camere super annata rectorie terrarum ruralium de Officaire et Benandfada, Akadensis diocesis, cuius fructus etc., sedecim marcharum sterlingorum communi extimacione, vacantis per non promocionem ad sacerdocium, collate eidem Rome apud S. Petrum, anno ut supra [1443], xvij kal. Novembris, anno terciodecimo.

154. Dicta die [20 Novembris] Thomas Macabrechun, principalis, obligavit se camere super annata decanatus ecclesie Akadensis, cuius fructus etc., dedem [rectius decem] marcharum sterlingorum communi extimacione vacaturi per privacionem faciendam, collati eidem Rome apud S. Petrum, anno etc., mcccccxliij, xiij kal. Novembris, anno terciodecimo.

1444
160. Dicta die [12 Augusti], Roricus Macdonchyd, principalis, obligavit se camere super annata monasterii beate Marie de Asdara, ordinis Sancti Augustini, Akadensis diocesis, cuius fructus etc., quadraginta marcharum sterlingorum communi extimacione, vacaturi per privacionem Cornelii Mactearryd de ipso faciendam, collati eidem Rome apud S. Petrum, anno etc., mccc[c]liiij, non. kal. Augusti anno quarodecimo.
161. Die x eiusdem [Julii] j bulla pro Carolo Omochan super perpetua vicaria parrochialis ecclesie de Killarchata, Akadensis diocesis, cuius fructus etc., quinque marcharum sterlingorum communi extimacione. Item j bulla pro eodem super perpetuo beneficio, rectoria terrarum ruralium noncupato, dicte diocesis, cuius fructus quinque marcharum similium communi existimacione, restituta sine obligacione quia infra taxam.

1446
165. Dicta die [3 Junii], Johannes Oracuiad [vel Oracniad], principalis, obligavit se camere super annata monasterii beate Marie de Asdara, ordinis S. Augustini, Akadensis diocesis, cuius fructus etc., quadraginta librarum sterlingorum, communi extimacione, vacaturi per privacionem Cornelii, moderi abbatis, collati eidem Rome apud S. Petrum, anno etc., mccccxlvj, undecimo kal. Maii, anno sextidecimo.
166. Die dicta [17 Octobris], Tatianus Okearnayd, principalis, obligavit se camere super annata rectorie terrarum ruralium de Oficary et Benfada, Akadensis diocesis, cuius fructus etc., sedecim marcharum argenti communi existimacione, vacature per privacionem Johannis Oclunian faciendam, collate eidem Rome apus S. Petrum, anno etc., ut supra [1446], pridie id. Septembris, anno sextodecimo. Gratis pro Deo.

1460
172. Dicta die [4 Julii], Malachias Omachan, principalis, obligavit se camere super annata rectoria terrarum ruralium de Dachoran et de Muta noncupate, Akadensis diocesis, cuius fructus etc., vigentiquinque marcharum sterlingorum, vacantis per obitum Bernardi Macdenchid extra curiam defuncti, et collate eidem sub data Petreoli, Senensis diocesis, xij kal. Junii, anno secundo. De mandato domini thesaurarii quia Ybernicus.

1461
179 Die xiiij eiusdem [Decembris], Donatus Ocluayn, principalis, obligavit se camere super annata monasterii beate Marie de Asdara, ordinis Sci. Augustini, Akadensis diocesis, cuius fructus etc., trigenta marcharum sterlingorum, vacaturi per privacionem Wiallialmi Macserray extra curiam in forma iuris faciendam, et conferendi eidem sub data Rome, quinto id. Julii, anno tercio.

1463
188. Die xj eiusdem [Augusti] Mauricius Macdonnchaid, principalis, obligavit se camere super annata monasterii beate Marie de Easdara, ordinis Sci. Augustini, Akadensis diocesis, cuius fructus etc., trigenta marcharum sterlingorum, vacaturi per privacionem Willialmi Macscarrayd in forma juris faciendam, et conferendi eidem Mauricio sub data Tibure, xij kal. Augustin, anno quinto.

1465

192. Die xxviiij eiusdem [Aprilis], una bulla pro Bernardo Ochoneam, canonico Akadensi, super provisione parrochialis ecclesie de Kilmiataig et Bennada, Akadensis diocesis, valoris octo marcharum sterlingorum communi extimatione, vacature per privacionem Johannis Ohara in forma iuris extra curiam faciendam, sub data Rome, sextodecimo kal. Martii, anno primo. Restituta, quia infra taxam etc. Gratis pro Ibernico paupere.

1472

213. Die xxxj eiusdem mensis [Januarii], dominus Donaldus Micdonchid, ordinis fratrum Predicatorum, Akadensis diocesis, principalis, obligavit se camere apostolice pro annata monasterii beate Marie de Asdara, ordinis S. Augustini, dicte Akadensis diocesis, cuius fructus trigenta marcharum sterlingorum communi extimatione, vacantis per obitum Mauricii, olim ipsius monasterii abbatis, extra Romam curiam defuncti, et mandatur provideri dicto Donaldo de dicto monasterio, sub data Rome, tertio kal. Decembris, anno primo. Et promisit solvere annatam dicti monasterii eidem camere infra sex menses immediarte a die habite possessionis computandos, sub penis etc. etc. Restituta, de mandato domini mensarii, quia pro Hibernico et in bulla narratur intrusus etc.

1473

215. Dicta die [31 Maii], una bulla pro Mauricio Yara, canonico Akadensi, super unione de perpetua vicaria parrochialis ecclesiede Kilmattaic, Akadensis diocesis, cuius fructus sex marcharum sterlingorum, rectorie dicte ecclesie facienda. Patet per bullam sub data Rome, quarto non. Aprilis, anno secundo. Restituta, quia non ascendit summam etc.

216. Die xij eiusdem [Junii], una bulla pro Will. Ocluain, clerico Akadensis diocesis, super provisione perpetue vicarie ecclesie de Kyllnaheind, dicte diocesis, cuius fructus sex marcharum sterlingorum communi extimatione, alias certo modo vacantis. Patet per bullas sub data Rome, sexto kal. Maii, anno secundo. Restituta, de mandato, quia dicte marche non ascendunt summam.

1475

219. Die predicta [29 Novembris], una bulla pro Ludovico Occonnuochan, presbytero Akadensis diocesis, super provisione vicarie parrochialis Clonneochille, Akadensi diocesis, cuius fructus quinque marcharum sterlingorum, communi extimatione, vacantis certo modo. Patet per bullam sub data Rome, pridie kal. Novembris, anno quinto. Restituta de mandato, quia non ascendit summam etc.

1477

226. Dicta die [13 Februarii], Tatheus Yheara, clericus Archadensis (sic), principalis, obligavit se camere apostolice pro annata canonicatus et de Killudeyn noncupate prebende Ackadensis, quorum fructus sexdecim; rectorie parrochialis ecclesie de Wykare et de Kalludrin, Akadensis diocesis, cuius [fructus] octo marcharum sterlingorum communi extimacione, vacantium alias certo modo, et mandantur uniri insimul, et de quibus mandatur provideri dicto Thateo sub data Rome, id. Januarii, anno sexto. Et promisit solvere annatam dictorum canonicatus et prebende et rectorie huiusmodi camere apostolice aut collectori infra sex menses immediate a die habite possessionis computandos, sub penis etc. etc. Restituta quia pro Hibernico.

227. Dicta die [26 Februarii], Thomas Ocongulann. decanus ecclesie Akadensis, principalis, obligavit se camere apostolice pro annata decanatus ecclesie Akadensis, cuius fructus decem marcharum sterlingorum communi extimatione, vacantis per obitum quondam Bernardi Oconnean, olim ipsius ecclesie decani, apud sedem apostolicam defuncti. Et providetur dicto Thome de dicto decanatu sub data Rome pridie kal Februarii, anno sexto. Et promisit solvere annatam dicti decanatus camere apostolice aut collectori in partibus infra sex menses immediate a die habite possessionis computandos, sub penis etc. etc. Restituta, de mandato, quia pro Hibernico etc.

1478
232. Dicta die [27 Februarii], dominus Cormacris Oheara, clericus Akadensis diocesis, principalis, obligavit se camere apostolice pro annata decanatus ecclesie Akadensis, cuius fructus decem marcharum sterlingorum communi extimatione, vacantis per obitum quondam Bernardi Ocomean, olim ipsius ecclesie decani, apud sedem apostolicam defuncti, et mandatur providi dicto Cormaco dicto decanatu sub data Rome, non. Februarii, anno septimo. Et promisit solvere annatam dicti decanatus camere apostolice hic in curia infra sex menses immediate a die habite possessionis computandos, sub penis camere etc. Restituta de mandato dominorum camere, domino Antonio refferente, quia pro Hibernico.

233. Die xxviij Februarii, una bulla pro Johanne Ohara, canonico Akadensi, super provisione perpetue vicarie parrochialis ecclesie de Kylmactahaic, ac rectorie prebende noncupate parrochialis ecclesie de Kylmactahayt, Akadensis diocesis, quarum fructus octo marcharum sterlingorum communi extimatione fructus non excedunt, que insimul unio mandantur et de quibus mandatur providi eidem Johanni. Patet per bullam sub data Rome, kal. Februarii, anno septimo. Restituta, de mandato, quia non ascendit summam etc.

1484
252. Dicta die [26 Maii], reverendus pater dominus Thomas, electus Achadensis, ut principalis et privata persona, obligavit se camere apostolice nomine domini Magonii Macclonchyd, abbatis monasterii Sancte Trinitatis de Lochque, Premonstratensis ordinis, Elphinensis diocesis, pro annata monasterii beate Marie de Asdara, ordinis Sancti Augustini, Akadensis diocesis, cuius fructus etc. trigenta marcharun sterlingorum secundum communem extimationem valorum annuum non excedunt, vacantia per obitum quondam Mauricii Macdonhyd, ipsius monasterii dum viveret abbatis, extra Romanum curiam defuncti, et mandatur commendari dictum monasterium beate Marie eidem Magonio, sub data Rome, decimoseptimo kal. Junii, anno tertiodecimo. Et promisit solvere annuatam dicti monasterii beate Marie infra sex menses a die habite possessionis computandos, sub penis etc. etc. Data, sub prefata obligatione, quia non fuit repertum in taxa, et quia pro Hibernico etc.

1493
303. Die dicta [1 Julii], Donaldus Onachon, presbiter Akadensis diocesis, principalis, obligavit se camere pro annata parrochialis ecclesie de Hanleon, dicte diocesis, certo modo vancantis, cuiusque fructus etc. duodecim marcharum sterlingorum non excedunt, et de qua providi mandatur, vocatis vocandis, dicto Donaldo sub data xvij kal. Julii, anno primo. Et promisit solvere dictam annuatam infra duos menses post assecutam possessionem collectori in partibus. Quia narratur intrusus.

1494

311. Dicta die [10 Septembris], dominus Roricus Ohara. clericus Akadensis diocesis, principalis, obligavit se camere apostolice pro annata decanatus ecclesie Akadensis, cuius fructus etc. duodecim marcharum sterlingorum secundum communem extimationem valorum annuum etc. non excedunt, vacantis tanto tempore quod eius collatio est devoluta, licet quidam Cormacus etiam Ohara dictum decanatum temere et de facto detinuerit prout detinet de presenti, et mandatur conferri dictus decanatus eidem domino Rorico sub data Rome, tertio kal. Junii, anno secundo. Et promisit solvere annatam predictam infra annum et mensem in forma etc. Juravit etc. Pro Ibernico.

1505

332. Die dicta [12 Junii], dominus Thomas Ochocolan canonicus ecclesie Acchadensis, obligavit se pro annata prepositure ecclesie Acchadensis ac rectorie parrochialis ecclesie de Clerandirach alias terrarum ruralium de Culein, et unius [beneficii] Acchadensis diocesis, vacantium per devolutionem, quarum [fructus] insimul sexdecim marcharum sterlingorum non excedunt, de quibus mandatur provideri eidem sub data nono kal. Junii, anno secundo. Et promisit solvere dictam annatam infra mensem post possessionem etc. sub penis. videlicet collectori. Juravit etc.

1507

[Elphin] Die xvi dicti [Octobris], dominus Roricus Macmayrgurthasynd, canonicus ecclesie Akadensis, obligavit … pro annata prioratus monasterii per priorem soliti gubernari Beate Marie de Insula Macnayr, ordinis Sancti Augustini, Elfinensis diocesis …

1548

349. Die 23 eiusdem [Maii], frater Terentius Ococonbayr, ordinis fratrum Predicatorum professor, obligavit se pro annata, prioratus monasterii per priorem gubernari soliti Beate Marie de Cillinoirnasinna. ordinis Sancti Augustini canonicorum regularium, Elphinensis dioc., necnon rectorie de Cillarachata ac illius de Gogealna parrochialium ecclesiarum predicte et Achadensis dioc., perpetuarum vicariarum, certo modo vacantium, quorum fructus etc., 50 auri de camera non excedunt. Et providetur eidem per bullam etc. sub data kal. Augusti, anno xiii. Et promisit solvere annatam huiusmodi, more Hybernicorum.

APPENDIX TWELVE: FRANCISCAN GUARDIANS IN BALLYMOTE
Liber Lovaniensis; for complete list up to 1826 see Swords, *A Hidden Church*, appendix 39, 421–3

Francis O'Conor, 5 Dec. 1647; John Tuite, 18 Feb. 1645; Anthony Teigg (Tighe), 4 Feb. 1648; Bonaventure Dillon, 17 Aug. 1650; vacant, 9 Oct. 1658; Anthony Fox, 5 Mar. 1670; Bernard Higgins, *lector jubilatus,* 21 Nov. 1672; James Blake, 23 Aug. 1675; Peter Neherney (Nerney), 23 Jan. 1676; Peter Nerney, 24 Aug. 1678; Peter Nerney (*loco refugii*), 28 Apr. 1680; Francis McDonnell (*loco refugii*), 14 Mar. 1681; Anthony McDonagh (*loco refugii*), 13 June 1683; Anthony McDonagh, 23 Aug. 1684; Anthony McDonagh, 27 Jan. 1685; Anthony McDonnell, 15 Aug. 1687; Anthony

McDonnell, 5 May 1689; Anthony McDonagh, 24 Aug. 1690; Francis Farry, 18 Feb. 1693; Daniel Kelly, 25 July 1697; Bernard O' Lorkan (*electus*), 26 July 1699; Terence O'Hart, 17 Oct. 1700; Peter Donnellan, 9 June 1702; Anthony O'Cullane, 13 Nov. 1703; Anthony McDonagh, 9 June 1705.

APPENDIX THIRTEEN: PRIESTS
(*Cal. Par. Rolls, I James I,* 20–4, 29)

Gillepatrick McDey, priest, Cowllone (Collooney); Dollove O'Dowgenane (Ó Dubhdagáin, Dowdican), priest, Ballindowne; Henry McEclerie (Mac Cléirigh, MacCleary, Clarke), priest, Clony-Mahine (Cloonamahon, Ballysadare or Cloonameehan, Cloonoghill); James O'Flanelly (Ó Flainghaile, O'Flannelly), priest, Rathlie; James McFearill (MacFhearghail, MacCarrell), student, Grangemore (Killala); Moyellmorie (Maol Mhuire) McDonnell, priest, Ardneglass (Killala); James Mc-Encarie, priest, Skreen; Hugh McDonnell, priest, Skreen; Dermot Glasse O'Mwllvihilly, priest, Bonanydanie; Shane O'Mochane (Ó Mocháin, Maughan), priest, Bonanysdanie; Melaghlin McDonnough, priest; Fearill (Fearghal, Fergal, Farrell) More, priest; Owen (Eoghan) Carragh O'Donilly (Ó Donnghalaigh, Donnelly), priest, Inileaghefadda (Emlafad); Mark McDonnell, student, Ballymote; Turlough McEparson (Mac an Phearsúin, MacPharsons, Parsons), student, Ballymote; Brian McRorie McGowane (Mac Gobhann, MacGowan), priest, Ballymote; Donatus O' Clawne (Ó Clúmháin, Coleman), priest, Killwohrine (Killoran); Hugh O'Derige (Ó Deirg, Derrig), priest, Cowrteroriballagh (Court); Arte (Art) McManes (Mac Maghnuis. MacManus), priest, Cowrteroriballagh); Will. O'Henygane (Ó hÉanacháin), friar, Tullynegloge (Tullynaglug, Tourlestane) (Court); Rorie McChristine (Mac Cristín, MacGriskin), priest, Ballyara; Owen O'Hart of Accadensis, bishop; Moriasse (Muirgheas, Maurice) O'Conoghane (Ó Connachain, Conaghan, Cunningham), priest, Achonry; Irriell (Irial) McMoelrony (Maol Ruadháin) O'Higgin, friar, Moygara; Brian O'Ferries (Ó Fearghuis, Fergus, Ferris, etc.), priest; Rossonever, priest; Will. Bickar, priest, Castleloghdargen.

APPENDIX FOURTEEN: DOMINICAN FRIARS

St Thomas' Urlaur
1622 Stephen Lynch, prior, with one priest for the education of many novices. See Flynn, *Irish Dominicans*, 160 n.d.: 'five priests, namely, Dominicus Keninus (Kerin), Donatus Carlan, senex, Hugo Gruagan, David Muril, Thomas Casside and four or fiveyouths whose names I forget,' *SOCG,* vol. 294, f.103v, n.d. (1635), Hugh Grugan, prior, 10 Aug. 1658, Pater Dominicus Dillon, prior Urlarensis See *Coll. Hib.,* vol. 15, 32, 18 Aug. 1703, visitation of Ambrose O'Connor, provincial, Peter Costello, prior, Richard MacMorishroe, Edmund MacMorishroe, John Mc Daniel, Raymond Costello. see Fenning, *Irish Dominicans,* 32, 1706 Edmond Mac Morrissy, Miler MacMorissy, Miler MacPhilip, John MacDonnell, Pierce Costello, Redmond Costello. O'Heyne, *Irish Dominicans,* 229–31, Holy Cross, Straide, 10 Aug. 1658, Pater Petrus Costely

(Costello), superior Stradensis, 16 Sept. 1702, James Cullen (of Burrishoole), prior, Anthony Hynagan, James Nicholas, Raymund Heneghan, Cormac Corcrane, Fenning, *Irish Dominicans*, 31.

APPENDIX FIFTEEN: LIMERICK, 12 OCTOBER 1561, DAVID WOLFE'S LETTER 1601
TO CARDINAL GIOVANNI MORONE

La vera pace ed amore di Gesu Christo Sre. nostro sia nelli cuori nostri.

Ho scritto in questi giorni passati con Sig. Guillelmo Neon a V, Revma. ed Illma. Sigria circa il stato della chiesa Ibernica in questa parte di Momonia: ed ora essendo il portatore di questa lettera Donaldo Mac Gomgayll meco in tutta la mia peregrinazione per la Ibernia ho giudicato piu espediente per dar buon conto del tutto, di mandarlo in persona per esser persona di giudizio ed esperta in queste parti ed ancora avendo (come diró dapoi) da fare costi.

Essendo questo Donaldo meco nella parte di Conacia avemo visto e non visitato l'Arcivescovo Tuamense et il Vescovo Clonfertense, li quali secondo il mondo sono uomini dabbene. Tutti due hanno dati suoi voti alla Regina come giá ho scritto delli altri di Momonia a V. Rma. ed Illma. Signia. Quello ArcicescovoTuamense per nome Cristoforo Botteghin, ebbe suo arcivescovado (secondo che si dice da ognuno) per forza d'armi et auctoritate regia, e non mi ha voluto dire né mostrare qualmente l'avuto, salvo che mi diceva che la buona memoria del Cardinal Polo fece una composizione fra lui ed un certo Arturo O'Frehir vero et legitimo Arcivescovo, il quale vive ancora ed é espulso da quell' Arcivescovato dal detto Cristoforo. Questi Cristoforo tiene l'Arcivescovato Tuamense insieme con lo Vescovato Duacense, Enachdunen. et Magdunen. le quali Enachdunen. et Magdunen. secondo che lui dice erano uniti da molti anni con Tuam; ed altri dicono che no, ma lui stesso propria et regia auctoritate ha gionto ancora Duacen, con quelle altre. Mi ha detto che ha avuto la resignazione dell' Arcivescovato dal detto Arturo ed in effetto se fossa accetta dal Sommo Pontefice mi pareria molto piu al proposito che il detto Arturo, perche é un uomo di governo ed ha gran credito appresso li Signori di quelle bande. Ed essendo questa chiesa per 300 anni per fortezza nelle mani di gentil uomini, senza messa ne altro officio divino, lui l'ha tolto per forza dalle mani loro con grande pericolo della sua persona, e dove prima erano cavalli ed altri animali, ora si canta e si dice messa in essa, e lui stesso suole essere in coro ogni giorno, abbinche non vi siano in quella terra Tuamense piu di 20 case o 30. Ha buona fama ed é ben voluto da ognuno ed ancora dalli suoi avversari li quali tenevano quella chiesa per il tempo passato.

Un certo Malachia O'Molonno, Canonoco Duacen, ha fatte false dispensazioni come V. Rma ed Illma. vedrá per la copia che gli mando qui annessa ed in quella ha incolpato quel Cristoforo con dire che lui l'abbia visto ed approvato, ma il detto Cristoforo mi ha giurato sopra l'Evangelio che mai ha visto né approvato tal decreto Aplico allegandomi molte ragioni, e trovo che il detto Malachia e falsario litterarum Aplicarum, e non ha voluto presentarsi avanti di lui quando era citato e perció io desidero di sapere che cosa dobbiamo fare di quel Malachia in tal caso, essendo liu ribelle e non avendo alcuna originale alla quale dovessimo dar fede.

Bernardo O'Huyghin, Escovo Elfinen, ha rassegnato il suo Vescovato a un Padre dell' ordine di S. Domenico Priore di Slyghvach per nome Andrea Crean, uomo assai religioso e di buona fama ed ha gran credito appresso alli secolari non tanto per la sua dottrina quanto per la buona conversazione bontá. Questo Bernardo é stato uomo da bene e religioso quanto a se stesso ma non era grato al popolo e vedendo lui di aver perso assai della sua temporalitá per esser cosí odioso al popolo, ha eletto quel Andrea il quale é molto amabile ad ognuno per recuperare tanto quanto lui ha perso. Il detto Andrea va adesso per (con permesso) [illegible].

notitia del suo Vicario Provinciale a Roma per obtinere quel Vescovato insieme con la resignazione del detto Bernardo: e volse aver le mie lettere testimonianali, ed io ha poca practica della sua persona nondimeno sento la sua fama buona sparsa per tutto il paese del che ne rendo testimonio. Va ancora col detto un compagno per nome Owen ovvero Eugenio O'Harty, frate del detto ordine, gran Predicatore ed uomo di buona vita e zeloso dell' onore di Dio, il quale é stato otto anni o incirca in Parigi ed io giudico (abbenche non va per tal effetto, ne anche pensa niente) che lui fusse buono per esser vescovo. Ed in caso che il detto Andrea (essendo la morte ad ognuno commune) fusse morto, quel Padre Eugenio saria buono in suo luogo non obstante che la resignazione non fosse fatta in suo nome. Ed ancor che la volontá di Dio che il detto Andrea viveria e fosse Vescovo Elphinen, anchora potria esser Vescovo Accaden. il quale vescovato vaca per la morte della buona memoria di Cormaco O'Coyn del detto ordine di S. Francesco. Quella chiesa Accadense é adesso per fortezza in mani di gentil'uomini e non via sia vestigio di Religione e credo che il detto Eugenio con li suoi esempi e buono vita insieme con ajuto delli suoi amici potra pigliar quella chiesa dalli mani dei gentil'uomini e far in quella come ha fatto Cristofero Tuamense. Il portatore di questa lettera Donaldo Magonigail fu compagno nelle parte di Connacia e non sia persona in tutta Ibernia che sa dar conto migliore di lui di ogni cosa ed io la mando per due effetti: 1, per dar quel conto di me stesso ed ancora delli Vescovi, Arcivesci e Prelati & c. 2, Essendo morto il Vescovo Rapotense non trovo persona che fusse atta a tal dignitá miglior di lui: é ben dotto seconda la dottrina di questa patria ed é ben boluto d'ognuno ed é stato in Roma l'anno passato.

Sono partiti d'Ibernia da 14 persone senza le mie lettere delle quali uno é il Decano Rapotense per impetrar quel Vescovato e questo Decano secondo che sento da persone degne di fede é uomo piutosto di guerra che di chiesa. Guardasi Vtra. Rma ed Illma. Sigria. che non gli dia fede se dirá di non saper della mia venuta in Ibernia non vi sia eretica né cattolica che non sa del mio venire, percho ho mandato un editto per tutta la patria: ed essendo la nave apparecchiata di partirsi adesso non diró altro, salvo raccomandar queste tre persone a V. S. Illma. e Revma. insieme con quel Sig. Guilelmo Neon gia mandato, pregando il Sig. Dio di conservarla la sanitá del corpo e dell'anima a gloria ed utilitá di questa misrea patria.

Di Limerico alli 12 di Ottobre, 1561

Di V. Sigria. Rma. et Illma.

Servo indegno,

David Wolf.

APPENDIX SIXTEEN: INTERVENTIONS OF EOGHAN Ó HAIRT
AT THE COUNCIL OF TRENT

1. Wed., 3 June 1562. General Congregation held in the Church of Mary Major regarding response to the King of France.
Achadensi placet (Rapotensis vacat. [Concilii Tridentini Actorum, VIII, 517])

2. Fri., 3 July 1562, 7 p.m. General Congregation regarding four canons on use of Sacrament of Eucharist.
Achadensi 1 & 2 cum notationibus Granatensis; [Archbishop Petrus Guerrero (1546–76) of Granada 3 placet ac 4; ibid., 648].

3. Thur., 9 July 1562, 7 p.m. General Congregation on four canons on use of Sacrament of Eucharist.
Acadensi placent canones et doctrina placent cum notationes Mutinensis [Bishop Aegidius Foschararius OP of Modena; ibid., 676].

4. Sun., 14 July 1562, 10–13 p.m. General Congregation, canons of reformation examined.
Achadensi placent notationes Veronensis [Bishop Hieronymus Trevisanus of Verona et Idruntini; Archbishop Petrus Antonius de Capua (1536–79); ibid., 684].

5. Wed., 26 Aug. 1562, 12–3.30 p.m. General Congregation examined same canons and doctrine regarding the sacrifice of the Mass.
Achadensis. Doctrina ponatur cum declaratione Bracarensis, [Archbishop Bartolomaeus de Martiribus OP of Braga, Portugal, primate of Spain, et Christum se obtulisse expiatorie; alias quomodo vetera sacrificia erant expiatoria, si hoc ipsum Christi in coena non fuit expiatorium? Et si illa erant expiatoria in virtute passionis Christi, quam figurabant multo magis hoc ab ipsomet Christo, qui est figuratum oblatum. Non expiavit autem cum illa reservata fuerit cruci; et quaestio haec potest omitti; ibid., 785].
Rapotensis probavit notationes patrum. [Uberior Seripandus (Barb. Lat. 817, f.368r) 'Moderatissima de hoc quaestione fuit sententia Rapotensis Hibernici, nihil certi hac de re pronuntiari posse, graviter et pie asseverantis.' Nisi Seripandus erraverit in persona, loco praecedentes ep. Achadensis. (it is more likely that Cardinal Hieronymous Seripandus OAS, second legate of the council, was referring to Achonry and mistakenly called it Raphoe as the latter is recorded as simply agreeing with the comments of the fathers.)]

6. Sat., 5 Sept. 1562, 12 o'clock. General Congregation examination of the concession of communion under both species.
Achadensis totum negotium remittendum censet ad Smm D.N. [ibid., 866].

7. Mon., 7 Sept. 1562. General Congregation, 12–17.30 p.m. Beginning of the examination of the doctrine and canons of the sacrifice of the Mass [ibid., 915]
Achadensi placet.

8. Sun., 13 Sept. 1562. General Congregation on examination of the same reform canons and abuses in the Mass.
Achadensi canones placent cum notationibus patrum [ibid., 939].

9. Mon., 14 Sept. 1562, 19–24 p.m. General Congregation – Profession of Faith of the Patriarch of the Assyrians is read and reform canons on the reform and abuses of the Mass are proposed.
Achadensi placet. [ibid., 941].

10. Tues., 15 Sept. 1562. General Congregation examining the first decree on the concession of the chalice.
Achadensis. Totum negotium Smo. D. N. remittatur absque decreto [ibid., 946].

11. Wed., 16 Sept. 1562, 13–17 p.m. General Congregation, another decree on the concession of the chalice is proposed.
Achadensi placet cum notationibus Cavensis. [Bishop of Amalfi-Cave deTirreni].

12. 17 Sept. 1562. Decretum super petitione concessionis calicis publicatum in eaem sessione …
R. D. Achadensis placet cum declaratione quod Smus D.N. utatur suprema potestate [ibid., 968–9].

13. Fri., 4 Dec. 1562. 16–19 p.m. General Congregation – canons and doctrine of the sacrament of orders examined.
Achadensis probat censuras Mutinensis. [Bishop Aegidius Foschararius OP of Modena. Doctrina et canones placent, Quoad septimus respondit, iurisdictionem episcoporum esse a Summo Pontce. Nam alias, si eam immediate a Deo haberent, vana esset iurisdictio summa (data Petro), et alias non esset in ecclesia hierarchia ecclesiastica, quia tot essent capita, quot episcopi, et pontifex eam auferre non posset. Falsa etiam est opinio, quod iurisdictio in consecratione detur, cum episcopus possit esse absque iurisdictione. Omnis igitur iurisdictio episcopi est a Summo Pontce tamquam a causa secunda. Quare in hoc 7. canone non addatur iure divino, cum etiam esset favere haereticis.
Rapotensis probat sententiam Achadensis. ibid., ix, 204].

14. Tues. 12 Jan. 1563, 20–24 p.m. General Congregation examined the decree on residency.
Achadensis dixit nullatenus determinandum residentiam esse de iure divino, quia ex hoc saeculares expellerent episcopos a consiliis regum cum maximo damno religionis Christianae. Assignavitque duo exempla circa hoc, quae contigerunt episcopis in Hibernia temporibus reginae Mariae et Elisabeth. *Deinde petiit, ut alicui in Hibernia concedantur facultates recipiendi haereticos et absolvendi ab omnibus casibus cum ibi nec sint legati Apci inquisitores.
Rapotensis petiit declarari residentiam esse de iure divino. [Et alii dixit in scriptis, quae non potuerunt intellegi.]
[Similia habet idem Achadensis in voto scripto de sacramento ordinis, supra n.61. vide etiam Paleottum (Theiner, II, 637, Mendham 458, s.v. N. Hibernicus)].

15. Weds. 9 June 1563, 10–14 p.m. General Congregation examined the same canons on abuses in the sacrament of orders.
Achadensis. 1. canonem reprobavit, cum nominatur populus. Idem in eo, quod dicitur de populo quoad ordinationem. Nollet, ut Galli ita instanter peterent electiones episcoporum; quin immo [magis] expediret, ut omnia reducerentur ad Summum

Pontcem, et praesertim propter reginam Angliae, et in 1. canone sequitur Quin-
queecclesiensem [Bishop Georgius Drascovitius of Funfkirchen. et Almeriensem;
Bishop Antonius Corrionera (1557–71) of Almeria, Spain.] 2. et 3. placent. Quoad
4. canonem censet, episcopis titularibus non esset dandum iuramentum. In 5. deleatur
quod dicitur de populo. In 6. deleatur quod dicitur de Archidiacono. In 7. deleatur
quod dicitur de Romana curia, quia non possumus [neque debemus loqui de Romana
curia. 8. placet; decernatur, nullum episcopum posse aliquid facere in eius ecclesia,
nisi habita prius confirmatione a Sede Apla, et quod episcopi non confirmati ab eadem
Sede non possint administrare sacramenta. 9. non placet; nam expellendi sunt pueri a
beneficiis. Et quoad aetatem clericorum non esset recedendum a dispositione
antiquorum canonum. Deleatur quod dicitur de privatione privilegii. In 10. remittit
se D. Senensi, [Bishop of Siena or Sénez (France). et tollatur abusus de paupertate
sacerdotum. in 11. restituantur functiones ordinum minorum, vel minores ordines
non conferentur absque subdiaconatu]. In 12. placet quod promotio sacerdotum sit
30 annorum. In 13. non placet quod dicitur, diaconos et sacerdotes teneri ad
praedicandum verbum Dei. 14. non placet, sed quod omnes quoad praedicationem
et ministerium sacramentorum habeant licentiam ab episcopo. 15. et 16. placet.
[O'Hart was last of eight speakers. Ross also spoke.] [ibid., 578].

16. Monday 12 July 1563, 9–15 p.m. General Congregation. Finished the examination
of reform canons regarding abuses in the sacrament of orders.
Achadensis. 1., 4., et ultimus differantur; quoad alia sequitur Hydruntinum.
[Archbishop Petrus Antonius de Capua (1536–79); ibid., 615].

17. Fri. 30 July 1563, 10–14 p.m. General Congregation examined the decree on
sacrament of matrimony.
Achadensis. In 1. et 2. sequitur Lotharingum [Cardinal Charles de Guize of Lorraine.
et Hydruntinum; see above 12 july 1563. in reliquis Mutinensem; see above 4 Dec.
1562. In 6. ponatur anathema. Quoad decretum de clandestinis non placet quod
dicitur de aetate, sed stetur iure communi, et in omnibus sequitur sententiam
Hyprensis; ibid., 676].

18. Fri. 20 Aug. 1563, 19–23 p.m. General Congregation examined the canons and
decrees on the reform of marriage.
Achadensis, 7. canon maneat ut iacet. Quoad decretum de clandestinis placet, ut
nomen clandestinorum tollatur. Quoad id quod dicitur de filiis familias et de aetate
non placet. circa decreta reformationis episcopi dispensat in 4. gradu. In reliquis
sequitur sententiam maioris partis patrum [Raphoe and Ross wanted all clandestine
marriages be declared invalid.] [ibid., 734].

19. 30 Sept. 1563. General Congregation. Twenty-one reformation canons examined.
Achadensis. In 1. tollatur quodcumque ius habent. Non placet quod dicitur de
iuramento cardinalium, et quoad cardinales sequitur Callaritanum. [Archbishop
Antonius Parragues de Castellegio of Cagliari, Sardinia. In 2. decidatur modus
procedendi in concilio provinciali et qui habent vota decisiva. Deleatur quod dicitur
contra statuta regularium; sufficit quod dicatur contra regulam. Omnes enim, qui non
vivunt regulariter, subiici debent episcopis. In 4. regulares arcendi non sunt, ut possint
in eorum ecclesiis praedicare. In In 6. capitula omnia subiiciantur suis episcopis. Non

placet quod dicitur quorum consilium sequi non teneantur. In 7. sequitur Granatensem. Archbishop Petrus Guerrero of Granada (1546–76). In 8. non placet, quod aliquid de Scriptura vertatur in linguam vulgarem. In 10. tollantur verba qui non subiiciuntur capitulis generalibus. In 13. non concedatur abesse canonicis nisi per duos menses iudicio episcopi ex rationabili causa. In 14. non placet quod dicitur de consensu regum et principum. In 18. sequitur Namurcensem; Bishop of Namur, Belgium. et Civitatensem. 19. non placet. In 20., si concedatur indignis, episcopus possit revocare, non autem si concedatur dignis. 21. non placet, quia videtur derogare canoni quinto, necnon praeiudicat iuri naturali.

Absolutaque congregatio hora 16].

20. Sat., 6 Nov. 1563, General Congregation on twenty reform canons about general reformation.

Achadensis. In 2. tollatur abusus obedientiae regni Neapolitani. In 3. servetur ius commune. In 3. causae minores episcoporum cognoscantur a concilio provinciali. In 5. sequitur Mutinensem. *Bishop Aegidius Foschararius OP of Modena, Italy. In 6. tollantur verba ex delicto occulto. In 9. non placet exceptio. 17. extendatur ad omnia curata. In 18. examinatores eligantur ab episcopo. [habeatur ratio insulanorum] [ibid., 943].

21. Thurs. 18 Nov. 1963, 15–19 p.m. General Congregation – examination of fourteen reform canons finished.

Achadensis. Placent petitiones Lotharingi. [Cardinal Charles de Guize of Lorraine.

22. comprendat regularia. 24. fiat clarior. 25. Coadiutoriae non tollantur. 26. Lotharingus. 27. Clausula in fine posita non placet, quia tangit Summi Pontificis autoritatem; statuens scil. quod etiam Summus Pontifex causas in partibus decidendas iudicibus illis dioecesanis committat. 30. cum Messanensi; Bishop of Messino, Italy. 31. cum Cretensi et Lancianensi; Bishop of Crete & Bishop of Lanciano, Italy. 32 non placet, et multis minus poenae positae. 33. extendatur ad … Reliqui placent; ibid., 1029].

APPENDIX SEVENTEEN: SPEECH OF Ó HAIRT ON HOLY ORDERS

22. Sententia Episcopi Achadensis Hybernici de Doctrina et canonibus Sacri Ordinis. [Vat. Lib., MSS Barberini Latini, 817 (XVI, 24), ff.270r–275v, microfilm N.L. pos. 868; printed in *Concilii Tridentini Actorum, pars sexta* (17 Sept. 1562 – 1 Dec. 1563)]

Illustrissimi Domini reverendissimiq Patres

Post exactissimas auctoritates et rationes pro approbatione huius reformatae doctrinae allatas a R.mis Dominis meis Idruntino et Mutinensi doctrina universaliter mihi placet. Canones similiter non displicent. Quoad septem autem canonem, in quo omnes Patres gradus sistunt, et diversi diversa sentiunt et adhuc post gravissimas exhortationes Illust.morum Dnorum meorum Legatorum, aliqui non desunt, qui prolixe suas sententias dicunt: sic et nostrum, licet exiguum, symbolum in medium afferre libet, quod alias praestaturus non eram, nec praestare poteram, ut ingenue fateor. Et quia, qui tenent illam opinionem. nempe omnem iurisdictionem Episcoporum esse immediate a Deo habent suos auctores, suas auctoritates, suasque rationes, iisque firmiter adhaerent, nec gravissimis auctoribus, et auctoritatibus ab aliis allatis credere volunt: visum est igitur mihi ad intentionem explicandam uti eo modo. quo utitur Aristotyles in primo Physicorum agens contra alios philosophos male sentientes de principiis naturalibus. Agit enim contra illos ex concessis ab iis. Hoc igitur modo tribus brevissimis consequentiis et unica ratione meam mentem declarabo, praemittens singulis consequentiis singulas propositiones in quibus consentimus, et e diverso dissentimus. Protestor autem quod non animo contradicendi alicui sed animo declarandi contradictionem propositionum ad exprimendam veritatem procedo.

Qui igitur tenent illam propositionem, fatentur nobiscum, Romanum Pontificem habere universalem iurisdictionem in Ecclesia Dei. Sit igitur prima consequentia:

Omnis iurisdictio Episcoporum est immediate a Deo; ergo nulla iurisdictio mediat inter ipsos et Deum. Consequentia bona est, quia anticedens huius enthymematis est probativum consequentis. Si enim [im]mediate excludit omne medium, ergo nulla iurisdictio mediat inter ipsos et Deum. Sed consequens est falsum ergo, et illud ex quo sequitur. Minor non eget probatione, quia conceditur ab utraque parte; ergo falsa est illa opinio (271r), et sibi ipsi contraria.

Ad Secundum

Qui tenent illam opinionem, tenent etiam nobiscum, unam esse hierarchiam in Ecclesia Dei, sub summo hierarcha Christi in terris Vicario Romano Pontifice. Sit igitur secunda consequentia ex eodem fundamento: Omnes Episcopi sunt immediate a Deo, etiam quoad potestatem iurisdictionis; ergo nulla est hierarchia in Ecclesia Dei. Probo consequentiam. Ubi tot capita, et in solidum nulla est hierarchia, et est probatio Philosophi in duodecimo Metaphisices sub aliis verbis; [It appears that 11 Metaphysics should be substituted, where in the beginning of chapter 10 Aristotle shows that there cannot be order in the home and family unless the children and servants obey the rule of the father of the family. Pariis 1850 II 609] ergo nulla est hierarchia in Ecclesia Dei. Sed consequens est falsum, ergo et illud ex quo sequitur, Minor non eget probatione, quia conceditur ab utraque parte; ergo falsa est illa opinio et unitatem capitis in hierarchia Ecclesiastica excludit et sibi ipsi est contraria.

Ad Tertiam

Qui tenent illam opinionem, tenent etiam, Romanum Pontificem (271v) ministerialiter tantum concurrere in iurisdictione Episcoporum, et tenent etiam Romanum Pontificem posse suspendere iurisdictionem Episcoporum ex quacumque causa. Sit igiter tertia consequentia:

Romanus Pontifex concurrit ut minister tantum in Iurisdictione Episcopi; ergo non potest suspendere iurisdictionem semel datam episcopo. Probe consequentiam a simili. Episcopus non potest facere, quod ordinatus semel ab eo sacerdos non sit sacerdos quia ut minister tantum agit. Et si dicatur quod possit impedire executionem, respondeo breviter quod hoc non facit, ut minister tantum sed ut habens auctoritatem. Ulterius non potest facere sacerdos, ut baptizatus semel non sit baptizatus, nec ut absolutus semel ab eo non sit absolutus. Similiter dicendum est discurrendo per omnes functiones quae fiunt ministerialiter tantum in ecclesia Dei; ergo nec Romanus Pontifex agens ut minister tantum potest suspendere iurisdictionem semel datam. Sed consequens est falsam ergo et illud, ex quo sequitur. Minor non egit probatione quia conceditur ab utraque parte. Falsa est illa opinio et sibi ipsi contraria.

Ad rationem.

Qui tenent illam opinionem tenent etiam omnem iurisdictionem episcoporum fluxisse a consecratione eorum. Sit igitur haec brevis ratio: Si verbi gratia Reginae Angliae in meum episcopatum unum Episcopum mitteret haereticum consecratum tamen a Catholicis et ego vellem probare adversus eum, mihi deberi episcopatum potiori iure, allegando quod sim electus a clero: diceret et ipse, quod sit electus a clero et populo. Si dicerem quod sim vocatus: diceret et ipse quod sit vocatus a Deo tamquam Aaron. [Hebrews 5, 4] Si dicerem, me missum: diceret et ipse, se missum a Spirito Sancto. Si dicerem me consecratum, diceret et ipse, se consecratum. Non est igitur evidentior ratio, qua possim eum convincere, quam allegando adversus eam me esse creatum episcopum auchoritate Romani Pontificis, ipse vero auctoritate saecularis potestatis. Quia igitur hoc sola ratio eum convincit iudicio cleri et populi, sequitur, illam opinionem esse falsam quae dicit, omnem iurisdictionem Episcoporum fluxisse a consecratione eorum, cum multos videmus consecratos non habentes iurisdictionem. Concludo igitur, omnem iurisdictionem episcoporum dependere a Romano Pontifice, tamquam a causa secunda habente commissionem sive executionem a causa prima. Sicut enim videmus in aliis causis secundis naturalibus, et quemadmodum inquit. Philosophus: necesse est hunc mundum inferiorem rationibus superioribus esse subiectum, ut inde omnis virtus gubernetur. [Aristotelis, Opera Omnia (pariis 1848 sq.) I, 411, Rhetorica ad Alexandrum]. Ita necesse est ut omnis potestas ecclesiastica sit subiecta Romano Pontifici et haec est mea sententia.

Quod vero allatum est a multis patribus quod damnare debemus haereses: damnare quidem debemus, ad summo tamen opere cavere debemus, ne dum volentes evitare Schyllam incidamus in Carybdem, ne, inquam, evitare indirectas consequentias haereticorum, incidamus directe in eorum opinionem. Nam regina Anglia negat, episcopos creatos a Romano Pontifice esse veros episcopos, sed dicit se ipsam supremum caput ecclesiae Anglicanae et Hibernianae, et ideo non placet mihi, quod illa verba opponerentur in canone, ex quibus directe vel indirecte faveretur huic opinioni. Quoniam, si illa verba, episcopos esse superiores presbyteris jure divino, hunc faciunt sensum, videlicet, omnes episcopos immediate esse a Deo quoad utramque potestatem ut [a] pluribus ex patribus dictum est: non aliquis est adeo deoculatus haereticus, qui non infert unam aut reliquam ex iis consequentiis: aut Romanum Pontificem nullam habere iurisdictionem super alios episcopos, aut reliquos omnes parem habere cum eo iurisdictionem et haec est directe opinio haereticorum.

Unum quod allatum est a quodam ex patribus [Bishop of Lucca especially and Aliphano] praeterire non possum videl. quod auctoritas Petri nihil contulit auctoritati Pauli; nec me latet quod ipse Paulus dicit ad Galatos 2, 6: *Nihil mihi alii contulerunt.* Mihi enim, qui videbantur esse aliquid, nihil contulerunt. ['those, I say, who were of repute, added nothing to me.'] Sed dum intueor sententiam Petri in 15 Actorum non possum non admirari ['Peter rose and said to them, "Brethren, you know that in the early days God made choice among you that by my mouth the Gentiles should hear the word of God and believe ... [God] made no distinction between us and them ... we believe that we shall be saved through the grace of the Lord Jesus, just as they will."] *si eius sententia nihil contulit. Quare Paulus in 2 caput [v.2] ad Galatos dicit: Ne forte in vanum currerem aut cucurissem? ['lest somehow I should be running or had run in vain.'] Si nihil inquam contulit, sequeretur, quod sententia lata a Iudice pro

aliqua parte nullam confert auctoritatem illi parti, quod est omnium rerum ordinem
pervertere. Et sic relinquo quodlibitum hoc discutiendum D.V. submittens me ex qua
dixi corectioni S.D.V.

APPENDIX EIGHTEEN: INQUISITION OF ACHONRY EPISCOPACY 18 AUGUST 1585

Inq' capt' apud Aghonra infra com' Sligo 18 Augusti 1585, coi' Danile Darens' Epo'
    p saramentu pboy etc quorum nomina subsequuntur, Brian McMolroni, Darbicis
    Bren, Teige O'Harte, Phelim O'Connor, Melaghlin McDonogh, Melaghlin
    McDonogh de Clowney, Joh' O'Mulconra, Connor Cahen, Carolus McDere,
    Manus Reagh McTeag boy, Brian O'Dowde, Erevan Mc Swyne, Miler McManus
    Ror'McGinella, Cahill McHeugh, Johannes Glass, Brian oge McPersun, John
    O'Hart, Muredac' McManus, Lucas McBreghun, Roric' O'Dowde, Carol' ø'Synan,
    & Brian McSwyne.
qui dic' quod Episcopat' Aghaden' infra
Dioch' (diocese) Aghaden' val' p ann' 10£,
Dicanat' (Deanery) Aghaden' val' p ann' 20s,
ppositus (Provost) Achaden' val' p ann' 6s/8d
Archionat' (Archdeaconry) Aghaden cu viccar' de Kilbrowryh (Kilturra) infra dioc'
    pdic' 4s,
vicar' de Kilvardnaha (Kilvarnet) 4s,
vicar de Killowran (Killoran) 10s,
Id de ann' val' vicarie de Kilmcteig (Kilmactigue) infra dioc' pdic' ignorant q' vastal',
Id vicar de Killesy (?) val' p ann' 2s,
" " Attemas (Attymass) nihil q' vast'
" " Strade (Straide) 4s,
" " Killodan (Killedan) 5s,
" " Killconnow (Kilconduff) nihil q' vast',
" " Kilveigh (Kilbeagh) 4s,
" " Moyconra (Moyconra) nihil q' vast'
" " Templemanrys (Templevanny) 5s,
" " Kilcolman 3s,
" " Killara (Killaraght) 3s,
" " Killosalvan (Kilshalvey) 2s,
" "Jumlehaedys (Emlefad) 3s " 4d,
" "Tumore (Toomour) 3s,
" "Kilmorchoi (Kilmorgan) 20d,
" "Clonoghill (Cloonoghill) 8s,
Rectoria de Cowlaven (Coolavin) 6s " 8d,
vicar' de Cowlavin " 3s " 4d,
Rectoria de Slewloa (Sliabh Lugha) 10s,
" " Bowcowlye (Bohola) 2s " 8d,
Rectoria voc' "inter duos amnes 3s " 4d,
" de Killownan 13s " 4d.

Registratum Episcopatus Acchadensis assumptum a Dno Henrico Hart Jurisperito et olim dicti Episcopatus officialis [recte officiale, judge of the bishop's court]. ac a Dno Joanne Henigane procuratore ac continuo quasi censore ejusdem di(o)ecesis sic prout noverint et viderint fuisse in exercitio et praxi tempore Eugenii O'Hart olim Catholici Episcopi ejusdem Episcopatus.

De Terris Episcopi Accadensis in Baronia de Leyney
Primo, habet 4 quarterias in Achonry scilicet in Episcopatus sede, viz. quarteria de Cloghbrandane, quarteria de Lisochat, quarteria de Tirahan, quarteria de Clanshearny divisa ut seqr. Lecharuane, Lismrane, Ardclunta, na clunta, viz Declune beg, Duclune mor, Laconlostrane, Cluniruane Cluny, terra mensalis et immunis a censu Regis et comitatus.

2. In Kilmacteige habet duas quarterias terrae viz quarterias Muintitclearug, Carrow Muintirchleary, et haec similiter mensalis et immunis a censu Regis et Comitatus.

3. Balisodare habet 10 quarterias terrae in quarum tribus sont coloni, familia de Clongcollobby [MacAvoy.], et in aliis tribus Clanmacbrehony [Brehony, Judge], et in 4 caeteris Malachias M'Donogh [Melaghlin M'Donogh of Colloony, d. 15 Aug. 1597] de Colany [Colloony]. Annuatim solveantr. Epo. per quarteriam 6 solidi et octo denarii cum noxali equorum et famulorum sustentatione toties quoties mittebantur illuc, et majus exigebatur a Dno de Cooluny quam ab aliis incolis.

4. Habet 4 quarterias quae vulgo dicuntr Bailcancairne viz. Carrowanfailduff, Carrowancnucbane, Carrogormain, Carrowanchairne, simul cum Carrowrille, quas 5 quarterias dabat Episcopus ille Eugenius O'Hart ad libitum suum aliquando Dno O'Connor Sligo [Donogh O'Connor Sligo d.1609], aliquando O'Hara-boy (Cormac O'Hara d. 1612.), cum omnibus oneribus consuetis. Hae quarteriae sunt ipsius Episcopi sed non immunes a censu Regis et Comitatus.

5. In Killorin habet 8 quarterias terrae et coloni erant muintir Chluane qui solvebant Episcopo 5 solidos p. quarteriam annuatim cum noxali pueris et equis sustentatione toties illuc mittebantur et aliis consuetis oneribus et Oeconomo 3 denarios per quem movebantur seu ejiciebantur hi coloni ad libitum Episcopi.

6. In Kilvarnad unam quarteriam cum semiquarteria hi coloni erant familia de Finane et solvebant Epo 10 (s) cum noxali et Oeconomo proportionaliter ut supra et cum pueris et equis sustentatione ut supra et movebantur ad libitum Episcopi.

7. In Tully Hugh vas(s)ali erant Sloight an aspuick Ruoigh [Sliocht an easbaig ruaidh, sept of the Red Bishop O'Hara who died in 1439; *AFM*]. annuatim solvebant Epo. 3 solidos cum 4 denariis et Oeconomo duos denarios.

In Baronia de Corran
Primo, in Kilmurghan habet unam quarteriam. Vassali erant familia de Dyer, solvebant Epo. annuatim 7s. cum 24 quartis butiri [butyri] et 12 meda [meadar] tritici mensurae 8 quartis per meda et Oeconomo 4 denarios et noxale et aliis oneribuus consuetis.

2. Emlifad habet duas quarterias in quibus solvebantur 7s. cum noxali et aliis oneribus consuetis ut supra et oeconomo 3 denarios.

3. Habet 5 quarterias de Sloight an asbuick Ruoigh solvere debent Epo. 5s. per quarteriam cum noxali et ejus Oeconomo 3 denarios.

4. Habet duas quarterias de Morhy in quibus sunt vassali Clanmulroony Fin annuatim solvebant Epo. 5s. p, quarteriam cum noxali et ejus Oeconomo 3 denarios.

5. Clunoghill habet duas quarterias terrae. Coloni erant Muintirchonnuchain qui solvebant Epo. per quarteriam annuatim sex solidos et octo denarios et habuerunt hoc in scriptis ab Epo.

6. In Kiloshalvy habet tertiam partem baile vulgo trian. Coloni erant Muintir Shealbhaigh qui solvebant Epo. annuatim sex solidos et octo denarios cum noxali et Oeconomo 4 denarios.

In Coolavin, primo, habet in Kilaraght 4 quarterias terrae. Coloni erant muintir Mochain. Solvebant Epo annuatim 6s. cum 8d. per quarteriam cum noxali ejusque Oeconomo 4 denarios.

2. In Kilfree habet unam quarteriam ad ipsum solumodo spectantem quam ad libitum dabat cui volebat, et a tenente habuit 5s. quotannis cum noxali et omnibus aliis assuetis oneribus ut supra et ejus Oeconomo 4 denarios.

3. Dnus O'Gara [Irriel O'Gara of Moygara] dabat quotannis Epo. pro Anagh duos solidos et ejus Oeconomo unum denarium.

In Baronia de Costello
Primo. In Kilmavee 4 quarterias terrae juxta templum et aliam q. vulgo dicitur Scrataith. In his Clain Enry qui solvebant Epo. annuatim 6 solidos et 8 denarios cum noxali et aliis oneribus consuetis ut supra ejusq. Oeconomo 4 denarios.

In Baronia de Gailleng
Primo. In Kinasfe habet duas quarterias terrae cujus coloni erant Mu(i)nt(h)ir Uggin qui solvebant Epo. 10s. annuatim p. quarteriam cum noxali ejusq. Oeconomo 6 denarios et mittebantur inde ad arbitrium Epi.

2. In Killiadain duas quarterias terrae cujus coloni erant Clan Coisdealbh [Costello] qui solvebant annuatim Epo. 10s. cum noxali ejusque Oeconomo 6 denarios per quarteriam.

3. In Milic unam cartron [one quarter of a quarter] ex quo solvebantur 6s. & 8d. cum noxali et ejus Oeconomo 4d.

4. In Kilcondufe Feairn Cairtagh [land held by charter] et solvebatur Epo unus solidus et ejus Oeconomo unus denarius.

De Jure Decani

1. Habet vicariatum de Achonry et duas parcellas terrae quae vulgo dicitur Gort Segart [Gort (na) Sagart, priest's field] sitas in orientali parte de Achonry ab utraque via(e) regis parte et domum teampol mure [teampall Muire] sine horto et aliqua parcella vel parte terrae juxta illam domum.

Habet etiam quartem partem decimarum per illam parochiam. Debet Epo. 6s. & 8d. cum noxali et Oeconomo 4d. cum aliis assuetis oneribus.

De Archiadiaconi

Archidiaconus habet vicariatum de Kiltorrow [Kilturra, part of the modern parish of Bunninadden] cum quarteria terrae quae vassali eranr Muintir Gormsuiligh [Gormleys] qui solvebant Archiadiaco annuatim 13s. cum 4 denariis. Quilibet dignitarius, ut Deaconus Propositq. Rectoresq. omnes solvebant Archidiacono annuatim 4 testilia, et quilibet vicarius 8 denarios, ipse vero Archidiaconus solvebat Epo. 6s. & 8d. cum noxali et aliis assuetis oneribus ejusq. Oeconomo 4 denarios.

De Rectoribus (Rectories consisted of a number of parishes united into a single benefice often bestowed on students who intended to take orders.)

In Baronia de Leyney Rectoria de Kilmactighe currit per terras O'Hara Riabac [Riabhach (grey), one of the two main branches of the O'Haras residing at Balliara near Tubbercurry] exceptis terris Epi et prebendae de Dogharn et terris in quibus currit praepositura et debet Epo. 6s. & 8d. cum noxali et aliis assuetis oneribus ejusq. Oeconomo 4 denarios.

Rectoria de Killorin

Currit p. terras O'Hara flavi [O'Hara Buidhe (yellow.) Cormac was chief in 1785 and lived in his castle in Coolaney.] exceptis terris Epi. et abbatis Balisodare. Solvit Epo. ut supra, ejusq. Oeconomo ut supra.

In Baronia de Gailling

1. Rectoria de Sancti Delphisi de C (B)ucholla [Bohola] currit per parochias de Bocholla, Killiadane, Millick et Kilcunduf et per 13 quarterias et cartron parochiae de Killasair, quae sunt terrae Muintir Eadhra. Debet Epo. quotannis 6s. et 8d. cum noxali et aliis assuetis oneribus, et Oeconomo 4d.

2. Rectoria Sancti Nicolai de Templemore currit per parochias de Templemore, Athianvaisse, Tuomore, Killuanegarvane, in quarteria de Rahii et per 12 quarterias parochiae de Killaishir, quae sunt – et solvebant Epo. quotannis ut supra ejusq, Oeconomo 4d.

In Baronia de Corren

Rectoria Sancti Columbae de Emlifad currit per illam Baroniam exceptis terris Epi. Monasterium de Bul [Abbey of Boyle.] et terris ordinis Sti Francisci et solvebant Epo. quotannis 10s. & 8d. cum noxali et aliis consuetis oneribus ejusq. Oeconomo 4d.

In Coolavin – Rectoria de Killaraght quae currit per parochias de Killaraght et Kilfree, exceptis terris Epi. et solvebant Epo. quotannis 7s. et 8d. cum noxali et aliis consuetis oneribus ejusq. Oeconomo 4d.

In Baronia de Costelloe – Rectoria de Kilmovey currit p. 24 Bailte fearin [Bailte fearainn, townlands.], Slaibh loghain, viz. [Sliabh Lugha, territory anciently belonging to the O'Garas, comprising the part of barony of Costello in the diocese of Achonry.] in parochia de Kilmavee, Kilbeagh, Templemuire et Kilcolman. exceptis terris Epi. et solvebant quotannis Epo. 7s. 8d. cum noxali et aliis consuetis oneribus ejusq. Oeconomo 4d.

De praepositura seu ut vulgo dicitur Cantoria [provost, precentor or chantor was a canon with a prebend and had care of souls.]
Praepositus habet duas quarterias terrae q. vulgo vocantur Kilasbuig [Cill Easpaig, the bishop's church.] habet duas quarterias decimarum preter 11 quarterias terrae cum dimidio, viz. p. quarterias de Achonry, p. duas de Kilasbuig, p. 4 de Balteorue [not identified but maybe Tullyhugh and Bailcancairne.] et quarteriam, de Carrowrejel [Carrowreilly.] et semiquarteriam Killuigh. Solvit Epo. annuatim 6s. 8d. cum noxali et consuetis oneribus.

De Prebendis
In Baronia de Leyney – Prebendae de Kilmacteige, in duabus quarteriis; Prebendae de Killorin in 8 quarteriis; Prebendae de Kilvarnad, in una cum semiquarteria; Prebendae de Moymlogh [Moymlough or Meemlough in parish of Coolaney where O'Hara-boy had a castle.] in 3tia parte seu vulgo trine; Prebendae de Dochoring [Doheran, townland between Tubbercurry and Coolaney.] (in) 8 quarteriis terrae.

In Baronia de Corran – Prebendae de Kilmorchun in una quarteria; Prebendae de Emlifad in duabuas quarteriis; Prebendae de Clunoghil in duabus quarteriis; Prebendae de Kiltorrow in una parte seu vulgo trine; Prebendae de Killoshalvy in terris Epi.

In Coolavin – Prebendae de Killaraght in 4 quarterias; Prebendae de Kilfree in una quarteria.

In Baronia de Costello – Prebendae de Kilmovy in 3 quarteriis ubi est Templum et in quarteria quae vulgo vocatur Scralig.

In Baronia de Galling – Prebendae de Killaffe et Killiadain in terra Epi, scilicet in 4 quarteriis terrae. Hi omnes debent assistere in Choro Civitatis Ecclesiae de Achonry. [Each canon had a stall in the choir of the bishop's church in Achonry and a voice in the chapter.]

De jure Parochi
Parochus habuit primitias seu Beart Arrabh et Cud corgus [First fruits consisted of Beart Airbh, a sheaf of corn [oats], paid at harvest time and Cuid Carghas, Lenten

dues, first born of livestock due in spring.] nempe, primitias farenae avenae, divisim et conjunctim de uniquoq. aratro, vulgo Seisrach et Mesgan primhe [Meascán príomh, the first pat of butter.] et oblationes, viz. duos denarios in festo nativitatis Dni et duos in paschate ejus aquae bajulans, [water-carrier, humblest vicar was expected to have his house-boy to make his bed and look after his horse.] 1d unaq. vice ex istis. In monasteriis Episcopatus habuit quartem partem funeralium ['at every burial of any person of worth the people yeild offerings which are divided between the priests and the friars and part for the scholars educated in seminaries beyond the seas; and priests make collections at the keeping of "months minds" of the deceased principal men and women.' *Pat. Rolls, 16 Jas. I.* qtd in Tracts relating to Ireland, 49n.] et alteram partem habuit parochiam et monasterio debet dimidium totius. Hujus quisque parochus solvebat Epo. 10 testilia cum noxali et omnibus oneribus assuetis ut supra.

De iis parcellis injuste scissis Parochiis
De Kilconduffe sex quarterias terrae quae vocantur vulgo Baliuslane de Kilassair, quarteriam de Collour et hae fuerunt conjunctae olim suis parochiis, ut supra dicti affirmant se novisse et vedisse, tempore supradicti Epi Eugenii O'Hart.

Parochia de Ballisidare fuit olim tempore Eugenii O'Hart divisa in duas parochias, scilicet in parochiam de Balisodare & parochiam de Anagh quae sita est e parte orientali pontis Killivorlin non nisi sinistro modo conjuncta sunt.

De Monachis
Abbas de Ballisodare habuit ibidem tres quarterias terrae et tertiam partem seu trian baile et habuit vicariatum de Ballisodare, Kilnagarvane et Drumratt et Rabarain in quarteria quae vulgo dicitur Carrow aite na scholle. [Ceathrú áite na scoile Institutio parochi erat Episcopi in istis locis et ipse Abbas debebat 6d (s.) cum 8 denariis in ipso monasterio cum noxali in uno quoque vicariatu respective prefatis.]

Abbas de Boyle habuit sex quarterias in Tempillavanny, duas in Corgin, unam in Ballinamanagh et unam in Anaghbeg. In his habuit Episcopus solumodo visitationem, procurationes et noxal(i)a cum institutione ad praesentationem monachorum sicut in locis pertentibus ad Ab(b)atem de Ballisadare.

In Coolavin habent Carmelitae monasterium cum una quarteria terrae, scilicet Kinockmore. Epus. habuit visitationes ut supra.

Fratres Ordinis Sti Francisci
In Court habent monasterium cum duabus quarteriis terrae junctis et unam quarteriam de Kilcomen.

In Balimote habent monasterium cum una et semiquarteria terrae annexae et aliam quarteriam de Balinaglogh. In his habuit Episcopus visitationem ut supra.

Fratres Predicatorum
Habent monasterium de Strade. Olim dicebatur filia de Sligae. Habent quatour quarterias terrae et una Balanamore. Illae 4 quarteria(s)e erant olim tantum(m)odo d(at)ae sed malitia hominum laicorum possidentium a Rege sic divisae in 4 quarterias ut supra. In hoc territorio parochus S. Nechah [Nicholae] de Templemore baptisavit,

matrimonio assistebat et curam animarum gerebat. Vero emolumenta ad fratres praedictos spectabat.

Habebant praedicti fratres monasterium de Urlare cum quatour quarter(u)iis terrae annexis. Parochus de Kilmavey habuit curam animarum &c. ut supra. Item habuit monasterium de Cloonivahane [Cloonameehan in Bunninadden parish.] alias Runnirogue cum una quarteria. Ibidem parochus de Clunoghil habuit curam animarum &c. ut supra.

Fratres Erimitarum S. P. Augustini habent monasterium de Banada cum una et semiquarteria terrae annexae ibidem cum altera parcella terrae in monte quae vulgo dicitur Mianagieragh. [Mían na gCléireach, Meenagleeragh, 'the smooth green field of the clergy'.] Parochus qui est rector de Kilmacteige habet curam animarum ut supra. Emolumenta ut supra.

APPENDIX TWENTY: POEM BY TADHG DALL Ó HUIGINN

Bráthair Bréige, Knott, *A Bhfuil againn dár chum Tadhg Dall Ó hUiginn,* nos 38 & 39

1   Ca talamh duit, a bhráthair?
    dona grásuibh bheith umhal;
    innis sgéala gan aincheas,
    nách beam i n-ainbheas umad.

2   An cuid dod riaghail chrábhaidh?
    léara a bhráthair, is innis
    créad tug di bhróga fallán,
    is h'atán do bheith brisde?

3   D'éis ar siubhlais do roide,
    a bhráthair choisflich chalma,
    iongnadh leam gloine t'asán,
    is h'atán lán do salchar.

4   An raibhe id riaghail chrábhaidh,
    a bhráthair ó chrích Connacht,
    cruas do bhróg agus t'asán,
    is h'atán do bheith robhog?

5   Dar leam ní faicim éanlocht
    ar t'éadach fada fallán,
    a bhráthair chroidhe cheóilbhinn,
    acht nach fiú feóirling h'atán.

6   Idir chóta agus chaipín,
    idir aibíd is asán,
    tar gach éanchuid dod chuladh
    ní maith do cumadh h'atán

7   Ní dot aibíd atámuid,
    a bhráthair as díol masán,
    féach id dhíaidh is féach romhad
    mar tá brollach ar hatán.

8   Th'atán, ar mhacaoimh léighinn,
    gi bé i nÉirinn ór gadadh,
    ní hatán duine dhílis
    bhíos dá sírreic i bhfalach.

9   Ní hé a chuma go lochtach,
    ní hé olcus a dhatha,
    tug gan a dhíol san Chabhán,
    acht é 'na atán ghada.

10 Beith 'ga bhélreic, a bhráthair,
    is tríd tánaig do mhilleadh;
    baile so in ndéantar nathán:
    'mairg tug hatán go Sligeach'.

11 Fulang gada do bhráthair
    ní do gnáthaibh an Iarla;
    dá seóltar tú 'na dhathán
    biaidh an t'atán go riabhach.

12 Maith do léine agus d'ionar,
    deas do siobhal ar chlachán,
    's is áluinn fós do mhatal,
    's is olc ghabhus tú h'atán.

13 Créad do-bheir th'aibíd goirid,
    's th'falluing go noige do sálaibh,
    agus h'atán fliuch fada
    ca talamh duit, a bhráthair?

A False Friar

1   Of what land art thou, friar? humility is one of the graces: give us plain information that we may not be in ignorance about thee.
2   Is it a part of thy Rule? explain, friar, and relate, why are thy shoes sound and thy hat tattered?
3   Considering all the swamp thou hast travelled, thou valiant wet-footed friar, I marvel at the cleanness of thy hose whilst thy hat is covered with dirt.
4   Was it in thy rule, thou friar from Connacht, that thy shoes and hose should be stout and thy hat very frail?
5   Methinks I see not a single fault in thy long and correct costume, beloved, melodious friar, save that thy hat is not worth a farthing.
6   Including coat and cap, habit and hose, more than any other article of thy dress has thy hat been ill-fashioned.

7   I make no complaint of thy habit, thou contemptible friar; look behind thee and before, for there is a rent in thy hat.

8   Thy hat, student, from whomsoever in Ireland it has been stolen, that it is not the hat of an honest man, which is ever been secretly offered for sale.

9   It is not its faulty fashioning, it is not the badness of its colour, prevented it been sold in Cavan, but the fact that it is a stolen hat.

10 Uttering it for sale, friar, that is what has brought about thy ruin; here is a proverb made, 'alas for him who brought a hat to Sligo.'

11 It is not the Earl's practice to suffer a friar to steal: if thou art sent in ... (?) the hat will be striped.

12 Good are thy shirt and thy vest, neat is thy step on the causeway, fone moreover is thy mantle, but badly doth thy hat become thee.

13 Why is thy habit short, and thy cloak down to thy heels, and thy hat damp and high, of what land art thou, friar?

APPENDIX TWENTY-ONE: POEMS OF MAOLMUIRE Ó HUIGINN

O'Rahilly, Thomas F., *Measgra Dánta, miscellaneous Irish poems*, part II, 52 & 53, 139–44 & 204–5

52. A fhir théid go Fiadh bhFuinidh,
mo-chean toisg dá dtriallfaidhir!
críoch naomhdha thirlinnte the,
maordha an fhirminte uaiste.

53. Slán uaim don dá aoghaire
'gá bhfuil an R 'na dtosach; [He expressed in some refined Irish verses sent from Belgium to Réamonn Ó Gallchobhair (O'Gallagher), Bishop of Derry, and Risteárd Mac Brádaigh of Kilmore, his ardent desire to return to his native country, which the nobleman, Roger O'Flaherty, accurately translated into Latin poetry.]

> d'uamhan fhear na saobhthuigse
> ní bhiú níos sia dá nochtadh.
> Ar eagla na buaidhearta
> géabhad an raon is réidhe;
> créad fá mbeinn re fuairleithribh?
> do-chímid croidhe a céile.
> Tig saoirse i ndiaidh róbhruide
> tar éis dubhaidh tig soineann;
> fuilngeam feadh an órlaigh-se
> mar do caitheadh an choinneal.
> Tig an uair saoilfidh,
> grás is cabhair ón gCoimdhe
> gear uaim am an fhaoithighe,
> fogas lá don ré dhoirche.

Ag Dia atá gach ordachadh;
ní feas duinn tráth tar neamhthráth;
ól an dighe domblasta
meinic fhóireas an t-easlán.

Greetings to the two shepherds
Whose names begin with an 'R';
To any foolish-thinking one
it's not worth revealing more.
For fear of trouble
I'll take the easiest route
Why should I use cold letters
We see each other's hearts.
After oppression comes freedom.
After foul weather comes fair weather
I'll suffer for the time being,
While the candle burns out.
When least expected,
grace and help came from God.
Not far away is the time of relief,
within a day of darkness.
God has the deciding of all things;
We don't know one time from another.
Drinking bitter medicine,
Often improves bad health.

Translation by Máirtín Mac Nioclás

APPENDIX TWENTY-TWO: 1603 GENERAL PARDON

General Pardon to Donnough O'Connor Sligo, of Sligo … Owen Grany Mc Moylroni finn of Templevanny, gent. Keodagh McMoylrony Fin of the same, kerne, Brian boy Mc Moilrony Fin of the same, kerne, Rorie oge Mc Moilrony Fin of the same, kerne, Arte Mc Gillylworin of the same, labourer, Gilleduffe McBrien buy of the same, labourer. Will. boy o'Gibbellanie of the same, kerne, Donald Mc Gilliworyne of the same, kerne, Moriasse Mc Gillilworanie of the same, labourer, Edw. Mc Gillylwornie of the same, kerne, Moriertagh Glas Mc Moilrony Finn of the same, labourer, Cahell Duffe Mc Dwalty, of the same, labourer, Dermot O'Lapane of the same labourer … Melaghlin Mc Donnogh of Inileaghefadda, priest, Fearill More of the same, priest, Cahell McEnilly of the same, labourer, Ulline Mc Ellay of the same, surgeon, Owen Carragh O'Donilly of the same, priest, Hugh boy O'Connor of Ballymote, gent. Thadeus boy Mc Donnell Chrone of the same, gent. Cormac Mergagh Mc Donnell Chronie of the same, horseman, Gilleduffe Mc Rorye of the same, horseman, Connogher Grany of the same, kerne, Donald oge Mc Donnell Chrone of the same, kerne, Rory Mc Hugh boy of the same, gent. Gillepatrick Cam Mc Eward of the same, rymer, Donald Mc Eward of the same, rymer, Geoffrie Mc Eward of the same, rymer, Moilmory Mc Eward of the same, rymer, Connoghor Mc Donnogh Reogh of the same, labourer, Donald Cam O'Coman of the same, labourer, Mark Mc Donnell of the same, student, Donatus Mc Sheaffrie Morrey of the same, kerne, Thadeus oge Mc Rorie of the same, kerne, Brian buy O'Clabby of the same, piper, Carbrie O'Brien of the same, labourer, Connoghor oge O'Brien of the same, galloglas, Phelim O'Birne of the same, galloglas, Thadeus O'Birne of the same, shot, Brien O'Birne of the same, galloglas, Shane O'Birne of the same, shot, Moriasse O'Birne of the same, shot, Thadeus Mc Donnogh of the same, kerne, Tirrelagh Mc Eparson, student, Shane O'Cahane of the same, messenger, Rorie O'Gilligan of the same, labourer, Will. Cwlkine of the same, labourer, Edw. Mc Cwlkine of the same, labourer, Gilleduffe Mc Evrehune of the same, horsekeeper, Gillegroma Mc Gworine of the same, kerne, Gillepatrick Mc Gworine of the same, kerne, Thadeus Mc Gworine of the same, kerne, Conillagh Mc Gworine of the same, kerne, Brian Mc Rorie Mc Gowane of the same, priest, Connor Mc Dermot O'Harte, of the same, husbandman, Will. Mc Shane Mc Dermot O'Harte of the same, kerne, Gillepatrick Mc Connor O'Hart, of the same, labourer, Fearill Mc Gloyne of the same, kerne, Shane Mc Dermot O'Conillan of the same, labourer, Will. O'Hart of the same, labourer, Brian oge Mc Hugh of the same, labourer, Oyne Mc Donnogh of the same, labourer, Connoghor Reogh O'Lauderne, of the same, labourer, Hugh Ballagh Mc Conbany of the same, tucker, Gillepatricke Reogh O'Callille of the same, labourer, Owen O'Mowrigane of the same, harper, Shane roe O'Clabby of the same, husbandman, Moellony O'Daly of the same, harper, Rorie Magloyne of the same, shot, Donatus Cwuwaghane of the same, shot, Brian O'Clwanie of the same, labourer, Hubert Mc Philip of the same, labourer, Rorie Duffe Mc Enilly of the same, labourer, Shane O'Lavine of the same, labourer, Shane Mc Moricrtagh Reogh of the same, labourer, Thadeus O'Creavoyne of the same, labourer, Thomas Bentfield of the same, serving-man, Tomoltagh McGwollrick of the same, kerne, Gillepatricke O'Birne of the same, labourer, Dermot Mc Hugh O'Hart of the same, labourer, Donald O'Helly of the same, keard, Owen O'Helly of the same, labourer, Owen Duffe Mc Tomoltagh of the same, husbandman, Thadeus boy Mc Tomoltagh, of the same, husbandman, Donald Mc Tomoltagh of the same, husbandman, Hugh O' Coane of the same, husbandman, Tomultagh Mc Cormucke of the same, kerne, Cormac O'Harie, otherwise O'Harie boy of Teaghtemplae, gent. Une ny Gallothoire, wife of said Cormac, Cormac oge O'Harie of the same, gent. Irrill O'Harie of the same, gent. Moriertagh Glas Mc Enchae, labourer, Kyen Mc Dermot O'Harie of the same gent. Will Duffe Mc Manes of the same, kerne, Rorie Gortagh of the same, labourer, Moilrony Mc Encha of the same, labourer, Donald Mc Dermot O'Harie of the same, gent. Cowconnaght O'Higgen of the same, kerne, Donell O'Harie of the same, gent. Ulick Mc Richard Mc Edw. Sallagh, horseman, Donald McCwne O'Harie, gent. Shane O'Cwigley of the same, carpenter, Philip O'Reilly of the same, kerne, Hugh oge mc Hugh Mc Brien of the same, kerne, Shane buy Mc Hugh Mc Brien of the same, kerne, Cormac Mc Will. O'Comane of the same, kerne, Dermot Duffe O'Harie of the same, kerne, Brien O'Comane of the same, kerne, Donald O'Clwayne of the same, labourer, Gillepatrick O'Mollrony of the same, labourer, Brien Dorrogh O'Higgen of the same, kerne, Cowconaght O'Higgen of the same, kerne, Brien O'Mowlgihie of the same, kerne, Donald O'Moulgihie of the same, labourer, Owen

roe O'Moullgihie of the same, labourer, Donatus O'Mowlgihie of the same, labourer,
Owen Duffe O'Mowlgihie of the same, labourer, Donald Duffe of the same, labourer,
Thadeus buy O'Harie of Twllihugh, gent. Moriertagh Mc Manes of the same,
horseman, Thadeus Mc Manes of the same, husbandman, Rorie oge Mc Shane
Nebacky of the same, horseman, Thadeus Reogh Mc Brien Dorrogh of the same, shot,
Moillrony O'Fennygane of the same, labourer, Donatus O'Clawne of Killwohrine,
priest, Henry O'Clawne of the same, kerne, Melaghlin O'Glawin of the same, labourer,
Owen O'Harie of Cowllany, gent. Brien O'Harie of the same, gent. Mortagh Duffe
O'Harie of the same, gent. Rorie O'Harie of the same, gent. Irriell Mc Fearill O'Harie
of Monielagh, gent. Kyen Mc Fearill O'Harie of the same, gent. Hugh O'Derige of
Cowrteroriballagh, priest, Arte Mc Manes of the same, priest, Phelim O'Harie of
Twillyneglock, gent. Will O'Harie of the same, gent. Cahell O'Harie of the same, gent.
Shane oge O'Harie of the same, gent. Will. Mc Eleray of Tullynegloge, kerne, Hugh
Mc Elrarie of the same, kerne, Brien Moile Mc Elearie of the same, kerne, Teige Mc
Owen Mc Elearie, of the same, labourer, Brian oge Mc Elearie of the same, labourer,
Brian Ballagh O'Brinane of the same, smith, Dermod Reogh O'Harie of the same,
gent. Will. O'Hennygane of the same, friar, Dermot O'Henigane of the same,
husbandman, Manes Mc Tomoltagh O'Harie of Beallacleare, gent. Will. Mc
Tomoltagh O'Harie of the same, gent. Rorie Mc Feardorogh O'Harie of the same,
gent. Art Mc Edward buy of the same, gent. Moriasse Mc Gillidwine of the same,
labourer, Donald Mc Gillyedwn of the same, labourer, Teige Keogh Mc Fearill Carragh
of Balliarie, gent. Teige Mc Tomoltagh of the same, gent. Dermot Keogh Mc Shane
oge of the same, gent. Hugh Mc Shane oge of the same, gent. Donnogh Mc Eleary of
the same, labourer, Rorie Mc Christine of the same, priest, Brien Mc Rorie Mc
Christeine of the same, kerne, Will. O'Higgin of Dwacharny, rymer, Twoholl O'Higgin
of the same, rymer, Cormuck O'Higgin of the same, rymer, Gillenewf O'Higgin of
the same, rymer, Teige oge Mc Teige Daile O'Higgin of the same, rymer, Dermod
O'Brinane Mc Gillepatrick of the same, husbandman, Cahell Mc Etire, shoemaker,
Richard Brennagh of the same, smith, Owen O'Hart of Accadensis, bishop, Moriasse
O'Connoghane of Archonerie, priest, Cormuck O'Connoghane, of the same, harper,
Gillepatricke O'Finane of the same, harper, Shane boy O'Fynane of the same, harper,
Edmond oge O'Finane of the same, harper, Brian Dorrogh O'Finane of the same,
harper, Fearill Mc Rorie of Ballinwihi, gent. Philip Mc Philip of the same, gent.
Dermot Crone of the same, horseman, Cormuck Mc Rorie of the same, kerne,
Dualtagh Mc Shane Glas of the same, horseman, Rorie oge O'Connoghor of the same,
horseman, Ed. Mc Swiny of the same galloglas, David Brennagh of the same, smith,
Shane Reogh Brennagh of the same, smith, Shane Mc Garay of the same, labourer,
Irriell O'Garie of Moygarie, gent. Rorie O'Garie of the same, gent. Farginannyne
O'Garie of the same, gent. Owen O'Garie of the same, gent. Teige O'Garie of the
same, gent. Manes Keogh Mc Brien Reogh O'Garie of the same, horseman, Dermot
Mc Brien Reogh O'Garie, horseman, Gillegroma Mc Dermot of the same, kerne,
Hugh boy Mc Manes Keogh of the same, kerne, Ferrill Mc Tomoltagh of the same,
kerne, Dermot roe Mc Moellronye of the same, kerne, Edw. oge Mc Edward of the
same, husbandman, Brien Mc Owen Mc Rorie of the same, husbandman, Gillegroma
Mc Riccard of the same, shot, Brian Mc Manes O'Garie of the same, kerne, Connor
Mc Brien of the same, husbandman, Rorie roe Mc Brien of the same, husbandman,

Thomas Duffe Mc Dermot Reogh of the same, husbandman, Kyen O'Garie of the same, gent. Manes O'Garie of the same, kerne, Owen boy Mc Fearagheir of the same, surgeon, Cahell O'Cahasey of the same, husbandman, Brin O'Spillane of the same, labourer, Melaghlin O'Coman of the same, labourer, Irriell Mc Donnell Keogh O'Higgin of the same, harper, Irriell Mc Moelrony O'Higgin of the same, friar, Donnell oge O'Higgin of the same, husbandman, Owen O'Higgin of the same, harper, Fearfeassa O'Dwgenaine of the same, rymer, Edw. O Cahasie of the same, husbandman, Brian Carragh O'Cwneanie of the same, husbandman … Tomoltagh Mc Kelly of Templevanny, labourer, Brian Mc Kelly of the same, labourer … Carberie O'Bearne of Bonenaddane, Dermod Mc Carbrie O'Bearne of the same, husbandman … Owen Ulltagh Mc Shane oge of Ballimote, Margaret Duffe, Donnogh Ultagh Mc Shane of the same, surgeon, Teige Mc Moreine of Ballimote, Richard O'Fallon, Brein Mc Moreine, Melaghlin Mc Moreine of the same, yeoman … 19 Apr. 1st.

APPENDIX TWENTY-THREE: 23 JULY 1575 LETTER OF EOGHAN Ó HAIRT TO CARDINAL COMO, ROME IN FAVOUR OF MILER O HIGGINS ENTRY TO COLLEGIO GERMANICO UNGARICO, ROME

Ille ac Rme Dne
Ineffabilem illam Ierosolimorum mutationem quam lamentabiliter propheta Jeremias descripsit. Huic nostrae ecclesiae Hibercanae hoc calamitose tempore accidisse conspicio. Clericis namque meis a nova ista religione Anglicana dissidentibus neque propria vita secura est eis permissa aut tutus regni pateat exitus. Nam marini portus diligentissime observantur. Si contra Reginae edictum exire volentium deprehenderentur, aut capitis pena plecterentur aut perpetuo carceri maxima ex gratiam tamquam regni exploratores deputarentur. Si qui fortuna favente clanculo exire ut (et T.F.) curiam ? peterent (peterem T.F.) possint(.) consulo conscientias ipsorum tefas? (nefas, sinful T.F.) et remorsas illic sanare, aut vitam quietam ducere studeant. Impetravent aliquam nova a sede ipsam opus non habent nisi maiorem persequtionem hereticorum adversos seipsos excitare vellent. Quoquomodo ? (quomodo, T.F.) plura respita (respira, take a respite, T.F.) apli-? [torn] (applicare, to attach, apply, devote oneself to, T.F.). apud me absconsa teneo impetrantes in hiis procedere nolunt. Quia nil commodi ex illis opess-? [torn] Senes nostri clerici in hac tempestate defecerunt, neque in portis aut plateis apparent. Iuvenes pariter de choro psallentium perierunt. Dilectus igitur hic meus praesentium lator, Milerus O'Huigin, presbyter bene morigeratus, atque litteratus et ecclesiae nostrae cathedralis decanus, cernens hunc regni nostri miserabilem statum, Romam de licentia nostra petere optavit. Ut suae hereditatis partem quam vi et potentia hereticorum amisit, in studiis bonarum litterarum cum Dei adiutorio illic recompensaret. Ea propterea, illustrissime et reverendissime domine inexhaustam D.V. pietatem obnixe rogamus, ut huic nostro prefato Milero in Collegio Germanico, cuius fama divulgta est, favere, si placet cunctis et sit rem nobis gratam et ecclesiae nostrae utilem fore speramus. Ex ecclesia Achadensi in Hibernia. Julii 23 scripserat 1575. Illustrissime et Reverendissime Domine, D.V. humilis servus Eugenius Achadensis episcopus. ASV Fondo Borghese, Serie III 9 C f.240r.

('I see in the terrible upheaval of the inhabitants of Jerusalem which the prophet Jeremias sorrowfully described, this calamitous time that has befallen our Irish church. For my clergy who refuse to accept this new English religion, their very lives are in danger and there is no safe way of leaving the kingdom, for sea-ports are carefully scrutinised. Spies are dispersed throughout the kingdom to such an extent that if those wishing to leave contrary to the Queen's proclamation are apprehended they are either condemned to death or, with the greatest leniency, to life imprisonment. If those who can with good luck leave secretly to seek refuge, I advise them to cure their sinful and troubled consciences there or strive to lead a peaceful life. If any of them by the favour of good fortune, be able to get out covertly, I would also repair to the Curia. I counsel their sinful consciences and also to heal those troubled consciences, or to study how to live a quiet life T.F.) From their new home they get something itself, they have no work unless they wish to excite greater persecution by the heretics against themselves. I will not say how I kept hidden at home for several – [torn], the impetrantes unwilling to show their faces in these parts. Because nothing suitable from here – [torn] At this time our older clergy are demoralised, refusing to show their faces in doorways or in the streets. Similarly the young have disappeared from the office in choir.)

APPENDIX TWENTY-FOUR: INVESTIGATION OF THE DIOCESE OF ACHONRY

Inq. o 15 Episcopat' Accaden
Inq' capt' apud Aghonra infra com' Sligo 18 Augusti 1585, coi' Danile Darens' Epo' p sacramentu pboy etc quorum nomina subsequuntur, Brian McMolroni, Darbicis Bren, Teig O'Harte, Phelim O'Connor. Melaghlin McDonogh, Melaghlin McDonogh de Clowny [Coolany], Joh' O'Mulconra, Connor Cahen, Carolus McDere, Manus Reagh McTeag boy, Brian O'Dowde, Erevan McSwyne, Miler McMcManus. Ror' McGinella, Cahill McHeugh, Johannes Glass. Brian oge McPersun, John O'Hart, Muredac' McManus, Lucas McBreghun, Roric' O'Dowde, Carol' O'Synan, & Brien McSwyne.
qui dic' quod Episcapat' Aghaden' infra
Dioc?' Aghaden' val' p ann' 10£
Dicanat' Aghaden' val'p ann' 20s,
ppositus Achaden' 6s/8d
Archionat' Aghaden cu viccar' de Kilbrowryh [Kilturrow] infra dioc pdic' 4s,
Vicar' de Kilvardnaha [Kilvarnet] 4s,
Vicar' de Killowran [Killoran]10s,
Id de ann' val' vicarie Kilmcteig [Kilmactigue] infra dioc' pdic' ignorant q' vastal',
Id vicar' de Killesy [Killasser?] val' p ann' 2s,
" " Attemas [Attymas] nihil q' vast',
" " Strade [Straide] 4s,
" " Killodan [Killedan] 5s,
" " Killconnow [Kilconduff] nihil q' vast'
" " Kilveigh [Kilbeagh] 4s,
" " Moyconra nihil q. vast'

" " Templemanrys 5s,
" " Kilcolman 3s,
" " Killara [Killaraght] 3s,
" " Killosalvan [Kilshalvy] 2s,
" " Iumlehaedys [Emlefad] 3s .. 4d,
" " Tujmore [Toomour] 3s,
" " Kilmorchor [Kilmorgan] 20d,
" " Clonoghill [Cloonoghill] 8s,
Rectoria de Cowlaven [Coolavin] 6s .. 8d
Vicar' de Cowlavin [Coolavin] 3s .. 4d
Rectoria de Slewloa [Sliabh Lugha] 10s,
" " Bowcowlye [Bohola] 2s .. 8d
Rectoria voc' "inter duos amnes ['between two rivers'] 3s .. 4d,
" de Killownan [Killoran] 13s .. 4d,

Bibliography

ARCHIVES

Austria
Vienna, Kaiserlich und Konigliches Haus-, Hof-, und Staatsarchiv. Conciliacten V

Belgium
Brussels
ms. 3947 (Analecta Hibernica, 1934, 25) Donatus Mooney OFM

England
London
National Archives, Kew, Surrey.

France
Paris
Archives Nationales

Ireland
Dublin
Royal Irish Academy
Brockliss & Ferté, 'Prosopography of Irish Clerics who studied in France in the 17th and 18th centuries, in particular at the universities of Paris and Toulouse' (unpublished typescript)

Italy
Rome
Archivio Segreto Vaticano
Vatican Library
Barberini Latini (part 1), f.272r–275v, microfilm, Nat. Lib., Dublin, 817, *Sententia episcopi Achadensis Hibernici de doctrina et canonibus sacri ordinis.*
2877, f.14v, poverty of Andreas, Eugenius and Donaldus.
2880, f.24v, Thomas O'Fighil, appointed to Achonry, 15 Jan. 1547
2932, f.3r. (pos. 872), Thomas de Rivis appointed to Achonry. 8 Oct. 1492
8648 (part 1) ff.218r–219v, Rossetti to Barberini, 5 Oct. 1640. Petitions by Conte di S.
Albano and by the Marchioness of Winchester that Dominic de Burgo OP be made Bishop of Achonry.

Spain
Simancas Archives. *Secretaria de Estado, Legajo* 819, f.182

PRINTED MATERIAL

All Salamanca and its province (Barcelona 1978).

Annala Connacht; the Annals of Connacht AD 1224–1544, ed. A. Martin Freeman (Dublin 1970).

Annals of Loch Cé, ed. William M. Hennessy (Dublin 1939).

Annala Rioghacta Eireann. Annals of the kingdom of Ireland by the Four Masters from the earliest period to the year 1616, ed. John O'Donovan, 7 vols (Dublin 1851).

Annala Uladh: Annals of Ulster: a chronicle of Irish affairs from A.D.431–A.D.1540, ed. with a translation and notes by William M. Hennessy, 4 vols (Dublin 1887–1901).

'Annals of Ireland from the year 1443–1468, translated by Duald Mac Firbis for Sir James Ware in the year 1666' in *The Miscellany of the Irish Archaeological Society* (Dublin 1846).

Barraclough, Geoffrey, *Papal Provisions Aspect of Church History, Constitutional, Legal and Administrative in Later Middle Ages* (Oxford 1935).

Barry, John, 'The Coarb and the Twelfth-century Reform', in *IER*, 88; 17–25, 'The Erenagh in the Monastic Irish Church', 'The Coarb in Medieval Times', in *IER*, 89, 424–32, 24–35,'The Lay Coarb in Medieval Times', in *IER*, 91, 27–39, 'The Appointment of Coarb and Erenagh', in *IER*, 93, 361–4, 'The Distinction between Coarb and Erenagh', in *IER*, 94, 90–5, 'The Status of Coarbs and Erenaghs', *IER*, 94, 147–53, 'The Duties of Coarbs and Erenaghs, *IER*, 94, 211–18.

Bartlett, John R. & Kinsella, Stuart D., *Two Thousand Years of Christianity and Ireland* (2006).

Bayne, C.G., *Anglo-Roman Relations*, Oxford Historical and Literary Studies, ii (Oxford 1913), 196–204.

Beirne, Francis, ed., *The Diocese of Elphin, People, Places and Pilgrimage* (Dublin 2000).

Bellesheim, Alphons, *Geschichte der Katholischen Kirche in Irland von der Einfuhrung de Christenthums bis auf die Gegenwart*, 3 vols (Mainz 1890–1).

Bergin, Osborn, *Irish Bardic Poetry.*

Berrueta, Juan Domínguez, *Enciclipeda Gráfica Salamanca* (Salamanca 1931).

Bossy, John, 'The Counter-Reformation and the People of Catholic Ireland, 1596–1641' in *Historical Studies*, viii (Dublin 1971), 155–69.

Boyle, P., *The Irish College in Paris* (Dublin 1901).

Bradshaw, Brendan & Keogh, Daire, eds, *Christianity in Ireland. Revisiting the Story* (Dublin 2002); *The Dissolution of Religious Orders in Ireland under Henry VIII* (Cambridge 1974).

Brady, Maziere William, *Episcopal Succession in England, Scotland and Ireland a.d. 1400–1875*. With appointments to monasteries and extracts from Consistorial Acts taken from MSS (Rome 1876–7).

Burgo, Thomas de, *Hibernia Dominicana* (reprinted 1970).

Butler, Alban, *The Lives of the Saints*, 12 vols, revised by Herbert Thurston (London 1926).

Byrne, F.J. 'The Trembling Sod: Ireland in 1169' in *A New History of Ireland*, xiv, 111–42.

Calendar of Entries in the Papal Registries relating to Great Britain and Ireland, xx vols (Dublin).

Calendar of Entries in the Papal Registers relating to Great Britain and Ireland. Papal Letters, vols i, 1198, xiv, 1492 (London 1893–1960), i, 1198–1304, Innocent III, Honorius III, Gregory IX, Innocent IV, Alexander IV, Urban iv, Clement IV, Gregory X, Nicholas III, Martin IV, Honorius IV, Boniface, VIII, Benedict XI, ed., W. H. Bliss (London 1893), ii, 1305–42, Clement V, John XXII, Nicholas V, anti-pope, Benedict XII, ed. as above (London 1895), iii, 1342–62, Clement VI, Innocent VI, ed., W. H. Bliss & C. Johnson (London 1897), iv, 1396–1404, Urbane V, Gregory IX, Clement VII, anti-pope, Urbane VI, Boniface IX, ed., (London).

Calendar of Papal Registers, i, Petitions to the Pope 1342–1419, ed. W. H. Bliss (London 1896), ed. W. H. Bliss & J. A. Twemlow (London 1902), v, 1396–1404, Boniface IX, ed. as above (London 1904), vi, 1404–15, Innocent VII, Gregory XII, Alexander V, John XXIII, ed. as above (London 1904), vii, 1417–31, Martin V, ed. as above (London 1906), viii, 1427–47, Martin V, Eugenius IV, ed. as above (London 1909), ix, 1431–47, Eugenius IV, ed. as above (London 1912), x, 1447–55, Nicholas V, ed. as above (London 1915), xi, 1459–64, Calixtus III, Pius II, ed. as above (London 1921), xii, 1458–71, Pius II, Paul II, ed. as above (London 1903), xiii, part i, 1471–84, ed. J. A. Twemlow (London 1955), xiii, part i, 1471–84, Sixtus IV, part ii, 1471–84, Sixtus IV, ed. J. A. Twemlow (London 1955), xiv, 1484–92, Innocent VIII ed. as above (London 1960), xv, 1484–92. Innocent VIII, ed. Michael J. Haren (Dublin 1978), xvi, 1492–1503, Alexander VI Lateran Registers, part i, 1492–8, ed. Anne P. Fuller (Dublin 1998), xvii, part ii 1492–1503, Alexander VI, Vatican Registers, 1492–1503, ed. as above (Dublin 1998), xviii, 1503–13, Pius III and Julius II, Vatican Registers, Lateran Registers (1503–8), ed. Michael J. Haren (Dublin 1989), xix, 1503–13, Julius II, Lateran Registers, part ii, ed. as above (Dublin 1998), xx, 1513–21, Leo X, Lateran Registers part i, ed. Anne P. Fuller (Dublin 2005).

Calendar of Documents, Ireland, 1171–1251, ed. H. S. Sweetman (London 1875), same, 1252–84 (London 1877), same, 1285–92 (London 1879), 1293–1307 (London 1881), same, 1302–7, ed. same & Gustavus Frederick Handcock (London 1886).

Calendar of Fiants of Elizabeth, i, 1558–86, 11th report of the deputy keeper of the Public Records of Ireland, 31–242, 12th report, 17–174, 13th report, 16–220, 15th report, 15–174 (Dublin 1879), ii, 1586–1603, 16th report, 17–278, 17th report, 29–276, 18th report, 27–150 (Dublin 1884), iii, 21st report, index, 33–862 (Dublin 1889).

Calendar of State Papers, Carew, 1515–74, ed. J. S. Brewer & William Bullen (London 1867), same, 1875–88, ed. as above (London 1868), same, 1589–1600, ed. as above, same. 1601–3, ed. as above (London 1870), same, 1603–24, ed. as above (London 1873).

Calendar of the State Papers relating to Ireland of the reigns … 1509–1670, 24 vols (London 1860–1910), *Henry VIII* (1509–47), *Edward VI* (1547–53), *Mary* (1553–8), *Elizabeth I* (1558–1603), 1509–73, ed. Hans Claude Hamilton (London 1860), *Elizabeth I* (1558–1603), 1574–85, ed. Hans Claude Hamilton (London 1867), 1586–July 1588, ed. Hans Claude Hamilton (London 1877), Aug. 1588–

Sept. 1592, ed. Hans Claude Hamilton (London 1885) 1592–6, ed. Hans Claude
    Hamilton (London 1890), 31 July 1596–Dec. 1597, ed. Ernest George Atkinson
    (London 1893), 1598–9, ed. Ernest George Atkinson (London 1893), 1599–1600,
    ed. Ernest George Atkinson (London 1893), 1600, ed. Ernest George Atkinson
    (London 1893), Mar.–Oct. 1600, ed. Ernest George Atkinson (London 1903), 1
    Nov. 1600–31 July 1601, ed. Ernest George Atkinson (London 1905), 1601–3, 1
    Nov 1600–31 July 1601, ed. Ernest George Atkinson (London 1912).
Calendar of State Papers, Rome, Elizabeth, 1558–1578, 2 vols, i, 1558–71, J. M. Rigg
    (London 1916), ii, 1578–1603, ed. (London ?).
Calendar of State Papers, Ireland: Tudor Period 1566–1567, ed. Bernadette Cunningham
    (Dublin 2009).
Calendar of State Papers, Ireland 1571–1575, ed. Mary O'Dowd (London & Dublin
    2000) *James I* (1603–25), *1603–06,* ed. C. W. Russell & John P. Prendergast
    (London 1872), *1606–08,* ed. as above (London 1874), *1608–1610,* ed. as above
    (London 1874), *1611–14,* ed. as above (London 1877), *1615–25,* ed. as above
    (London 1880), *Charles I* (1625–49), *1625–32,* ed. Robert Pentland Mahafy
    (London 1900), *1633–47,* as above (London 1901), *1625–60, Charles II*
    (1649–85), *1660–2,* ed. as above (London 1903), *1642–1659, Adventurers for
    Land,* ed. as above (London 1903), *1663–65,* ed. as above (London 1907), *1666–
    69,* ed. as above (London 1908), *Sept. 1669–Dec. 70,* ed. as above (London 1910).
*Calendar of State Papers relating to English Affairs, preserved principally at Rome in the
    Vatican Archives and Library,* 2 vols (1916–26).
Calendar of Patent Rolls, James I (London 1830), *Fiants Eliz.* 5865; *Cal. Patent Rolls,*
    ed. Morrin.
Callus, Daniel A., *Oxford Studies presented to D. Callus,* Oxford Historical Studies
    (1964), xvi.
Charles-Edwards, Thomas M., *Early Christian Ireland* (Cambridge 2000).
Cochrane, Rupert, 'The Ecclesiastical Remains at Sligo Abbey' (revised by H. G. Leask)
    in *Sligo Abbey,* 1–15.
Commentarius Rinuccinianus (Dublin 1941).
Connellan, 'Knockmore Carmelite Convent' in *Whitefriars,* Sept–Oct 1955.
Cosgrove, Art, ed., *Marriage in Ireland* (Dublin 1985); 'Irish Episcopal Temporalities
    in the Thirteenth Century' in *Arch. Hib.* (1974), xxxii, 63–71.
Cotton, Henry, *Fasti Ecclesiae Hibernicae. The succession of prelates and members of
    Cathedral bodies in Ireland.* iv, The Province of Connaught (Dublin 1850).
Davies, John, *The complete prose works of Sir John Davies,* ed. A. B. Grossart, 3 vols
    (London, 1869–76); *A discovery of the true causes why Ireland was never subdued
    … until … his Majesty's happy reign* (London, 1612), facsimile reprint (Shannon
    1969); 'Letter to Salisbury', in Morley, *Ireland under Elizabeth and James I* (London
    1890), 213–312.
Derricke, John, *Image of Ireland, with a discovery of Woodkarne,* 1581 (Edinburgh
    1883).
Dictionary of Irish Biography, 9 vols, eds James Maguire & James Quinn (Dublin 2009).
Dictionary of the Middle Ages, 11 vols (New York 1982).
Dodd, Romuald, 'Vatican Archives: Instrumenta Miscellanea' in *Arch. Hib.,* xix, 135 ff.

Doherty, J. E., *A Chronology of Irish History* (Dublin 1989).

Dolley, Michael, *Anglo-Norman Ireland* (Gill History of Ireland, 1972).

Doyle, Alexander, 'Fearghal Ó Gadhra and the Four Masters' in *IER* (July–Dec. 1963), 100–14.

Duby, Georges, *The Knight, the Lady and the Priest, The Making of Modern Marriage in Medieval France* (translated from the French).

Dunning, P. J. 'Letters of Innocent III as a source for Irish History', in *Proceedings of the Irish Catholic Committee*, 1958 (Dublin 1959), 1–15.

Edwards, R. Dudley, 'The Irish Reformation Parliament of Henry VIII 1536–7' in *Historical Studies*, vi, 59–80.

Edwards, Ruth Dudley, 'Ecclesiastical Appointments in the Province of Tuam 1399–1477' in *IER* (1975), xxxiii, 91–100.

Egan, Bonaventure, Cathaldus Giblin, Cuthbert McGrath, 'Irish Students ordained in Rome (1625–1710)' in *IER* (1943), lxxxi, 116–24.

Ehses, Stephanus, ed., *Concilium Tridentinum, Diariorum, Actorum, Epistolarum Tractatum* (Friburg 1919, 1923), viii, 517, 648, 676, 685, 785, 866, 905, 915, 939, 941, 946, 954, 969; ix, 204, 351, 578, 615, 676, 734, 871, 943, 1029. *Concilii Tridentini Actorum, pars sexta* 17 Sept. 1562–1 Dec. 1563 (Friburg 1924), 205–6, 'Sententia episcopi Achadensis Hibernici de doctrina et canonibus sacri ordinis 4 decembris, 1562' ('Opinion of Eugene O'Hart, Bishop of Achonry on the doctrine and canons of holy orders').

Eubel, Conrad, *Hierarchia Catholica Medii Aevii*, i, 1198–1431, ii (Regensberg 1914), ii, 1431–1503, iii, 1503 (Regensberg 1910).

Fenning, H., 'Irish Material in the Registers of the Dominican Masters General (1390–1649)' in *Archivium Fratrum Praedicatorum*, 39 (1969).

FitzPatrick, J. E., 'Ballymote Castle' in *JRISA*, lvii, part ii, 81–99 (1927).

Flynn, Thomas S., *The Irish Dominicans 1536–1641* (Dublin 1993).

Ford, Alan, *The protestant reformation in Ireland 1590–1641* (Frankfurt 1985).

Foster, J., *Alumni Oxonienses*, 4 vols (Oxford 1891).

Fryde, E. B., *Handbook of British Chronology*.

Gams, Pius Bonifacius, *Series Episcoporum Ecclesiae Catholicae* (Graz 1957).

Gauchat, Patritius, *Hierarchia Catholica Medii Aevii*, iv (Regensberg 1935).

Giblin, Cathaldus, *Liber Lovaniensis, A Collection of Irish Franciscan Documents, 1629–1717* (Dublin), 'The Irish Colleges on the Continent', in Swords, *The Irish-French Connection*, 9–20. 'Catalogue of material of Irish interest in the Collection Nunziatura di Fiandra, Vatican Archives, part 1, vols 1–50' in *Coll. Hib.* (1958), no. 1, 7–134; same as above, part 2, vols 51–80, in *Coll. Hib.* (1960), no. 3, 7–144; same as above. part 9, vols 148–52, in *Coll. Hib.*, no. 13 (1970), 61–99; 'Vatican Library: MSS Barbarini Latini', in *Arch. Hib.* (1955), xviii, 67–129.

Glasscock, R. E., 'Land and People c. 1300' in *A New History of Ireland*, ii, Medieval Ireland (1169–1534), 205–39.

Gleeson, Dermot & Gwynn, Aubrey, *A History of the Diocese of Killaloe*, part 1. The early period by Aubry Gwynn, part II–IV. The Middle Ages by Dermot F. Gleeson (Dublin 1962).

Gleeson, Dermot F, 'Your Parish and its History', in *IER* (1960), 93, 1–18.

Gougaud, Louis, *Christianity in Celtic Lands* (Dublin 1992).

Graham, J. M. 'Rural society in Connacht, 1600–1640', in *Irish Geographical Studies*, 192–208.

Grattan Flood, W. H., 'The Episcopal Succession of Achonry (1219–1561)' in *IER* (1922), xx, 474–83.

Gwynn, A & R. N. Hadcock, *Medieval Religious Houses Ireland* (London 1970, reprinted Dublin 1988).

Gwynn, Aubrey, 'The Black Death in Ireland' in *Studies* (1935), xxiv, 25–42. 'Ireland and the English Nation at the Council of Constance', 202–17 in *RIA Procs.*, lvi, section C, no. 8. 'The Centenary of the Synod of Kells', in *IER* (Mar–April 1952), vol. 77, 161–77, 250–64. 'The Medieval Councils: Lateran 1 to Vienne 1123–1211' in *IER* (Jan–June 1963) xcix, 147–56.

Hagan, J., 'Miscellanea Vaticano-Hibernica' in *Arch. Hib.* (1915), iv 264–7, 284–7, v, 74–163 (1916), vi, 97, 141.

Hanly, John, *The Letters of Oliver Plunkett, 1625–1681 Archbishop of Armagh and Primate of All Ireland* (Dublin 1979).

Harbison, Peter, *Our Treasure of Antiquities* (2001).

Haren, Michael J., 'Clogher Cathedral in the early sixteenth century', in *Clogher Record* (1985) 48–77; 'Vatican Archives as a Historical Source to *c*.1530', in *Catholic Record Society of Ireland* (1984), 3–12.

Herity, Michael, *Ordnance Survey Letters, Mayo* (Dublin 2009).

Hinnebusch, W. A., 'Foreign Dominican Students and professors at the Oxford Blackfriars' in A. B. Enden, *Oxford Studies presented to Daniel Callus* (1964).

Hogan, Edmund, *Distinguished Irishmen of the sixteenth century* (London 1894). *Onomasticon Goedelicum Locorum et Tributum Hiberniae et Scotiae* (Dublin 1910). *Holinshed's Irish Chronicle* 1577 (1979).

Hughes, Kathleen, *Traveller to the Early Irish Church* (London 1977, 2nd edn 1997); *Early Christian Ireland: Introduction to the Sources* (London 1972).

Hyde, Douglas, *Amhráin Diadha Chúige Connacht* (London-Dublin 1906).

Jedin, Hubert, *Crisis and Closure of the Council of Trent* (London 1967).

Jennings, Brendan,'Brussels MS 3947: Donatus Moneyus de Provincia Hiberniae S. Francisci' in *Anal. Hib.* no. 6 (1934); 12–131; 'Miscellaneous Documents ii 1625–1640' in *Arch. Hib.*, xiv (1949), 1–49; 'Ireland and Propaganda Fide, 1672–6' in *Arch. Hib.*, xix (1956), 1–60; 'Ecclesiastical Appointments in Ireland, Aug 1643–Dec 1649' in *Coll. Hib.* (1959), no. 2, 18–65.

Jones, Frederick M., 'The Counter-Reformation', in Corish (ed.), *A History of Irish Catholicism*, 1–53.

Kearns, Conleth, 'Archives of the Irish Dominican College, San Clemente, Rome: a summary report' in *Arch. Hib.*, xviii, 145–9.

Kelly, Matthew, *Calendar of the Irish Saints, The Martyrology of Tallagh* (Dublin 1857).

Kelly, Michael J, 'The Belt-Sharine from Moylough, Sligo', *JRSIA*, lxxxxv, 149–87.

Kenney, J. F, *Sources for the Early History of Ireland, i, Ecclesiastical* (New York 1929).

Kirby, T. F., *Annals of Winchester College*.

Knott, Eleanor, *A Bhfuil Againn dár chum Tadhg Dall Ó Huiginn (1550–1591)* (London 1920); ed. *The Bardic poems of Tadhg Dall O hUiginn (1550–1591)*, 2 vols (London 1922, 1926); *An introduction to Irish Syllabic poetry of the period 1200–1600, with selections, notes and glossary* (Cork 1928).

Knox, Hubert Thomas, *The History of the County of Mayo to the close of the Sixteenth Century* (Dublin 1908); *Early Tribes of Connaught*.

Lawlor, H. J., 'A Fresh Authority for the Synod of Kells 1152' in *Proceedings of the Royal Irish Academy*, xxxvi, section C, no. 3, 16–22 (Dublin 1922).

Le Plat, Josse, *Monumentorum ad historiam Concilii Tridentini potissimum illustrandum spectantium amplissima collectio*, 7 vols, i (Louvain, 1781).

Leask, Harold G., *Irish Churches and Monastic Buildings*, 3 vols, i, The first phases and Romanesque, ii. Gothic Architecture to AD 1400, iii, Medieval Gothic, the last phases (Dundalk 1955, 1958, 1960).

Littleday, Richard Frederick, *A Short History of the Council of Trent* (London 1888).

Lynch, Anthony, 'Religion in Late Medieval Ireland', *Catholic Record Society of Ireland* (1981), 3–15.

Lynch, John, *De Praesulibus Hibernicis*, ed. John Francis O'Doherty (Dublin 1944).

McDonnell, Thomas, *The Diocese of Killala from its institution to the end of the penal times* (Ballina 1976).

Mac Fhinn, Eric, 'Dha Athuinge as Achad Chonaire,' *Galvia* viii, 27–30.

MacGrath, Kevin, 'Irish Priests transported under the Commonwealth, 1649–58' in *Arch. Hib.*, xiv, 92 ff.

McKenna, Lambert, ed., *The Book of O'Hara* (Dublin 1980).

Mac Niocaill, Gearóid, 'Obligationes pro Annatis Diocesis Elphinensis', in *Arch. Hib.*, xxii (1959), 1–2.

Mhág Craith, Cuthbert, *Dán na mBráthar Mionúir*, 9, 38–51, 27, 127–51 (Dublin 1967).

Martin, F. X., & Meijer, A. de, 'Irish Material in the Augustinian General Archives, Rome, 1354–1624' in *Arch. Hib.*, xix, 61–113 (1956); 'Archives of the Irish Augustinians: a summary report' in *Arch. Hib.*, xviii, 157–63.

Martin, F. X., 'The Council of Trent' in *IER* (July–Dec 1963), 18–30; 'The Irish Augustinian Reform Movement in the Fifteenth Century', 230–64 in *Medieval Studies presented to Aubrey Gwynn SJ* (Dublin 1961); 'The Irish Friars and the Observant Movement in the Fifteenth Century' in *Proceedings of the Irish Catholic Historical Committee* (1960), 10–16.

Memoirs of the Taaffe Family (Vienna, 1856).

Millet, Benignius, 'Archbishop Edmund O'Reilly's Report on the State of the Church in Ireland, 1662', in *Coll. Hib.,* no. 2, 105–14. 'Calendar of *Scritture riferite nei congressi, Irlanda*', ff.470rv, 481r–482, v, in *Coll. Hib.*, nos 6 & 7 (1963–4), 18–211. 'Catalogue of Irish Material in vols 140–3 of the *Scritture oriiginali riferite nelle congregazioni generali* in Propaganda Archives' in *Coll. Hib.*, no. 13 (1970), 21–60. 'Calendar of Volume 2', in *Coll. Hib.*, no. 16 (1973), 11–45. 'Calendar of Volume 13 of the *Fondo di Vienna* in Propaganda Archives: part 2, ff.201–401' in *Coll. Hib.*, no. 25 (1983), 30–62.

Miscellany of the Irish Archaeological Society (Dublin 1846).

Montgomery, 'Account of the bishops …', in Shirley ed., *Papers relating to the Church of Ireland*.

Moody, T. W., F. X. Martin, F. J. Byrne, eds *A New History of Ireland*, iii, 1534–1691.

Mooney, Canice, 'The First Impact of the Reformation', in Corish, ed. *A History of Irish Catholicism*, 1–40; 'The Irish Church in the Sixteenth Century' in *IER* 99 (Jan.–June 1963), 102–13.

Moran, P. F. 'The See of Achonry in the Sixteenth Century' in *IER*, i, 209–17 (1865). *History of the Catholic Archbishops of Dublin since the Reformation*, i, 77–81, 417–19 (Dublin 1864).

Morley, Henry (ed.), *Ireland under Elizabeth and James the First. Described by Edmund Spenser, by Sir John Davies and by Fynes Morrison* (London 1890).

Moryson, Fynes, 'A description of Ireland', in Morley, Henry, ed. *Ireland under Elizabeth and James the First* (1890).

New Catholic Encyclopedia, 15 vols, 2nd edn (Washington 2003).

Nicholls, K. W., 'Rectory, Vicarage and Parish in the Western Irish Dioceses', in *JRSAI.*, ci, 53–82 (1971); 'Medieval Irish Cathedral Chapters', in *IER*, xxxi (1923), 102–11; *Gaelic and Gaelicised Ireland in the Middle Ages* (Gill History of Ireland 1972).

O'Brien, A. F., 'Episcopal Elections in Ireland 1254–72' in *Proceedings of the Royal Irish Academy* (1973) lxxiii, section C, no. 5, 129–68.

O'Doherty, D. J. 'Students of the Irish College, Salamanca' in *Arch. Hib.*, vi, 1ff.

O'Doherty, J. F., *'Obligationes pro Annatis Provinciae Tuamensis'*, in *Arch. Hib.* (1963), xxvi (from the transcript by M. A. Costello), 56–117.

O'Donovan, John, *The Martyrology of Tallagh, A Calendar of the Saints of Ireland* (Dublin 1864); *The Genealogies, Tribes and Customs of Hy-Fiachrach* (Dublin 1844); *Ordnance Survey Letters Sligo 1936, Mayo 1938*, see O'Flanagan *Ordnance Survey Name Books*.

O'Dowd, Mary, *Power, Politics and Land: Early Modern Sligo 1568–1688* (Belfast, 1991).

Ó Duáin, Odhrán, *Rógaire Easpaig* (Dublin 1975).

Ó Duinn, Seán, *Where Three Streams Meet: Celtic Spirituality* (Dublin 2002).

O'Dwyer, Peter, *Towards a History of Irish Spirituality* (Dublin 1995); *The Irish Carmelites* (Dublin 1988).

Ó Fiaich, Tomás, in Diarmaid Ó Doibhlinn, ed., *Ón Chreagán go Dubhrann, aisti*.

O'Flaherty, Roderick, *A chorographical description of West or h-Iar Connaught written 1684*, ed. James Hardiman. (Dublin 1846).

Ogygia, seu rerum Hibernicarum chronologia (London 1685), trans. James Hely, 2 vols (Dublin 1793).

O'Flanagan, Michael, *Ordnance Survey Letters, 1836, County Sligo* (Bray 1928); *Ordnance Survey Letters, 1838, 2 vols, County Mayo* (Bray 1927).

O'Hanlon, John, *The Lives of the Irish Saints,* 10 vols (Dublin 1875–1903).

Ó hEodhasa, Bonabheantúra, *Truagh liom, a chompáin, do chor* in *An Teagasg Críosdaidhe* 2nd edn (Rome 1707); in Mág Craith, *Dán na mBráthar Mionúir*, 38–51 (Dublin 1967).

Ó Moghráin, Pádraig, 'Pól Ó hUiginn', in *Béaloideas*, XV (1945–6), 86–107.

Ó Muraíle, Nollaig, *Mayo Places, their Names and Origins* (Dublin 1985); *The Celebrated Antiquary Dubhaltach Mac Fhirbhisgh c.1600–1671. His Lineage, Life and Learning* (Maynooth 2002); ed. *The Great Book of Irish Genealogies*, 5 vols (Dublin 2004–5).

O'Rahilly. Thomas F., *Measgra Dánta, miscellaneous Irish poems* (Cork 1927).

O'Rorke, Terence, *History, Antiquities and Present State of the Parishes of Ballysadare and Kilvarnet* (Dublin, n.d. 1878); *The History of Sligo Town and County*, 2 vols (Dublin, 1889).

O'Sullivan, M.D., 'Italian Merchant Bankers and the Collection of Customs in Ireland, 1275–1311', 168–85 in *Medieval Studies presented to Aubrey Gwynn.*

Oxford Dictionary of National Biography, 60 vols (2004).

Pastor, Louis, *History of the Popes from the Close of the Middle Ages* (1938–61).

Pio, G.M., *Delle Vite degli Huomini Illustri d. S. Dominico*, 3 vols (Bologna 1607–13).

Potthast, Augustus, *Regesta Pontificum Romanorum*, ii, 1198–1243 (1875), iii, 1243–1304.

Purcell, Mary, *The First Jesuit* (Dublin 1956).

Renehan, Laurence F., *Collections on Irish Church History* (Dublin 1861).

Ritzlier, Remigius & Sefrin, Perminius, *Hierarchia Catholica Medii et Recentioris Aevi* (Patavii 1952).

Roche, Richard, *The Norman Invasion of Ireland* (Tralee 1970).

Rogers, Patrick, Henry VIII and the Irish Monasteries', in *Bonaventura* (Autumn 1937), 115–45.

Sauval, *Histoire et Antiquites de la Ville de Paris*, 494.

Sheehy, Maurice P., *Pontificia Hibernica, Medieval Papal Chancery Documents concerning Ireland 640–1261*, 2 vols (Dublin 1965); 'Unpublished Medieval Notitiae and Epistolae', in *Coll. Hib.*, nos 6 & 7 (1963–4), 7–17.

Shirley, Evelyn Philip, *Original Letters and Papers in illustration of the history of the church of Ireland, during the reigns of Edward VI, Mary and Elizabeth, with notes from autographs in the State Paper Office (London 1851) relating to the Church of Ireland.*

Silke, John J., 'The Irish Abroad', 1534–1691', in *A New History of Ireland*, iii, 615–32.

Simington, Robert C., *Books of Survey and Distribution, ii, County of Mayo* (Dublin 1956).

Smith, Aquilla ed., 'Annals of Multyfarnham, Annales de Monte Fernande', in *Tracts relating to Ireland i* (printed for the Irish Archaeological Society), v–viii, 1–16 (Dublin 1843).

Smythe, William J., *Map-making, Landscapes and Memory: A Geography of Colonial and Early Modern Ireland, c.1530–1750* (Cork 2006).

Spenser, Edmund, 'A view of the state of Ireland', in Morley, Henry, ed *Ireland under Elizabeth and James the First*, 32–212.

Stokes, Whitley, ed. *Felire hui Gormain: The Martyrology of Gorman* (from a MS in the Royal Library, Brussels) (London 1895); *Felire Oengusso Celi De: The Martyrology Oengus the Culdee* (London 1905).

Stubbs, William, ed. Gesta *Regis Henrici Secundi Benedicti Abbatis* (London 1867).

Swords, Liam, *Soldiers, Scholars, Priests* (Paris 1985); *College des Lombards, souvenir tricentenaire* (Paris 1977); *The Flight of the Earls. A Popular History* (Dublin 2007).

Theiner, Augustinus, *Vetera Monumenta Hibernorum et Scotorum Historia Illustrantia* (Rome 1864).

Timoney, M. A, 'A Wooden Trough from Cloonahinshin, Ballymote, Co Sligo', 18 in *The Corran Herald*, 2004/2005.

Todd, James H., & Reeves, William, ed. *Felire na Naomh nErennach: The Martyrology of Donegal. A Calendar of the Saints of Ireland*, translated from the Irish by John O' Donovan (Dublin 1864).

Venn, J. & J. A, *Alumni Cantabrigienses*, 4 vols (1922–7).

Walsh, Katherine, 'The Opening of the Vatican Archives 1880–1' in *Arch. Hib.*, xxxvi (1981), 34–43.

Walsh, Reginald, 'Irish Manners and Customs in the sixteenth century' in *Arch. Hib.,* v, 17–19 (1916).

Walz, Angelo, *I Dominicani al Concilio di Trento* (Roma 1961).

Ware, Sir James, *History of the Bishops of Ireland* (Dublin 1739).

Watt, John A., 'The Irish Church in the Middle Ages' in Bradshaw & Keogh, eds *Christianity in Ireland* (Dublin 2002); 'The Papacy and Episcopal in Thirteenth Century Ireland' in *Proceedings of Irish Catholic Historical Committee 1959*, 1ff. (Dublin 1960).

Welch, Robert, ed. *Oxford Companion to Irish Literature* (Oxford 1999).

Wood-Martin, W. G., *History of Sligo, County and Town from the Accession of James I to the Revolution of 1688* (Dublin 1889).

Woulfe, Patrick, *Slointe Gaedheal is Gall* (Dublin 1922).

Wyse Jackson, Robert, *Archbishop Magrath – the scoundrel of Cashel* (Cork 1974); 'Two Letters of Dr Lyon, Protestant Bishop of Cork, written in 1596' in *IER*, vii, 490–503).

Index